America's National Battlefield Parks: A Guide

A Confederate volunteer. Library of Congress.

America's National Battlefield Parks
A Guide

By Joseph E. Stevens

Maps by Beth Silverman

University of Oklahoma Press : Norman and London

By Joseph E. Stevens

Hoover Dam: An American Adventure (Norman, 1988)
America's National Battlefield Parks: A Guide (Norman, 1990)

Library of Congress Cataloging-in-Publication Data

Stevens, Joseph E. (Joseph Edward), 1956–
    America's national battlefield parks : a guide / Joseph E. Stevens ; maps by
Beth Silverman. — 1st ed.
        p.   cm.
    ISBN 0-8061-2268-4 (alk. paper)
    1. National parks and reserves—United States—Guide-books.
2. Battlefields—United States—Guide-books.   3. United States—
Description and travel—1981—Guide-books.   4. United States—History,
Military.   I. Title.
E160.S72   1990
917.304′928—dc20   89-40739
                                                                              CIP

The paper in this book meets the guidelines for permanence and durability of the
Committee on Production Guidelines for Book Longevity of the Council on Library
Resources, Inc.⊚

CONTENTS

Midwest

South

West

ILLUSTRATIONS

MAPS

PREFACE

I grew up in Cambridge, New York, a small town located less than an hour's drive from Saratoga National Historical Park, site of one of the great battles of the American War of Independence. Every spring my schoolmates and I were bussed off to the park and turned loose on the fields where, in 1777, a patriot rabble defeated an invading British army and breathed new life into the faltering American Revolution.

In my mind I always tried to people the vacant landscape, conjuring up romantic images of Daniel Morgan's buckskin-clad riflemen, of Baron Von Riedesel's black-gaitered Hessians, and of the magnificent, mercurial Benedict Arnold leading the patriot charge against Breymann Redoubt. There was something thrilling about standing on the very spot where these men had fought and died; it was the electric excitement of making direct, physical contact with the past, and it fired my imagination in a way that no textbook or teacher could do.

I still feel that spark when I visit a battlefield today; the technicolor fantasies of boyhood are gone, but the excitement of treading hallowed ground, of walking shoulder-to-shoulder with the ghosts of history, remains. For myself and millions of other Americans, the National Battlefield Parks are places where time stands still, where Pickett is forever poised to begin his charge, where Custer eternally fights his last battle, where Jackson stands for all time like a stone wall.

As we walk down Bloody Lane at Antietam, cross the Old North Bridge at Concord, sit beneath the peach trees at Shiloh, or stand behind the stone fence at Gettysburg's High Water Mark, we salute the courage and devotion of the men who made these ordinary places extraordinary. We also ponder the genius and nobility, the stupidity and cruelty, that war seems to draw forth in equal measure. Finally we honor the dead, whose supreme sacrifice has shaped our nation's history.

The military heritage of America—both heroic and tragic—is embodied in the National Battlefield Parks, and it is my hope that this book will help visitors understand and appreciate that legacy more fully. In writing the book I have tried to focus on the human dimensions of each battle, describing not just the tactical whys and wherefores, but the real-life experiences of the participants. To make the battlefields come alive—to recreate the ebb and flow of combat, to connect the trails, landmarks, and monuments with the flesh-and-blood people who gave them meaning—has been my goal.

Without the cooperation and assistance of many individuals it would have been impossible to finish this book. I owe a special debt of gratitude to the men and women of the National Park Service and to the reference librarians at the Santa Fe Public and New Mexico State libraries. I would also like to thank Robert M. Utley and Edwin C. Bearss, past and present Chief Historians of the National Park Service, for reading and commenting on the manuscript.

To my mother and father, who nurtured my interest in military history, and to my wife Anastasia, who has cheerfully accompanied me on long and exhausting off-trail jaunts at Gettysburg, Vicksburg, and Custer battlefields, I would like to express my deep gratitude and love.

Joseph E. Stevens

Santa Fe, New Mexico

America's National Battlefield Parks: A Guide

CHAPTER 1

BUNKER HILL MONUMENT
BOSTON NATIONAL HISTORICAL PARK
(Revolutionary War)

Charlestown Navy Yard
Boston, Massachusetts 02129
Telephone: (617) 242-5601

On June 17, 1775, 2,500 British regulars commanded by General William Howe attacked a force of several thousand patriots entrenched on Breed's Hill on the Charlestown Peninsula north of Boston. Twice the British advanced up the hillside, only to be repulsed with terrible casualties. Finally, on their third attempt, the redcoats overran the patriot position. Bunker Hill Monument, a unit of Boston National Historical Park, stands on the site of the American redoubt, focal point of the bloodiest battle of the Revolutionary War.

Getting to the Park: The Bunker Hill Monument is located in Charlestown, approximately a mile north of downtown Boston. The Bunker Hill Pavilion is located on Constitution Avenue, just off the Charlestown Bridge. From the pavilion, follow the Freedom Trail—a red line marked on the sidewalk—to the monument. The walk takes about seven minutes.

Gas, food, lodging: In Boston.

Visitor Center: The Boston National Historical Park Visitor Center is located at 15 State Street, across from the Old State House unit. The Bunker Hill Pavilion offers a dramatic multimedia presentation on the battle. The Bunker Hill Lodge, next to the Monument, houses exhibits.

Activities: Interpretive talks by park personnel.

Handicapped Access: Ramps lead up to the monument, but to reach the top visitors must climb 294 eight-inch steps.

News of the Battle of Lexington and Concord, fought on April 19, 1775 (see Chapter 3), ignited the spirit of rebellion in the American colonies. All over New England, militia units were hastily raised and sent to Boston, where several thousand Massachusetts minutemen had bottled up a British army commanded by General Thomas Gage.

By the beginning of May the patriot force encircling Boston had swelled to over 10,000, more than double the number of troops Gage had at his disposal. The Americans were poorly organized and armed, however, and were led by inexperienced officers, few of whom possessed any real military aptitude. The British soldiers, on the other hand, were well trained and equipped and led by battle-tested officers, including General William Howe, a decorated veteran of the French and Indian War and the British army's leading expert on light infantry tactics. The forty-six-year-old Howe was a highly capable soldier, much respected by the Americans who had served with him at the Battle of Quebec in 1759. It would fall to him to lead the Boston garrison in its bid to break the patriot siege.

The Americans Fortify the Charlestown Peninsula

One of the keys to controlling Boston was the Charlestown Peninsula, a lumpy, triangular piece of land that jutted into the estuary formed by the Charles and Mystic rivers. Just beyond the "Neck," the low, narrow isthmus that connected the peninsula to the mainland, was Bunker Hill, a smooth, round elevation 110 feet high. Approximately 2,000 feet to the south was Breed's Hill, 75 feet high, used as a hayfield and pasturing ground. Southeast of Breed's Hill, the land sloped down to a rocky beach at Moulton's Point; to the southwest lay the small community of Charlestown.

On June 15 the Americans decided to fortify the Charlestown Peninsula. Colonel William Prescott and 1,200 Massachusetts and Connecticut soldiers marched over the Neck on the night of June 16, bypassed Bunker Hill, and dug in on Breed's Hill, erecting an earthen redoubt measuring 160 feet by 30 feet.

At sunrise on June 17, the people of Boston were flabbergasted to see a dark crown of fresh-turned earth on the crest of Breed's Hill, three-quarters of a mile to the north across the waters of the Charles. British warships in the harbor and land batteries on Copp's Hill opened fire on the American entrenchments while the royal officers gathered for a council of war. It was decided that the position must be captured, but how? Sir Henry Clinton proposed that a landing be made in the American rear, near the Charlestown Neck. This move would prevent the patriots from receiving reinforcements and block their only retreat route; when their food ran out in a few days the Americans would be forced to surrender.

Clinton's strategy promised a bloodless victory, but General Gage refused to adopt it. He deemed it unsoldierly to maneuver in the presence of an enemy who had challenged him to a fight. A powerful frontal assault, he decided, would teach the rebellious colonists an unforgettable lesson, and he ordered General Howe to make preparations for the attack at once.

Meanwhile, Prescott's soldiers were extending their fortifications by building a breastwork northward from the redoubt on Breed's Hill. Around 3 p.m., Colonel John Stark's New Hampshire regiment arrived on the peninsula and took up a position behind a rail fence that ran down the northeast slope of Breed's Hill to the water. The New Hampshiremen propped bunches of hay against the rails to create a serviceable, albeit flimsy, barricade, and also built three arrow-shaped shelters, called fleches, to cover the area between the Breed's Hill breastwork and their wood-and-hay wall. To protect the right flank, several detachments of militia took up snipers' positions in deserted Charlestown. All told, several thousand New Englanders were now arrayed

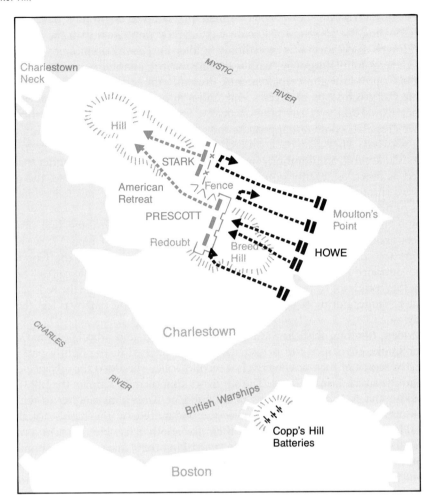

Bunker Hill, June 17, 1775

in a zigzag line across the middle of the peninsula, waiting to meet the British onslaught.

Howe Attacks

Just before noon on the 17th, six British regiments—approximately 2,500 troops—paraded on Boston Common in full battle gear, then marched to Long Wharf and North Battery to board boats that would carry them over the river to the Charlestown peninsula. They landed at Moulton's Point shortly after 1:00 P.M., and then sat and chewed on rations while Howe inspected the patriot defenses. Finally, at about 3:30 P.M., the British general was ready to make his attack: the main objective would be the rail fence, but diversionary thrusts would also be launched against the Breed's Hill redoubt and the American left flank on the Mystic River beach.

In their brilliant scarlet jackets, buff breeches, and glossy black boots, the British soldiers made a colorful show as they formed into ranks to begin their advance. Spectators crowding the rooftops of Boston were greatly impressed with the martial display. "Howe's disposition was exceedingly Soldier-like, in my opinion it was perfect," wrote General John Burgoyne, who was studying the panorama through a spyglass from the Copp's Hill gun emplacements. Presently the red-and-white lines began to move up the green slope of Breed's Hill, and it appeared to the awestruck observers that they would roll over anything or anyone foolish enough to stand in their path.

Howe's regulars could not appreciate the grand spectacle they were making as they moved forward. They had been ordered to advance carrying all their gear—pack, rations, blanket roll, ammunition—and were staggering and panting under loads that weighed as much as seventy pounds per man. To make matters worse, the ground they were traversing was muddy and uneven, and there were rail fences and large clumps of brambles to climb over or through.

Behind their fortifications, the Americans watched the glittering line of British bayonets draw closer, and struggled to quell a rising sense of panic. It was at this moment, according to legend, that Israel Putnam, commander of the Connecticut troops, cautioned his men not to fire "until you see the whites of their eyes." Some of the patriots could not restrain themselves and began shooting while the redcoats were still out of range, but most dutifully waited until the leading rank was less than fifty yards away.

A sudden, blinding flash lit the top of the rail fence, and a boiling cloud of gray powder smoke enveloped the British. Great gaps opened in the tightly packed formations as scores of men pitched over; a second volley shredded the advance companies, and the attack disintegrated. The survivors stumbled back down the hill with the resounding cheers and war whoops of the jubilant Americans ringing in their ears.

Although he had lost heavily, Howe was undaunted by the repulse of the first attack. He rallied his men and formed them for another try. He also sent a message back to Boston requesting reinforcements and asking that Charlestown be bombarded to flush out the marksmen who had been sniping at his left flank all afternoon. This done, he led the scarlet line forward, over the bodies of dead and wounded comrades, into the teeth of the deadly patriot musketry; once again, the British ranks were shattered by a hail of lead from the American fortifications.

Trying to rally the bloody shambles of his command after the second charge, Howe nearly lost heart, but the galling thought of being beaten by a colonial rabble, and the arrival of reinforcements from Boston, revived his fighting spirit. He ordered his soldiers to prepare for yet another attempt. This time the heavy packs would be left behind, and the entire force would bypass the rail fence and concentrate on the breastwork and redoubt on top of Breed's Hill.

Artillery fire from the Boston batteries had set Charlestown aflame, and plumes of dark smoke swirled around Howe's sweating, powder-grimed soldiers as they dressed their ranks for the third assault of the afternoon. Exhibiting iron discipline and raw courage, they set out again, up the corpse-strewn slope toward the American position.

Now it was the patriots' turn to quail: they had smashed two charges, inflicting devastating losses on the enemy, but the redcoats were stubbornly refusing to accept defeat. To make matters worse, ammunition was almost gone—many men had only one round left—and no reinforcements had arrived to bolster the Breed's Hill line.

On their third assault, British troops overran the American redoubt on Breed's Hill. Painting by John Trumbull, *Battle of Bunker's Hill,* Copyright Yale University Art Gallery.

One weak volley was all that could be hurled against the oncoming attackers, and then it was stones, bare fists, and musket butts against British bayonets.

There was a brief, furious struggle inside the redoubt, then the Americans scrambled for the rear. Some units held together and fought tenacious rearguard actions, but most fell apart in the rush to get away from the slashing, stabbing bayonets. "In God's name," roared Israel Putnam, "form and give them one shot more!" but his efforts to rally the patriots were in vain. By 5:30 P.M., the last of the surviving Americans had fled across the Neck into Cambridge, leaving the exhausted British regulars in sole possession of the Charlestown Peninsula.

A Costly Victory

The redcoats had won their hill, but at a fearsome cost. Of the 2,500 soldiers who participated in the three assaults, 1,054 had been killed or wounded—42 percent of the effective force. General Howe had escaped physical harm despite personally leading all the charges, but psychologically he would never be the same. When he relieved Gage as commander in chief of British military forces in America in October 1775, he could not shake the memory of the battle. His old combativeness was gone, replaced by hesitancy and caution, and he would prove an ineffective leader in the war to stamp out the rebellion.

The Americans had lost between 400 and 600 men in the struggle for Breed's Hill, and learned a bitter lesson in the process: individual gallantry and patriotic fervor were no substitute for tactical planning and battlefield discipline. Better military organization and more forceful leadership would be required if they were ever to meet the British army on equal terms. The first step in this direction was taken barely two weeks after the battle when General George Washington arrived in Cambridge to assume command of the new Continental Army and direct the siege of Boston.

Touring the Park

The Bunker Hill Monument is a granite obelisk, built between 1827 and 1843. It stands on the site of the Breed's Hill redoubt, focal point of the battle.

Begin your tour at the Bunker Hill Pavilion on Constitution Avenue, just off the Charlestown Bridge. After viewing the multi-media presentation, follow the Freedom Trail—a red line marked on the sidewalk—to the monument. The walk takes about seven minutes. In the lodge, next to the monument, you will find exhibits explaining the battle and a park ranger to answer any questions.

CHAPTER 2

FORT STANWIX NATIONAL MONUMENT
(Revolutionary War)

112 East Park Street
Rome, New York 13440
Telephone: (315) 336-2090

Between August 3 and August 22, 1777, the garrison of Fort Stanwix in west-central New York was besieged by a large army of British regulars, American loyalists, and Iroquois Indians. The 800 patriot soldiers, led by Colonel Peter Gansevoort, withstood all attacks, and the British commander, Colonel Barry St. Leger, was forced to withdraw his force to Canada. Fort Stanwix National Monument is an authentic, full-scale reproduction of the log-and-earth fort as it appeared in 1777.

Getting to the Park: Fort Stanwix National Monument is located in downtown Rome, New York. Leave the New York State Thruway (I-90) at Exit 33 and drive into Rome on State Route 365 (Erie Boulevard East). Turn right on James Street (State Route 26), then left on West Liberty Street. The parking areas will be on your left.

Gas, food, lodging: In Rome.

Visitor Center: The Visitor Center is located in the West Barracks, at the door marked GREGG. (West Barracks will be on your left as you enter the Parade Ground.) Museum and gift shop; film on the Fort Stanwix siege.

Activities: Interpretive talks and walking tours are conducted by park personnel. Between Memorial Day and Labor Day a full living-history program is offered, including close-order drill and weapons firing demonstrations by volunteers in period dress, as well as exhibitions of colonial-era crafts, cooking, and barracks life. Inquire at Visitor Center for a complete schedule.

Handicapped Access: The parking lot is two blocks from the site. Visitor Center is completely accessible. Gravel walkways run through the grounds; inclines instead of stairs have been provided. Assistance is available from park personnel.

On July 26, 1777, a long, colorful procession passed through the gates of Fort Oswego at the settlement of Oswego, New York, and marched southeast toward the

Mohawk Valley. It was composed of British regulars, smartly turned out in red-and-white uniforms, American tories clad in drab leather and homespun, and Iroquois Indian warriors, garishly got up in paint and feathers. This strange collection of allies, numbering 1,700 in all, was bound for Albany and a linkup with General John Burgoyne's army, which was advancing southward from Canada along the Lake Champlain–Hudson River waterway. The column's commander, Colonel Barry St. Leger, knew that all that stood between him and Albany was a small patriot garrison at Fort Stanwix, situated between Wood Creek and the Mohawk River in central New York.

Fort Stanwix: Guardian of the Oneida Carry

During colonial times it was possible to travel by boat all the way from the Great Lakes to New York City. The only gap in the waterway was a mile-wide neck of land between the Mohawk River and Wood Creek, where the modern-day city of Rome, New York, stands. This portage was called De-O-Wain-Sta by the Indians and the Oneida Carry by the British; in any language it was an area of great strategic importance because all commercial and military traffic had to funnel through it.

To guard the Oneida Carry, the British army built a star-shaped fort in 1758. Named after its builder, General John Stanwix, this frontier outpost served as a base of operations during the French and Indian War and as a trading center after the British conquest of Canada in 1763.

When the Revolutionary War began in the spring of 1775, American military leaders recognized the importance of controlling the Mohawk Valley water route. Patriot soldiers occupied Fort Stanwix in mid-1776, and began refurbishing it in anticipation of British incursions into the valley. Colonel Peter Gansevoort, a twenty-eight-year-old officer from Albany, arrived to take command in early 1777, and the work of strengthening the fort was speeded up as rumors of an impending British attack circulated throughout western New York.

Fort Stanwix Besieged

St. Leger's invasion column arrived in the vicinity of Fort Stanwix at the beginning of August 1777. On August 3, the British commander formally called on the garrison to surrender; Colonel Gansevoort rejected this demand "with disdain," and the British forces surrounded the fort and began siege operations. Although his force—some 800 New York and Massachusetts infantrymen—was badly outnumbered, Gansevoort was confident that St. Leger would be unable to seize Stanwix. He knew that the British did not have cannon capable of pounding the fort into submission, and that General Nicholas Herkimer and 900 men of the Tryon County militia had mustered at German Flats on the Mohawk River, fifty miles to the east, and were marching to his aid.

Unbeknownst to either Gansevoort or Herkimer, St. Leger had learned of the relief column's approach and sent a large portion of his army to intercept it. This detachment of Indians and tories set an ambush in a wooded ravine near Oriskany, six miles southeast of Fort Stanwix, and waited for the approach of the American militia.

On August 6, Herkimer and his soldiers stumbled into the trap that had been laid for them. The loyalists and Indians opened fire at close range, killing scores of the Americans and fatally wounding many others, including General Herkimer. The patriot militiamen refused to panic, however. Quickly forming a defensive perimeter, they traded volleys with their attackers and forced them to fall back. When the Indians and tories stormed forward again there was a ferocious hand-to-hand struggle in which knives, tomahawks, and musket butts were used and no quarter was given.

While this savage melee was underway at Oriskany, Gansevoort ordered his second-in-command, Lieutenant Colonel Marinus Willet, to lead a sortie out of Fort Stanwix. Willet and his men barged into the undefended British and Iroquois encampments and looted them of everything that could be carried away, including food, clothing, cooking kettles, regimental colors, and the personal papers of St. Leger and his officers. When news of this raid reached Oriskany, the loyalists and Indians broke off the fight with Herkimer's force and rushed back to their camps, only to find them ransacked and in ruins.

The Hon-Yost Schuyler Stratagem

Although the Battle of Oriskany ended in a draw, the exhausted and bloodied American militia had to give up its effort to relieve Fort Stanwix. St. Leger's force had lost heavily, too, but the British colonel managed to rally his men, and they resumed the siege.

With his stocks of food and ammunition rapidly dwindling, Gansevoort again turned to Marinus Willet, asking him to slip through British lines and carry word of the garrison's plight to American army headquarters at Albany. Willet managed to evade capture and get to Albany, and a second relief column was hastily organized and dispatched to Fort Stanwix.

General Benedict Arnold, commander of the relief column, knew that he would be outnumbered when he reached the fort, and so he decided to employ a clever stratagem to sap St. Leger's strength. The Americans had recently captured a man named Hon-Yost Schuyler, a mentally retarded loyalist who was regarded by St. Leger's Iroquois allies as a prophet. Arnold told the half-wit Hon-Yost to go to the Indian camps around Fort Stanwix, pretend that he had just escaped from his American captors, and spread the rumor that Arnold's approaching men were "as numerous as the leaves on the trees."

This outrageous ploy proved remarkably successful. The Iroquois, stung by the casualties they had suffered at Oriskany and angry about the lack of plunder, deserted en masse. The loyalists soon followed suit, and St. Leger found himself commanding a force that was one-third its original size. Disgusted and downhearted, he called off the siege on August 22 and ordered his shrunken army to return to Fort Oswego. Two days later, Arnold and his column marched triumphantly into Fort Stanwix and relieved Peter Gansevoort and his 800 men.

British Disaster

St. Leger's failure to capture Fort Stanwix and push on to Albany ruined the British strategy for reestablishing royal authority in New York State. Burgoyne's invasion from the north bogged down too, and at Saratoga his army was defeated and forced to surrender (see Chapter 4). This double disaster effectively ended Britain's bid to crush patriot resistance in New England and the Mid-Atlantic region and brought France into the war on the side of American independence.

Touring the Park

Begin your tour at the Visitor Center, where a film and exhibits provide information on the history of Fort Stanwix and the role it played in the Revolutionary War. Of particular interest is the large and varied display of eighteenth-century artifacts found by archaeologists excavating the fort grounds prior to the reconstruction in the 1970s. This display can be seen in the West Casemate, directly behind the Visitor Center.

Except for the headquarters building, the guardhouse, the sally port, the necessary, and the ravelin, the fort is an accurate reconstruction of the original as it appeared in 1777, the year of the siege.

Stop 1. West Barracks (Visitor Center). The structure that now serves as the Visitor Center was originally a barracks with two small rooms for officers and two larger rooms for enlisted soldiers.

Stop 2. West Casemate (Museum). Casemates were log structures built into the walls of the fort to provide shelter from artillery bombardment. The rooms in this casemate originally served as enlisted men's quarters. They now house the fort museum.

Stop 3. North Casemate. The rooms in this casemate served as officers' quarters.

Stop 4. Northeast Bastion. The diamond-shaped protrusions at the corners of the fort were called bastions. Each one had six embrasures for cannon, the embrasures angled so as to create a cross-fire pattern. During the siege, the fort had only eleven cannon.

Stop 5. East Barracks. The smaller rooms on either end of the barracks were officers' quarters, while the two larger rooms housed soldiers. During the siege, both the east and west barracks were evacuated because they offered little protection from artillery fire.

Stop 6. Southeast Bastion. The fort's bakehouse was located under this bastion. The extra embrasure was the entrance to the necessary, or outhouse, which has not been reconstructed.

Stop 7. Storehouse (Rest Rooms). This building was originally used to store provisions. It now houses the public rest rooms.

Stop 8. Southeast Casemate. Behind the storehouse is the southeast casemate, which housed approximately forty men.

Stop 9. Main Gate and Drawbridge. When the fort was under siege, the drawbridge was raised. The small door within a door, on the lefthand side, is the wicket gate, used to let people in or out without opening the larger door.

Stop 10. Southwest Casemate (Gift Shop). The civilian carpenters, masons, and sawyers who rebuilt the fort before the 1777 siege stayed in this building. It now houses the gift shop.

Stop 11. Southwest Bastion and Bombproof. Bombproofs—dugouts with heavy timber roofs covered with three to four feet of earth—were located under three of the fort's four bastions. They could withstand a direct hit from a cannon ball. This bombproof served as a hospital during the siege.

CHAPTER 3

MINUTE MAN NATIONAL HISTORICAL PARK

(Revolutionary War)

174 Liberty Street
P.O. Box 160
Concord, Massachusetts 01742
Telephone: (617) 369-6993

On the morning of April 19, 1775, British regulars fired on American minute-men at Lexington Green and began the Revolutionary War. Several hours later there was a second clash at North Bridge in the village of Concord. Following this skirmish, the British retreated under fire all the way back to Boston. Minute Man National Historical Park preserves sites associated with the fighting of April 19, 1775, and commemorates the events that marked the beginning of the War of the American Revolution.

Getting to the Park: Minute Man National Historical Park is located approximately 15 miles northwest of Boston. The Battle Road Visitor Center is located on Massachusetts State Route 2A in Lexington; North Bridge Visitor Center is located off Lowell Road in Concord.

Gas, food, lodging: In Lexington, Lincoln, and Concord.

Visitor Centers: Museum and gift shop; electric map and film at Battle Road Visitor Center.

Activities: Interpretive talks and walking tours led by park personnel. Tours of The Wayside mid-April through October. Inquire at Visitor Centers for schedule and locations.

Handicapped Access: Both Visitor Centers are fully accessible. North Bridge and the Minuteman statue are accessible via a hard-packed earth path. Inquire at Visitor Center about accessibility of other park areas.

Small, sedate, and quiet, the town of Lexington, Massachusetts, seems a most unlikely site for a battlefield. It was in this sleepy village, however, shortly after sunup on April 19, 1775, that a column of British regulars, marching toward Concord six miles to the west, fired on a straggling line of seventy-seven American militiamen and began the War of the American Revolution.

To the Brink of War

The minutemen who stood shoulder-to-shoulder on Lexington Green in the chill dawn of April 19, 1775, had no idea they were about to change history. In fact, as they gripped their muskets in sweaty palms and watched the British troops advance toward them across the dew-sprinkled grass, they fervently hoped that a showdown could be avoided.

To start a revolution was the last thing they intended; complete independence from Britain was the last thing they wanted. On the contrary, their aim was to preserve their rights as Englishmen and to restore home rule to the colonies—the political status quo as they understood it.

The conflict over home rule had begun in 1763 at the conclusion of the Seven Years' War between Britain and France, known in America as the French and Indian War. Britain emerged victorious from that struggle, but deep in debt: the war had cost 70 million pounds and the expense of ruling newly won territory—much of it in North America—was high. To the British government it seemed only fair that the American colonies should help foot the bill for garrisoning the conquered lands on their western and northern frontiers, and a series of tax measures were passed.

The colonists, particularly those in New England, were shocked and outraged by these taxes. For generations they had governed themselves with only minimal supervision from the mother country, and they considered this the established system. Their colonial assemblies had consented to a handful of tax acts before 1763, but these laws had been flouted with almost total impunity. Now the British Parliament had decreed that those old laws be vigorously enforced and that new taxes be levied *without* colonial consent.

Meetings were held, manifestos written, and petitions drafted and signed, all opposing the tax measures. There was violent resistance too, especially in the city of Boston, where unruly mobs hounded tax collectors and vandalized customs offices.

The British government could not ignore this outbreak of lawlessness, and troops were sent to Boston to quell the unrest. Their arrival produced exactly the opposite effect, however. The Bostonians threatened and harassed the redcoats at every turn, provoking confrontations that often degenerated into ugly brawls. The worst of these occurred on March 5, 1770, when a group of British regulars fired their muskets into a crowd that was pelting them with stones and snowballs. Several colonists were killed, and the "Boston Massacre," as the episode was called, greatly inflamed hostile passions.

In 1773, tensions were raised again when Parliament passed the Tea Act, giving the British East India Company a monopoly of the American tea market. The incensed colonists vowed to resist this high-handed move, and the first shipment of East India Company tea to arrive in Boston was flung into the harbor. Angered by this rebellious act, Parliament decided to close the port of Boston and put Massachusetts colony under martial law.

The man responsible for enforcing these draconian edicts was General Thomas Gage, fifty-six-year-old commander in chief of His Majesty's forces in North America and military governor of Massachussetts. At his disposal Gage had approximately 4,000 regular troops—a formidable army, but one that would be outnumbered if Massachusetts's many small militia companies banded together to oppose it.

The punishment Parliament had intended proved ineffective as the other colonies came to Massachusetts's aid, sending food and supplies to the beleaguered city of Boston. More worrisome to General Gage were the warlike preparations being made in the small towns surrounding Boston. The local militia companies had stepped up their drilling, and cannon, gunpowder, and other military stores were being stockpiled in large quantities. It was clear that any move by the Boston-based British forces to reestablish their authority in the rest of Massachussetts would be violently resisted.

The British March

Under pressure from King George III to bring the unruly colonists to heel, General Gage decided to act. His spies told him that a large cache of arms and ammunition had been hidden in Concord, just twenty miles west of Boston. If he could seize and destroy those supplies, he would nip the Massachusetts militia's military buildup in the bud.

Plans were made and orders issued: a column composed of twenty-one companies of grenadiers and light infantry—some 700 men in all—would march to Concord, destroy the military stores, and return to Boston, all within a twenty-four-hour period. The expedition was to be led by Colonel Francis Smith, a corpulent old soldier whose only qualification for the assignment was his length of service and friendship with General Gage. Major John Pitcairn of the Royal Marines, one of the best-liked and most able of the officers in Gage's army, was to be second-in-command.

On the night of April 18, 1775, the British expeditionary force mustered on Boston Common. The sky was clear and starry, and a brisk, brine-scented wind blew out of the east, chilling the regulars as they formed into regiments on the grassy field. By 10:30 P.M. they were organized, and on command from their officers, they marched down to the banks of the Charles River, where a fleet of longboats waited to ferry them across to Lechmere Point, the place where the march to Concord would begin.

General Gage had tried to keep the expedition a secret, but all of Boston, it seemed, knew of his plans before the British soldiers even began to assemble. While the redcoats were still milling about on the Common, Paul Revere, a forty-year-old silversmith who carried messages for the patriot leaders, had rowed across the Charles and was riding hell-for-leather toward Concord, spreading the alarm along the way.

A mounted British patrol, sent out the day before to scout the route the regulars would follow, captured Revere west of Lexington, but another patriot, Dr. Samuel Prescott, escaped and rode on. Thus by 1 A.M. all the towns that the British column would pass through had been alerted, and the local militia companies were gathering, muskets ready, to confront the redcoats. Meanwhile, Colonel Smith and Major Pitcairn were still trying to get their 700 men across the Charles and into position to begin the march.

April 19, 1775: A Deadly Skirmish on Lexington Green

In Lexington, Captain John Parker and some 130 members of the town's militia company turned out after Paul Revere's midnight alarm. They waited on the village green for over an hour, but when there was no sign of the British, they dispersed, some going home to bed, others congregating in the tap room of Buckman Tavern, which was conveniently located on the northeastern edge of the green.

While the militiamen were warming themselves by the tavern's fireplace, the cold, wet British regulars were slogging along the road to Concord. Around 4 A.M. they reached the outskirts of Menotomy (now called Arlington), less than ten miles from their starting point. At this rate it would take them several more hours to reach their objective, and Colonel Smith decided to send Major Pitcairn and six companies of light infantry ahead to secure the bridges leading into Concord.

As the men of Pitcairn's advance force double-timed through Menotomy and pushed on toward Lexington, they could hear the tolling of alarm bells and the banging of signal guns in the hills on either side of the road. Presently they were met by the patrol that had captured Paul Revere earlier: these men reported that the country ahead was crawling with militia. Moments later, scouts stopped a man in a carriage who told them 600 armed colonials were waiting in Lexington, spoiling for a fight.

This wildly exaggerated claim was accepted as fact by Major Pitcairn, and he ordered his nervous soldiers to stop and load their muskets. They approached Lexington just as the sun was coming up; from the village they could hear the rattle of a drum, beating out the call to arms. Certain now that a battle was in the offing, Pitcairn commanded the leading companies to fix bayonets and move into town on the run.

The road into Lexington forked in front of a two-and-a-half story high meetinghouse; one branch angled right toward Bedford, the other left toward Concord. In the crux of the V formed by the diverging roads lay the triangular village green, flanked by houses, yards, and Buckman Tavern.

When he learned that the British were approaching, Captain John Parker, forty-

---

The Minutemen

Since the time of the Pilgrims and Plymouth Plantation, every Massachusetts man between the ages of sixteen and sixty had been required to belong to his town's militia company. At least four times a year the companies mustered for drill, and the citizen-soldiers were schooled in the manual of arms and the rudiments of close-order marching.

The younger, more active members of the militia also had to be prepared to go quickly to the aid of neighboring towns. They were supposed to be ready to depart "at a minute's notice," and so they were called "minutemen."

The minutemen had minimal equipment: a musket, a powder horn, a bullet pouch or cartridge box, and a bag of extra flints. Officers were chosen in elections, and important decisions affecting the company were usually debated and voted on.

Despite their loose organization and unsoldierly appearance, the minutemen performed well at the Battle of Lexington and Concord. They responded quickly to the call to arms and, for the most part, fought bravely. Only the lack of a coherent strategy and command structure prevented them from cutting off and annihilating the entire British force.

The Minuteman statue stands near Old North Bridge in Concord. Eastern National Parks and Monuments Association, photograph by Chris Stein.

five-year-old veteran of the French and Indian War, hastily lined up seventy-seven men of the Lexington militia company in two long ranks on the northern side of the green, about one hundred yards behind the meetinghouse. Parker and the militiamen had decided earlier that unless the regulars began destroying property they would let them pass by unopposed. The Lexington men would stand their ground, maintaining the honor of the town, but would not pick a fight with the much larger British force.

A crowd of onlookers had gathered on the fringe of the green, and they gasped as the red-coated infantry burst into view, coming on the run around the side of the meetinghouse. Captain Parker was taken aback, too. He had just given the order:

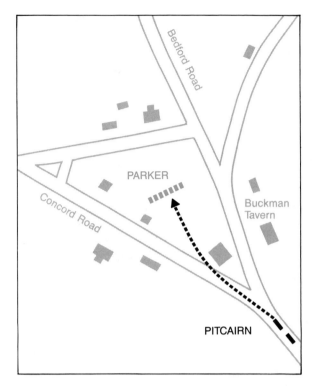

Lexington, April 19, 1775

"Stand your ground. Don't fire unless fired upon," in expectation that the regulars would simply march by along the Concord road. Instead, they were charging directly toward his little formation, bayonets flashing in the early morning sunlight.

Fearing that his men would be captured and have their muskets confiscated, Parker gave the order to disperse. Most of the militiamen obeyed with alacrity; a few stood where they were, determined not to run in the face of the British.

Major Pitcairn, who had just ridden up, saw Parker's men melting away, and screamed at them: "Lay down your arms, ye damned rebels, lay down your arms!" Then, to his own frenzied men, he shouted: "Soldiers don't fire! Keep your ranks and surround them!"

At this instant a single shot rang out. It has never been determined who pulled the trigger, but there is no doubt that the British soldiers, hearts pounding after their charge, nerves jangling in fear and anticipation, were itching for a fight.

"Fire, by God! Fire!" bellowed a junior officer, and the regulars loosed a volley at the backs of the retreating militia. A few of Parker's men tried to return fire, but a second, heavier volley sent them scrambling for safety. With wild shouts the British troops followed, brandishing their bayonets and chasing the fleeing patriots among the houses that surrounded the green.

The melee lasted until Colonel Smith and the main body of the expeditionary forced reached Lexington, fifteen minutes after the first shot had been fired. When order was finally restored, the regulars discharged a volley to celebrate their victory, then resumed the march to Concord, stepping along to the music of fife and drum.

The brief skirmish had shattered the Lexington militia. Of the seventy-seven men who mustered on the green, eight were dead and ten wounded. The British had suffered no casualties.

The Tables are Turned at North Bridge

By 7 A.M., some 250 minutemen had congregated in Concord, and when news of the Lexington fight reached them, they set off down the road to meet the advancing scarlet column. The two forces came together about a mile east of town. The Americans saw that they were outnumbered, and without offering a fight they turned around and marched back to Concord, followed closely by the British troops.

The commander of the Concord militia, Colonel James Barrett, knew that most of the military stores the redcoats were after had either been hidden or carried off to safety, so he ordered his men to retreat through the center of Concord, across North Bridge on the western edge of town, and into a position on Punkatasset Hill, where they could safely wait for reinforcements.

After arriving in Concord, Colonel Smith conferred with his officers and then sent six companies of light infantry to hold North Bridge. The rest of the column went from house to house in Concord, looking for gunpowder, muskets, and other munitions. All they found were several wooden gun carriages, which they piled up and set on fire.

The American force on Punkatasset Hill had swelled to over 400 as minutemen from surrounding towns continued to arrive, but Colonel Barrett and the other officers could not agree on a course of action. Some were in favor of making an attack, while others wanted to avoid bloodshed if at all possible. A thousand yards away, they could see three of the British light infantry companies guarding North Bridge; three more were marching on toward the nearby Barrett Farm.

Colonel Barrett and the others continued to argue until someone spotted a dark cloud of smoke rising above Concord.

"Would you let them burn down our town?" cried Lieutenant Joseph Hosmer.

"No!" replied a chorus of angry voices, and the minutemen loaded their muskets, formed into a long column, and moved down the hill toward North Bridge.

The 100 British soldiers guarding the span were not prepared for this sudden, threatening advance. They fell back, firing warning shots into the Concord River, but still the Americans came on. As the lead company set foot on the bridge, the British muskets spat flame, and two men in the patriots' front rank fell dead.

For a moment, as the guns' report echoed and powder smoke drifted across the sun-dappled stream, the advance halted. In spite of all that had happened that morning, many of the Americans found it hard to believe they were actually being shot at.

"God damn it, they are firing ball!" swore Timothy Brown, but the rest of the minutemen had fallen into a shocked silence.

The spell was finally broken by Major John Buttrick: "Fire!" he yelled. "For God's sake, fire!" Responding mechanically, the minutemen leveled their muskets and unleashed a withering blast at the British soldiers gathered on the east end of the bridge.

Old North Bridge at Concord, Massachusetts, where American minutemen fired the "shot heard 'round the world." National Park Service, photograph by Richard Frear.

Eleven regulars crumpled to the ground, and the rest turned and sprinted back toward Concord.

The tables had been turned on the victors of Lexington.

The British Run a Deadly Gauntlet of Fire

After the fight at North Bridge, the British regrouped in the center of Concord while the patriot militia rested on a nearby hill. At noon, Colonel Smith got his column moving back toward Boston, its flanks and rear covered by companies of light infantry. The patriots followed, moving through fields and woods on either side of the road, staying just out of musket range.

At Meriam's Corner, a mile east of Concord, the British had to bunch together to get across the narrow bridge spanning Mill Brook. When the redcoats began jamming up at this bottleneck, the Americans boldly moved closer. The light infantry tried to drive them back with a crashing volley, but the minutemen continued to press in on the flanks of Smith's column. Taking cover behind fences, stone walls, and the buildings of the Meriam Farm, they opened fire, lashing the scarlet line with a hail of musket balls.

The banging of discharging guns grew louder and louder as fresh militia companies from all over eastern Massachusetts arrived on the field and got into position to shoot at the redcoats. The tired British troops would have to run a deadly gauntlet for the rest of the afternoon.

Near the Job Brooks House in Lincoln, where the road curved sharply through thick woods, hundreds of minutemen poured fire into Colonel Smith's column at point-blank range, killing eight and wounding many more. A mile farther on, Captain John Parker and the remnants of the Lexington militia had been waiting in ambush since 11 A.M., determined to avenge their comrades who had fallen earlier in the day. At 2 P.M., when the retreating redcoats drew abreast of their concealed position, Parker's men blasted them with a heavy volley. One of the many casualties in this fierce attack was Colonel Smith, who pitched from his horse, a musket ball embedded in his thigh.

The British infantry staggered on, but when yet another fusillade swept their ranks, they began to panic. Some men sat down by the side of the road and refused to go on; others dropped their muskets and ran wildly toward Lexington. Major Pitcairn tried to rally the fleeing soldiers, but his horse was shot from under him, and the rout continued.

Had the Americans been better organized and led, they could have blocked the road and captured or annihilated Colonel Smith's entire force. However, the minutemen were fighting as individuals, not as an army, and so no thought was given to strategy. The exhausted British soldiers were allowed to stagger into Lexington, where 1,000 reinforcements, commanded by General Hugh Percy, came to their rescue.

Percy's relief column, which had marched from Boston that morning after receiving news of the Lexington fight, arrived in the nick of time. The redcoats rolled up two cannon and opened fire on the swarming minutemen, holding them at bay while Smith's weary soldiers caught their breath and regained their composure. After a half-hour respite, they set out again, shielded by Percy's fresh troops.

Patriot Marksmanship

One of the enduring myths of the Lexington and Concord battle is that the minutemen who took part were crack shots, able to pick off the brightly dressed British soldiers at long range. In fact, their marksmanship was extremely poor.

One historian has calculated that the Americans discharged a minimum of 75,000 shots during the fighting. They scored just 247 hits—only one ball in 300 found its target. Had half of the Americans who fought hit their mark once, the entire British force would have been wiped out.

Why was the patriots' marksmanship so bad? The smoothbore muskets they used had an effective range of 100 yards or less. Many of the minutemen never came this close to the British column because they were afraid of being bayoneted by the light infantrymen guarding its flanks. Those who did close the distance fared only slightly better: nerves and lack of shooting practice caused all but a few of their shots to fly high and wide.

British light infantrymen tried to drive the minutemen back with musket volleys, but the Americans continued to press the attack. National Park Service, photograph by Richard Frear.

The combined force entered Menotomy at 4 P.M., and as it passed through the center of town, the battle reached a furious crescendo. Hundreds of minutemen had run ahead of the slow-moving British column to find concealed shooting positions in buildings lining the road; they now rained fire down on the redcoats.

Infuriated by this deadly sniping, Percy's troops forced their way into houses flanking their route, terrorizing the occupants, looting valuable possessions, and setting fires. Three homes went up in flames and more than twenty colonists, including boys and old men who had taken no part in the fighting, were shot or bayoneted.

The brutal combat continued as the redcoats grimly pushed on, through Menotomy and into Cambridge. There, in the waning daylight, the patriots made a last-ditch effort to cut off the retreat. The bid failed, however, and the scarlet infantry trudged into Charlestown, where under cover of darkness a large fleet of boats evacuated them to Boston and safety.

Twelve hours after it began, the battle was over.

The Aftermath

General Gage and the other British officers were stunned by the events of April 19: 73 of their soldiers had been killed, 200 were wounded or missing, and the rest of the army was trapped, under siege, in Boston.

Perhaps most disturbing, however, was the courage and resolution demonstrated by the Americans. Gage and the others had deluded themselves into thinking that the minutemen were a cowardly rabble who would run at the first sign of a fight. Now they knew better. As General Percy wrote in his report of the battle: "I never believed, I confess, that they [the minutemen] would have attacked the King's troops, or have had the perseverance I found in them yesterday."

The Massachusetts patriots had lost forty-nine men killed and forty-six wounded, but had won a momentous victory. In defense of their liberty and property, they had vanquished the vaunted British regulars, electrifying New England—and eventually all of the colonies—with the spirit of rebellion. In time, this spirit would deepen into a fierce determination to win independence from Britain. At Lexington and Concord, the War of the American Revolution had begun.

Touring the Park

Begin your tour at either the North Bridge or Battle Road Visitor Center, where exhibits and maps will help you gain a better understanding of the events of April 19, 1775.

As you travel east along the Battle Road from Concord toward Lexington, there are ten stops along the way.

Stop 1. North Bridge Area. In the vicinity of Old North Bridge, minutemen offered the first effective forcible resistance to British rule in America. Take the foot trail from the Visitor Center to the North Bridge (the structure you see is a reproduction, built in 1956). Cross the bridge, where the "shot heard 'round the world" was fired, and view the Minuteman statue by Daniel Chester French, unveiled on April 19, 1875, to commemorate the citizen-soldiers who battled the British here.

From the North Bridge Visitor Center, return to Concord and and the Battle Road.

Stop 2. The Wayside. The Wayside was the house of Samuel Whitney, muster master for the Concord minutemen. It was later home to several important American literary figures, including Nathaniel Hawthorne, Bronson Alcott, and Louisa May Alcott.

Between mid-April and October, Friday through Tuesday, the Wayside is open to visitors. There are exhibits and an audiovisual program. Park personnel lead thirty-minute tours of the house on the half hour (limited to ten persons).

Stop 3. Meriam's Corner. The British soldiers retreating from Concord had to bunch up to get across a narrow bridge over Mill Brook on the Meriam Farm. Using the Meriam House and barn as cover, the minutemen moved in close and opened fire, starting the running battle that would last all afternoon as the redcoats struggled to get back to Boston.

Stop 4. Hardy's Hill. Minutemen from Sudbury and other towns to the south arrived here in time to join the fighting on the afternoon of April 19, 1775. As the British column passed this point, it was hit by fire from both flanks.

Stop 5. Bloody Angles. The Battle Road curved sharply through thick woods at this point. Concealed among the trees, hundreds of minutemen from Woburn and other communities poured fire into the British ranks at close range. The fusillade killed eight redcoats and wounded many others, including the commanding officer, Colonel Francis Smith.

Stop 6. Hartwell Tavern. This structure, built in 1775 and enlarged in later years, was the tavern of Ephraim Hartwell. It provided bed and board to travelers and was a popular gathering place for local people.

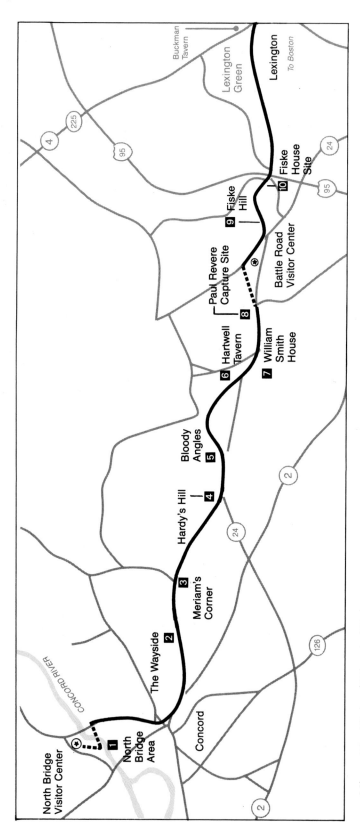

Minute Man National Historical Park

The British column was reeling as it retreated past this point on the afternoon of April 19. The losses suffered at the Bloody Angles, and the continuous musket fire from the minutemen swarming on all sides, brought home to the redcoats just how desperate their situation was.

Stop 7. William Smith House. This restored eighteenth-century house was the home of William Smith, captain of the Lincoln minutemen.

Stop 8. Paul Revere Capture Site. During the early morning hours of April 19, Paul Revere rode west from Charlestown toward Concord, warning townspeople along the way that the redcoats were coming. Near this point, Revere, Dr. Samuel Prescott, and another patriot courier named William Dawes were intercepted by a mounted British patrol. Revere was taken prisoner, Dawes lost his horse and had to return to Lexington on foot, but Dr. Prescott managed to escape and ride on to alert Concord.

Stop 9. Fiske Hill. Minutemen posted on this rocky bluff threatened to cut off the British retreat. Major Pitcairn, who had become acting commander when Smith was wounded, led the light infantry in a charge that cleared the hill and allowed the column to move on. Pitcairn's horse was shot from under him during this skirmish, and his pistols were captured by minuteman Israel Putnam. The pistols are now on display at the Lexington Historical Society.

Stop 10. Fiske House Site. The rows of stones you see mark the foundation of the Fiske House. There was intense, close-quarter fighting in this area as the redcoats struggled to get to Lexington. It was at this point that panic swept the British ranks. Wrote one officer: "[The rebels] kept the road always lined and a very hot fire on us without intermission; we at first kept our order and returned their fire . . . but when we arrived a mile from Lexington, our ammunition began to fail and the light [infantry] companies were so fatigued with flanking they were scarcely able to act . . . so that we began to run rather than retreat in order."

Minute Man National Historical Park ends here. However, you may wish to continue on to Lexington to see Lexington Green, where the first shots of the Revolution were fired, and visit the Lexington Visitor Center and Lexington Historical Society.

CHAPTER 4

SARATOGA NATIONAL HISTORICAL PARK
(Revolutionary War)

R.D. #2, Box 33
Stillwater, New York 12170
Telephone: (518) 664-9821

In fierce clashes on September 19 and October 7, 1777, American forces commanded by General Horatio Gates defeated the British army of General John Burgoyne. This decisive victory breathed new life into the patriot cause and encouraged France to enter the war on the American side. Saratoga National Historical Park preserves the scene of the fighting as well as several historic buildings associated with the Saratoga campaign.

Getting to the Park: Saratoga National Historical Park is located 30 miles north of Albany, New York. Take U.S. 4 from Albany to Stillwater. The park's main entrance is approximately 3 miles north of Stillwater.

Gas, food, lodging: In Schuylerville, 8 miles north of the main entrance on U.S. 4.

Visitor Center: Located approximately 1.5 miles from main entrance. Museum and gift shop; twenty-minute film on the battle.

Activities: Interpretive hikes led by park personnel during the summer months. Living history demonstrations by volunteers in period dress at the John Neilson House and the Schuyler House during the summer. Inquire at Visitor Center for schedule and locations.

Handicapped Access: The ramp from the parking lot to the Visitor Center is steep, and assistance may be required. Surfaced walkways at the tour stops throughout the park are accessible, but historic houses have one or two steps at their entrances.

The winter of 1776–1777 found British forces in North America frustrated in their efforts to crush the American Revolution. Two years of hard fighting had failed to subdue the recalcitrant colonists, and the war's cost was becoming worrisome to the royal government.

In London, the British high command approved plans for a spring campaign aimed at bringing a quick end to the conflict. General John Burgoyne—"Gentleman Johnny" to his troops—was to lead an army south from Canada along Lake Champlain, Lake George, and the Hudson River to Albany in east-central New York. At the same time, a smaller force commanded by Colonel Barry St. Leger would march east from Lake Ontario through New York's Mohawk Valley. After converging on Albany, Burgoyne and St. Leger would link up with General Sir William Howe's army advancing north from New York City. This would give Britain undisputed control of the strategic Lake Champlain–Hudson River waterway, cut New England off from the rest of the colonies, and break the back of the rebellion.

Burgoyne Invades New York

On June 17, 1777, Burgoyne's invasion column, made up of 4,200 British regulars, 4,000 German mercenaries, and several hundred Canadians and Indians, left St. Johns, Canada, and advanced down Lake Champlain into New York. The general's first objective was Fort Ticonderoga, a star-shaped stone citadel guarding the approaches to the Hudson River Valley. He captured the fort after a four-day siege, and then pursued the fleeing defenders, routing them in sharp skirmishes at Skenesboro, Fort Ann, and Hubbardton, Vermont.

News of Burgoyne's triumph at Ticonderoga greatly boosted British morale: "I have beat them! I have beat all the Americans!" King George III is said to have exclaimed when he heard of the fort's fall. But rather than crumbling in the face of the British invasion, American resistance stiffened. The patriots felled trees to block roads, tore down bridges, destroyed crops, and drove off livestock herds, slowing Burgoyne's advance to a crawl. Reaching Fort Edward at the southern end of Lake George on July 30, the British general was forced to call a halt to rest and resupply his army.

It took all of August for Burgoyne's soldiers to receive provisions from Canada, and this long delay allowed the Americans to take the initiative. At Fort Stanwix (see Chapter 2) and Oriskany in western New York, they blocked St. Leger's march down the Mohawk Valley and forced him to return to Canada. Then, on August 16, they surprised and destroyed an 800-man detachment that Burgoyne had sent from Fort Edward to nearby Bennington, Vermont, to seize patriot supplies.

The Bennington disaster brought home to Burgoyne the precariousness of his army's position: it was isolated deep in enemy territory, threatened by a large and growing American force. Still, orders were orders, and he decided to push on to his objective. On September 13, he and his troops crossed to the west bank of the Hudson and began marching south along the River Road toward Albany.

An American army commanded by General Horatio Gates was waiting to intercept the British invasion column in a fortified position, four miles north of the village of Stillwater. Approximately 9,000 patriots had dug in on Bemis Heights, a series of bluffs overlooking the River Road. If Burgoyne's troops tried to get by on the road they would be hammered by American artillery; if they moved inland they would run

British general John Burgoyne, known to his troops as "Gentleman Johnny," led an invasion column south from Canada along the Lake Champlain–Hudson River waterway during the summer of 1777. Painting by Sir Joshua Reynolds, Copyright The Frick Collection.

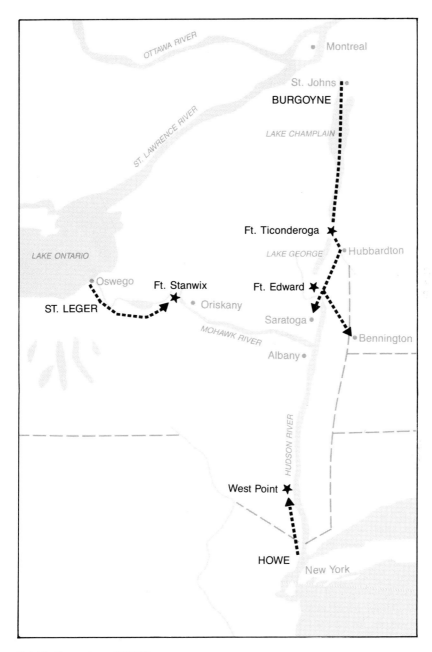

British Campaign of 1777

General Horatio Gates com-
manded the American forces
at Saratoga. Painting by
C. W. Peale, Independence
National Historic Park
Collection.

into a bristling line of fortifications, laid out by Colonel Thaddeus Kosciuszko, a
Polish engineer serving on Gates's staff.

Freeman's Farm: September 19, 1777

On the cool, foggy morning of September 19, Burgoyne's army, divided into three
columns, approached the American line. One of the columns, composed of German
troops led by Baron Von Riedesel, moved down the River Road. The other two, led
by General Simon Fraser and by Burgoyne, advanced through thick woods on the
high ground above the Hudson.

When Gates learned from his scouts that the British were approaching, he sent
Colonel Daniel Morgan's corps of riflemen to determine the enemy's strength and
exact position. At 12.30 P.M. a group of Morgan's soldiers encountered British skirmishers in the open fields of Freeman's Farm. They opened fire and drove the redcoats
back, only to be thrown into retreat themselves by heavy volleys from the main body
of Burgoyne's column, which had just emerged from the woods.

Colonel Morgan realized that a battle was in the offing, and he began blowing
frantically on a turkey call, a signal for his men to rally to him. They soon did, and he
quickly placed them in a line on the southern boundary of Freeman's Farm, where
they could take cover behind trees and brush. Burgoyne ordered his troops to fix

bayonets and attack, but the rapid, deadly accurate rifle fire from the concealed Americans shattered the charge. Trying to exploit the enemy's confusion, Morgan launched a counterattack, but the British managed to reform their ranks in time to repel it.

For more than three hours the fighting raged back and forth across the farm as both sides struggled desperately to gain the upper hand. The British used their bayonets to hold the Americans at bay, while the Americans relied on scathing rifle fire to fend off the repeated charges of the redcoats.

Late in the afternoon American reinforcements came up and under the direction of General Benedict Arnold moved to attack Burgoyne's right flank. The British line was

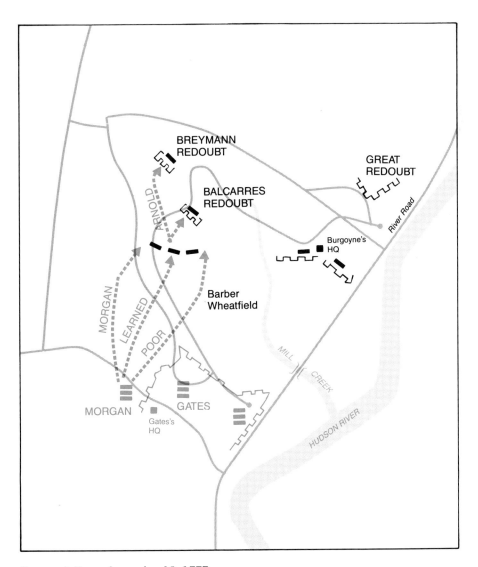

Freeman's Farm, September 19, 1777

wavering and about to break when 550 of Von Riedesel's Germans burst out of the forest and struck the American right, saving the day for Burgoyne. As darkness fell, the Americans withdrew to their fortifications leaving the exhausted, bloodied British to regroup and lick their wounds.

Burgoyne Waits in Vain

Although he could claim victory in the Freeman's Farm fight because he was in possession of the battlefield, Burgoyne knew that his army had come within an eyelash of being destroyed. Abandoning the offensive, he ordered his soldiers to build a zigzag line of forts and log redoubts stretching from Freeman's Farm east two miles to the river. They would wait in these entrenchments for the reinforcements Burgoyne believed were on their way up the Hudson from the British stronghold at New York City.

For his part, General Gates was content to sit back and let the redcoats make the next move. Every day the American army grew stronger thanks to the arrival of militia companies from the surrounding countryside. In just three weeks the size of the patriot force jumped from 9,000 men to 13,000.

By contrast, Burgoyne's situation was rapidly deteriorating. His supplies were running out, many of his German mercenaries were deserting, the weather was growing colder, and there was no sign of help coming from the south, where the British advance up the Hudson had come to a halt at West Point. He was forced to make a difficult choice: retreat back to Canada, 200 miles away, or attack and break through to Albany. Reluctantly, he decided to attack.

The Second Battle of Freeman's Farm: October 7, 1777

At noon on October 7, Burgoyne led 1,500 of his most experienced men out of the fortifications and toward the left flank of the American line. He intended to probe the patriot position and find a weak spot against which he could later launch a full-scale attack.

The column moved slowly through the forest for two-thirds of a mile, then halted and deployed in battle formation in a wheatfield on the Barber Farm. This was the opportunity Gates had been waiting for: "Order on Morgan to begin the game," he said when he learned of the British advance.

Soon Morgan's riflemen, accompanied by the infantry brigades of Generals Ebenezer Learned and Enoch Poor, were moving north toward the Barber Wheatfield. Poor's brigade attacked first, smashing into Burgoyne's left and rolling it back. Morgan's riflemen followed with a savage assault on the right, pouring fire into the ranks of redcoats and mortally wounding General Fraser. As the battle roared toward its climax, Benedict Arnold galloped onto the field and led Learned's brigade in a fierce charge against Burgoyne's center.

The hard-hit British line bent and then broke, as panicky soldiers scrambled back through the woods toward the shelter of their fortifications. In less than an hour, 400 of Burgoyne's veterans had been killed, wounded, or taken prisoner, and the Americans were not through yet. Urged on by Arnold, they followed the retreating redcoats

Benedict Arnold, Traitor

At the battles of Quebec, Valcour Island, and Saratoga, Benedict Arnold proved himself to be the Continental Army's finest fighting officer. "A bloody fellow he was," recalled a veteran of the Arnold-led assault on Breymann Redoubt. "He didn't care for nothing; he'd ride right in. It was 'Come on, boys!' 'twasn't 'Go boys!' . . . there wasn't any waste timber in him." This opinion was seconded by General George Washington, who wrote: "He . . . always distinguished himself as a judicious, brave officer of great activity, enterprise and perseverance."

General Benedict Arnold. National Archives.

But for all his success on the battlefield, Arnold was a bitter, chronically disappointed man who believed that he had been denied the plaudits he was justly due. Egotistical and quarrelsome, he made many enemies among his fellow officers, and as a result was passed over for promotion and accused of having loyalist tendencies.

As the war progressed and the attacks on his character mounted, the thin-skinned Arnold grew ever more disillusioned and resentful. "Having made every sacrifice of fortune, ease and domestic happiness to serve my country, I am publicly impeached," he declared. Finally, in a fit of rage and despair, he contacted British officials and offered his services as a spy. The offer was accepted, and from May 1779, to September 1780, Arnold provided military intelligence to the redcoats.

When his treachery was at last discovered, Arnold escaped to New York

City, where he joined the British army as a brigadier general. He subse-
quently led raids against the patriot strongholds of Richmond, Virginia,
and New London, Connecticut, and at war's end he sailed for London,
never to return to the land of his birth.

Sadly, it was as a traitor that Arnold won the immortality that should
have been his as the patriot army's best and bravest combat officer. The
tragic irony of this was not lost on his contemporaries, who wondered
how such an outstanding soldier could have betrayed the cause he had
fought so valiantly for. "How black," lamented General Nathanael Greene,
"how despised. Loved by none, hated by all—once his country's idol, now
her horror!"

back to the Freeman Farm and launched a series of ferocious assaults on Balcarres
Redoubt, the strongest of the British earth-and-log forts.

These charges were repulsed, but as twilight settled over the battlefield, Arnold led
several fresh American units in a successful attack on Breymann Redoubt, located just
north of Balcarres Redoubt. One of the German defenders shot Arnold in the leg, but
it was not enough to stem the American tide. The fieldwork was captured, and its
fall made Burgoyne's entire position untenable. He evacuated Balcarres Redoubt
under cover of darkness and withdrew to Great Redoubt, located a mile and a half to
the east.

Retreat and Surrender

After burying General Fraser in the Great Redoubt on the night of October 8,
Burgoyne and his battered army retreated northward. They got as far as Saratoga
(present-day Schuylerville) before being cut off and surrounded by Gates's army,
which now numbered 20,000 men. With supplies exhausted and no prospect of help
arriving from Canada or New York, Burgoyne was forced to surrender. On October
17, 1777, 5,800 weary, hungry soldiers—all that remained of the once-proud British
invasion force—marched out of camp, stacked their arms, and became prisoners
of war.

Turning Point of the Revolution

The victory at Saratoga breathed new life into the patriot cause at a time when another defeat might have spelled the end of the Revolution. American soldiers who
had begun to doubt their ability to defeat the better trained and equipped British
regulars were greatly heartened, and American civilians, many of whom had remained
neutral during the first two years of the war, now had reason to back their countrymen
in the struggle for liberty. Even more importantly, the surrender of Burgoyne's army
in the field, an event unprecedented in British military annals, inspired France to join
the war on the American side. It was French logistical and military assistance that
would enable the Americans to fight on for four more years and ultimately win their
independence.

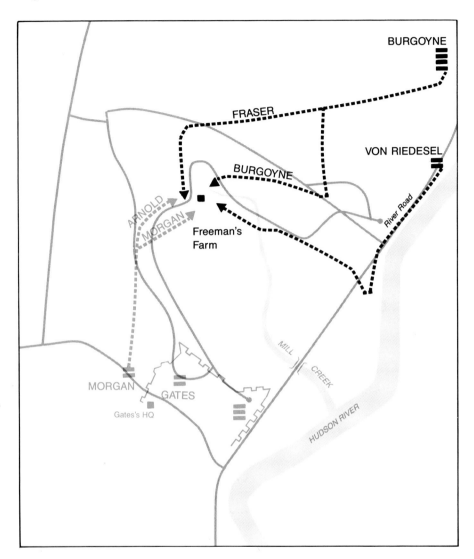

Second Battle of Freeman's Farm, October 7, 1777

Touring the Park

Begin your tour at the Visitor Center, where maps, exhibits, and an audiovisual program will help you to gain a clearer understanding of the Saratoga campaign and the critical part it played in the American Revolution.

A nine-mile tour road (open from April 1 to November 30 as weather permits) runs through the park. Ten stops mark the key historic points on the battlefield.

Stop 1. Freeman's Farm Overlook. The fields in front of you were part of Freeman's Farm, scene of fierce fighting on the afternoon of September 19, 1777. Colonel Daniel Morgan's riflemen intercepted Burgoyne's advancing column here. After three

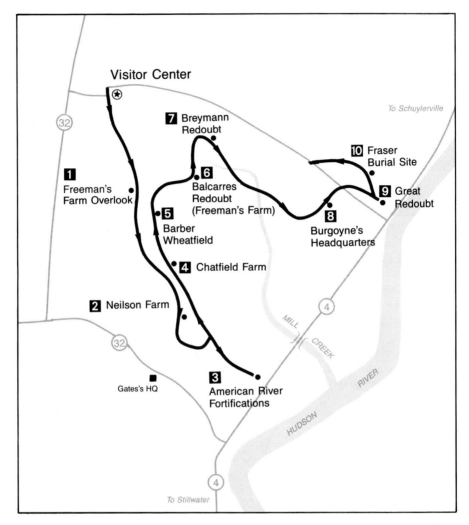

Saratoga National Historical Park

hours of combat, it appeared that the Americans would drive the British from the field, but the arrival of 550 German troops turned the tide for Burgoyne. As darkness fell, the Americans retreated to their camp at the Neilson Farm, one mile to the south, or to your right. The British began constructing fortifications, including Breymann and Balcarres redoubts, half a mile to the east, or in front of you.

Stop 2. Neilson Farm (Bemis Heights). The farm of John Neilson was at the center of the fortified line held by the Americans on Bemis Heights in September and October 1777. White stakes show where the line extended to the southeast and southwest. The farmhouse has been restored to its 1777 appearance; it was used for quarters by Generals Benedict Arnold and Enoch Poor. About a quarter mile to the south, across Route 32, are the sites of General Gates's headquarters and the field hospital where the American wounded were treated.

Stop 3. American River Fortifications. From this high ground, batteries of American cannon commanded the River Road, Burgoyne's route to Albany. The guns sited here by Colonel Thaddeus Kosciuszko, a Polish engineer serving with the patriots, forced Burgoyne to abandon the road and attack the American line on the wooded bluffs to the west.

Stop 4. Chatfield Farm. From this ridge, which was part of the Asa Chatfield Farm in 1777, American scouts watched the British line during the weeks leading up to the October 7 battle. Burgoyne's movement toward the Barber Farm was first seen and reported by the patriots manning this outpost.

Stop 5. Barber Wheatfield. In this field, and in the field to the west beyond the first row of trees, the Americans attacked Burgoyne's advancing column on the afternoon of October 7. In less than an hour, 400 British soldiers were killed, wounded, or taken prisoner, and the rest were forced to retreat to Balcarres Redoubt, half a mile to the northeast.

Stop 6. Balcarres Redoubt (Freeman's Farm). After the fight on September 19, the British entrenched along a two-mile line extending from the river to Freeman's Farm. The strongest fortification was Balcarres Redoubt, a 1,500-foot long, 14-foot high log-and-earth barricade. After being routed at the Barber Wheatfield on October 7, the survivors of Burgoyne's column sought shelter here. Led by Benedict Arnold, the Americans stormed the redoubt repeatedly but failed to capture it, suffering heavy casualties in the process. The outline of the redoubt is marked by stakes.

Stop 7. Breymann Redoubt. After failing to capture Balcarres Redoubt, Benedict Arnold led the Americans in a successful assault on this 600-foot-long log breastwork, which is now outlined by stakes. Arnold was wounded in the leg as he charged into the redoubt; the nearby "Boot Monument" commemorates this event. The capture of Breymann Redoubt forced Burgoyne to evacuate Balcarres Redoubt on the night of October 7.

Stop 8. Burgoyne's Headquarters. The path from the parking area leads to the site of Burgoyne's headquarters, established after the September 19 fight. The headquarters was a large tent, pitched near a spring.

Stop 9. Great Redoubt. The British fortifications located on this hill and on the two hills to the north were called the Great Redoubt. They protected the field hospital and the supply depot on the river flat. It was to this area that Burgoyne and the British army retreated after the fighting of October 7.

Stop 10. Fraser Burial Site and Trail. A one-mile loop trail leads past the grave site of General Simon Fraser, who was mortally wounded by an American rifleman at the Barber Wheatfield on October 7. Beyond Fraser's grave, the trail passes the site of of the British field hospital, the artillery park and baggage area, and the Taylor House, where Fraser died.

To reach the Schuyler House and Saratoga Monument, return to U.S. 4, turn left, and drive to Schuylerville, eight miles to the north.

General Philip Schuyler House. Located in Schuylerville (historic Saratoga), this large, two-story white frame house was the country home of General Philip Schuyler. Schuyler rallied American forces in upstate New York to oppose Burgoyne's advance, but was relieved of command by General Horatio Gates a month before the battle. The first house to stand on this site was burned by the British army; the present structure was built in 1777, shortly after Burgoyne's surrender.

The Schuyler House is open from late June to Labor Day. Living-history demonstrations are presented by volunteers in period dress. Inquire at the Visitor Center for hours and the schedule of events.

Saratoga Monument. This 155-foot-high granite obelisk, completed in 1883, commemorates the surrender of Burgoyne's army on October 17, 1777. The monument stands on the site of Burgoyne's camp during the final days of the campaign. A winding staircase leads to the top, where an observation floor offers a panoramic view of the battlefield area.

CHAPTER 5

ANTIETAM NATIONAL BATTLEFIELD
(Civil War)

P.O. Box 158
Sharpsburg, Maryland 21782
Telephone: (301) 432-5124

The Battle of Antietam on September 17, 1862, marked the climax of the first Confederate invasion of the North. The Union Army of the Potomac, commanded by General George B. McClellan, forced Robert E. Lee's Army of Northern Virginia to abandon its foray into Maryland. In twelve hours of fighting, 23,000 men were killed or wounded, making Antietam the bloodiest one-day battle in American history.

Getting to the Park: Antietam National Battlefield is located approximately 1 mile north of Sharpsburg, Maryland, on Maryland 65 (the Hagerstown Pike).

Gas, food, lodging: Along U.S. 40 east of Hagerstown, Maryland, 10 miles from the park.

Visitor Center: Museum and gift shop; audiovisual program on the battle and the Maryland Campaign.

Activities: Park personnel present interpretive programs at Dunker Church (Stop 1 on the auto tour) and the National Cemetery (Stop 11 on the auto tour). Inquire at the Visitor Center for schedule and locations.

Handicapped Access: All Visitor Center facilities and most tour exhibits are readily accessible.

On a golden, warm September afternoon in 1862, young Leighton Parks stood on the Maryland bank of the Potomac River and witnessed a scene he would never forget. Coming toward him from the Virginia side, splashing knee-deep through the placid waters of White's Ford, was a long column of soldiers dressed in butternut and gray. "They were the dirtiest men I ever saw," Parks wrote years later, "a most ragged, lean, and hungry set of wolves. . . . Many of them were from the far South and spoke a dialect I could hardly understand. They were profane beyond belief and talked incessantly."

"A most ragged, lean, and hungry set of wolves," was the way one civilian described the Confederate infantrymen who invaded Maryland in the summer of 1862. Library of Congress.

On they came, all that day and the next, thousands of gaunt, bright-eyed Confederates, wading across the river with their muskets and cartridge boxes held high. Many had no shoes and were limping along on bruised and blistered feet, but they managed to look jaunty nonetheless. They were the tough, proud veterans of the Army of Northern Virginia, embarked on the South's boldest military venture of the Civil War: an invasion of the North.

Maryland, My Maryland

Robert E. Lee faced a difficult decision after his brilliant victory at the Battle of Second Manassas on August 29–30, 1862 (see Chapter 10). Having sent the Union army scrambling in disarray back to Washington, he was in a position to go on the offensive, but his command was too small and the Federal capital too strongly fortified to risk a frontal assault. His options were either to stay put near Manassas or to bypass Washington and strike out to the north. "We cannot afford to be idle," he concluded, and on September 3 he ordered his troops to head north toward Maryland.

From a strategic standpoint, an invasion of Maryland held great promise for the

Confederacy. First, it would draw the Union army away from battle-scarred Virginia and allow the state's farmers to harvest their crops in peace. Second, it would give the Marylanders, many of whom were southern sympathizers, a chance to support the Confederate cause actively. Third, and most enticingly, it might induce Great Britain to recognize the Confederacy, putting immense pressure on the war-weary North to negotiate a peace.

There was an important practical benefit, too: a thrust into the verdant Maryland countryside would enable Lee to seize the food, clothing, and horses his army desperately needed to carry on the fight.

McClellan Marches

On September 7, the Army of the Potomac, commanded by General George B. McClellan, marched northward in pursuit of Lee's invasion force. The Union troops arrived in the town of Frederick on the 13th; the Confederates had departed days earlier, but on their abandoned campground an alert private discovered three cigars wrapped in a piece of paper. The paper turned out to be a copy of Lee's Special Order No. 191, detailing the general's plans for the Maryland campaign.

McClellan read the document and learned that Lee had divided his army, sending a detachment under General Thomas "Stonewall" Jackson southwest to capture Harpers Ferry, and another under General James Longstreet northwest toward Hagerstown. If McClellan moved swiftly, he could position his army between the two Confederate detachments and destroy them in turn.

The Army of the Potomac headed west the next day, following a route that would

General Robert E. Lee led the Confederate Army of Northern Virginia on its invasion of the North in 1862. Library of Congress.

General George B. McClellan commanded the Union Army of the Potomac at Antietam. National Archives.

take it over South Mountain by way of Turner's, Fox's, and Crampton's gaps. When Lee learned of this sudden move he became concerned: the Army of Northern Virginia had to be reunited as quickly as possible. To buy time, he ordered the small forces he had close at hand to move into the South Mountain gaps and delay McClellan's approach long enough to allow the rest of the army to concentrate at Sharpsburg, a little farming village on the banks of Antietam Creek, midway between Hagerstown and Harpers Ferry.

After a grueling, day-long fight on September 14, the Union columns succeeded in punching through the gaps. Lee was regrouping his scattered forces rapidly, however, and by the afternoon of September 16, the Army of Northern Virginia—with the exception of General A. P. Hill's division, which was still at Harpers Ferry—was together and deployed on a long, low ridge just west of Antietam Creek.

Lee had only 41,000 troops at his disposal, but he was confident that he could fend off McClellan, who, with a force of 87,000 men, was preparing to attack him.

Assault through Miller's Cornfield

A damp, gray mist shrouded the valley of Antietam Creek at dawn on September 17. The soldiers, Confederate and Union alike, shivered in the early morning chill, gripped their muskets with clammy palms, and tried to steel themselves mentally for the impending clash.

It began with a tremendous Union cannon barrage that shook the earth with its rolling, concussive thunder. The center of the maelstrom was Miller's Cornfield, a forty-acre patch of dry, yellow stalks on the extreme left end of the Confederate line. This position was held by Stonewall Jackson's men, and they suffered heavy casualties as shell fragments shredded the concealing corn, cutting it "as closely as could have been done with a knife," leaving the slain lying "in rows precisely as they had stood in their ranks a few moments before."

When the barrage lifted, 10,000 Union soldiers of General Joseph Hooker's corps advanced toward the Cornfield and the clumps of trees—called the East Woods and the West Woods—that flanked it on the left and right. The surviving Confederates rose and greeted them with withering point-blank volleys, but could not slow the momentum of the charge. Back stumbled Jackson's veterans, trying to find shelter in the West Woods; on came Hooker's men, firing and cheering as they approached the Dunker Church, a small, white building just south of the Cornfield.

It was now 7 A.M., and the sun was burning through the mist. The Confederate army was in danger of having its flank rolled completely up by Hooker's powerful assault. In desperation, Lee pulled units out of other parts of the line and sent them to the Dunker Church to reinforce his crumbling left. Jackson received these fresh troops and immediately launched a ferocious counterattack that drove the Federals back through the blood-soaked Cornfield. Suddenly the tables were turned, and it was Hooker's men who were reeling and on the brink of collapse.

Slaughter in the West Woods

Just when it appeared that Hooker and his troops would be routed, General Joseph Mansfield's corps arrived on the field and halted the Confederate onslaught in its

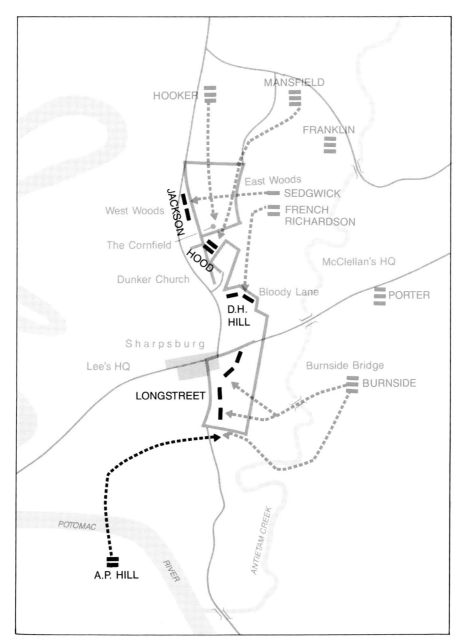

Antietam, September 17, 1862

tracks. Mansfield was mortally wounded but his troops swept the Rebels back across Miller's Cornfield and drove a salient deep into the gray line between the West Woods and the Dunker Church.

General Alpheus Williams, who had assumed command when Mansfield was shot, sent word to the Union headquarters that he could break through and win the battle if reinforcements were sent to him immediately. One division was already on its way, moving through the East Woods toward the scene of the fighting, but there would be a delay before it got into position. Stonewall Jackson took advantage of this lull to bring up more Confederate reinforcements and place them in the West Woods where they could devastate the advancing Union column.

Shortly after 9 A.M., the blue ranks of General John Sedgwick's division emerged from the East Woods, filed across the Cornfield, and passed into the West Woods, where Jackson's men lay in wait. Sheets of flame erupted from the shadows as the concealed Confederates opened fire, ravaging the densely packed Union column. In twenty minutes of concentrated carnage, nearly half of Sedgwick's division, 2,200 men, were shot down. The rest fled in panic, followed by Williams's troops, who could not hold on to their salient without support.

Bloody Lane

The soldiers of General William French's division, who had been marching behind Sedgwick's troops, veered to the south and avoided the West Woods trap. They were

Bloody Lane, where more than 5,000 men were killed or wounded in savage fighting. National Park Service, photograph by Cecil W. Stoughton.

crossing the open fields of the Roulette Farm when they came upon an old country lane that wagon wheels and the wash of rain had worn beneath the level of the ground. Posted in this sunken road were some 2,500 Confederates commanded by General D. H. Hill. As the men in blue approached, stepping along as if on parade, Hill's soldiers blasted them from the shelter of the road embankment. The Federals stumbled backward in the face of this savage, unexpected fire, but soon rallied and charged again.

What had begun as a chance encounter quickly escalated into an all-out struggle as both sides threw more troops into the fray. General Israel Richardson's division buttressed French's sagging formation, while General Lee sent the last Confederate reserves forward to bolster Hill. "For three hours and thirty minutes the battle raged incessantly, without either party giving way," wrote a Union officer. Waves of Union soldiers continued to press the attack, suffering appalling losses as they swept up the ridge toward the flickering line of muzzle flashes.

Just before 1 P.M., a Confederate unit misunderstood an order and retreated from its position in the line. Union infantry rushed into the breach and began pouring fire down the length of the sunken road, turning it into a slaughter pen. Within minutes bodies lay so thick that it was impossible to walk without stepping on them. The survivors of Hill's force ran from the deadly, snapping bullets, fleeing south toward Sharpsburg; henceforth the sunken road would be known as "Bloody Lane."

The way was now open for McClellan to smash through the center of Lee's line and destroy the Army of Northern Virginia. "There was no body of Confederate infantry in this part of the field that would have resisted a serious advance," recalled one of Lee's officers. A fresh Union corps was massed and ready to deliver the coup de grace, but at the critical moment McClellan wavered. "It would not be prudent to make the attack," he announced after examining the situation, and thereby squandered the golden opportunity for victory that had been created at such terrible cost.

Burnside's Bridge

At the far end of the battlefield, southeast of Sharpsburg, another bitter struggle was underway. Since 9:30 A.M., 14,000 Union troops led by General Ambrose Burnside had been trying to cross a stone bridge over Antietam Creek. On the steep slope just beyond the bridge, 500 Georgians were dug in with their muskets trained on the stone span and its approaches. Again and again blue columns stormed onto the bridge only to be driven back by a hail of lead from the rifle pits above.

Finally, at 1 P.M., the Federals managed to get across Burnside's Bridge and onto the west side of the creek. After a two-hour delay to rest and reorganize, the powerful force began to advance toward Sharpsburg. Lee had stripped this part of his line to reinforce Stonewall Jackson at Dunker Church and D. H. Hill at Bloody Lane, and there was little left to stand in the way of Burnside's divisions. They swept forward inexorably, brushing aside feeble resistance, and approached the village. Lee was in danger of having his line of retreat cut; the outnumbered Army of Northern Virginia was about to be hemmed in and destroyed.

A Confederate disaster was in the making, but then A. P. Hill's division, which had left Harpers Ferry at 6:30 A.M., arrived on the field. Exhausted from marching seventeen miles in seven hours, Hill's soldiers nevertheless rushed directly to the attack, smashing into the left flank of Burnside's advancing column. The Federals were staggered by this unexpected onslaught, and their drive toward Sharpsburg stalled. Soon they were retreating back toward the heights above the creek, and as the sun finally set the battle sputtered to a close.

Somehow, Lee and his troops had withstood the hammer blows of McClellan's much larger army, but they could not stand any more. The next evening they began withdrawing across the Potomac River, heading south for Virginia's Shenandoah Valley. McClellan did not pursue. The first Confederate invasion of the North was over.

America's Bloodiest Day

In all of America's wars, from the Revolution to the present, no single day has been bloodier than September 17, 1862. In twelve hours of virtually nonstop fighting, the Union army lost 12,410 men; the Confederates 10,700. One soldier out of every four who went into action at Antietam was killed or wounded.

This dreadful carnage brought neither side a decisive victory, but it did alter the strategic and political complexion of the conflict. Lee's hopes of enlisting Maryland's aid and winning foreign recognition for the Confederacy were dashed, while Union morale was boosted. Even more importantly, the repulse of the invader allowed President Lincoln to proceed with issuing the Emancipation Proclamation, freeing all slaves in states still in rebellion against the United States. Thus, the terrible trial by

America's bloodiest day. These Confederates were killed in fighting along the Hagerstown Pike, just west of the Cornfield. Library of Congress.

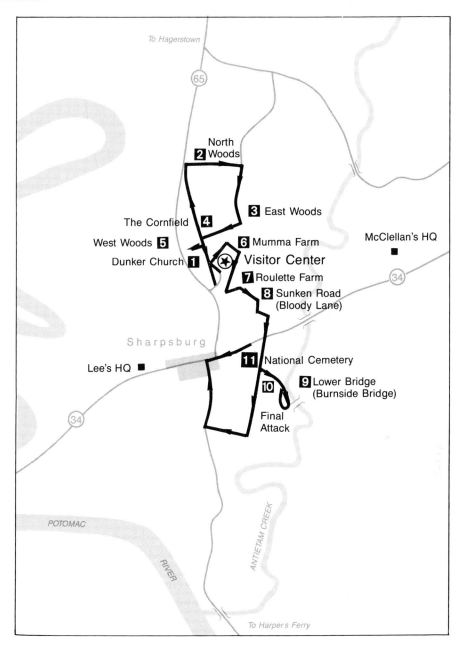

North
2 Woods

3 East Woods

The Cornfield **4**

West Woods **5**

6 Mumma Farm

McClellan's HQ

Dunker Church **1**

⊛ Visitor Center

7 Roulette Farm

8 Sunken Road
(Bloody Lane)

Sharpsburg

Lee's HQ ■

11 National Cemetery

10

9 Lower Bridge
(Burnside Bridge)

Final
Attack

To Hagerstown

65

34

34

POTOMAC

RIVER

ANTIETAM CREEK

To Harper's Ferry

Antietam National Battlefield

fire that was the Battle of Antietam transformed the Civil War into a struggle not just to preserve the Union, but to end slavery.

Touring the Park

Begin your tour at the Visitor Center, where museum exhibits and an audiovisual program provide an overview of the battle and of the campaign that preceded it.

A self-guided auto tour will take you around the battlefield. Eleven numbered stops, marking major points of interest, are arranged according to the sequence of the battle.

Stop 1. Dunker Church. Hundreds of men on both sides died in the seesaw fighting that raged around this small, whitewashed brick building during the early morning hours of September 17, 1862. Ironically, the church belonged to a pacifist group, a German Baptist sect called the Dunkers. It was restored to its wartime appearance in 1962.

Stop 2. North Woods. The assault that opened the battle began here shortly after 6 A.M. General Hooker's corps, 10,000 men strong, swept past the Miller Farmhouse and across the Cornfield, half a mile to the south. The Union advance was halted by a Confederate countercharge launched from the vicinity of the Dunker Church.

Stop 3. East Woods. The second Union attack, made by General Mansfield's corps, began here. Mansfield was mortally wounded near this spot, but his soldiers drove Stonewall Jackson's Confederates back across the Cornfield toward the West Woods, half a mile to the southwest.

Stop 4. The Cornfield. Between 6 A.M. and 9 A.M., the blue and gray battle lines swept back and forth across this forty-acre field. The cornstalks were cut down by bullets and shell fragments, and hundreds of men were killed or wounded in the repeated charges. "The fire and smoke, flashing of muskets and whizzing of bullets, yells of men, etc., were perfectly horrible," wrote a Union soldier of the Cornfield combat. Said another: "I do not see how any of us got out alive."

Stop 5. West Woods. Around 9:15 A.M., Union general John Sedgwick's division, moving to support Mansfield's corps, emerged from the East Woods (Stop 3), advanced west past the Cornfield (Stop 4) and the Mumma Farm (Stop 6), and entered this forested area. Here they were ambushed by Stonewall Jackson's concealed troops. Within twenty minutes, half of Sedgwick's command, 2,200 men, were gunned down.

Stop 6. Mumma Farm. Fighting raged across the farm of Samuel Mumma all through the morning of September 17. The crash of muskets and the screams of the wounded terrified the farm's dairy herd, which stampeded back and forth trying to escape the awful din. "I remember I was more afraid just then of being run over by a cow than of being hit by a bullet," wrote a Georgia soldier. Eventually, the Confederates were forced to abandon their position, and as they withdrew to the south and west, they torched the Mumma Farm buildings to prevent Union sharpshooters from being posted in them.

Stop 7. Roulette Farm. General William French's Union division, advancing toward the fighting at about 9:30 A.M., veered southwest to avoid the West Woods trap that had closed around Sedgwick and his men (Stop 5). French's troops marched across these fields, which belonged to farmer William Roulette, and collided with a Confederate force posted in the sunken road. Later, another Union division, led by General Israel Richardson, passed this point on its way to assault the sunken road.

Stop 8. Sunken Road (Bloody Lane). This country lane, which formed the boundary between the Roulette and Piper farms, had been worn several feet below ground level by rain and the pressure of wagon wheels. About 2,500 Confederate soldiers commanded by General D. H. Hill were positioned here, and they blasted French's division as it advanced from the north across the fields of the Roulette Farm. The Union troops continued to press the attack, and after three hours of almost indescribable carnage, they succeeded in driving the Confederates out of the sunken road. More than 5,000 men were killed or wounded in the desperate struggle for "Bloody Lane."

Stop 9. Lower Bridge (Burnside's Bridge). At 9:30 A.M., McClellan ordered General Ambrose Burnside to advance across Antietam Creek and attack the Confederate right flank south of Sharpsburg. Burnside's corps, totaling nearly 14,000 troops, spent the next three hours trying to seize this stone bridge, which was defended by a few hundred Georgians dug in along the ridge on the creek's west bank. Shallow fords, where the Union soldiers could have waded across the stream, existed a few hundred yards above and below the bridge.

Stop 10. The Final Attack. At 1 P.M., after a three-hour struggle, Burnside's troops succeeded in capturing the Lower Bridge. After regrouping for another two hours, they advanced across these hills toward Sharpsburg and were threatening to turn Lee's right flank and cut off his line of retreat, when a fierce attack by A. P. Hill's Confederate division, just arrived from Harpers Ferry, drove them back. Learning of Burnside's retreat, McClellan decided to halt the fighting, thereby bringing the Battle of Antietam to a close.

Stop 11. Antietam National Cemetery. This hillside cemetery holds the remain of 4,776 Union soldiers. Most of the Confederate dead are buried in Hagerstown and Frederick, Maryland, and Shepherdstown, West Virginia.

CHAPTER 6

FORT McHENRY NATIONAL MONUMENT AND HISTORIC SHRINE
(War of 1812)

Fort McHenry National Monument
Baltimore, Maryland 21230
Telephone: (301) 962-4299

A British attempt to capture Baltimore on September 12–14, 1814, was thwarted, in part, by the defense of Fort McHenry. After watching the bombardment of the star-shaped masonry structure, Francis Scott Key was inspired to write the words to "The Star Spangled Banner." Fort McHenry National Monument and Historic Shrine preserves the fort and surrounding grounds.

Getting to the Park: Fort McHenry National Monument and Historic Shrine is located in Baltimore, Maryland. From I-95 take Exit 55 (Key Highway/Fort McHenry National Monument) and follow the blue and green signs on Key Highway to Lawrence Street. Turn left on Lawrence Street and then left on Fort Avenue to the park.

Gas, food, lodging: In Baltimore.

Visitor Center: Museum and gift shop; sixteen-minute film on the Battle of Baltimore and the writing of "The Star Spangled Banner."

Activities: Guided tours by park personnel. Cannon-firing demonstrations, drills, and special ceremonies by the Fort McHenry Guard during summer months. Flag Day and Defenders' Day (battle anniversary) special programs. Inquire at Visitor Center for schedule and further details.

Handicapped Access: Visitor Center is fully accessible. Trail around the fort is wheelchair negotiable with assistance. Ramps are provided to all buildings where first floor exhibits are displayed. Audio stations on battlements are inaccessible by wheelchair because of stairs.

In April 1814, Napoleon abdicated his throne and went into exile, ending the twenty-two-year-old world war between France and Great Britain. Cessation of hostilities in Europe meant that the British military could devote its full attention to the War of 1812, which had been sputtering along for nearly two years. The high com-

mand mapped out a strategy for defeating the United States, and transports loaded
with veteran soldiers set sail for North America.

The Chesapeake Campaign

A fleet of twenty British warships commanded by Admiral Alexander Cochrane entered Chesapeake Bay and sailed up the Patuxent River in mid-August 1814. Cochrane was intent on attacking Washington and giving the Americans "a complete drub-
bing" that they would not soon forget.

The fleet landing force—3,400 seasoned troops led by General Robert Ross—went
ashore at Benedict, Maryland, on August 19 and marched northwest. On August 24
at Bladensburg, barely a mile from the boundary of the District of Columbia, Ross's
army routed a force of American militia. After occupying the capital and burning
government buildings, including the Capitol and the White House, the British soldiers returned to Benedict and reembarked. Their next target was Baltimore.

The Battle of Baltimore

The water approaches to Baltimore were guarded by a large, star-shaped fort located
on Whetstone Point. This masonry structure had been built in the late 1790s and was
named Fort McHenry in honor of James McHenry, secretary of war in the administration of President John Adams.

With its fifty-seven guns and 1,000 defenders, Fort McHenry prevented Admiral
Cochrane from making a direct assault on Baltimore. Instead, he landed Ross's infantry, reinforced by 600 marines, on North Point, a spit of land extending some ten
miles into Chesapeake Bay. The soldiers would march up this peninsula and attack
Baltimore from the landward side while Cochrane's warships neutralized the fort.

The British began marching up North Point on the morning of September 12. A
detachment of American skirmishers intercepted them around 2 P.M. and fired several
volleys; one of the bullets struck General Ross in the chest, mortally wounding him.
Colonel Arthur Brooke assumed command, and the redcoats continued to advance
until they ran into 3,200 American militiamen in the vicinity of Bear Creek. A sharp
battled ensued; the Americans eventually were driven back toward Baltimore, but not
before they had inflicted 300 casualties.

While the fighting was going on at North Point, Admiral Cochrane was busy
moving five bomb ships—vessels armed with mortars that fired heavy, explosive
shells—and a rocket ship into position to bombard Fort McHenry. On the drizzly
morning of September 13, these ships opened fire, raining projectiles down on the
fort's red-brick bastions. The thunder of the guns, the crash of exploding shells, the
billowing flames and powder smoke were impressive, but little real damage was done.
Cochrane had hoped that the Americans might panic and evacuate the fort, but they
held their ground as the cannonade continued through the afternoon.

On shore the British army had pushed ahead to the eastern outskirts of Baltimore,
only to be stopped by the Rodgers Bastion, a menacing line of earthworks, ditches,
and palisades manned by 15,000 Americans. A frontal assault in daylight was out of
the question, but a surprise night attack might succeed in stampeding the defenders,
most of whom were inexperienced militiamen. Colonel Brooke decided to take the

Fort McHenry, built in the late 1790s, guarded the water approaches to Baltimore during the War of 1812. National Park Service.

risk. He scheduled the attack for 3 A.M. and sent a messenger to Admiral Cochrane asking the navy to make a feint toward Ridgely's Cove on the western side of Baltimore to divert the Americans' attention from the main thrust against Rodgers Bastion.

Shortly before midnight, twenty boats carrying 300 men rowed away from the British fleet and headed for Ridgely's Cove. It was raining and pitch-dark. Eleven of the craft became lost; the remaining nine rowed on.

At 1 A.M. Cochrane's bomb ships opened up on Fort McHenry with the heaviest fire yet. Shell fuses and rockets traced glowing arcs across the sky, the rain clouds were underlit by red and yellow flames, and the buildings of Baltimore shook as huge 200-pound mortar rounds exploded over the fort. At 2 A.M. rooftop observers were surprised to see muzzle flashes to the west of Whetstone Point: American gunners had spotted the nine British rowboats heading toward Ridgely's Cove and were lashing them with cannonballs.

Cochrane had done his best to create the requested diversion, but in front of Rodgers Bastion Colonel Brooke had lost his nerve. To the consternation of the British soldiers, who were spoiling for a fight, he ordered a withdrawal back to North Point. He would not risk an assault on the strongly held American earthworks.

In the harbor the nine rowboats managed to return to the fleet, and the bombardment finally ended. Between 1,500 and 1,800 rounds had been fired at Fort McHenry, but little damage had been done and only four members of the garrison had been killed. In the gray dawn of September 14, the Stars and Stripes still rippled over the parade ground, signaling to all that the fort had not fallen.

Cochrane's ships withdrew to North Point to pick up Colonel Brooke and his dispirited troops, and then sailed down Chesapeake Bay. The Battle of Baltimore was over; the British had been vanquished.

Touring the Park

Begin your tour at the Visitor Center, where exhibits and a film describe the history of the fort and the writing of "The Star Spangled Banner." From the Visitor Center a foot trail leads to the fort. There are fifteen numbered stops along the way.

Stop 1. Armistead Statue. Across from the Visitor Center entrance is a statue of Major George Armistead, commander of the Fort McHenry garrison during the 1814 bombardment. Behind the statue you may be able to make out the foundation outlines of several original service buildings.

Stop 2. Old Tavern Site. A tavern stood on this site in 1814.

Stop 3. Dry Moat. Fort McHenry's layout—a star shape with five bastions—followed a French design. On the right, as you approach the fort, you will see a raised mound, all that remains of the dry moat that encircled the fort and protected many of its defenders during the bombardment.

Stop 4. Ravelin. This V-shaped outwork—called a ravelin—protected the fort's entrance from a direct attack. The underground magazine was added after the 1814 battle.

The Star Spangled Banner

One American who had a ringside seat for the twenty-five-hour bombardment of Fort McHenry was a young Washington lawyer named Francis Scott Key. In the company of Colonel John Skinner, Key had sailed out to the British fleet on a flag-of-truce sloop to try to arrange the release of William Beanes, an elderly Maryland doctor taken prisoner during the fighting around Washington.

Admiral Cochrane agreed to let Beanes go, but to protect the secrecy of his Baltimore operation he detained both Key and Skinner until the attack had run its course. Thus, Key was aboard the flag-of-truce sloop in the Patapsco River when the British bomb ships opened up on Fort McHenry. All through the rainy night of September 13, the young lawyer and his companions watched helplessly as the storm of mortar shells and rockets descended on the American bastion.

At dawn Key trained a spyglass on Fort McHenry and saw that the Stars and Stripes was still flying over the battlements. Overjoyed, he pulled an envelope from his pocket and began jotting down couplets, which he later incorporated into a full-length poem. The poem was published in a Baltimore newspaper on September 16 under the title "Defense of Fort M'Henry," and was an instant success. Renamed "The Star Spangled Banner" and reprinted in newspapers from Georgia to Maine, the poem continued to grow in popularity and soon was being sung to the tune, "To Anacreon in Heaven."

This song was made the national anthem of the United States in 1931, immortalizing the gallant defense of Fort McHenry and the stirring poetry of Francis Scott Key.

Stop 5. Sally Port. The sally port was the only entrance to the fort. The archway was constructed after the battle. The bombproofs flanking the sally port sheltered some of the fort's defenders during the bombardment. Later, during the Civil War, they were used as cells for holding Confederate prisoners.

Stop 6. Cannon. The cannon you see on the parade ground are believed to have been used in the 1814 defense of Baltimore. The monogram of King George III appears on one of them.

Stop 7. Flag Pole. On the parade ground, just beyond the sally-port opening, is the site of the flagpole from which flew the huge forty-two-by-thirty-foot American flag that inspired Francis Scott Key to write "The Star Spangled Banner."

Stop 8. Guardhouses. On both sides of the sally port are guardhouses and prison cells built in 1835. They were used to house Confederate prisoners during the Civil War.

Stop 9. Bastion. Fort McHenry has five projecting angles called bastions. From the battlement (top wall) of this one, you can see the Patapsco River, where the British fleet lay at anchor in 1814. Be sure to listen to the tape at the audio station. It describes the fort's strategic importance.

Stops 10 and 11. Soldiers' Barracks. The fort's regular sixty-man garrison lived in these buildings. They now contain exhibits depicting the history of Fort McHenry.

Stop 12. Junior Officers' Quarters. The first floor of this building housed the garrison's junior officers.

Stop 13. Powder Magazine. The fort's ammunition was stored in this magazine. During the 1814 bombardment, a 186-pound mortar bomb scored a direct hit on the structure, but failed to detonate. The magazine was later rebuilt and enlarged to its present size.

Stop 14. Commander's Quarters. These restored quarters were reserved for the fort's commanding officer. Major Armistead used them as his command post during the Battle of Baltimore.

Exit the fort and turn right to tour the outer grounds.

Stop 15. Civil War Batteries. Gun emplacements were dug here during the Civil War, replacing the earlier battery near the waterfront.

The statue of Orpheus, a mythological Greek hero of music and poetry, was erected in 1922 in honor of Francis Scott Key.

CHAPTER 7

FORT NECESSITY
NATIONAL BATTLEFIELD
(French and Indian War)

Route 40 East, Box 528
Farmington, Pennsylvania 15437
Telephone: (412) 329-5805

In the spring of 1754, Colonel George Washington and a small band of Virginia militia ventured into the upper Ohio Valley to confront French forces there. Washington's men were victorious in a skirmish at Jumonville Glen on May 28, 1754, but were defeated at Fort Necessity on July 3 and forced to retreat to Virginia. These two small battles enflamed hostilities between Britain and France and led to a seven-year-long world war. Fort Necessity National Battlefield preserves the sites of the Jumonville Glen and Fort Necessity battles.

Getting to the Park: Fort Necessity National Battlefield is located 11 miles east of Uniontown, Pennsylvania, on U.S. 40.

Gas, food, lodging: In Uniontown.

Visitor Center: Museum; slide presentation.

Activities: Interpretive talks by park personnel. Inquire at Visitor Center for schedule.

Handicapped Access: Visitor Center is accessible. Inquire about condition of trails.

During the 1750s, the rivalry between France and Great Britain for control of North America intensified into armed conflict. The flash point was the upper Ohio Valley in what is now western Pennsylvania. British fur traders, advancing northward from colonial Virginia, clashed with French traders moving south from Canada. The French responded to these confrontations by sending 1,800 troops to the valley in February 1754.

Lieutenant Governor Robert Dinwiddie of Virginia was alarmed by this military buildup, and he sent twenty-one-year-old George Washington to the Ohio Valley to warn the French to withdraw. Predictably, they refused. Dinwiddie then sent an expedition to build a fort at the forks of the Ohio River where the city of Pittsburgh now stands. The French drove this force away and built a stockade of their own, called Fort Duquesne, on the site.

This was the final straw for Dinwiddie. He requested money and troops from the Virginia legislature and made plans for an expedition against the French in the Ohio Valley. On April 18, 1754, a small band of Virginia militia, led by newly commissioned Lieutenant Colonel George Washington, set out from Winchester for Wills Creek (now Cumberland, Maryland). From there, they would build a military road into the Ohio Valley in preparation for Dinwiddie's campaign against the French.

Skirmish at Jumonville Glen

Washington and his militiamen camped at Great Meadows, in what is now southwestern Pennsylvania, on May 24. Three days later, Seneca Indian scouts reported that a French detachment was approaching from the west. This thirty-two-man force, commanded by Joseph Coulon de Villiers, Sieur de Jumonville, had bivouacked for the evening in a glen near Chestnut Ridge, seven and a half miles northwest of Great Meadows.

Although the night was cold and a steady rain was falling, Washington set out at once with forty of his soldiers. Joined by a dozen Seneca scouts, they reached Chestnut Ridge shortly after dawn on May 28 and surrounded the enemy camp. Some of the French were still asleep; others were cooking breakfast, unaware that they were in mortal danger.

Suddenly there was a flash and puff of smoke, and the report of a musket shattered the early morning calm. The French frantically scrambled for their weapons as more muskets discharged and bullets whizzed overhead. Jumonville's men returned fire, but their defense was disorganized and ineffective. After fifteen minutes the skirmish was over; ten Frenchmen, including Jumonville, had been killed, and twenty-one taken prisoner. One man escaped, however, and made his way back to Fort Duquesne to tell the commander there about the incident.

Fort Necessity

Washington returned to Great Meadows well pleased with the results of the Jumonville Glen fight. He had struck a hard blow against the French while losing only one of his own men. He knew that the French army at Fort Duquesne outnumbered his small command, however, so he set his soldiers to building a circular log palisade, which he named Fort Necessity.

On June 9, reinforcements arrived from Virginia, bringing supplies and nine swivel guns to arm the fort. With the size of his force now increased to over 300 men, Washington could begin carrying out his original assignment, constructing a military road west toward the forks of the Ohio. Good progress was made on the road until July 1, when it was learned that the French were on the march from Fort Duquesne. Washington ordered his men to retreat to Fort Necessity and prepare for battle.

Around noon on July 3, 600 French soldiers and 100 Indian warriors reached Great Meadows and advanced to the attack. Washington's troops tried to make a stand on open ground, but soon were forced to seek shelter behind the walls of the fort.

Fighting continued for eight hours in the midst of a torrential downpour, with both sides suffering modest losses. Finally Washington realized that he was hopelessly out-manned and agreed to a proposal by the French commander that terms of surrender be negotiated.

The next morning the French permitted Washington and his soldiers to depart for Virginia. They then destroyed Fort Necessity and marched back to Fort Duquesne.

A World on Fire

The British government was stung by the French triumph at Fort Necessity, and the following year General Edward Braddock and 1,200 troops were sent to seize the Ohio Valley. On July 9, 1755, this army was ambushed and destroyed by 900 French and Indians, eight miles east of Fort Duquesne. Braddock died of wounds suffered in the battle and was buried about one mile west of the ruins of Fort Necessity.

With this bloody debacle, the skirmishing between Britain and France in the Ohio Valley escalated into full-scale hostilities. The conflagration spread from North America to Europe in 1756, where the fighting would continue until 1763. The battles of Jumonville Glen and Fort Necessity, although brief and seemingly incon-sequential, had sparked a world war. As British statesman Horace Walpole put it: "A volley fired by a young Virginian in the backwoods of America set the world on fire."

Touring the Park

Begin your tour at the Visitor Center, where exhibits and an audiovisual program tell the story of the Ohio Valley campaign and the battles of Jumonville Glen and Fort Necessity.

Fort Necessity. From the Visitor Center a foot trail leads to the stockade, store-house, and entrenchments reconstructed on the site of old Fort Necessity.

Jumonville Glen. From the Visitor Center, drive 4.9 miles west on U.S. 40 to Mount Summit. Turn right on the Jumonville Road and drive 2.5 miles north. The glen has changed little from the morning, more than 230 years ago, when George Washington's soldiers fired on French troops and began a world war.

CHAPTER 8

FREDERICKSBURG AND SPOTSYLVANIA COUNTY BATTLEFIELDS MEMORIAL NATIONAL MILITARY PARK

(Civil War)

1013 Lafayette Boulevard
Fredericksburg, Virginia 22401
Telephone: (703) 373-6122

Between 1862 and 1864, four major Civil War battles were fought in the vicinity of Fredericksburg, Virginia. Robert E. Lee and the Confederate Army of Northern Virginia decisively defeated the Union Army of the Potomac in the battles of Fredericksburg (December 11–13, 1862) and Chancellorsville (May 1–4, 1863). In the Battle of the Wilderness (May 5–6, 1864) and at Spotsylvania Court House (May 8–21, 1864) the two armies fought to a bloody draw. Fredericksburg/Spotsylvania National Military Park preserves the scene of the four battles as well as four historic buildings associated with them.

Getting to the Park: The Fredericksburg Visitor Center is located in Fredericksburg, Virginia, on U.S. 1 at the foot of Marye's Heights. A National Cemetery lies across U.S. 1 to the southwest. The Chancellorsville Visitor Center is located on the Chancellorsville Battlefield, 10 miles west of Fredericksburg on Virginia Highway 22. The Wilderness Battlefield Unit is located approximately 15 miles west of Fredericksburg on Virginia Highway 3. The Spotsylvania Court House Battlefield Unit is located approximately 7 miles southeast of the Wilderness Unit on Virginia Highway 613.

Gas, food, lodging: In Fredericksburg.

Visitor Centers: Museum and gift shop; audiovisual programs.

Activities: Interpretive talks by park personnel. Inquire at Visitor Centers for schedule and location.

Handicapped Access: The Fredericksburg Visitor Center is in an older building with five steps leading up to a porch. The newer Chancellorsville Visitor Center is fully accessible. Inquire at Visitor Centers about accessibility of historic buildings.

The Fredericksburg/Spotsylvania National Military Park is unique in that it commemorates not one, but four major Civil War battles: Fredericksburg, Chancellorsville, the Wilderness, and Spotsylvania Court House.

Prelude to Fredericksburg

Following the Battle of Antietam on September 17, 1862 (see Chapter 5), the Union Army of the Potomac failed to pursue the Confederate Army of Northern Virginia as it retreated out of Maryland. General Robert E. Lee's severely weakened force was allowed to spend the entire month of October recuperating near Culpeper, Virginia, undisturbed by any Union offensive.

Exasperated by this lack of action, President Abraham Lincoln relieved the commander of the Army of the Potomac, George B. McClellan, and replaced him with General Ambrose Burnside. Burnside at once began organizing a campaign to capture the city of Richmond. His plan called for Federal forces to cross the Rappahannock River at Fredericksburg and then advance south fifty miles to the Confederate capital.

The key to success, from Burnside's point of view, was a quick crossing of the Rappahannock, before Lee's army could occupy the heights behind Fredericksburg. Pontoons for bridge building were not immediately available, however, and by the time preparations were complete, in early December, the Confederates had dug in along the Fredericksburg ridges with their guns carefully sighted on the ground the Union army would have to traverse. "A chicken could not live on that field when we open up on it," boasted a Confederate artillery officer.

Despite the strong defensive position held by the Army of Northern Virginia, Burnside decided to proceed with the river crossing. He divided his force, which

General Ambrose Burnside commanded the Army of the Potomac at the Battle of Fredericksburg. National Archives.

A wartime view of Fredericksburg, taken from Stafford Heights on the north bank of the Rappahannock River. Library of Congress.

totaled about 120,000 men, into three Grand Divisions—right, center, and left. The right Grand Division, commanded by General Edwin Sumner, would bridge the Rappahannock at Fredericksburg. The left Grand Division, commanded by General William Franklin, would cross several miles downstream. The center Grand Division, under General Joseph Hooker, would be held in reserve.

Union engineers began laying the pontoon bridges over the Rappahannock in the predawn darkness of December 11. On the left, Franklin's men met with little resistance and quickly finished their task, but in Fredericksburg Confederate sharpshooters concealed in riverside buildings made work nearly impossible for Sumner's pontoniers. Union artillery bombarded the town for an hour, trying to blast the snipers from their hideouts, but it was not until infantry was ferried across the river to flush the Confederates out at bayonet point that the bridge building could be finished.

The next day, under cover of thick fog, long columns of Union troops filed across the pontoon bridges into Fredericksburg. By evening, the Grand Divisions of Franklin and Sumner were on the south bank making preparations for an assault on the heights behind the city.

Attack on Prospect Hill

Fredericksburg was again shrouded by fog on the morning of December 13; the mists finally burned away at midday, allowing the Union attack to begin. Franklin's troops moved forward to strike the Confederate right at Prospect Hill, but were halted by the fire of a single Confederate artillery battery, which boldly moved out into the open to intercept their advance. When the Federals finally got moving again, the massed guns of General Thomas "Stonewall" Jackson's corps opened up on them. An avalanche of shot and shell slammed into the blue ranks, sending them reeling back.

Union artillery arrayed along Stafford Heights on the opposite bank of the Rappahannock now engaged Jackson's guns in a noisy duel. For an hour and a half the

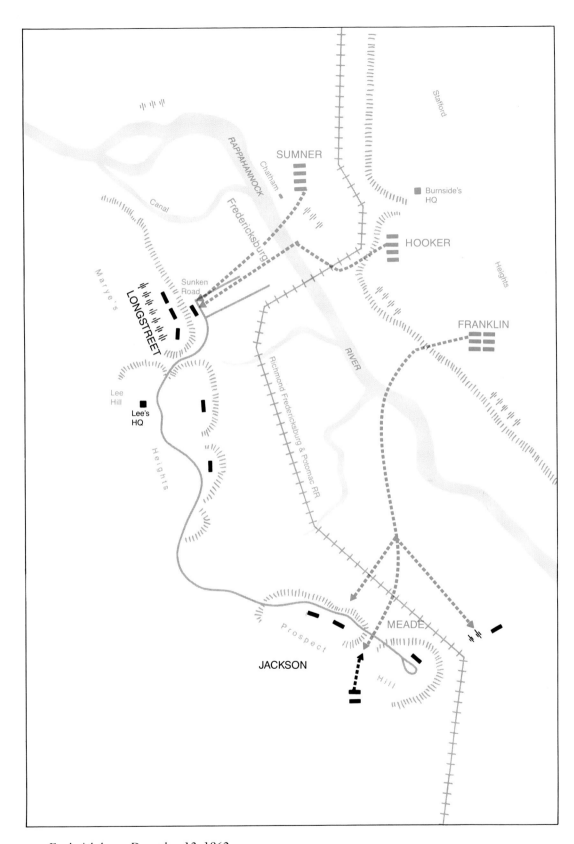

Fredericksburg, December 13, 1862

cannon thundered at each other; then the Union infantry advanced again. A single division—4,500 Pennsylvanians led by General George Gordon Meade—found a hole in the Confederate line and broke through into the rear. Had reinforcements been available to exploit this penetration, a great Union victory might have been won. Instead, the Confederates launched a savage counterattack that drove Meade's men back and sealed the breach they had made.

Slaughter at Marye's Heights

Shortly after Franklin's Grand Division launched its assault on the Confederate right, the other wing of the Federal army began massing to strike a blow against the Confederate left at Marye's Heights. "It appeared to us there was no end to them," said a Rebel cannoneer as the thousands of blue-uniformed soldiers formed into ranks on the plain below.

General James Longstreet, commander of this segment of the Confederate defenses, was not worried by the size of the attacking force, however. His position was extraordinarily strong: a sunken road, flanked by a four-foot-high stone wall, ran along the base of the heights. In this ready-made breastwork, a brigade of Georgians and North Carolinians waited with muskets ready. Behind them, along the ridge top, the dark snouts of canister-loaded cannon protruded from mounded earthworks, and a solid phalanx of Confederate soldiers—six men to every yard—calmly awaited the expected onslaught.

"General," Longstreet said to Lee, "if you put every man now on the other side of the Potomac in that field . . . and give me plenty of ammunition, I will kill them all before they reach my line."

The Federals began their attack, but as they approached the stone wall a storm of Rebel bullets shredded their ranks and left the ground littered with blue bodies. They stumbled back, regrouped, and moved forward again only to suffer the same dreadful scourging.

It was obvious that further charges against the Confederate position would be suicidal, but the Union soldiers kept rushing forward in long, sweeping waves that broke in blood against the flaming barrier of the stone wall.

"Oh great God!" cried one of Burnside's generals as he watched the almost unbelievable carnage among the attacking units. "See how our men, our poor fellows, are falling!"

The attacks continued as Burnside fed his reserves into the meat grinder. Half a dozen attempts were made to storm the heights, but they all failed to get past the stone wall. Finally, as darkness fell, General Hooker ended the slaughter. "Finding that I had lost as many men as my orders required me to lose," he bitterly wrote, "I suspended the attack."

Union Disaster

Beaten and bleeding, the Army of the Potomac withdrew across the Rappahannock, having suffered one of the most lopsided defeats of the war. Union losses were a horrific 12,653 men; the Confederate casualty total, 5,309, was less than half that number.

A disheartened Union supporter summed up the debacle this way: "It can hardly be in human nature for men to show more valor, or generals to manifest less judgment, than were perceptible on our side that day."

Hooker Takes Command

After the Fredericksburg bloodbath the morale of the Army of the Potomac plummeted. "I am sick and tired of disaster and the fools that bring disaster upon us," wrote a New York corporal, echoing the sentiments of his fellow soldiers. The cynical, jeering phrase "all played out" was heard in the ranks whenever there was talk of resuming the offensive, and officers feared that the enlisted men would mutiny if General Burnside ordered another attack.

A change of command was desperately needed, and in January 1863, President Lincoln relieved Burnside and replaced him with General Joseph Hooker. Hooker took immediate steps to restore morale and halt the flood of desertions that was threatening to wreck the army: rations were improved with the addition of fresh vegetables and soft bread, unsanitary camps were cleaned up, six months' back pay was distributed, and a system of regular furloughs was established. "Cheerfulness, good order, and military discipline at once took the place of grumbling, depression, and want of confidence," recalled an impressed Union soldier, and by spring the Army of the Potomac was again ready to take the field.

Hooker knew from intelligence reports that his command of 135,000 men outnumbered Lee's Confederates better than two to one. He intended to take advantage of this by splitting his force into two attack groups, one to strike each flank of Lee's

General "Fighting Joe" Hooker took command of the Army of the Potomac after the Fredericksburg debacle. His timidity and indecision cost the Union heavily at the Battle of Chancellorsville. National Archives.

General Thomas J. "Stonewall" Jackson led three Confederate divisions on an audacious flanking march around the Union army at Chancellorsville. National Archives.

army, which was still entrenched in the vicinity of Fredericksburg. If this maneuver was successful, the Rebels would be caught in a vise and crushed. "My plans are perfect," Hooker concluded after studying his maps and reviewing his troop dispositions. "When I start to carry them out, may God have mercy on Bobby Lee; for I shall have none."

On April 27 the Union army broke camp; the main attack group marched west up the Rappahannock River, while the other group marched downstream. Two days later both columns crossed the river and began converging on Fredericksburg.

Although caught off guard by Hooker's sudden advance, Lee refused to consider retreat. Discerning that the main Federal thrust was coming from the west, he moved swiftly to block it. Five divisions were dispatched to the crossroads hamlet of Chancellorsville, where the bulk of Hooker's army was gathering. Only one division was left behind to hold Fredericksburg against the second Union attack group.

May 1, 1863: Hooker Pulls Back

The clear, warm dawn of May 1 found General Hooker in high spirits. So far his plan had worked to perfection, and he felt confident that this would be the day he achieved a smashing victory over the heretofore invincible Robert E. Lee. At 10 A.M., after carefully organizing and positioning his attack columns, he started forward toward Fredericksburg, ready to deliver the knockout blow.

At almost exactly the same moment, some four miles to the east, Stonewall Jackson was ordering the Confederate divisions to advance toward Chancellorsville. Lee had told him the night before to "make arrangements to repulse the enemy," and the ever-aggressive Jackson had interpreted this to mean attack.

Shortly before noon an explosion of musket and cannon fire heralded the collision of the two armies. The officers leading the Union advance prepared to drive forward and overwhelm the smaller Confederate force, but they were stopped in their tracks by a peremptory order from Hooker: retreat back to Chancellorsville without delay. Stunned and perplexed by this sudden, unexplained abandonment of the battle plan, they sent word to the general that they had "open country to the front and a commanding position." Hooker was adamant, however. Jackson's audacious approach had rattled him, and he now believed that it would be safer to fight a defensive battle than to risk an attack.

Back trudged the disheartened Union troops, retracing the route they had followed that morning. Forward came the the Confederates, advancing cautiously lest the Yankee retreat prove to be a ruse luring them into a trap. Hooker intended no trickery, however. "It is all right," he told his commanders, explaining why he had surrendered the initiative to the Confederates. "I have got Lee just where I want him; he must fight me on my own ground."

His listeners were unimpressed. They believed that Hooker had lost his nerve just when resolute boldness was most called for. "I left his presence," wrote General Darius Couch, "with the belief that my commanding general was a whipped man."

The Cracker Box Council

Lee rode out from Fredericksburg to join his army on the afternoon of May 1. He was puzzled by Hooker's precipitous withdrawal, and thinking that it might have been caused by some gap in the Federal line, he personally reconnoitered with an eye toward launching an attack. But instead of a weak spot, he found that the enemy "had assumed a position of great natural strength, surrounded on all sides by a dense forest filled with tangled undergrowth, in the midst of which breastworks of logs had been constructed."

At dusk he returned to his field headquarters, located a mile southeast of the Chancellorsville crossroads, where he was joined by General Jackson. The grizzled, glowering Stonewall sat on a tree stump while Lee seated himself on an empty cracker box, and the two quietly discussed what should be done. Both men agreed that "a direct attack upon the enemy could be attended with great difficulty and loss," but they were loath to pass up the opportunity Hooker had so surprisingly offered them.

The answer to their dilemma came in the form of a scouting report from Confederate cavalry commander J. E. B. Stuart: the Federal right flank, west of the Wilderness Church, was uncovered and could be turned by a surprise attack. The two generals quickly made a decision: Jackson would take three divisions, make a twelve-mile flanking march across the front of the Union army, and then strike its right rear. Lee, with just two divisions—barely 15,000 men—would hold Hooker's 75,000 in check until Jackson was in position, then join him in the attack.

The scheme involved a breathtaking gamble. If Hooker discovered that Lee had divided his force, he could easily use his overwhelming numerical superiority to crush the two Rebel detachments in turn. If, on the other hand, the strategy worked, the undermanned Confederates might surprise and destroy the Army of the Potomac, effectively ending the war.

May 2, 1863: Jackson's March

Jackson's column moved out at 7:30 A.M., marching along a narrow dirt road that wound through a sun-dappled forest of scrub oak and pine. As the morning passed, the long line of Rebel infantry and supply wagons extended until it was six miles long, snaking slowly west and south across the Union front.

After 9 A.M. reports of the Confederate movement began to arrive at Hooker's Chancellorsville headquarters. The general briefly considered the possibility that his right flank was threatened, but decided it was much more likely that Lee was retreating toward Gordonsville. Acting on this false assumption, he ordered his commanders to prepare for a pursuit the next day, and sent word to General John Sedgwick, the officer in charge of the Union attack group before Fredericksburg, to capture the city. "We know the enemy is fleeing," he wrote in his dispatch.

Meanwhile, Jackson's men were making steady progress, moving ever closer to Hooker's exposed right flank. At 2:30 P.M., two Union divisions led by General Daniel Sickles overwhelmed the gray column's rear guard, but failed to recognize what the true purpose of the Confederate march was. "We had heard that Lee was retreating and supposed this unfortunate regiment had been sacrificed to give the main body a chance to escape," wrote a cavalryman in Sickles's command. "One of [the captured Rebels] defiantly said 'You may think you have done a big thing just now, but wait till Jackson gets around on your right.' We laughed at this harmless bravado."

Around 5 P.M., as dusk began to gather in the woods west of Chancellorsville, the Confederates reached their destination and deployed to begin the attack. Just

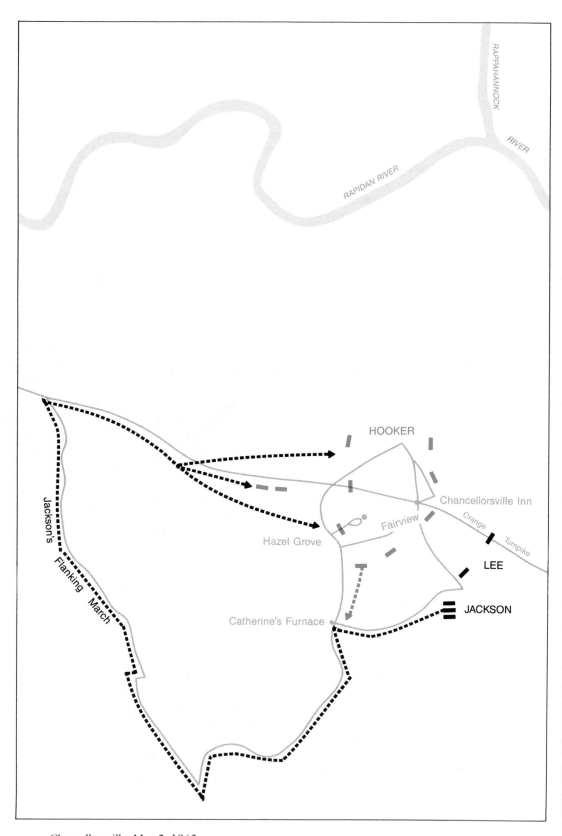

Chancellorsville, May 2, 1863

ahead of the massed gray formations, screened by a dense tangle of underbrush, lay the Union right flank held by two regiments of infantry numbering barely 900 men. These soldiers—many of them recent German immigrants—had their muskets stacked and were lounging about waiting to eat supper. Suddenly a herd of deer burst from the forest and raced through their camp, followed by a flock of scampering rabbits and squirrels. Before the startled Federals could divine the meaning of this strange behavior, they heard the high-pitched keening of "that hellish [Rebel] yell" and saw the glittering bayonets of the Confederate battle line bearing down on them.

"Press them, press them!"

Jackson's surprise attack exploded with fearsome impact against the vulnerable Union flank, sending the soldiers in blue running as fast as their legs could carry them. "More quickly than it could be told," wrote General Oliver O. Howard, commander of the corps that bore the brunt of the onslaught, "with all the fury of the wildest hailstorm, everything, every sort of organization that lay in the path of the mad current of panic-stricken men, had to give way and be broken into fragments."

At twilight on May 2, 1862, the Confederates completed their flanking march and launched an attack against the Union right. The attack succeeded, but in the confusion General Jackson was accidentally shot by his own men; he died eight days later. Anne S. K. Brown Military Collection, Brown University Library.

Flushed with excitement, gesticulating exultantly, urging his men to "push right ahead," Stonewall Jackson rode just behind the gray assault wave as it rolled up the Federal line. A subordinate cried out: "They are running too fast for us. We can't keep up with them," but Jackson would have none of it. "They never run too fast for me, sir," he snapped. "Press them, press them!"

The attack roared ahead until darkness and the exhaustion of the footsore Confederate troops slowed its momentum. Hooker had finally realized what was happening and rushed up reinforcements to try to stem the Rebel tide, but Jackson had no intention of being stopped. He ordered the fresh division of General A. P. Hill to take the point and drive on toward the Rappahannock three miles ahead, cutting the Army of the Potomac's only retreat route.

At this moment of supreme triumph and opportunity for the Confederacy, tragedy struck. Riding toward the battle line, Jackson was accidentally shot by his own men. Bleeding profusely, he was taken to the rear in an ambulance, where surgeons amputated his left arm. Shortly after Jackson's fall, Hill was struck in the legs by Union shell fragments. The loss of both commanders ended any chance of the Rebel forces making another assault before dawn, which in turn gave Hooker time to reorganize his badly shaken command.

May 3, 1863: Lee Resumes the Attack

Robert E. Lee waited impatiently for sunrise on May 3, anxious to resume the battle. Jackson's attack had been successful, but the Confederate army was still divided and vulnerable to a counterstroke by Hooker's numerically superior forces. At 3 A.M. Lee sent a message to J. E. B. Stuart, who had assumed command of Jackson's corps, ordering him to advance at first light in an effort to unite the army's two wings.

What Lee could not know was that Hooker had been unnerved by the previous day's events and was thinking only of holding his present position. To shorten his defensive line, he ordered Union troops to abandon a hilltop clearing called Hazel Grove. This opened the way for Stuart to link up with Lee, and also gave the Confederate artillery a perfect position from which to blast the Federal entrenchments around Chancellorsville.

After occupying Hazel Grove, the gray army pressed northeastward toward another forest clearing called Fairview. The Federals contested this advance, and a ferocious, swirling fight ensued in dense undergrowth, where units became separated and much of the combat was hand to hand. "With high-wrought, supreme earnestness, and with a savage, fiendish purpose, all strained themselves to the very utmost to wound and kill," wrote one of the participants. "This close, murderous contest continued for a solid half hour."

Eventually, the heavy fire of the Confederate cannon at Hazel Grove forced the Union troops to retreat from the knoll at Fairview. Solid shot also rained down on the Chancellorsville Inn, the building Hooker was using as his headquarters. The general was on the porch, leaning against a wooden pillar, when a ball shattered it, hurling him to the ground and knocking him unconscious. Upon recovering, he rode away from the fighting in a daze, and presently gave the order for the entire army to withdraw toward the Rappahannock fords.

As the blue troops obediently broke off the fight and retreated toward the river, the jubilant Confederates surged forward and captured the Chancellorsville Inn, which had been set afire by the earlier bombardment. Lee galloped up moments later, and was greeted with a thunderous ovation. It was, wrote an awestruck officer, "one long, unbroken cheer, in which the feeble cry of those who lay helpless on the earth, blended with the strong voices of those who still fought, rose high above the roar of battle and hailed the presence of the victorious chief. He sat in the full realization of all that soldiers dream of—triumph. . . . I thought that it must have been from such a scene that men in ancient times rose to the dignity of gods."

Fight at Salem Church

Hooker was beaten, but now Lee had to turn his attention to a new threat: the Federal force under Sedgwick that had captured Fredericksburg earlier in the day and was moving west along the Orange Turnpike toward Chancellorsville and the Confederate rear. Reluctantly Lee divided his army again, sending General Lafayette McLaws and 7,000 men to block the advance of Sedgwick's 22,000, while he remained at Chancellorsville with a scant 37,000 troops to hold Hooker's command at bay.

At 4 P.M., at Salem Church, a small red-brick building midway between Fredericksburg and Chancellorsville, Sedgwick's column made contact with McLaw's Confederates. "A tremendous roar of musketry met us from the unseen enemy, one hundred feet away, posted behind a fence and a ditch," a Federal soldier wrote of the action. "Men tumbled from our ranks dead, and others fell helpless with wounds." The lead Union division was hurled back, and before the rest of the force could be brought forward to make another attack, darkness fell.

The Army of the Potomac Withdraws

On May 4, Lee boldly decided to concentrate his efforts on destroying Sedgwick's detachment, gambling that Hooker would remain passive and not go over to the offensive. He reinforced McLaws at Salem Church, but the assault on the three Union divisions began late, at 6 P.M., and soon fizzled out. That night Sedgwick withdrew his force across the Rappahannock to safety.

The following day, under cover of a drenching rainstorm, Hooker also began pulling his troops back over the river. By midmorning on May 6 they were all gone, much to Lee's disgust. He had won a brilliant tactical victory, but failed to destroy his opponent; the casualty totals were 17,287 killed, wounded, or missing for the Federals, 12,821 for the Confederates.

One Confederate casualty overshadowed all the others: On May 10, Stonewall Jackson died of pneumonia contracted after the amputation of his left arm. "The daring, skill, and energy of this great and good man are now lost to us," Lee announced to the Army of Northern Virginia. It was a turning point in the war, for without Jackson, Lee would never again be able to give free rein to his own aggressive instincts or to exploit to the full the magnificent fighting spirit of his troops.

Spring 1864: Grant Moves South

On May 4, 1864, exactly a year after the Chancellorsville battle, the Army of the Potomac again marched south into central Virginia, heading toward the Confederate

Care of the Wounded

"The doctors kill more than they cure," lamented a Confederate soldier after visiting a field hospital during a battle. Sadly, his statement was accurate. Heavy, hollow-based .58-caliber minié balls and shrapnel from exploding shot and shell inflicted dreadful wounds that Civil War surgeons lacked the skill to treat properly.

The worst shortcoming of battlefield medicine as practiced during the Civil War was ignorance of sterile surgical technique. Chest and abdominal wounds were probed with bare fingers and contaminated instruments; shattered arms and legs were amputated with unwashed knives and bone saws, and the stumps were sewed up with unsterilized silk. "We operated in old blood-stained and often pus-stained coats," recalled Dr. W. W. Keen. "We used undisinfected instruments. . . . We knew nothing about antiseptics and therefore used none."

The result in almost every case was infection, followed by the onset of gangrene, septicemia, tetanus, or one of the other so-called "surgical fevers." Mortality rates exceeded 50 percent, and in the case of gunshot wounds to the abdomen, approached 90 percent.

The hellish atmosphere prevailing in the field hospitals was described in chilling detail by Colonel T. D. Kingsley, who was wounded in the Battle of Port Hudson on May 26, 1863: "All around on the ground lay the wounded men; some of them were shrieking, some cursing and swearing and some praying; in the middle of the room was [sic] some 10 or 12 tables . . . covered with blood; near and around the tables stood the surgeons with blood all over them and by the side of the tables was a heap of feet, legs and arms. . . . I never wish to see another such time as the 27th of May."

capital at Richmond. The strategic objective was the same as in 1863, but the soldiers' outlook was entirely different. Hapless "Fighting Joe" Hooker was gone, replaced by Ulysses S. Grant, conqueror of Vicksburg and hero of Chattanooga (see Chapters 32 and 17). Grant did not cut as imposing a martial figure as Hooker: one officer described him as "stumpy, unmilitary, slouchy, and western-looking," but his reputation as a fighter and his businesslike demeanor more than made up for his unimpressive appearance. "We all felt at last that *the boss* had arrived," wrote a Chancellorsville veteran, and as the ranks trudged south to confront Robert E. Lee and his Army of Northern Virginia, there was a feeling that this time the outcome would be different.

Grant's plan for victory was based on simple arithmetic: his command totaled nearly 120,000 men while Lee had only 62,000 troops at his disposal. If the Army of the Potomac smashed forward, applying relentless pressure, the Confederate force must eventually be ground to dust by the sheer weight of Union numbers. It was a brutal, inelegant strategy, but it promised decisive results. Grant set it in motion on May 4, 1864, sending his long blue columns splashing across the Rapidan River southeast toward Richmond.

Wounded soldiers at a field hospital outside Fredericksburg. National Archives.

May 5–6, 1864: The Battle of the Wilderness

When Lee learned of the Federal advance, he moved at once to block it. He intended to give battle in an area where the terrain and ground cover would negate, at least partly, Grant's overwhelming numerical advantage. This region, located just west of the Chancellorsville battlefield, was known locally as the Wilderness. It was a jungle of vines, brambles, and scrub-oak and pine thickets, where men could see only a few feet ahead in any direction and where it was extraordinarily difficult for infantry units to maneuver in an organized manner.

The two armies came together near Wilderness Tavern on the morning of May 5. Blue divisions of General Gouverneur K. Warren's corps, advancing down the Orange Turnpike, barreled into the lead elements of General Richard Ewell's Confederate corps and threw them back. A spectacular counterattack by two Rebel brigades halted the Federal thrust, and the combat quickly spread from the turnpike into the woods on either flank, where it became, in the words of one of the participants, "a battle of invisibles with invisibles."

Regiments and companies became separated in the smoke-shrouded, bullet-slashed tangle and stumbled about with no sense of direction, firing "by earsight" into the gray-green murk. "It was simply bushwacking on a grand scale," a veteran declared, "in brush . . . where such a thing as a consistent line of battle on either side was impossible."

Grant had not anticipated a fight in the Wilderness, but he was not going to shy away now that one had started. "If any opportunity presents itself for pitching into a part of Lee's army, do so without giving time for disposition," he told his officers.

Around 4 P.M. Union General Winfield S. Hancock acted on these instructions when he encountered the two Confederate divisions of A. P. Hill's corps on the Orange Plank Road, approximately two miles southeast of where the other battle was raging. Hancock's Federals advanced, 30,000 strong, into the woods just east of the Widow Tapp Farm, and a vicious struggle ensued. The gray soldiers were badly outnumbered, but broken terrain and dense foliage helped them to hold Hancock's troops at bay until darkness ended the day's combat.

During the night both Grant and Lee made plans for attacking in the morning. Grant would hit hard on the Orange Plank Road, where Hancock had almost scored a breakthrough late that afternoon. Lee intended to strike in the same area once General James Longstreet's corps arrived from Gordonsville.

The Army of the Potomac was able to get in the first punch, beginning at daybreak on May 6, and it was nearly a knock-out blow. "The men seemed to fall back upon a deliberate conviction that it was impossible to hold the ground and, of course, foolish to attempt it," a Confederate officer wrote of the gray retreat down the Orange Plank Road toward the farm of Widow Tapp.

In the Tapp barnyard, artillery commanded by Colonel William Poague went into action, firing charges of canister into the brush through which the Federals were advancing. The Union charge was delayed just long enough for the lead element of Longstreet's corps—General John Gregg's brigade—to reach the field. Gregg's Texans and Arkansans were about to launch their counterattack when Robert E. Lee galloped to the front as if to lead the assault. All movement stopped, and hoarse shouts rose along the battle line: "Lee to the rear! Lee to the rear!"

Finally a soldier seized the bridle of the general's mount and physically prevented him from riding forward. "Go back, General Lee," he croaked, "go back. We won't go unless you go back." Lee finally understood, and turned around. The Texans and Arkansans then charged ahead, joined by Benning's Georgia brigade, which had also just arrived on the field.

The whooping Confederates ran straight into the onrushing bluecoats, and the woods exploded in smoke and flame. The clatter of musketry rose to a fearful crescendo as slowly, grudgingly, the Federals were driven back to their starting point. "It ain't no battle," one of the soldiers cried of the confused, swirling fighting. "It's all a damned mess! And our two armies ain't nothing but howling mobs."

Now it was Lee's turn to go over to the offensive. Under the direction of General Longstreet, four Confederate brigades maneuvered around the left flank of Grant's line, near the Brock Road–Plank Road intersection, and launched a fierce attack. The Union flank was rolled up "like a wet blanket," and elation swept through the Rebel ranks as the troops realized that a second Chancellorsville was in the making.

The Chancellorsville parallel grew even more striking—and unpleasant—around noon, when Longstreet was accidentally shot by his own men. He was carted away in an ambulance, bleeding from the neck and shoulder, and without his guidance the Confederate assault ran out of steam. Many units became lost or separated in the impenetrable Wilderness undergrowth, and when the attack resumed at 4 P.M. the Federals had gathered themselves to meet it and no more progress could be made.

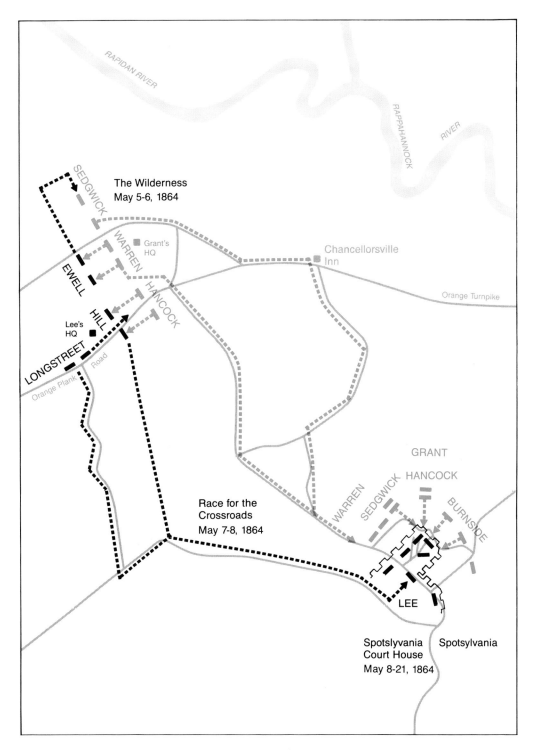

The Wilderness and Spotsylvania Court House, May 5–21, 1864

At 5:30 P.M. Lee rode to the far end of his battle line, along the Orange Turnpike, to confer with General Ewell and see if an attack could be made in that sector. A half hour later the brigades of Generals John Gordon and Robert Johnston hit the Union right flank and surged ahead for a mile, taking over 600 prisoners before darkness fell. Gordon would thereafter maintain that had this attack been made earlier while several hours of daylight remained, it "would have resulted in a decided disaster to the whole right wing of General Grant's army, if not in its entire organization."

The specter of disaster had been looming over Grant all day, but he remained calm, giving orders "without any external sign of undue tension or agitation." Despite having both his flanks turned and seeing his army suffer some 17,000 casualties in forty-eight hours, he remarked that "this is a crisis that cannot be looked upon too seriously," and told a reporter who was about to depart for Washington: "If you see the President, tell him, from me, that, whatever happens, there will be no turning back."

The Union troops were inclined to be skeptical about this as they waited for orders the next day. The Rebels, having spent themselves in the attacks of May 6, were now solidly entrenched, and a frontal assault against their rifle pits and log breastworks would be suicidal. Most of the bluecoats, and many of the Confederates as well, concluded that Grant was whipped and that "another skedaddle" was in the offing. This was how the Army of the Potomac's Virginia forays had always ended: McClellan, Burnside, and Hooker had all limped back toward Washington after being bested by Robert E. Lee.

But Ulysses S. Grant was cut of different cloth. Although he had been drubbed in the Wilderness, his strategy of victory by attrition was still in force. The Army of Northern Virginia had suffered approximately 8,000 casualties in the two-day battle, losses that could never be made up, and it was Grant's intention to maintain the pressure until his opponent was too weak to continue. Thus, on the afternoon of May 7, the orders went out to the Federal divisions along the battle line: there would be no retreat. Instead, under cover of darkness, the Army of the Potomac would sidestep around Lee's right flank and press on to the south, marching toward a cross-roads hamlet named Spotsylvania.

Race for the Crossroads

With intuition honed by three years of combat experience, Robert E. Lee foresaw what the Federals' move would be. "Grant is not going to retreat," he told a flabbergasted subordinate who was sure that the bluecoats were about to withdraw to the north. "Spotsylvania is now General Grant's best strategic point."

It was obvious to Lee that if the Army of the Potomac reached the Spotsylvania crossroads first, the Confederates would be cut off from their supply base at Richmond. The capital would fall, and in all likelihood the war would come to a quick end. To forestall this disaster, he immediately set his troops in motion, racing against Grant's soldiers to arrive at the vital intersection first.

The lead elements of the two armies—the Confederate corps of General Richard Anderson and the Union corps of General Gouverneur K. Warren—marched southeast on parallel routes toward Spotsylvania. As they approached the vital objective they were neck and neck, but then, just two miles short of the crossroads, Federal skirmishers ran into a roadblock thrown up by Confederate cavalrymen. As the main body of gray troops drew closer to Spotsylvania, they were met by a desperate cavalry courier. "Run for our rail piles!" he shouted. "The Federal infantry will reach them first if you don't run!"

The Confederate brigades heading up the advance gamely sprinted toward the barricade and reached it just in time to open fire on their blue counterparts, who were only sixty yards away and also coming on the run. The Army of Northern Virginia had won the nine-mile race to Spotsylvania by less than a minute. "With the blessing of God," Lee wired president Jefferson Davis, "I trust we shall be able to prevent General Grant from reaching Richmond."

May 12, 1864: The Battle of Spotsylvania Court House

Unable to get his army between the Confederates and their capital, Grant found himself in the same tactical situation he had sought to escape by ordering the flanking march out of the Wilderness. The Rebels were again entrenched on terrain strongly favoring the defensive, manning a seven-mile line of log-and-dirt breastworks bristling with bayonets and the ominous black snouts of artillery pieces. To advance upon these works seemed hopeless, but Grant had committed himself to slugging it out with Lee toe to toe, and he would not back down. "I am sending back . . . for a fresh supply of provisions and ammunition, and propose to fight it out on this line if it takes all summer," he wrote in a dispatch to Washington.

Despite the bloody repulse of two Union probing attacks on May 10, Grant forged ahead with his plan for a full-scale frontal assault against Lee's Spotsylvania line. At 4:30 A.M. on May 12, a Federal corps numbering approximately 20,000 men charged through dense fog toward a vulnerable point in the Confederate defenses, a U-shaped salient called the "Mule Shoe." The outnumbered gray troops posted there were quickly overwhelmed; many of them never got off a shot because rain and fog had dampened their gunpowder.

Faced with the prospect of having his army cut in half, Lee launched a desperate counterattack to stem the blue tide pouring through the ruptured line. This move succeeded in containing the initial Union advance, but then another Federal corps smashed into the left side of the Mule Shoe. More Confederates were rushed into the fray, and more Federals, until the salient became so jammed with soldiers that those on the battle line could neither fall back nor move laterally, only press forward and come to grips with their opponents.

Like a smoking cauldron suddenly boiling over, the Mule Shoe—now dubbed the "Bloody Angle"—exploded with the most ferocious hand-to-hand combat of the Civil War. Point-blank musket fire gave way to bayonets, which in turn gave way to knives and clubs, which finally gave way to rocks and bare hands in an orgy of blind violence that bordered on insanity.

Hour after hour the hideous struggle continued, fresh units moving into the cataclysm like pieces of meat being pushed into a grinder. Rain fell and mixed with blood to turn the battlefield into a thick crimson quagmire that swallowed up bodies and sucked hungrily at the feet and legs of the living. But still the fighting raged on. Company commanders sent word to the rear that combat of this intensity was beyond

"Your Dying Son"

The mortal cost of Civil War battles can be hard to grasp; casualty figures numbering in the tens of thousands are so overwhelming, so far beyond the range of normal experience, that the identity—and the humanity—of the slain tends to become blurred or lost. Yet every soldier who fell was a distinct individual, a young man whose hopes and dreams for the future died with him on the battlefield, a son or husband who would never go home.

This letter, written to A. V. Montgomery of Camden, Mississippi, by his mortally wounded son, conveys the tragedy of a single loss, one of thousands at Spotsylvania Court House in the spring of 1864.

Spottsylvania County, Va.
May 10, 1864

Dear Father

This is my last letter to you. I went into battle this evening as Courier for Genl Heth. I have been struck by a piece of Shell and my right shoulder is horeribly mangled & I know death is inevitable. I am very weak but I write to you because I know you would be delighted to read a word from your dying Son. I know death is near, that I will die far from home and friends of my early youth but I have friends here too who are kind to me. My Friend Fairfax will write you at my request and give you the particulars of my death. My grave will be marked so that you may visit it if you desire to do so, but is optionary with you whether you let my remains rest here or in Miss. I would like to rest in the grave yard with my dear mother and brothers but is a matter of minor importance. Let us all try to reunite in heaven. I pray my God to forgive my sins & I feel that his promises are true that he will forgive me and save me. Give my love to all my friends. My strength fails me. My horse & equipments will be left for you. Again a long farewell to you. May we meet in heaven.

Your dying son,
J. R. Montgomery

human endurance, yet somehow it continued, past sunset and into darkness. Finally, at midnight, after twenty hours of nonstop savagery, the Confederates disengaged, staggering backward to a new line that stretched across the neck of the Mule Shoe. The Bloody Angle was left empty—empty save for thousands of grotesquely trampled corpses.

"Dogged Pertinacity"

For nearly three days after the battle it rained without letup, a steady, soaking downpour that fell, wrote a South Carolina soldier, "as if Heaven were trying to wash up the blood as fast as the civilized barbarians were spilling it." The men of both armies squatted amid the mud and desolation, pondering their wretched state and growing

A dead Confederate at the Bloody Angle, Spotsylvania Court House, May 1864. Library of Congress.

increasingly bitter as the futility of the ordeal they had just endured became apparent. A Union artilleryman could have been speaking for all when he said: "We fought here. We charged there. We accomplished nothing."

Grant was not through, however. Bidding again for a breakthrough, he ordered a second frontal attack against the Mule Shoe on the morning of May 18. This assault was crushed by Confederate artillery fire almost before it got started. "We found the enemy so strongly intrenched," wrote General George Meade, "that even Grant thought it useless to knock our heads againt a brick wall, and directed a suspension."

Stalemate had been achieved. The Union commander remembered his well-publicized vow to "fight it out along this line if it takes all summer," but he now realized that this was neither possible nor desirable. The Army of the Potomac had lost nearly 18,000 men at Spotsylvania compared to the Army of Northern Virginia's 14,000 casualties, grim arithmetic that could be accepted only because of the numerical superiority the Federals enjoyed.

But to keep bleeding the Confederates, Grant had to draw them out of their breastworks and into the open. So on May 21, displaying the "dogged pertinacity" that President Lincoln so admired in him, he abandoned the Spotsylvania line and sent his men on another flanking march around Lee's right, south toward Richmond and yet another bloodletting.

Touring the Park

Begin your tour at the Fredericksburg Battlefield Visitor Center, where maps, exhibits, and an audiovisual program will help you understand the four battles fought in the Fredericksburg vicinity.

A complete tour of the park requires a drive of approximately eighty miles. There are sixteen numbered stops along the way, corresponding to key historic points on the four battlefields. In addition, there are four historic buildings associated with the battles, as well as about twenty-five buildings in town.

Fredericksburg Units

Stop 1. Fredericksburg Battlefield Visitor Center. The Visitor Center is located at the base of Marye's Heights, the ridge held by Lee's Army of Northern Virginia throughout the Battle of Fredericksburg. From the parking lot behind the Visitor Center, a short foot trail leads to the area that was the heart of the Confederate defensive position during the fighting on December 13, 1862. A National Cemetery lies across the road, southwest of the Visitor Center.

The paved street you see running along the base of the heights was a sunken dirt road in 1862. It was flanked by a stone retaining wall that formed a perfect breastwork for Confederate infantrymen. Some 1,200 of them crowded behind it, on either side of where you are standing, and blazed away at the Union ranks advancing across the open plain from the direction of Fredericksburg. Thousands of the blue soldiers died in brave but futile attempts to carry this position by frontal assault.

Walk down the sunken road, which is well marked with interpretive signs. At the far end stands a section of the original stone wall that sheltered Lee's troops. The Innis House, which stood on this site during the battle, is preserved today as it appeared in 1862. Its interior is pockmarked with bullet holes from the combat that swirled around it.

Stop 2. Lee Hill. From the parking area climb the short, steep foot trail to the top of Lee Hill. It was from this vantage point that Generals Robert E. Lee and James Longstreet directed the Confederate defense of Marye's Heights.

As Lee watched the waves of blue attackers sweep across the open ground below and break against the smoke-shrouded barrier of the stone wall, he turned to Longstreet and said: "It is well that war is so terrible. We should grow too fond of it."

The cannon you see here are similar to the ones that fired in support of the Confederate infantry during the battle.

Stop 3. Federal Breakthrough. The Union assaults on the Confederate left (Stops 1 and 2) were bloody failures, but here, on the right, a Federal division commanded by General George Gordon Meade successfully breached the Confederate line. Meade's men penetrated as far as this point, but then were hurled back by a determined Rebel counterattack.

Stop 4. Prospect Hill. General Thomas J. "Stonewall" Jackson, commander of the Confederate right, positioned fourteen cannon on this hilltop. The fire from these

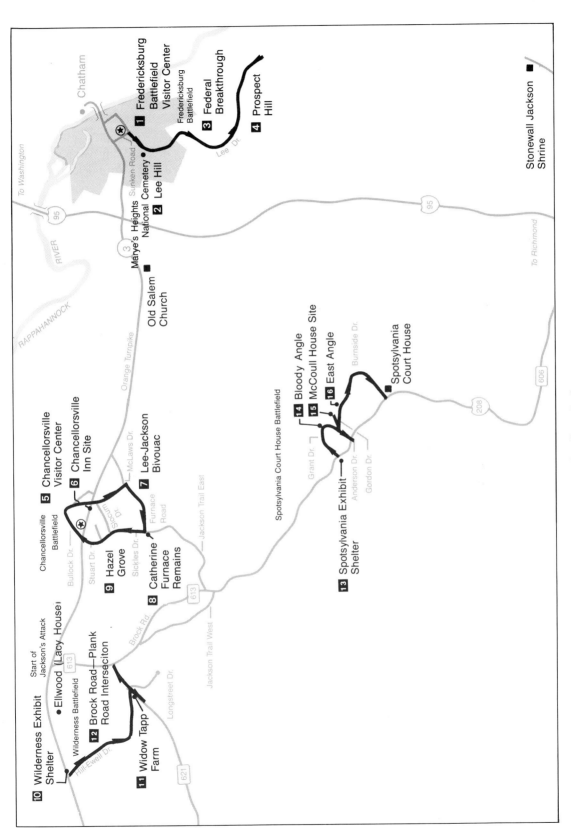

1 Fredericksburg Battlefield Visitor Center

2 Lee Hill

3 Federal Breakthrough

4 Prospect Hill

5 Chancellorsville Visitor Center

6 Chancellorsville Inn Site

7 Lee-Jackson Bivouac

8 Catherine Furnace Remains

9 Hazel Grove

10 Wilderness Exhibit Shelter

11 Widow Tapp Farm

12 Brock Road—Plank Road Interseciton

13 Spotsylvania Exhibit Shelter

14 Bloody Angle

15 McCoull House Site

16 East Angle

Stonewall Jackson Shrine

Old Salem Church

Chatham

To Washington

Marye's Heights

Sunken Road

National Cemetery

Fredericksburg Battlefield

Lee Dr.

RAPPAHANNOCK

RIVER

Orange Turnpike

McLaws Dr.

Jackson Trail East

Jackson Trail West

Chancellorsville Battlefield

Bullock Dr.

Stuart Dr.

Slocum Dr.

Sickles Dr.

Furnace Road

Brock Rd.

Longstreet Dr.

Hill-Ewell Dr.

Wilderness Battlefield

Start of Jackson's Attack

Ellwood (Lacy House)

Spotsylvania Court House Battlefield

Spotsylvania Court House

Burnside Dr.

Grant Dr.

Anderson Dr.

Gordon Dr.

To Richmond

95

95

3

613

613

621

208

606

Fredericksburg and Spotsylvania County Battlefields Memorial National Military Park guns wreaked havoc on the Union ranks advancing in the vicinity of the large stone pyramid, which is visible through the trees, beyond the railroad, to your left.

Chancellorsville Units

Stop 5. Chancellorsville Visitor Center. The Visitor Center contains exhibits related to the Battle of Chancellorsville and features a twelve-minute audiovisual presentation.

Stop 6. Chancellorsville Inn Site. The inn that stood at this crossroads was used by Union General Joseph Hooker as his headquarters during the battle. It was here, on May 1, 1863, that Hooker ordered his advancing army to halt and form a defensive line, thus surrendering the initiative to Robert E. Lee.

On the morning of May 3, 1863, Hooker was standing on the inn's porch when a cannonball shattered the pillar he was leaning against and knocked him unconscious. This close brush with death panicked the already rattled general, and he ordered the Union army to withdraw toward the Rappahannock and Rapidan river fords. Shortly thereafter, the attacking Confederates captured the crossroads and the inn, completing one of the most remarkable victories in the annals of warfare.

Today all that remains of the inn are traces of its foundation.

Stop 7. Lee-Jackson Bivouac. It was here, on the night of May 1, 1863, that Robert E. Lee and Stonewall Jackson held their famous "cracker box" council. Jackson sat on a tree stump and Lee on a cracker box while they hatched a daring plan for fighting the Battle of Chancellorsville. The two generals agreed to divide their badly outnumbered force and to send a large detachment, commanded by Jackson, on a long flanking march around the Federal right.

Stop 8. Catherine Furnace. The tumbled stone ruin you see here is all that remains of an early nineteenth-century iron furnace. On May 2, Stonewall Jackson's men swung past the furnace on their famous flanking march. The route of the march follows the road you are driving along.

Stop 9. Hazel Grove. This elevated clearing, called Hazel Grove, was one of the few sites on the heavily wooded Chancellorsville battlefield that was suitable for deploying artillery. Confederate troops seized Hazel Grove on the morning of May 3, 1863, moved thirty-six cannon into the clearing, and began a ferocious artillery duel with Federal batteries on a knoll 1,200 yards to the northeast. This knoll, known as Fairview, is visible at the far end of the corridor cut through the forest.

While the artillery duel was underway, Union and Confederate infantry fought in the surrounding woods. Eventually, the gray soldiers gained the upper hand and overran Fairview. The Confederate batteries advanced to the position, and began bombarding the Federal line near the Chancellorsville Inn (Stop 6).

If you wish, you may walk along a foot trail to Fairview, or drive to it via Berry-Paxton Drive.

Wilderness Units

Stop 10. Wilderness Exhibit Shelter. The displays here will help you gain a clearer understanding of the Battle of the Wilderness, fought on May 5–6, 1864.

Some of the most confused and desperate combat of the Civil War took place in the woods surrounding you. Units became lost in the dense undergrowth, and soldiers accidentally shot their comrades. Ambushes took a heavy toll, and to add to the horror, muzzle flashes set the brush on fire and hundreds of wounded men burned to death.

Stop 11. Widow Tapp Farm. On the morning of May 6, 1864, Union infantry attacked down the Orange Plank Road from the vicinity of Stop 12, and routed the Confederate Third Corps. As they approached the Tapp Farm, the Federals appeared to be on their way to a smashing victory, but canister spewing from Rebel cannon deployed in this clearing slowed their charge. Moments later, Gregg's Texas-Arkansas brigade and Benning's Georgia brigade arrived and prepared to counterattack. Robert E. Lee galloped to the front to lead the Confederate attack personally, but the soldiers refused to advance until he returned to the rear. Once their beloved commander had withdrawn to a position of safety, the Texans, Arkansans, and Georgians surged forward and threw the Union force back.

Stop 12. Brock Road–Plank Road Intersection. The area around this strategic point was the scene of heavy fighting on May 5–6, 1864. The Union assault that reached the Widow Tapp Farm (Stop 11) began and ended here. The Confederates later mounted a flank attack toward this position; it was during this action that Confederate General James Longstreet was severely wounded by friendly fire.

On the afternoon of May 7, Union commander Ulysses S. Grant ordered his army to maneuver around the Confederate right and march under cover of darkness to the crossroads at Spotsylvania Court House, nine miles to the southeast. All through the night of May 7, units of the Army of the Potomac trudged past this point, following the Brock Road to Spotsylvania.

Spotsylvania Court House Units

Stop 13. Spotsylvania Exhibit Shelter. The exhibits here explain the maneuvering and fighting that took place in the vicinity of Spotsylvania Court House on May 8–21, 1864. Nearby is a monument to Union general John Sedgwick. On May 9, 1864, Sedgwick, affectionately known to his troops as "Uncle John," was supervising the digging of breastworks. He had just reproved his men for flinching from sniper fire, saying, "They couldn't hit an elephant from this distance," when a bullet struck him just below the left eye, killing him.

Stop 14. Bloody Angle. Late on May 8, 1864, the Confederate divisions of Generals Edward "Allegheny" Johnson and Robert Rodes constructed a U-shaped line of entrenchments, called the "Mule Shoe Salient." The low earthen mounds you see are all that remain of the breastworks, which at the time of the battle stood shoulder high and were reinforced with logs.

Grant believed that the Mule Shoe was vulnerable, and at 4:30 A.M. on May 12 he launched a massive attack against it. Under cover of dense fog, some 20,000 Union troops rushed forward and captured or killed most of Johnson's division. Confederate reinforcements advanced to halt the Federal penetration of the salient, and for the next twenty hours the two armies struggled nonstop, through a pouring rainstorm, for control of what thereafter would be known as the "Bloody Angle."

The hand-to-hand combat at the Bloody Angle was the most savage of the Civil War, perhaps the most savage in American history. Bayonets, musket butts, rocks, and bare fists were used to maim and kill. The hail of bullets sweeping the battleground was so thick that an oak tree, twenty-two inches in diameter, was cut in half. "The dead and wounded were torn to pieces," recalled Private G. N. Galloway of the Union

Ninety-fifth Pennsylvania Regiment. "The mud was halfway to our knees. . . . Our losses were frightful."

Finally, at about 12:30 A.M. on May 13, the dazed, exhausted survivors broke off the fight and withdrew.

From the parking area, a loop trail covers the Bloody Angle battlefield. Interpretive signs along the way orient you and identify troop positions.

Stop 15. McCoull House Site. The McCoull House was located in the center of the Mule Shoe Salient and served as headquarters to Confederate general Edward "Allegheny" Johnson. The massive Union assault of May 12 was halted here. As at the Widow Tapp Farm (Stop 11), Robert E. Lee tried to lead the counterattack personally, but was forced to ride to the rear by the protests of his troops.

A one-and-a-half mile loop trail begins at the parking area, and follows the route of yet another Federal assault—this one made on May 18, 1864—to the line of earthworks that formed Lee's final line of defense at Spotsylvania.

Stop 16. East Angle. Union troops swarmed over the Confederate breastworks here on the morning of May 12. "I could see General Johnson with his cane striking at the enemy as they leaped over the works," wrote Confederate major Robert Hunter. "A sputtering fire swept up and down our line, many guns being damp. I found myself . . . in the midst of foes, who were rushing around me, with confusion and general melee in full blast."

The Federals captured these works and held them until May 21, when Grant once again ordered the Union army to swing around the Confederate right and march toward Richmond.

Historic Buildings

Chatham. Located on Stafford Heights, on the north bank of the Rappahannock River across from Fredericksburg, this large mansion was built between 1768 and 1771. During the Battle of Fredericksburg, the mansion served as headquarters, field hospital, and artillery and communications center. General Edwin V. Sumner directed the Federal attacks against Marye's Heights from here, while volunteers, including such notables as Clara Barton and Walt Whitman, tended wounded soldiers brought to the house from the battlefield across the river.

Old Salem Church. This small brick church building, located approximately three miles west of Fredericksburg on Virginia Highway 3 (Orange Turnpike), was built by Spotsylvania County Baptists in 1844. On May 3, 1863, a Union force under General John Sedgwick, advancing west from Fredericksburg to join the rest of the Army of the Potomac at Chancellorsville, ran into Confederates posted in the church and along the ridge it stands on. A fight erupted, and the Federals were thrown back. After the battle, Confederate surgeons used the church as a field hospital. Pockmarks from Federal bullets are visible in the church walls.

Stonewall Jackson Shrine. On the night of May 2, 1863, General Thomas J. "Stonewall" Jackson was accidentally shot by his own men. He was evacuated to a field hospital, where his left arm was amputated. On May 4, he was taken by horse-drawn ambulance to Fairfield Plantation at Guinea Station, some twelve miles south of Fredericksburg on the rail line to Richmond.

Jackson was quartered in this plantation office building, which is now preserved as the Stonewall Jackson Shrine. It was hoped that he would rest for several days, then journey on to Richmond for further medical treatment. Jackson contracted pneumonia, however, and on Sunday, May 10, 1863, with his wife and baby daughter in attendance, he died.

Dr. Hunter H. McGuire witnessed Jackson's passing and wrote: "A few moments before he died he cried out in his delirium, 'Order A. P. Hill to prepare for action! pass the infantry to the front rapidly! tell Major Hawks'—then stopped, leaving the sentence unfinished. Presently a smile of ineffable sweetness spread itself over his pale face, and he said quietly and with an expression, as if of relief, 'Let us cross over the river, and rest under the shade of the trees.'"

The building has been preserved as it was during the last six days of Jackson's life.

Elwood (Lacy House). Originally part of a plantation known as the Wilderness, Ellwood, or Lacy House, served as a hospital for Confederate forces during the fighting at Chancellorsville. General "Stonewall" Jackson's amputated arm was buried by Rev. Beverley Tucker Lacy in the family burial ground at Ellwood. A small stone near the house marks the location.

Ellwood derives its historical significance chiefly from its use as a Union army headquarters during the Battle of the Wilderness in May 1864; the three-day battle swirled just south of the house.

CHAPTER 9

GETTYSBURG NATIONAL MILITARY PARK
(Civil War)

Gettysburg, Pennsylvania 17325
Telephone: (717) 334-1124

In a mammoth three-day battle on July 1–3, 1863, the Union Army of the Potomac repulsed the second Confederate invasion of the North. This struggle, the bloodiest ever fought on the North American continent, marked a turning point in the Civil War. Never again would Robert E. Lee and his Army of Northern Virginia be able to mount an offensive of such magnitude. Gettysburg National Military Park preserves the scene of this decisive battle.

Getting to the Park: Gettysburg National Military Park is located 37 miles southwest of Harrisburg, Pennsylvania, off U.S. Highway 15.

Gas, food, lodging: In Gettysburg.

Visitor Center: Museum and gift shop; audiovisual program, electric map, and cyclorama.

Activities: Park personnel present interpretive programs at various battlefield locations, lead walks, and give talks at the Visitor Center. Inquire at Visitor Center for schedule and locations.

Handicapped Access: The Visitor Center is fully accessible, as are the tour exhibits. Most foot trails are wheelchair accessible; inquire at Visitor Center for more information.

The name Gettysburg reverberates through American history like a drum roll, a single, three-syllable word that evokes all the heroism and horror, the triumph and tragedy of the Civil War. It was on the outskirts of Gettysburg, a small farm town in the rolling hills of southern Pennsylvania, that the climactic battle between North and South was fought. During this titanic three-day struggle more than 51,000 men were killed or wounded. When it was over the shattered Confederate army withdrew to Virginia, never to go on the offensive again. The war would grind on for another two years, but its outcome was no longer in doubt. On the fields of Gettysburg the destiny of a nation had been determined.

A Summons to Richmond

On May 14, 1863, General Robert E. Lee, fresh from his brilliant victory at the Battle of Chancellorsville (see Chapter 8), was summoned to Richmond for a meeting with Confederate president Jefferson Davis and Secretary of War James Seddon. The two officials were deeply worried about events unfolding in Mississippi. A Union army commanded by Ulysses S. Grant had captured the city of Jackson and was preparing to advance on Vicksburg, threatening to seize undisputed control of the strategically vital Mississippi River (see Chapter 32). Davis and Seddon wished to ask their leading general how to avert this disaster. Lee had already considered the problem and concluded that "it becomes a question between Virginia and Mississippi." If part of his force was sent west to the relief of Vicksburg he feared that the Union Army of the Potomac, now licking its wounds in camp north of the Rappahannock River, would lunge south and take Richmond.

The thought of his beloved Virginia lying prostrate before the Yankee horde was too much for Lee, and so he proposed an alternative strategy: an invasion of the North. If this daring maneuver succeeded, it would draw the Federals away from the Confederate capital, ease the pressure on Vicksburg, and perhaps even end the war.

Lee's first foray into the North in the late summer of 1862 had ended with a bloody repulse on the banks of Antietam Creek in central Maryland (see Chapter 5). This time he intended to march rapidly through Maryland into southern Pennsylvania, where his army would destroy the Susquehanna River bridge at Harrisburg, severing the Pennsylvania Railroad, one of the main links between the Eastern Seaboard and the Midwest. "After that," he told the enthralled Confederate cabinet members, "I can turn my attention to Philadelphia, Baltimore, or Washington as may seem best for our interest."

The officials quickly approved his plan. It involved great risk, but after his triumphs at Fredericksburg and Chancellorsville Lee seemed unbeatable. He had proved himself the Confederacy's best soldier; who could presume to challenge his military judgment or question his ability to defeat the enemy on the field of his choosing? In the eyes of his countrymen he had ascended into the martial pantheon heretofore reserved for the great warriors of antiquity. As a Richmond lady wrote after he paid a social visit: "I recall the superb figure of our hero standing in the little porch. . . . It did not need my fervid imagination to think him the most noble looking mortal I had ever seen. We felt, as he left us . . . that we had been honored by more than royalty."

Lee, too, sensed this aura of invincibility, but believed that it emanated not from him, but from his soldiers. "There never were such men in an army before," he said. "They will go anywhere and do anything if properly led."

North to Pennsylvania

On June 3, 1863, the Confederate army broke camp at Fredericksburg and marched westward into the Shenandoah Valley. Screened by the barrier of the Blue Ridge, the long files of gray infantry wheeled north, crossed the Potomac River at Williamsport,

General George Gordon Meade commanded the Union Army of the Potomac during the Gettysburg Campaign. He reminded his soldiers of "a damned goggle-eyed old snapping turtle." Library of Congress.

General James Longstreet, who became Lee's second in command after the death of Stonewall Jackson, argued against the Confederate battle plan at Gettysburg. Cook Collection, Valentine Museum, Richmond, Virginia.

Maryland, and Shepherdstown, West Virginia, and moved on toward Pennsylvania. The advance was so rapid that Lee's soldiers joked about enjoying "breakfast in Virginia, whiskey in Maryland, and supper in Pennsylvania." By the end of June, a scant three weeks after setting out, Rebel divisions had occupied the towns of Chambersburg, Carlisle, and York, and were preparing to converge on Harrisburg.

Meanwhile, the Union army was undergoing a high-level shakeup. "Fighting Joe" Hooker, soundly trounced at Chancellorsville, was replaced by George Gordon Meade, a grizzled, grouchy forty-seven-year-old Pennsylvanian. The new commander reminded his soldiers of "a damned goggle-eyed old snapping turtle," but he moved with distinctly untortoise-like speed to get the Army of the Potomac on the march toward his home state and a confrontation with the invading Confederates.

At his bivouac in Chambersburg on the night of June 28, Lee learned from a spy that the Federals were fast approaching. He at once canceled the Harrisburg plan and ordered the scattered units of his command to concentrate for battle in the vicinity of Cashtown. Among the first troops to reach the gathering point were the men of Johnston Pettigrew's brigade. On June 30, while waiting for the rest of their comrades to arrive, they went on a foraging expedition to Gettysburg, eight miles to the east. There they collided with a column of Union cavalry, the outriders of Meade's advancing host. Chance had dictated that Gettysburg would be the site of the showdown between the two armies.

July 1, 1863: Gettysburg—Day One

The two cavalry brigades discovered by Pettigrew's men were commanded by John Buford, a hard-boiled regular who had fought Indians on the western plains. Buford had a good eye for terrain, and the ridges surrounding Gettysburg struck him as being ideal for conducting a defensive battle against Lee's force. He decided to hold the ground until the rest of the Union army could deploy on it, even though he knew it would be costly to his division. "They will attack you in the morning and they will come booming," he told one of his brigade commanders on the night of June 30. "You will have to fight like the devil until supports arrive."

True to Buford's words, the Confederates approached Gettysburg in strength early on the morning of July 1. Advancing down the Chambersburg Pike from the west, they came into contact with the Federal cavalrymen, dismounted, and spread out along McPherson Ridge at about 8 A.M. The battle was joined almost immediately as the gray infantry charged forward, impatient to shatter the thin blue line and capture Gettysburg.

Although badly outnumbered, Buford's troopers did enjoy one advantage: they were armed with breech-loading carbines that allowed them to get off as many as twenty shots a minute compared to the three or four possible with a standard-issue muzzle-loading Springfield. Bolstered by this extra firepower, the cavalrymen fought a desperate holding action until 10 A.M., when the vanguard of the Union infantry reached the field and reinforced them.

The commander of these infantry units, General John Reynolds, took over management of the battle, and sent word to General Meade and the rest of the Army of the Potomac to hurry forward and seize control of the hills and ridges to the east and south of Gettysburg. "Tell him the enemy are advancing in strong force, and that I fear they will get to the heights beyond the town before I can," he told the dispatch rider. "I will fight them inch by inch, and . . . hold them back as long as possible." A moment later a sharpshooter's bullet pierced his brain.

Although shaken by the loss of Reynolds, the Union soldiers fought on, grimly clinging to their position along McPherson Ridge and its northern extension, Oak Ridge. The pressure was mounting, however, as more Confederate units reached the battlefield and went into action. Shortly after 1 P.M., the division of General Robert Rodes, just arrived from Carlisle, struck the Federal flank on Oak Ridge. Two additional blue divisions came up to extend the Union right onto the plain north of Gettysburg, but they were hit in turn by Confederate formations advancing from the northeast down the Harrisburg Road.

It was at this moment, just as the collision of the two armies produced the critical mass necessary for a major battle, that Robert E. Lee came on the scene. He was unhappy with the way the early morning clash had escalated out of control: "I am not prepared to bring on a general engagement today," he peevishly told a subordinate. But he could also see that the chain reaction was beyond recall, and that a huge explosion of combat was inevitable.

Even as he watched, the Union line stretching across the Carlisle and Harrisburg

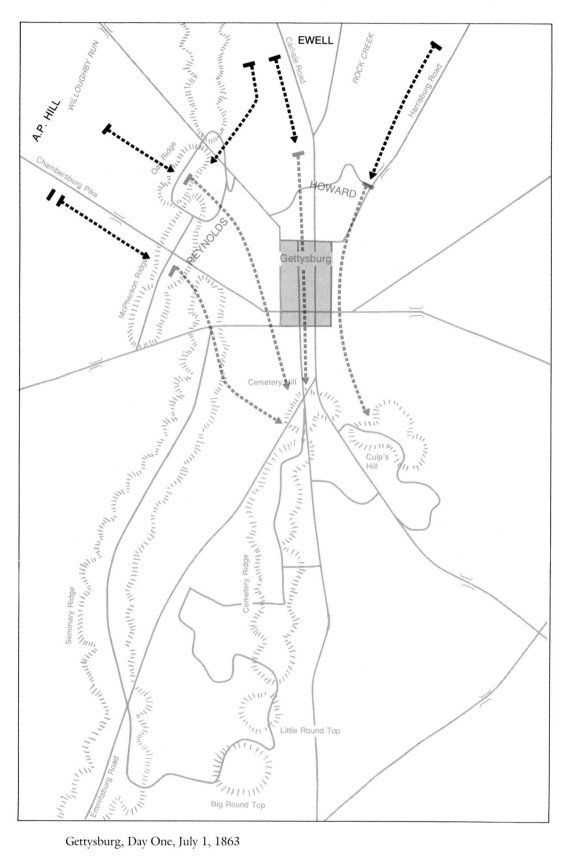

Gettysburg, Day One, July 1, 1863

roads suddenly broke, and the fragments were swept through the streets of Gettysburg toward Culp's Hill and Cemetery Hill, the dominant heights south of town. With their flank and rear exposed, the blue ranks on Oak Ridge had to give way, and they also retreated south, down Seminary Ridge, through Gettysburg, to the new rallying point on Cemetery Hill. The only Federals still holding their original position were the men on McPherson Ridge, and they were soon hurled back by a determined Confederate thrust down the Chambersburg Pike.

It was now 4:30 P.M., and the Army of Northern Virginia had suffered some 8,000 casualties while making its day-long series of attacks. Despite these heavy losses Lee, who earlier had wished to avoid a general engagement, now wanted to press the advantage. From Union prisoners he had learned that the bulk of Meade's army was coming fast, and he wanted to seize the high ground south of Gettysburg before the enemy could dig in on it. Consequently, he ordered General Richard Ewell, one of his three corps commanders, to "press those people" and capture Cemetery Hill.

Ewell, known as "Old Baldy" to his men, was in no position to act on Lee's order, however. He had his hands full trying to regain control of his command. His divisions had delivered the attack that shattered the Federal right, but in so doing they had become scattered and disorganized. Many soldiers were milling about Gettysburg, searching for Union fugitives or celebrating their victory. Federal snipers added to the confusion by taking potshots at the gray throng, and among those hit was General Ewell, who had lost a leg ten months earlier at the Battle of Second Manassas. The sharpshooter's bullet struck his artificial limb with a resounding thwack, but Old Baldy calmly rode on, remarking to the man next to him that "it don't hurt at all to be shot in a wooden leg."

Ewell's phlegmatic reaction to the sniping incident was indicative of his overall state of mind. He moved slowly to regroup his units, and by the time he had them in hand the sun was setting. Deciding that success was unlikely, he called off the attack, allowing the Federals to continue their frantic pick-and-shovel work on the crest of Culp's Hill and Cemetery Hill.

July 2, 1863: Gettysburg—Day Two

The tactical situation confronting Robert E. Lee on the morning of July 2, 1863, was far different from the one that had prevailed the night before. General Meade and the bulk of the Army of the Potomac had arrived around 3 A.M. and occupied a strong defensive position running from Culp's Hill and Cemetery Hill south two miles down Cemetery Ridge. The Confederate forces were arrayed parallel to the Union line, beginning on the southern outskirts of Gettysburg and extending down Seminary Ridge, which was separated from Cemetery Ridge by a shallow valley approximately two-thirds of a mile wide.

Lee was upset with Ewell for not storming Cemetery Hill, as ordered, on the evening of July 1, but still believed that the Federals could be dislodged from the high ground by a well-timed series of attacks. He decided to send General James Longstreet's corps against the Union left. Once that assault was under way, Ewell would hit the right at Culp's Hill.

Longstreet, Lee's most experienced and trusted lieutenant, was not enthusiastic about his chief's plan. The previous day he had advocated moving the Army of

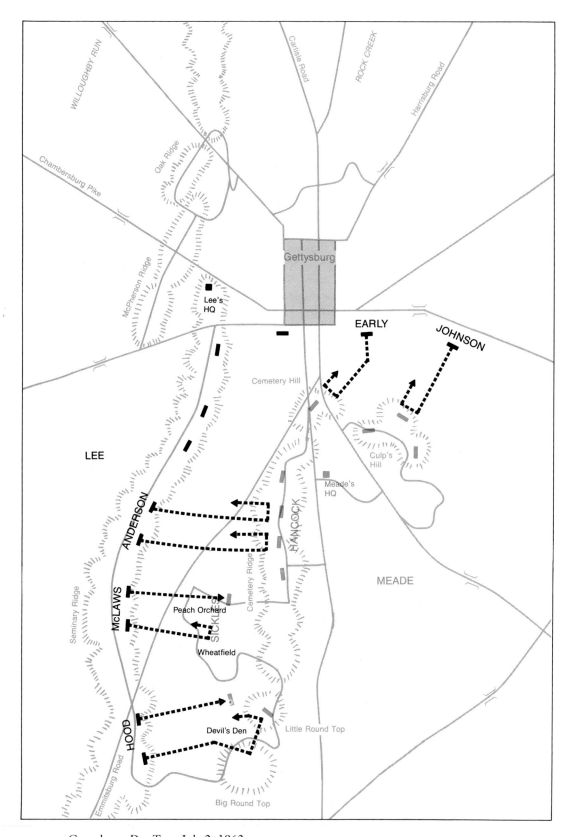

Gettysburg, Day Two, July 2, 1863

Northern Virginia to a new position well south of Gettysburg and fighting a defensive battle, along the lines of Fredericksburg (see Chapter 8). "No," Lee had said, pointing toward Cemetery Hill. "The enemy is there, and I am going to attack him there."

"If he is there," replied Longstreet, "it will be because he is anxious that we should attack him, a good reason, in my judgment, for not doing so."

"No," Lee had said again, with some heat. "They are there in position, and I am going to whip them, or they are going to whip me."

Longstreet gave up the argument, but he was very disturbed, believing that Lee was making a serious, perhaps fatal, blunder. Consequently he delayed getting his men on the move, and they did not reach the designated jump-off point, astride the Emmitsburg Road across from the southern extremity of Cemetery Ridge, until 4 P.M.

A surprise was in store for them there. The Union Third Corps, two divisions commanded by General Daniel Sickles, had come down from Cemetery Ridge and occupied a new line, in advance of the rest of the army. This salient ran from a peach orchard on the Emmitsburg Road, southeast through a large wheat field, to a jumble of glacial boulders aptly called the "Devil's Den." Sickles, a former New York City politician, had made this maneuver without the knowledge or approval of the Union high command. In so doing, he had unwittingly blocked Longstreet's route of attack, but had also placed his divisions in a position of great danger. Exposed and unsupported, they were about to pay in blood for their commander's rash move.

The Confederate attack got under way shortly after 4 P.M., launched in echelon from right to left by the divisions of John Bell Hood, Lafayette McLaws, and Richard Anderson. Hood's soldiers moved out first, heading not northeast along the Emmitsburg Road as Lee had ordered, but due east, toward the Devil's Den and the two rocky hills behind it, Big Round Top and Little Round Top.

The Federals posted in the Devil's Den took full advantage of the natural cover offered by the maze of boulders to inflict heavy punishment on the onrushing Confederates. Moments later the antagonists came to grips in wild hand-to-hand combat. Hood was carried from the field, bleeding from a severe arm wound, but his absence had little effect on the confused flow of the battle. "Every fellow was his own general," recalled one of the survivors. "Private soldiers gave commands as loud as officers; nobody paying any attention to either."

As the fighting among the rocks roared toward its climax, 500 Alabamians led by Colonel William Oates swung wide around the Devil's Den, scaled Big Round Top, then headed north to seize Little Round Top. This modest promontory was the key to the entire Union position. If the Confederates gained control of it, their artillery could rake the blue line that ran northward along Cemetery Ridge to Culp's Hill, causing almost unimaginable death and destruction.

At the last moment, General Gouverneur K. Warren, the Army of the Potomac's chief engineer, recognized the extreme peril and rushed Union troops to the defense of Little Round Top. They arrived just fifteen minutes before Oates's Alabamians, and a furious struggle ensued as the men in butternut and gray tried to carry the crest. The fighting seesawed up and down the hill's boulder-strewn slope—"blood stood in puddles in some places on the rocks," wrote Oates—but eventually the Federals pushed the Confederates back at bayonet point, averting disaster.

While Hood's men were battling for control of the Devil's Den and Little Round

Soldiers killed during the second day's fighting lie among shattered trees on the slope of Little Round Top. Library of Congress.

Top, McLaws's division swept into the Wheatfield and Peach Orchard. As the Rebel yell issued from thousands of throats and the rattle of musketry rose to a terrific crescendo, the blue ranks began to give way. General Sickles tried to rally his men, but a cannonball struck his right leg just above the knee, mangling it horribly; only the swift application of a tourniquet saved his life.

With their leader down and the pressure from the Confederates mounting by the second, the Federals fell back toward Cemetery Ridge. Three fresh divisions rushed to their aid, and now it was the Rebels' turn to stumble back through the smoking, blood-soaked Wheatfield. The assault through the Peach Orchard, spearheaded by Barksdale's Mississippi brigade, met with greater success. In what a Union colonel called "the grandest charge that was ever made by mortal man," the Mississippians overran the orchard, taking close to 1,000 prisoners, then continued straight on toward Cemetery Ridge. Massed batteries on the ridge's forward slope shattered the attack with vicious blasts of canister; the survivors of Barksdale's brigade retreated, minus their leader, who lay dying from gaping wounds in his chest and legs.

General Richard Anderson's division now took its turn, driving toward the center of the Union line on Cemetery Ridge. The commander in this sector, General Winfield Scott Hancock, desperately shifted units to meet the new Confederate threat. The First Minnesota Regiment was ordered to make a suicidal countercharge into the teeth of the Rebel advance while reinforcements were rushed up; the Minnesotans obeyed and lost 216 of 262 men in less than ten minutes. Their sacrifice gave Hancock time to buttress his position, however, and to get his men ready to absorb the impact of the charge.

"On they came like the fury of a whirlwind," wrote one of the Union soldiers crouching on the top of the ridge, waiting for the order to fire. When the command was given muskets crashed and cannon roared, tearing holes in the ranks of the attackers, but the gaps were quickly closed and the Confederates continued to push forward. Reaching the crest, the gray line held for a moment within eyesight of the white farmhouse Meade was using as his headquarters, then receded like a spent wave, washing back the way it had come. Without support the attackers' choices were capture, death, or retreat. They slowly streamed back across the shallow valley toward the shelter of Seminary Ridge, under fire every step of the way.

With the withdrawal of Anderson's division the attempt to crack the Union left was over. "I do not hesitate to pronounce this the best three hours' fighting ever done by any troops on any battlefield," said Longstreet, but his praise could not obscure the fact that nothing had been gained. Seven thousand men—almost a third of the 22,000 participating in the assault—had fallen trying to dislodge some 40,000 Federals from their positions on the high ground. "We have not been so successful as we wished," was Longstreet's terse summation of the results of an attack he had argued against in the first place.

Even as the Confederate effort on the left was sputtering to a conclusion, Ewell's corps was preparing to make its bid to break the Union right. At about 7 P.M., following a brisk artillery duel, the divisions of Edward "Allegheny" Johnson and Jubal Early advanced up the steep north slope of Culp's Hill and Cemetery Hill. These positions had been weakened considerably during the afternoon by the subtraction of units sent south to help deal with the threat to Little Round Top and Cemetery Ridge. Now, as twilight gave way to darkness, the hard-charging Rebels overran the top of Cemetery Hill. As with Anderson's division on Cemetery Ridge several hours earlier, it appeared that Early's men were about to pierce the Union line, but once again Federal reinforcements arrived in the nick of time. Grudgingly the Confederates retreated, stumbling down the dark hillside until they were back where they had started.

At midnight, after the fighting around Cemetery Hill had finally subsided, Meade called his corps commanders together for a council of war. He was reeling from the events of the past forty-eight hours; at the helm for less than a week, he had already suffered 20,000 casualties and would undoubtedly suffer more if he held his present position.

The question he put to the twelve generals who crowded into the parlor of the farmhouse headquarters was simple: withdraw, hold, or attack? The reply was unanimous: stay put and fight it out. As the meeting broke up, Meade took aside General John Gibbon, whose division held the center of the Union line, and said, "Gibbon, if Lee attacks me tomorrow it will be in your front."

Even as this prediction was being made, the Confederate commander was pondering his army's next move. From his perspective, the day's fighting could be analyzed in two ways. One point of view held that the attacks made against a numerically superior foe dug in on high ground had been doomed before they began, and that to continue in this vein was foolhardy. Conversely, it could be argued that both assaults had come within an eyelash of scoring a breakthrough and that with better coordination among the attacking units and better artillery preparation success could be achieved.

Aggressiveness was the essence of Lee's generalship. He had supreme, almost mystical, confidence in the fighting ability of his army, and he hungered for victory—complete, crushing victory that would destroy his opponents and end the war. He resolved to resume the offensive the next day, striking at the heart of Meade's position.

July 3, 1863: Gettysburg—Day Three

Dawn on July 3 was ushered in by the sound of cannon fire, reverberating along the south slope of Culp's Hill and through the rocky glen surrounding Spangler's Spring. The Federal forces ousted from this area the previous night were attacking, trying to regain the earthworks the Confederates had captured from them.

Riding along Seminary Ridge, Lee heard the rumbling of the cannonade to the northeast and correctly surmised that Ewell's corps was engaged. His mind was on the grand assault he intended to launch against the Union center, however. The division of General George Pickett, which had not seen action yet, would spearhead the drive, supported by the divisions of Generals Joseph Pettigrew and Isaac Trimble, who were standing in for their superiors Harry Heth and Dorsey Pender, both wounded during the first day's fighting. The total number of soldiers involved would be approximately 12,000; their advance was to be preceded by a heavy artillery bombardment aimed at paralyzing the enemy.

General Longstreet was dismayed when Lee outlined the battle plan and assigned him the task of coordinating the attack. The objective was a small grove of trees three-quarters of a mile distant on Cemetery Ridge; in between was an open, shallow valley that was within range of nearly every musket and cannon on the Federal line. "General," Longstreet said to Lee, "I have been a soldier all my life. . . . It is my opinion that no 15,000 men ever arrayed for battle can take that position."

The Confederate commander had made up his mind, however. He ordered the assault force to get ready and instructed Colonel Edward Porter to concentrate the army's artillery for the preliminary bombardment. Then he rode back and forth along the front for three hours, carefully studying the ground between the gray line and the copse of trees on Cemetery Ridge, positioning batteries and mentally mapping the routes he wanted the attacking units to follow. Longstreet wearily accompanied him, his heart in his boots: "Never was I so depressed as upon that day," he later wrote.

As noon approached, the fighting around Culp's Hill and Spangler's Spring came to an end, and an eerie hush descended on the battlefield; the air was oppressively hot and humid, and there was little breeze to stir it. The last of the Confederate cannon were dragged into place in a line running from the Peach Orchard northward two miles along Seminary Ridge. All told, 140 artillery pieces were loaded and aimed at the point of attack, the little grove marking the center of the Union line on Cemetery Ridge.

The minutes ticked away, and on both sides the soldiers lounged in the grass talking casually or napping. "Never was sky or earth more serene, more harmonious, more aglow with light and life," wrote one of the young men about to make the attack.

At precisely 1:07 P.M. the stillness was shattered by two cannon firing in quick succession. Moments later all 140 Confederate guns joined in, loosing an awesome, groundshaking blast. Dust and smoke erupted along the green crown of Cemetery Ridge as shot and shell smashed into the Union position, creating instant pandemonium. "The air was all murderous iron," recalled one of the blue infantrymen who desperately dived for cover as the bombardment exploded around him.

Union gunners held their fire for a few moments until they had located the position of the Confederate batteries, then opened up, adding to the tremendous din. Dark, billowing clouds of powder smoke soon shrouded the field, and all that was visible were the lightning flashes of explosions and flame stabs of discharging cannon. The thunder was incessant and deafening. Union soldiers manning the front line hugged the ground as metal fragments whined through the air and then fell in a hot, clattering shower around them. Despite the intensity of the fire, casualties were quite light. "All we had to do was flatten out a little thinner," explained one of the men who endured the great bombardment, adding sarcastically that "our empty stomachs did not prevent that."

The gun duel went on for nearly two hours, then Union fire slackened on orders from General Henry Hunt, the Army of the Potomac's chief of artillery. He wanted to conserve ammunition and let the gun tubes cool down in preparation for the Rebel assault he was sure was coming. Colonel Alexander, who was directing the Confederate batteries on Seminary Ridge, interpreted this lull to mean that his gunners had forced the Union artillery to withdraw, and he sent word to General Pickett that it was time to launch the attack.

Pickett rode up to Longstreet and asked, "General, shall I advance?"

Longstreet, choked with emotion, merely nodded in the affirmative. "My feelings had so overcome me that I could not speak, for fear of betraying my want of confidence," he later wrote.

Pickett saluted smartly. "I am going to move forward, sir," he said, then galloped back to his men and ordered them to advance.

As they cleared the line of trees on Seminary Ridge and moved out into the open fields that swept up toward the distant Union position, the Confederate infantrymen—sons of Virginia, Alabama, North Carolina, Tennessee, Mississippi, and Florida—saw clearly the near impossibility of the task that had been assigned them. "A passage to the valley of death," a major said of the long, gently sloping approach to the enemy line. Some men prayed; others sang a hymn. "June Kimble, are you going to do your duty?" one sergeant asked himself outloud as he gazed at the ground on which, in all likelihood, he would soon be wounded or killed. "I'll do it, so help me God," he finally murmured.

Among the Union defenders there was excitement and relief as the long gray lines of Confederates came into view. "Thank God! Here comes the infantry!" cried one of the Federals, intensely grateful that the terrifying artillery bombardment was over. Others watched the great martial display of the attack—12,000 men striding forward

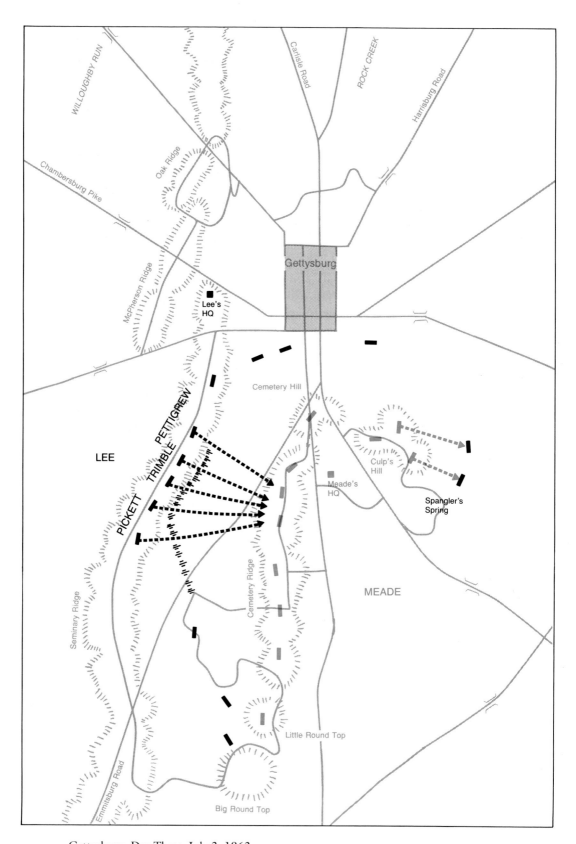

Gettysburg, Day Three, July 3, 1863

in neat, precise ranks, battle flags rippling, bayonets twinkling—with awe and admiration. "Beautiful, gloriously beautiful, did that vast array appear in the lovely little valley," wrote one. They had "the appearance of being totally irresistible," recalled another, as the formations drew steadily closer, covering 100 yards a minute. But now the time for killing was at hand, and as the Union batteries resumed their fire, beauty was replaced by butchery.

Bounding cannonballs knocked holes in the Confederate ranks, and the Federals cheered loudly like spectators at a sporting event. Flanking fire from the guns sited on Cemetery Hill and Little Round Top was particularly deadly, killing or wounding as many as a dozen soldiers with each shot. A brigade of Virginians on the far left of the advancing line could not bear the relentless pounding and broke for the rear, reducing the strength of the assault force. The right flank managed to keep going, but crowded toward the center, shying away from the deadly enfilading fire.

Like a wedge, the Confederate formations now crossed the Emmitsburg Road and drove toward the little clump of trees that was their objective. A stone wall running along this part of Cemetery Ridge veered outward to avoid bisecting the grove, then returned to its former course, creating an eighty-yard jog that the Union defenders had dubbed "the Angle." It was here that the attackers would come to grips with their opponents. But first they had to pass through a deadly cloud of minié balls and canister being fired at point-blank range.

The confusion and carnage were frightful; the Rebel ranks had been decimated, but somehow the survivors kept moving, stumbling toward the barrier of the stone wall. With only 100 yards to go, the Confederates halted and discharged a heavy volley of their own, the first they had fired since beginning the charge. Its effect was devastating. A Union battery was silenced, and a blue regiment broke from its position behind the wall and fled.

General Lewis Armistead, his black felt campaign hat resting on the point of his saber, now exhorted the men in gray to make the final, supreme effort. "Come on boys!" he screamed. "Follow me!" Covering the last bit of open ground, he clambered over the stone wall, laid his hand on the muzzle of one of the abandoned Union cannon, then pitched to the ground mortally wounded.

In the instant that the lead projectile ripped through Armistead's flesh, the Confederate attack—and the Confederate cause—reached its high-water mark. The 300 soldiers who had heroically followed the general into the Angle were quickly shot down or taken prisoner by counterattacking Federals. Those who were able to escape turned and began to make the long retreat back across the shot-swept valley toward Seminary Ridge. One of these was Sergeant June Kimball, who, having upheld his oath to do his duty, now retreated with his face toward the enemy so that if he was shot it would not be in the back.

As the survivors of the charge straggled toward the shelter of their own lines, Robert E. Lee rode out to meet them. "All this will come right in the end," he called out. "We'll talk it over afterwards. But in the meantime all good men must rally. We want all good and true men just now."

Pickett rode up, tears streaming down his cheeks. "General Lee, I have no division now," he stammered.

"Come, General Pickett," said Lee. "Your men have done all that men can do. The fault is entirely my own."

Retreat to Virginia

Of the 12,000 soldiers who made the attack on Cemetery Ridge on July 3, some 7,000—nearly 60 percent of the total—were killed, wounded, or taken prisoner. These losses, and those of the preceding two days, crippled the Army of Northern Virginia, but like a wounded animal it was still highly dangerous.

Many of the Confederates hoped that the Federals would attempt a counterattack, giving them a chance to even the score for the bloody failure of Pickett's Charge. Lee had ordered a contraction of the line in anticipation of a Union move against Seminary Ridge, and his soldiers were braced and ready. "We'll fight them, sir, till hell freezes over, and then, sir, we'll fight them on the ice," one soldier declared in response to a question about his unit's morale.

But it was not to be. Meade, having won a defensive victory in the greatest battle of the war, was not about to risk it by going over to the offensive. He decided not to move against Seminary Ridge "in consequence of the bad example he [Lee] had set for me, in ruining himself attacking a strong position."

Having lost a mind-boggling 28,000 casualties in the three-day struggle, Lee could not stay put for long. "We must now return to Virginia," he told his subordinates on the night of July 3, and at once began making plans to get what remained of his command back across the Potomac. The retreat began on the afternoon of July 4 with the departure of a wagon train, seventeen miles long, bearing the wounded; the able-bodied men followed later that night, marching southwest along the Hagerstown Road toward Maryland.

Although victorious, the Army of the Potomac had suffered almost as grievously as the Army of Northern Virginia. Slightly more than 23,000 of its soldiers had been killed, wounded, or captured, and the survivors were hungry, bone-tired, and low on ammunition. As a consequence, Meade was slow to pursue the withdrawing Confederates, and when he did it was with great caution, despite exhortations from Washington that he "Push forward and fight Lee before he can cross the Potomac."

The Confederates reached the Potomac at Williamsport, Maryland, on July 10, but were unable to ford it because the stream was swollen by rain. Grimly they dug in, expecting a massive Union attack at any moment. The Federals did not arrive until the 12th, however, and failed to get themselves organized for another two days. By then the river had dropped enough for a crude pontoon bridge to be built, and on July 13 Lee's bedraggled units crossed it to the safety of Virginia. Meade ordered an attack the next morning, but the advancing blue ranks found only empty trenches. The Confederate army had made good its escape; the Gettysburg Campaign was over.

"These Honored Dead"

Union victory at Gettysburg, and the simultaneous fall of Vicksburg on the Mississippi (see Chapter 32), marked the turning point of the Civil War. Robert E. Lee's bid to end the conflict by invading the North had failed, and at a cost the Confederacy could not bear. The flower of the Army of Northern Virginia, the soldiers Lee had declared "invincible," had fallen in the fields of Pennsylvania. They could not be replaced.

The Union, on the other hand, with its large reserves of man power, could absorb the losses at Gettysburg and come back stronger than ever. The only question was whether the resolve to fight, the willingness to pay the price for ultimate victory, could be sustained. President Abraham Lincoln, whose own steely determination to crush secession formed the very backbone of the northern war effort, saw this clearly. He decided to take the opportunity afforded by the dedication of a cemetery for the Union dead at Gettysburg to state the purpose of the war, as he saw it, and to justify the sacrifices that had been made, and those that still would be required, to conquer the Confederacy and reunite the nation.

So it was that on the chilly morning of November 19, 1863, the president made his way through the streets of Gettysburg to the new cemetery, laid out on the same ridge where Union and Confederate soldiers had struggled desperately four months earlier. A throng of 15,000 was on hand to listen to hymns, prayers, and a two-hour address by Edward Everett, the leading orator of the day. Then it was Lincoln's turn to deliver, in "a sharp, unmusical, treble voice," the "few appropriate remarks" the dedication committee had requested of him—remarks that have echoed down the years, calling on all Americans to honor and defend the trust bestowed upon them by their nation's founders and sanctified by the blood of the men who died at Gettysburg:

> Four score and seven years ago our fathers brought forth on this continent a new nation, conceived in liberty, and dedicated to the proposition that all men are created equal.
>
> Now we are engaged in a great civil war, testing whether that nation, or any nation so conceived and so dedicated, can long endure. We are met on a great battlefield of that war. We have come to dedicate a portion of that field as a final resting place for those who here gave their lives that that nation might live. It is altogether fitting and proper that we should do this.
>
> But, in a larger sense, we cannot dedicate, we cannot consecrate, we cannot hallow this ground. The brave men, living and dead, who struggled here, have consecrated it far above our poor power to add or detract. The world will little note, nor long remember, what we say here, but it can never forget what they did here. It is for us the living, rather, to be dedicated here to the unfinished work which they who fought here have thus far so nobly advanced. It is rather for us to be here dedicated to the great task remaining before us, that from these honored dead we take increased devotion to that cause for which they gave the last full measure of devotion; that we here highly resolve that these dead shall not have died in vain; that this nation, under God, shall have a new birth of freedom; and that government of the people, by the people, for the people, shall not perish from the earth.

Touring the Park

Begin your tour at the Visitor Center, where museum displays, audiovisual programs, and an electric map will help you gain a better understanding of the Gettysburg Campaign. You may also wish to visit the Cyclorama Center, located just south of the Visitor Center. A ten-minute film is shown here, and the Gettysburg Cyclorama, a huge (356 feet by 26 feet) circular painting of the climax of Pickett's Charge, is displayed. As you stand surrounded by the painting, a light and sound program highlights points on the canvas and recreates the atmosphere of the battle. Admission is charged.

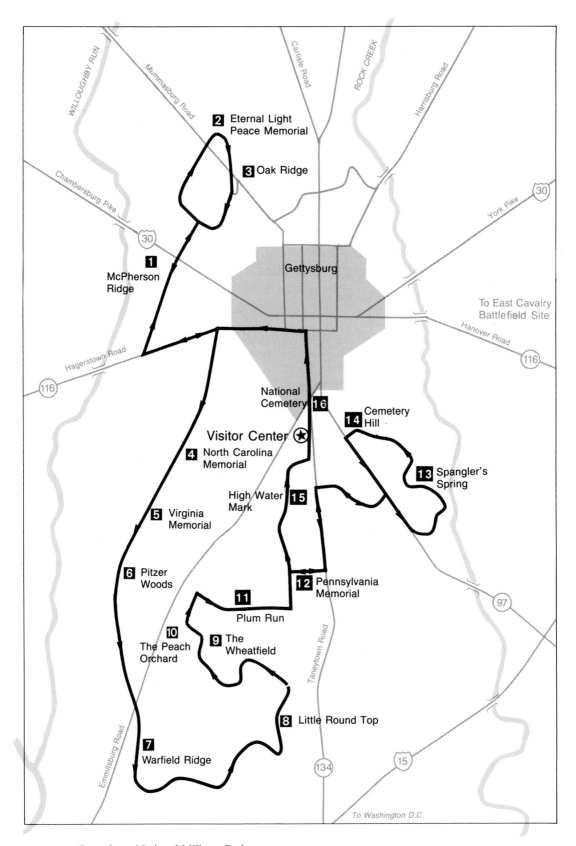

2 Eternal Light
Peace Memorial

3 Oak Ridge

ROCK CREEK

WILLOUGHBY RUN

Mummasburg Road

Carlisle Road

Harrisburg Road

Chambersburg Pike

30

York Pike

30

1

McPherson
Ridge

Hagerstown Road

Gettysburg

To East Cavalry
Battlefield Site

Hanover Road

116

116

National
Cemetery 16

Cemetery
14 Hill

Visitor Center ★

4 North Carolina
Memorial

13 Spangler's
Spring

High Water
Mark 15

5 Virginia
Memorial

6 Pitzer
Woods

12 Pennsylvania
Memorial

97

11

Plum Run

10 9 The
The Peach Wheatfield
Orchard

Taneytown Road

8 Little Round Top

7

Warfield Ridge

Emmitsburg Road

134

15

To Washington D.C.

Gettysburg National Military Park

A self-guided auto tour, which begins and ends at the Visitor Center, takes you around the battlefield. There are sixteen numbered stops along the way marking sites that figured prominently in the three-day struggle.

Stop 1. McPherson Ridge. The Battle of Gettysburg began here on the morning of July 1, 1863, when General John Buford's Union cavalrymen clashed with Confederate infantry advancing southeast down the Chambersburg Pike.

Through the morning and into the afternoon the Federals grimly held onto this high ground. General John Reynolds, who arrived with reinforcements around 10 A.M., was shot and killed in the woods just to your left. Finally, late in the afternoon, the Confederates forced the blue soldiers to abandon McPherson Ridge and retreat to Cemetery Ridge to the east.

Stop 2. Eternal Light Peace Memorial. In 1938, on the seventy-fifth anniversary of the battle, this monument was dedicated by President Franklin D. Roosevelt to "Peace Eternal in a Nation United."

The memorial stands on the hill occupied by Confederate general Robert Rodes's division on the afternoon of July 1, 1863. From here Rodes's men attacked south, driving the Federals from their defensive position on Oak Ridge (Stop 3).

Stop 3. Oak Ridge. The Union defensive line running along McPherson Ridge was extended northward to this high ground on the afternoon of July 1, 1863. The Federals stubbornly held the position for several hours, but were eventually outflanked and forced to withdraw to Cemetery Hill (Stop 14).

Stop 4. North Carolina Memorial. The thousands of North Carolinians who participated in Pickett's Charge on July 3 stepped off from this area of Seminary Ridge, marching east toward the Union position at the Angle (Stop 15).

Stop 5. Virginia Memorial. Here, on the crest of Seminary Ridge, the Virginians of General George Pickett's division were marshaled for the final, supreme effort on July 3. From this area they advanced across the open valley to the east, aiming for the Copse of Trees (Stop 15) on Cemetery Ridge. Robert E. Lee watched them go, and when the assault failed he rode forward from this point to rally the returning survivors.

Stop 6. Pitzer Woods. The Confederates of General Richard Anderson's division attacked from the shelter of these woods late on the afternoon of the battle's second day. Breaking through Sickles's salient north of the Peach Orchard, they pushed on toward the center of the Union line on Cemetery Ridge in the vicinity of the Pennsylvania Memorial (Stop 12). They managed to reach the crest of the ridge before being driven back.

Stop 7. Warfield Ridge. Shortly after 4 P.M. on July 2, the three divisions of Confederate general James Longstreet's corps advanced from this point, east and north, toward the Union left in the vicinity of Little Round Top (Stop 8), the Wheatfield (Stop 9), and the Peach Orchard (Stop 10). The assault was repulsed and approximately 7,000 men—almost a third of the attacking force—were killed or wounded.

Stop 8. Little Round Top. This small, rocky hill anchored the left flank of the Union defensive line. Incredibly, it was left undefended until the late afternoon of the battle's second day when General Gouverneur K. Warren rushed a brigade of Federals to guard its crest against a Confederate attack.

The Federals piled stones to form crude breastworks and fought desperately to hold the position. Repeated Rebel assaults were repelled by musket volleys and canister blasts from a six-gun battery that had been moved into firing position. Running low on ammunition, Union units countercharged with fixed bayonets and succeeded in driving the soldiers in gray down the hillside, ending the Confederate threat to Little Round Top.

Stop 9. The Wheatfield. Union general Daniel Sickles moved two divisions of troops down from Cemetery Ridge into the Devil's Den, this field, and the adjoining Peach Orchard on the afternoon of July 2, 1863, forming an exposed salient in the Federal line. Shortly after 4 P.M., Confederates of General James Longstreet's corps smashed into this salient. The combat seesawed back and forth through the field in which you are standing, leaving the wheat trampled and blood soaked. One of the many casualties was General Sickles, whose right leg was mangled by a cannonball. Eventually the weight of Confederate numbers told, and the Union survivors retreated back to Cemetery Ridge.

Stop 10. The Peach Orchard. Barksdale's brigade of Mississippians broke Sickles's salient here on the afternoon of July 2, 1863. After taking 1,000 prisoners, they resumed their attack to the east, driving toward the main Union line on Cemetery Ridge. Fire from artillery batteries and infantry massed on the ridge turned them back, but not before half their number had been cut down.

Stop 11. Plum Run. Union soldiers, retreating from the savage fighting in the Peach Orchard (Stop 10), crossed this ground on their way to Cemetery Ridge. Their withdrawal was covered by the fire of several Union cannon positioned here.

Stop 12. Pennsylvania Memorial. The nearly 35,000 Pennsylvanians who fought at Gettysburg are honored by this monument, one of the most elaborate on the battlefield.

Stop 13. Spangler's Spring. Although the Confederates failed to carry Culp's Hill on the evening of July 2, they succeeded in capturing this spring and the Union earthworks just north of it. Their triumph was short-lived, however. At dawn on July 3, the Federals counterattacked and retook the position.

Stop 14. East Cemetery Hill. Fleeing Union troops rallied and dug in here on the night of July 1. The next evening they repelled a determined Confederate assault that reached the crest of the hill and almost broke through their line.

Stop 15. High Water Mark. Pickett's Charge, the climactic Confederate infantry attack made on the afternoon of July 3, 1863, ended here. The soldiers in gray—12,000 strong—set out from the wooded ridge visible approximately three-quarters of a mile to the west of where you are standing. They advanced across the shallow, open valley under fire all the way, heading for the point marked by the Copse of Trees.

The assault reached its high water mark when some 300 Rebel infantrymen led by General Lewis Armistead entered "the Angle," the jutting salient marked by the stone wall. In a matter of minutes they were all killed, captured, or forced to withdraw, ending Robert E. Lee's desperate bid to break the Union line.

Take the one-mile-long loop trail that winds through the High Water Mark area. You will see regimental monuments, part of an artillery battery, the Copse of Trees, the stone wall forming the Angle, and the small white farmhouse that was General Meade's headquarters.

Stop 16. National Cemetery. Union soldiers who died in the Battle of Gettysburg are buried in this cemetery; the Soldier's National Monument commemorates their supreme sacrifice. A few steps to the south is the spot where Abraham Lincoln delivered his Gettysburg Address.

East Cavalry Battlefield Site. Three miles east of Gettysburg on Pennsylvania Highway 116 (Hanover Road) is the site of a fierce clash between Union and Confederate cavalry units on the afternoon of July 3, 1863.

The Confederate cavalry, led by J. E. B. Stuart, was trying to strike at the rear of the Federal line on Cemetery Ridge in support of Pickett's Charge. They were intercepted by General David M. Gregg's Union cavalry, however, and a pitched battle ensued. Charge and countercharge swept back and forth across this ground as the two sides struggled to gain the upper hand. One of the Union soldiers distinguishing himself in the combat was George Armstrong Custer, whose Michigan regiments stood fast against repeated Confederate onslaughts. After three hours of intense, often wild fighting, Stuart's troopers retired to the north of Gettysburg, unable to carry out their mission of raising havoc in the Union rear.

CHAPTER 10

MANASSAS NATIONAL BATTLEFIELD PARK
(Civil War)

P.O. Box 1830
Manassas, Virginia 22110
Telephone: (703) 754-7107

On July 21, 1861, Union and Confederate armies clashed along the banks of Bull Run creek in the first major battle of the Civil War. Thirteen months later, a second battle was fought on the same field. Manassas National Battlefield Park preserves the scene of the two battles as well as several historic structures associated with the Manassas campaigns.

Getting to the Park: Manassas National Battlefield is located 26 miles southwest of Washington, D.C. Take I-66 southwest from Washington to the Virginia Highway 234 Exit. Drive north 1 mile on Virginia 234 to the park entrance.

Gas, food, lodging: In Manassas, 13 miles southeast of the park on Virigina Highway 234.

Visitor Center: Museum and gift shop; audiovisual programs.

Activities: Interpretive hikes led by park personnel. Living-history demonstrations during the summer months. Inquire at Visitor Center for schedule and locations.

Handicapped Access: The Visitor Center is fully accessible. The foot trail on Henry Hill is moderately steep; the surface is grass. Access to the Stone House is impeded by three high entrance steps.

On April 15, 1861, two days after the fall of Fort Sumter (see Chapter 21), President Abraham Lincoln issued a call for 75,000 troops. Within a week, militia units from the northern states were arriving in Washington, coming first in a trickle and then in a torrent. They were made up of young, enthusiastic volunteers who knew nothing of soldiering but were eager to participate in what they believed would be a short, glorious war.

On to Richmond

During the tumultuous days of April and May 1861, the development of Union strategy was dictated as much by political considerations as by sound military principles. War fever was running rampant, and both the press and the public were clamoring for a quick campaign against the Confederate capital of Richmond, located only 110 miles south of Washington. It was widely believed that the capture of this Virginia city would lead to the breakup of the Confederacy. The difficulty of mounting such an expedition with an army of raw recruits was either down played or ignored.

The southern soldiers were just as green as their northern counterparts, but they had the advantage of being on the defensive. By the end of June, a Confederate army 22,000-men strong had taken up a position approximately thirty miles southwest of Washington, near the point where the Orange & Alexandria Railroad intersected the Manassas Gap line. The junction was strategically vital: if Union forces seized it, the best overland route to Richmond would be open to them.

Under the direction of General Pierre G. T. Beauregard, the Confederates positioned themselves along a narrow, meandering creek called Bull Run. There they waited with growing excitement and apprehension for the attack they were sure would come. Meanwhile, in Washington, the Union commander, General Irvin McDowell, was trying to delay any advance until his army could receive more training. Calls for action were growing louder, however. The newspapers had coined the battle cry, "On to Richmond!" and the people of the North were waiting impatiently for word that the campaign to end the war had begun. President Lincoln was also pushing for a prompt advance; the volunteers he had called for in April were obligated to serve just three months. That period would soon expire, and he wanted the decisive battle fought before these ninety-day enlistees left for home.

On July 16, 1861, McDowell reluctantly bowed to the pressure and put his army on the road to Manassas. The 35,000 Union troops made a stirring spectacle as they marched through the streets of Washington and out into the Virginia countryside. Bands played patriotic airs, swords and bayonets glittered in the sunlight, and brilliantly colored regimental flags rippled in the summer breeze. Caught up in the excitement, many prominent Washingtonians packed wicker baskets with food and wine and followed the advancing columns in buggies and carriages. The holiday mood soon spread to the volunteer soldiers, who behaved as if they were going to a picnic rather than a battle. They broke ranks to pick blackberries and refill their canteens, threw away their heavy equipment and full cartridge boxes, and ate up the rations that were supposed to last them several days.

At noon on July 18, the Union army finally reached Centreville, five miles east of Bull Run. It bivouacked there for two days while additional food and ammunition were brought forward and McDowell and his staff reconnoitered the enemy positions. The Confederates took full advantage of this lull to strengthen their defenses. Beauregard telegraphed Richmond requesting reinforcements, and on July 20, General Joseph E. Johnston and approximately 5,000 troops arrived from Winchester in the

During April 1861, thousands of enthusiastic young men rushed to join the Confederate and Union armies, eager to participate in what they thought would be a short, glorious war. Cook Collection, Valentine Museum, Richmond, Virginia.

Shenandoah Valley, after slipping away from a Union force that was supposed to hold them there.

Above left: General Pierre G. T. Beauregard commanded the Confederate army at the First Battle of Manassas. Library of Congress.

Above right: General Irvin McDowell led 35,000 Union troops at the First Battle of Manassas. Library of Congress.

Left: Union general John Pope ordered an all-out frontal assault against Jackson's Confederates at the Second Battle of Manassas, exposing his army to a devastating flank attack. Library of Congress.

First Battle of Manassas (Bull Run)

In the predawn hours of July 21, McDowell's army moved into position to commence the attack. The main column, composed of divisions commanded by Colonels David

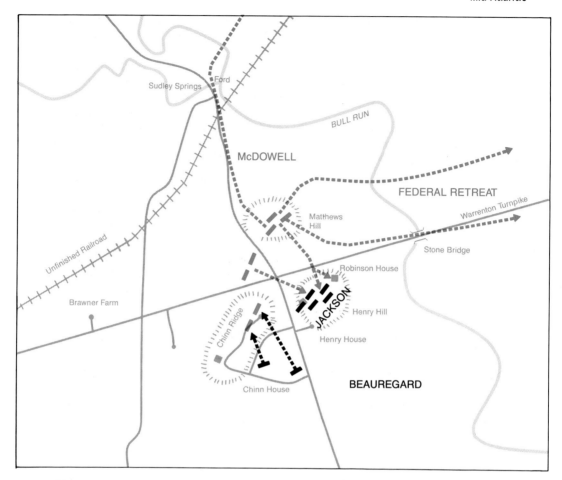

First Battle of Manassas, July 21, 1861

Hunter and Samuel P. Heintzelman, marched north and west toward Sudley Springs Ford, well beyond the Confederate left flank. The other two columns moved southwest toward Bull Run. They were to make diversionary attacks at Blackburn's Ford and the Stone Bridge, freezing the Confederates in place until Hunter and Heintzelman smashed into their left and rear.

The three-pronged assault was well thought out, but its success depended on speed, timing, and surprise. Night marches were difficult, even for experienced troops, and McDowell's amateurs simply could not execute the maneuver in the time allotted. They tripped and staggered along the narrow country roads in the dark, choking on thick dust as they tried to find their assigned jump-off points.

At about 5:30 A.M., there was a flash and roar as a Union cannon fired on the Confederate units defending the Stone Bridge. Presently other Union batteries in the vicinity of the bridge and Blackburn's Ford also opened up, and McDowell's diversionary columns made a show of beginning an attack. The real assault was scheduled to begin at 7 A.M., but the slow-moving divisions of Hunter and Heintzelman could not get into position on the Confederate left flank until 9:30.

Since 8 A.M. it had been apparent to the Confederates that the Union maneuvering at the Stone Bridge and Blackburn's Ford was a feint. This suspicion was confirmed when an observer with field glasses spotted the main Federal column approaching Bull Run at Sudley Springs Ford beyond the Confederate left. Swiftly, Colonel Nathan Evans withdrew the bulk of the force that was defending the Stone Bridge and rushed it northwest to Matthews Hill to fend off the Union flanking attack.

Evans's 1,000 Confederates had barely formed into a skirmish line when they were struck by 13,000 Federals. Volleys crashed out and a cloud of powder smoke billowed over the field. The gray line wavered momentarily, but then held as reinforcements—the brigades of General Bernard Bee and Colonel Francis Barton—shored it up.

The novice soldiers of both sides slugged it out on Matthews Hill for over an hour, becoming instant veterans in the flaming, thundering cauldron of battle. The pressure of Union numbers increased until it became irresistible, and the Confederate formations broke and streamed back toward higher ground near the Henry and Robinson houses. Sensing that victory was at hand, the blue ranks plunged ahead, pursuing their demoralized opponents.

The Confederate retreat might have become a rout, but in the midst of the wild confusion General Bee looked toward Henry Hill and saw the brigade of General Thomas J. Jackson arrayed across its crest. "There is Jackson standing like a stone wall!" bellowed Bee. "Rally behind the Virginians!"

As quickly as it had come, the panic gripping the Confederates dissipated. The retreating gray units stopped, reformed, and took up positions to the left and right of Jackson's now-famous "Stonewall Brigade." Generals Beauregard and Johnston soon arrived on the scene with additional reinforcements, and the Confederates braced themselves for the renewal of the Union assault.

It began at 2 P.M. with a furious artillery barrage that continued until a bold Confederate charge overran two of the Federal batteries. Now began a series of ferocious attacks and counterattacks as the opposing armies struggled desperately for control of Henry Hill. For an hour and a half the fighting raged under the hot sun with first one side giving ground, then the other.

Finally, at about 4 P.M., Beauregard sent several fresh brigades plowing into the Union right near the Chinn House. The blue line buckled, then broke. Exhausted by more than twelve hours of marching and fighting, the Union soldiers broke off and streamed back across Bull Run.

The retreat was orderly until the Federal troops reached Warrenton Pike, the road back to Centreville and Washington. There they ran into a traffic jam created by the carriages of the congressmen and other civilians who had driven out to watch the battle. A few well-placed Confederate cannon shots fell in the midst of this turmoil, and panic suddenly swept through the ranks. Throwing down their muskets and shucking off their knapsacks and blanket rolls, the ninety-day men ran wildly toward Washington, ignoring their officers' attempts to rally them. McDowell's army had disintegrated into a terrified mob.

Aftermath of First Manassas (Bull Run)

Had the Confederates pursued their fleeing foe aggressively late on the afternoon of July 21, the Union army might have ceased to exist as a fighting force. But Beauregard's soldiers were just as battle weary as McDowell's men, and just as disorganized in victory as their enemy was in defeat. No pursuit was made, and by the morning of July 22, the Federal forces were back behind the Washington defenses, pulling themselves together to fight another day.

Despite a casualty list that showed 387 dead and 1,582 wounded, the people of the South were elated by their army's victory at Manassas. Many believed the war was as good as over; the Confederate fighting man, it was said, had shown himself to be far superior to his Yankee counterpart, and southern independence soon would be secured beyond all doubt.

In the North, news of the defeat was received with shock and consternation: the Union army had lost 460 men killed and 2,436 wounded, captured, or missing. "On every brow sits sullen, scorching, black despair," wrote newspaper editor Horace Greeley. But the Manassas disaster also had a positive effect. It forced a previously overconfident public to face reality. The war would not be decided in a single day by a small force of ill-trained ninety-day volunteers. When President Lincoln called for more troops—three-year volunteers this time—tens of thousands of men responded, not with the naïve enthusiasm of their predecessors, but with a stern sense of resolve to see the war through to its bitter end.

Prelude to Second Manassas (Second Bull Run)

Within days of the Union debacle at the first Battle of Manassas, General George B. McClellan arrived in Washington to take charge of the disorganized and dejected Federal forces. He instituted a rigorous training program that soon transformed McDowell's amateur command into the powerful, disciplined, thoroughly professional Army of the Potomac. In March 1862, McClellan moved the bulk of the army—more than 100,000 men—to the tip of the York-James peninsula, 100 miles southeast of Richmond; approximately 40,000 troops were left behind to guard the approaches to Washington.

McClellan's end run forced the Confederate army, commanded by General Joseph E. Johnston, to leave the Manassas area and march south to meet the new Federal threat to Richmond. Through April and May the Army of the Potomac inched its way up the York-James peninsula until it was within sight of the spires of Richmond.

On May 31, Johnston attacked the Union forces in a desperate bid to save the Confederate capital. The bloody Battle of Fair Oaks ended with the repulse of Johnston's men and the wounding of the general himself. Richmond's fall, and the collapse of the Confederacy, appeared inevitable, but with victory in his grasp McClellan hesitated. The new Confederate commander, Robert E. Lee, took advantage of the Union inaction to reinforce his army, which he had named the Army of Northern Virginia, and to strengthen Richmond's defenses. On June 26 he went over to the offensive, pushing McClellan back down the peninsula in a series of savage encounters known collectively as the Seven Days' Battles (see Chapter 12).

While the Seven Days' Battles were underway, the scattered Federal units guarding

Washington were consolidated into the Army of Virginia and placed under the command of General John Pope. Pope was instructed to shield Washington while at the same time disrupting Confederate rail traffic at Gordonsville, thus relieving some of the pressure on McClellan. Lee dispatched Stonewall Jackson's corps to "suppress Pope," while the remainder of the Confederates kept an eye on the Army of the Potomac.

On August 9, Jackson attacked part of Pope's army at Cedar Mountain. Several days later, Lee learned that McClellan had been ordered to withdraw from the peninsula and join Pope; eager to strike the smaller Union army before it could be reinforced by McClellan's legions, Lee marched northwest to link up with Jackson. Pope was alerted to the Confederate move against him and retired across the Rappahannock River in the direction of Washington.

Time was running out for Lee. Within a few days Pope's Army of Virginia would unite with McClellan's Army of the Potomac, leaving the Confederates outnumbered better than two to one. Swiftly, Lee made a decision: he would divide his force, sending Stonewall Jackson and 24,000 troops on a wide flanking movement around Pope's right to get into the Union rear and cut the supply line to Washington.

Jackson's "foot cavalry" set out on their flanking march on August 25. Two days and fifty-one miles later, they seized Pope's supply depot at Manassas Junction. After gorging on captured rations, outfitting themselves with new blankets and shoes, and stuffing their pockets and haversacks with loot, they put the depot to the torch and pitched camp in woods northeast of the Brawner Farm, near the Warrenton Turnpike, barely two miles away from the First Manassas battlefield.

When Pope was told that Jackson was loose in his rear, he turned his army around and went after him. Lee also moved northward with General James Longstreet's corps, intending to reunite with Jackson at Manassas.

August 28, 1862: Slaughter at Brawner's Farm

The afternoon of August 28 was hot and still; Jackson's 24,000 soldiers lay about napping, playing cards, laughing, and talking. "The woods sounded like the hum of a beehive in the warm sunshine," recalled one of the men who was there.

Mounted on his horse, Jackson rode back and forth along a low ridge from which he could see the Warrenton Turnpike. He had been informed by scouts that Union troops were advancing from the southwest, and he was concerned that the armies of Pope and McClellan were about to link up at Centreville.

Just before sunset, a tightly packed blue column appeared, tramping along the dusty pike toward the Stone Bridge. Jackson conferred briefly with his officers, who then turned and galloped toward their concealed soldiers. "The men . . . knew what it meant," wrote an observer, "and from the woods arose a hoarse roar like that from cages of wild animals at the scent of blood."

Out from the shadows swarmed the Confederates. They formed into ranks and charged down the ridge toward the Warrenton Turnpike, yelling as they came. The Union column—2,800 Wisconsin and Indiana men commanded by General John Gibbon—was caught off guard, but did not panic. Wheeling to the left, it met and halted the Confederate onslaught in its tracks with several massed volleys. Jackson impatiently threw reinforcements into the fray; the blue line stubbornly held firm, and for two long hours the opposing forces blasted away at a range of less than 100 yards. Darkness finally ended the slaughter; some 2,000 men had been killed or wounded.

August 29, 1862: Second Manassas (Bull Run) —Day One

News of the fight at Brawner's Farm convinced Pope that Jackson was isolated and could be overwhelmed by the combined Union forces. Accordingly, he ordered the Federal columns to converge on Groveton on the morning of the 29th preparatory to launching an attack on Jackson's corps, which he believed would be in full flight.

The combative Stonewall had a different scenario in mind, however: he had set his soldiers to digging in along the grade of an unfinished railroad about half a mile north of the Warrenton Turnpike. The Confederates were spread out in a mile-and-a-half-long defensive line, using the mounded earth embankment of the grade as a breastwork, waiting for the shock of the Union assault and for the arrival of Longstreet's corps marching up from the southwest.

At his headquarters on the Warrenton Turnpike, Pope made plans for simultaneous blows against the left and right flanks of Jackson's line. A large part of his army was delayed getting into position, but he decided to make the attack anyway, throwing units forward piecemeal against the Confederate left near Sudley Springs. The fighting was ferocious as the blue ranks swept in waves up to, and sometimes over, the railroad grade held by the men in gray. At several points the Federals pierced the Confederate line only to be thrown back after desperate minutes of hand-to-hand combat.

Early in the afternoon, as the battle was raging near Sudley Springs, the 30,000 troops of Longstreet's corps arrived on the field. They deployed on Jackson's right flank, in position to threaten the exposed Union left. General Lee suggested that Longstreet move forward at once, but Longstreet declined, wanting to give his men a chance to rest and regroup after their long march.

Unaware that he was now facing the entire Army of Northern Virginia, Pope continued to hammer away at Jackson's left. Charge after charge was repulsed and the blanket of bodies in front of the railroad embankment grew thicker. The Confederate defenders were exhausted and running low on ammunition—one remembered spending the time between attacks "praying that the great red sun . . . would go down"—but they grimly refused to retreat.

Twilight finally did come, and with it an end to the day's fighting. The roar of musketry and rumble of cannon fire subsided and was replaced by the doleful chorus of wounded men calling for water.

August 30, 1862: Second Manassas (Bull Run) —Day Two

Despite the failure of all his assaults the previous day, Pope remained confident on the morning of August 30 that victory would soon be his. "We fought a terrific battle here yesterday," he wired the high command in Washington. "The enemy is still in our front, but badly used up."

At midday the Union general ascended a hill to reconnoiter the Confederate lines and somehow convinced himself that Jackson's soldiers were in retreat. Still unaware

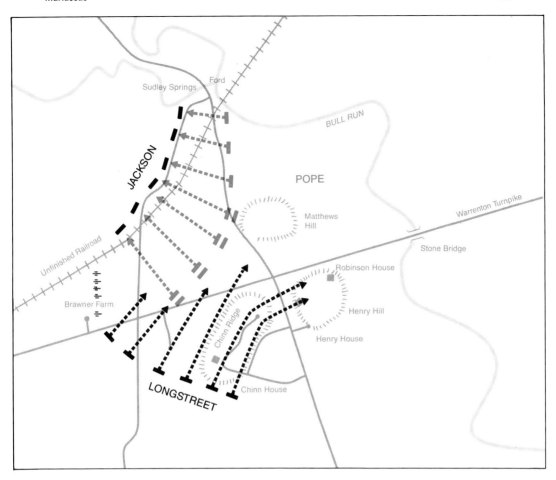

Second Battle of Manassas, August 30, 1862

that Longstreet was menacing his left, and believing that the decisive moment was at hand, he ordered his army forward.

Jackson had not retreated, and as the Federal columns advanced three lines deep toward the railroad embankment, his soldiers leveled their muskets and took aim. A sheet of fire tore through the tightly packed Union formations, leaving gaping holes, but the men in blue gallantly closed ranks and surged ahead. Thick clouds of sulfurous gunsmoke shrouded the field and bullets whizzed and hissed like a deadly plague of insects, but still the Federals pressed the attack, bending and almost breaking the gray line.

At the height of the struggle, Jackson's Confederates were firing so rapidly into the writhing blue mass in their front that their musket barrels became too hot to handle. The worst fighting took place in the area near a section of railroad bed known as the "Deep Cut." Here, the Union soldiers momentarily breached the gray line, only to be driven back after a wild hand-to-hand melee in which rocks, clubbed muskets, and bare fists were used by the desperate defenders.

It was approximately 3:30 P.M., and the battle had reached its climax. Pope's entire army was now committed to the headlong charge against Jackson's line, and Longstreet was at last ready to launch his counterattack. First, Confederate artillery batteries raked the exposed Federal ranks with lethal flanking fire, shattering entire units with a hail of iron. Then Longstreet's infantry bore down on the Union left, smashing into it with sledgehammer force, sweeping the stunned Federals to the northeast. Seeing the blue assault suddenly dissolve in front of them, Jackson's men raised the Rebel yell and joined the counterstroke. Like a set of powerful jaws, the long lines of gray infantry clamped down on Pope's fragmented command and ground it up.

On a low, grassy knoll, two New York regiments tried to stem the Confederate tide; one was quickly overrun, and the other was virtually destroyed, losing 70 percent of its strength in less than ten minutes. Longstreet's eager soldiers barreled ahead, moving along the crest of Chinn Ridge, coming on, wrote a bluecoat, "like demons emerging from the earth." Here and there on the ridge, isolated Federal units fought last-ditch holding actions, delaying the Confederates just long enough for Pope to organize a defensive line on nearby Henry Hill. As the sun set smoky red below the western horizon, Longstreet's men repeatedly stormed the hill but failed to dislodge the stubborn Union regiments holding it.

Darkness ended the fighting, and Pope's reeling army, which had come within an eyelash of destruction, withdrew across Bull Run and limped northeast toward Centreville and the shelter of Washington's defenses.

Lee Triumphant

The soldiers of both sides had fought with a skill and ferocity that far outstripped their performance at the First Battle of Manassas thirteen months earlier. The raw recruits of 1861 were hardened combat veterans now, capable of inflicting, and sustaining, horrific casualties: the Federals had lost 1,747 men killed, 8,452 wounded, and 4,263 captured or missing, while the Confederate losses were 1,553 men killed, 7,812 wounded, and 109 captured or missing. The total, nearly 24,000, was five times greater than the figure for First Manassas.

For Robert E. Lee and the Army of Northern Virginia, Second Manassas was a remarkable triumph. Three months earlier, Union troops had been at the gates of Richmond. Now, soundly thrashed, they were falling back on Washington, opening the way for a Confederate invasion of the North and a possible end to the war.

Touring the Park

Begin your tour at the Visitor Center, where displays and audiovisual programs will help you gain a better understanding of the two Battles of Manassas.

The one-mile-long Henry Hill foot trail loops around the area of critical fighting at First Manassas. Unnumbered interpretive signs and audiotape stations along the way describe the troop movements.

A twelve-mile self-guided auto tour takes you around the Second Manassas battlefield. There are twelve numbered stops along the way marking sites that figured prominently in the fighting.

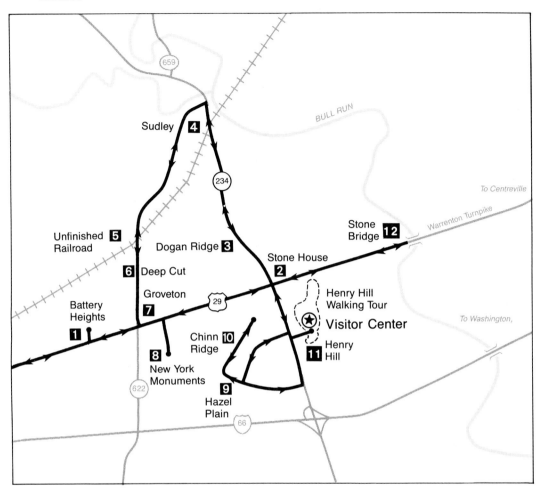

Manassas National Battlefield Park

First Manassas Battlefield Walking Tour. The one-mile loop trail begins behind the Visitor Center and leads to the rebuilt Henry House, around which fierce fighting raged on the afternoon of July 21, 1861. A few feet west of the house is the grave of the widow Judith Henry, the only civilian killed in the first battle. Also near the house is a stone monument to the "Memory of the Patriots who fell at Bull Run, July 21, 1861." From the Henry House the trail leads north to the Confederate artillery positions fronting Matthews Hill to the northwest. The cannon deployed here fired on the Federal columns advancing up the road from Sudley Springs Ford during the morning phase of the battle.

Next on the trail is the Robinson House, where Colonel Wade Hampton led the famed South Carolina Legion into battle. At this point the trail loops back to the south along the high ground held by General Thomas J. Jackson and his brigade. It was here that Jackson earned his famous nickname by "standing like a stone wall" in

The Stone House served as a field hospital during both battles of Manassas. It is open in the summer months. Virginia State Travel Service.

the face of the oncoming Union attack. The trail passes the site of the capture of Griffin's battery, an event that signaled an abrupt shift in the tide of the battle. The final stop overlooks Chinn Ridge to the west, where a Confederate attack rolled up the Union right flank and triggered the rout of the Federal army.

Second Manassas Battlefield Driving Tour. This twelve-mile driving tour covers twelve sites which figured prominently in the Second Battle of Manassas. Exercise caution when crossing or turning onto and off U.S. 29 and Virginia Highway 234.

Stop 1. Battery Heights. The Second Battle of Manassas began in the late afternoon of August 28, 1862, in this open field on the Brawner Farm. A column of Union troops, marching east along the Warrenton Turnpike (now U.S. 29), was attacked by Stonewall Jackson's soldiers, who had been concealed on a wooded ridge to the north. Although caught by surprise, the Union troops swung around and met the attack. Fighting raged for an hour and a half, with the battle lines only eighty yards apart in some places. By nightfall, some 2,000 men had been killed or wounded.

Stop 2. Stone House. During the fighting on August 30, Union general John

Pope had his headquarters directly behind this house. The interior was turned into a field hospital. The house is open during summer months.

Stop 3. Dogan Ridge. On and around this ridge on August 29, thousands of Federal troops formed into ranks to assault Stonewall Jackson's line, which lay about half a mile to the northwest along an unfinished railroad grade. The attacks were bloodily repulsed. Union artillery batteries were posted on the low ridges nearby.

Stop 4. Sudley. The extreme left of Jackson's line was located on a knoll just west of this point. Repeated Union attacks in this area on August 29 came to naught as the Confederate defenders stubbornly held their ground.

Stop 5. Unfinished Railroad Cut. The center of Jackson's mile-and-a-half-long defensive line was located in this area. The Confederate soldiers were posted along the bed of an unfinished railroad. The grade can still be seen, running into the woods on both sides of the road.

Stop 6. Deep Cut. At midday on August 30, General Pope ordered the Union army to advance toward the unfinished railroad, mistakenly believing that Jackson was withdrawing. Even when he learned that the Confederates were still in position, Pope let the attack continue. The 5,000 troops of General Fitz-John Porter's corps passed this point, crossed the road into the field to the west, and hit the gray line along a section of the railroad bed known as the "Deep Cut." Despite suffering terrible casualties as they moved forward, Porter's men momentarily breached the line, but then were hurled back in savage hand-to-hand fighting.

A foot trail, about a third of a mile long, begins at the road and follows the route of Porter's soldiers as they advanced, under heavy fire, toward the Deep Cut.

Stop 7. Groveton. This small, white frame building is one of just two Civil War–era houses remaining in the park. It marks the site of the wartime village of Groveton. The nearby cemetery contains the remains of approximately 260 Confederate soldiers, most of whom are unidentified.

Stop 8. New York Monuments. By 3:30 P.M. on August 30, Pope had committed himself completely to the attack against Jackson's line to the west. Confederate general James Longstreet's corps, which had arrived on the battlefield on the 29th and deployed on Jackson's right, now crashed into the exposed Union left flank. The Fifth and Tenth New York regiments tried to block the Confederate charge on this low hill but were overwhelmed. In five minutes the Fifth New York lost 123 men killed, the greatest loss of life in any single infantry regiment in any battle of the Civil War.

Stop 9. Hazel Plain (Chinn House). The stone foundation you see here is all that remains of Hazel Plain, the wartime home of Benjamin T. Chinn. At 5 P.M. on August 30, Longstreet's troops swept past this house as they attacked along the ridge to the northeast, rolling up the Union left flank.

Stop 10. Chinn Ridge. Along the crest of this ridge Federal units fought desperate holding actions against Longstreet's corps. They managed to delay the Confederate attackers just long enough to give Pope time to organize a defensive stand on Henry Hill (site of the Visitor Center) to the northeast. The granite boulder with bronze plaque you see is a monument to Colonel Fletcher Webster, son of Daniel Webster, who was killed leading the Twelfth Massachusetts Infantry into battle.

Stop 11. Henry Hill. As the sun set on August 30, Longstreet's men repeatedly assaulted this hill, but failed to dislodge Federal units making a stand in the bed of Sudley Road (Virginia Highway 234). Darkness ended the fighting.

Stop 12. Stone Bridge. The Union army was defeated but still intact after the fighting of August 30. Under cover of darkness it withdrew down the Warrenton Turnpike (U.S. 29), crossed the Stone Bridge, and limped away toward Centreville and Washington.

A 1.4-mile loop trail leads past the Stone Bridge and along Bull Run Creek.

CHAPTER 11

PETERSBURG NATIONAL BATTLEFIELD

(Civil War)

P.O. Box 549
Petersburg, Virginia 23803
Telephone: (804) 732-3531

For ten months, from June 1864 to April 1865, the Union Army of the Potomac besieged the Virginia city of Petersburg, a strategic railroad center supplying the Confederate capital of Richmond. During the course of the siege the Confederate Army of Northern Virginia was weakened by combat losses, disease, and hunger, until in early April 1865, it could no longer effectively resist the larger, stronger, and better supplied Federal forces. Petersburg National Battlefield preserves sites associated with the siege.

Getting to the Park: Petersburg National Battlefield's main unit and Visitor Center are located 2½ miles east of Petersburg on Virginia Highway 36.

Gas, food, lodging: In Petersburg.

Visitor Center: Museum and gift shop; audiovisual program.

Activities: Interpretive talks by park personnel; living history demonstrations during summer months. Inquire at Visitor Center for schedule and locations.

Handicapped Access: Visitor Center is fully accessible. The principal features of the park can be seen by automobile.

"We must destroy this army of Grant's before he gets to the James River. If he gets there it will be a mere question of time." So said Robert E. Lee in May 1864, when he learned that the 120,000-man Army of the Potomac, commanded by Ulysses S. Grant, had crossed the Rapidan River and was advancing south toward Richmond.

Grant was intent on destroying Lee's Army of Northern Virginia, which numbered about 62,000 men, and ending the war. Using his two-to-one advantage in troop strength, he planned to hammer away at the Confederates, applying relentless pressure until all resistance collapsed.

During the third week of June 1864, Ulysses S. Grant ordered the Union Army of the Potomac to circle around Richmond and attack the city of Petersburg. National Archives.

At the Wilderness and Spotsylvania Court House (see Chapter 8), Grant put his strategy into effect. The Confederates fought desperately to block the Union advance, inflicting heavy casualties, but the Army of the Potomac absorbed the losses and pushed ahead until it was less than ten miles from Richmond. On June 3, at Cold Harbor, the Federals launched a powerful frontal assault aimed at finishing Lee's army once and for all (see Chapter 12). The attack was repulsed with such dreadful slaughter that even the battle-hardened Grant was appalled. Realizing that his command could no longer sustain such punishment and remain in the field, he abandoned his effort to kick in the front door to Richmond and moved to try the back door. During the third week of June, the Army of the Potomac pulled out of its Cold Harbor entrenchments, crossed the James River, and headed south toward the city of Petersburg.

Petersburg under Attack

Petersburg, located only twenty-three miles from Richmond, was a strategically vital city. If it fell to the Federals, the railroads supplying Richmond from the south would be cut, and the Rebel capital would have to be evacuated.

Union forces made their first attempt to seize Petersburg on June 15; their attack was stoutly resisted by 3,500 Confederates manning the "Dimmock Line," a ten-mile-long chain of fortifications southeast of the city. The assault was renewed the next day, but only slight progress was made. Finally, on the night of the 17th, overwhelming Union pressure forced the defenders to abandon the Dimmock Line, but they simply withdrew a mile to the west and dug in again. The following morning Lee arrived with the Army of Northern Virginia to reinforce this new line.

Grant was disappointed that Petersburg had not fallen, and concerned about the poor performance of his officers and men. For three days Union forces had enjoyed overwhelming numerical superiority, but their attacks had been made in a disjointed and half-hearted fashion. The horror of Cold Harbor was haunting the army; some units had flatly disobeyed orders to assault the Rebel entrenchments, while others had advanced a few yards, then fallen to the ground and refused to get up and go on.

Deciding to put the best face possible on the situation, Grant declared himself "perfectly satisfied that all has been done that could be done," and ordered his army to dig in. "Now we will rest the men," he said, "and use the spade for their protection until a new vein can be struck."

The Battle of the Crater

It was the Forty-eighth Pennsylvania Infantry that struck the "new vein" Grant was looking for. This regiment was made up largely of men who had been coal miners before the war, and it was their idea to tunnel under the Confederate line and explode a huge mine, opening a gap in the enemy's defenses that Union troops could rush

Union infantrymen sit in a trench, waiting for orders to advance. National Archives.

through. If the scheme worked and a breakthrough was scored, Petersburg might be taken quickly and a long siege avoided.

The Pennsylvania miners began digging on June 25 and finished the tunnel three weeks later. It was 511 feet long, extending from the Union trenches to a point 20 feet directly underneath a Confederate fort; a 75-foot-long lateral gallery was excavated at the shaft's end and packed with 320 kegs of gunpowder.

Twelve hours before the giant mine was to be exploded, Grant suddenly changed the plan of attack. A division of black troops, which had been training for weeks to spearhead the assault, was replaced by a white division. It was a case of reverse racism: "If we put the colored troops in front and [the operation] should prove a failure," Grant later explained, "it would then be said . . . that we were shoving these people ahead to get killed because we did not care anything about them." Whatever the reason, the decision to withdraw the well-drilled black infantrymen and send the unprepared white soldiers in their place proved disastrous.

The mine was detonated just before 5 A.M. on July 30: "Without form or shape, full of red flames and carried on a bed of lightning flashes, [the explosion] . . . spread out like an immense mushroom whose stem seemed to be of fire and its head of smoke," wrote an awed observer. As soon as the dust cleared, the Union soldiers moved forward, but when they got to the immense crater where the Confederate fort

This wartime sketch shows Union soldiers advancing toward the crater following the huge explosion on July 30, 1864. Library of Congress.

Black Soldiers in the Civil War

"Is not a Negro as good as a white man to stop a bullet?" someone asked General William T. Sherman, a soldier noted for his blunt, ofttimes brutal views on war and its conduct.

"Yes," answered Sherman. "And a sandbag is better."

This exchange crystalized one of the great controversies dividing Union politicians and military leaders during the Civil War: should blacks be recruited into the armed forces, and if so, how should they be used?

Those in favor of enlisting blacks argued that pitting ex-slaves against their former masters would be an excellent way to punish "Rebel traitors." Those opposed feared that such an action would alienate the slaveholders in border states that had stayed in the Union. Eventually the North's need for additional military man power tipped the balance in favor of black recruitment. "The colored population," said President Abraham Lincoln, "is the great *available* and yet *unavailed* of, force for restoring the Union."

Beginning in 1863, black infantry, artillery, and cavalry units were formed and placed under the leadership of white officers. By the end of the war, 186,000 blacks—over 70 percent of them ex-slaves from southern states— had joined the Union army, even though they were discriminated against in matters of pay, equipment, and duty assignments.

Many Federal commanders, like Sherman, were openly prejudiced against black soldiers and considered them fit only for performing hard manual labor and occupying garrisons well away from the front lines. But other white officers, particularly those who volunteered to lead black units, fervently believed that blacks would make excellent fighters.

The first real test came on July 18, 1863, when the all-black Fifty-fourth Massachusetts Regiment spearheaded an assault against Confederate-held Fort Wagner near Charleston, South Carolina (see Chapter 21). The black soldiers gallantly charged through heavy fire and scaled the fort's parapets, where they fought hand-to-hand with the defenders. They were finally forced to retreat, but not before they had demonstrated conclusively that black troops could fight with just as much dash and courage as their white counterparts.

The arming of blacks and their use in combat outraged the South; Confederate soldiers were especially bitter, believing that the Union was trying to endanger their families by inciting a slave rebellion. In April 1864, Rebel cavalrymen led by Nathan Bedford Forrest exacted a bloody reprisal at Fort Pillow, Tennessee; after capturing the fort, they executed 208 black members of the racially mixed garrison. "The poor, deluded negroes would run up to our men, fall upon their knees and with uplifted hands scream for mercy, but were ordered to their feet and then shot down," reported a Confederate sergeant.

Despite such atrocities, or perhaps because of them, black units fought bravely and well for the duration of the war, distinguishing themselves at Fort Harrison (see Chapter 12), New Market, and Petersburg. In the process they won the respect, grudging but heartfelt, of many of their white comrades-in-arms. As one man put it: "Much credit is due to all of them for their gallantry. . . . they fought like veterans, and . . . their coolness and bravery I have never seen surpassed."

had been, they came to a stop, unsure what they were supposed to do next. To make matters worse, their commander, General James Ledlie, had remained behind in his dugout, too drunk to join the attack.

Instead of sweeping around the crater and punching through the gap opened in the Confederate defensive line, the confused attackers moved down into the rubble-strewn hole and took cover. They were joined there by two more divisions that were supposed to be making a follow-up assault. Soon the crater—170 feet long, 60 feet wide, and 30 feet deep—was teeming with a disorganized mob of more than 10,000 men.

The Confederates quickly recovered from the shock of the tremendous explosion and began to pour cannon and musket fire into the crater, turning it into a slaughter pen. An order was given for the Union troops to withdraw, but escape from the smoldering, body-choked pit was all but impossible. The massacre continued until early afternoon, when a savage bayonet charge finally ended the gory fiasco. The Army of the Potomac had lost 4,000 men in what Grant pronounced "the saddest affair I have witnessed in this war."

The Siege of Petersburg

After the debacle at the Battle of the Crater, Grant concluded that he would not be able to take the Confederate entrenchments by storm and resigned himself to a long, grinding campaign of attrition. Slow strangulation, rather than a knockout blow, would be his modus operandi, and he set out to build up his forces in anticipation of an extended siege.

The village of City Point, situated at the confluence of the James and Appomattox rivers, approximately nine miles northeast of Petersburg, was transformed into a sprawling supply center. Ammunition, food, equipment, and supplies of all kinds arrived aboard ships and barges and were dispatched to the Union siege lines via a railroad built and operated by U.S. military engineers. It was a staggering logistical operation, one that the Confederates could not hope to match, and Lee understood all too well what the long-term results would be. "Without some increase of our strength," he wrote to James A. Seddon, the Confederate secretary of war, "I cannot see how we are to escape the natural military consequences of the enemy's numerical superiority."

To stretch the Confederate defenses even thinner, Grant extended his lines to the south and west across the Petersburg & Weldon Railroad. In three days of bitter fighting beginning on August 18, Union troops succeeded in cutting the railroad in the vicinity of Globe Tavern; the Confederates struck back on August 25 at Ream's Station, five miles south of Globe Tavern, but despite capturing more than 2,000 Federals (many of whom chose to surrender rather than obey orders to advance and

A dead Confederate lies in a Petersburg trench. Library of Congress.

fight) they failed to dislodge the blue units. Again, in September and October, Grant extended his siege line westward, bleeding the Army of Northern Virginia and inexorably tightening the noose around Petersburg.

With each skirmish, with every bombardment, the Confederate man-power situation grew more desperate: "There is the chill of murder about the casualties of this month," said one officer as he tallied losses he knew could never be made up. Lee beseeched President Jefferson Davis to take "immediate and vigorous measures to increase the strength of our armies," but there simply were no more recruits to be had. As the gray, wet shroud of winter settled over southern Virginia, distress about the Confederacy's deteriorating military situation gave way to despair.

In muddy, rat-infested dugouts that carried such grim nicknames as "Fort Hell" and "Fort Damnation," the soldiers huddled in abject misery, trying to escape the cold rain, the sniping and constant mortar shelling. Living conditions were dreadful for both sides, but the Union troops at least had plentiful food and warm clothing. The Confederates were surviving on a pint of cornmeal and an ounce or two of moldy bacon a day. They were all clad in tatters, and many were barefoot despite the freezing temperatures. "We were shocked at the condition, the complexion, the expression of the men . . . even the officers," wrote a visitor to the Petersburg entrenchments. "In-

The interior of Fort Sedgwick, nicknamed "Fort Hell" by its Union garrison. Library of Congress.

deed, we could scarcely realize that the unwashed, uncombed, unfed, and almost un-clad creatures were officers of rank and reputation in the army."

Assault on Fort Stedman

The beginning of March 1865 found the Army of Northern Virginia defending thirty-seven miles of entrenchments with only 46,000 men, many of whom were too weak to perform any real military duties. It was clear to Lee that the Federals, who now enjoyed a nearly three-to-one advantage in troop strength, would either swing around his right flank or smash through a weak spot in the over-long defensive line, and take Petersburg and Richmond. He decided to try a breakout in the vicinity of Fort Stedman; if he could cut the Army of the Potomac's supply railroad, which lay just a mile beyond Fort Stedman, Grant would have to give up his positions to the west and his stranglehold on Petersburg would be broken.

At 4 A.M. on March 25, a Confederate assault force rushed from Colquitt's Salient in their line across a 150-yard wide no-man's land toward Union Fort Stedman. The garrison was caught by surprise, and the fort fell after a brief struggle. More Confed-erates came forward to try to widen the hole in the blue line, but the commotion had aroused the Federals in adjacent Fort Haskell, and they poured musket and cannon fire into Fort Stedman. The storm of projectiles pinned the attackers down, and when the sun rose it revealed a scene tragically familiar to veterans of the previous summer's fighting: it was the Battle of the Crater all over again, except this time the Confeder-ates were the ones caught in the deadly maelstrom, unable to fight back or flee. When the lopsided struggle ended, barely four hours after it began, 3,500 of them had been killed, wounded, or taken prisoner.

The Fall of Petersburg

The Army of Northern Virginia had shot its bolt at Fort Stedman, and Grant knew it; it was time to deliver the coup de grace. On April 1, General Philip Sheridan, commanding a large force of cavalry and infantry, struck the Confederate right at Five Forks, crushing the opposition and taking 5,000 prisoners. That night Grant ordered an all-out assault along a twelve-mile length of the siege line, to begin the next morning.

At dawn on April 2, 60,000 Union soldiers charged forward and overran the Confederate fortifications to their front. For a time it appeared that the war would end that afternoon with the remnants of the shattered Rebel army being hunted down in the streets of Petersburg. Six hundred Mississippians and North Carolinians in a small earthwork called Fort Gregg halted the Federal advance for two hours, however, and gave Lee time to rally his men.

Final defeat had been averted for the moment, but there was nothing the pitifully weak Confederate forces could now do to stem the rising blue tide. They abandoned Petersburg that night and set out on the road to Appomattox; surrender and the end of the Civil War were only a week away.

Touring the Park

Begin your tour at the Visitor Center, where maps, exhibits, and audiovisual programs will help you gain a better understanding of the Petersburg Campaign.

The four-mile Battlefield Tour runs through the park's main unit. There are eight numbered stops along the way. The sixteen-mile Siege Line Tour takes you to park areas south and west of Petersburg. There are seven numbered stops on this tour. You may also wish to visit the City Point Unit, located approximately 7.5 miles northeast of the Visitor Center off Virginia Highway 36.

Battlefield Tour Stop 1. Visitor Center. From the Visitor Center a short foot trail leads to the site of Battery 5 on the Dimmock Line, the original Confederate defensive line, which was abandoned to the Federals on June 15, 1864. Union artillerists placed a huge mortar called the "Dictator" in this gun emplacement, and used it to bombard Petersburg to the west.

Battlefield Tour Stop 2. Battery 8. On June 15, 1864, black troops of General Edward Hincks's division assaulted the Dimmock Line in this area. They overran Battery 8, taking some 150 Confederate prisoners in the process. The battery was renamed Fort Friend, and served as a Union artillery position for the duration of the siege.

Battlefield Tour Stop 3. Battery 9. Like adjoining Battery 8, this strongpoint on the Dimmock Line was captured by Hincks's black troops on the evening of June 15.

A short walking trail leads east to Meade Station, a supply and hospital depot on the military railroad that led from City Point to the siege area. Winter quarters of the Union Ninth Corps were located near here. The Soldier Hut and Sutler Store, located

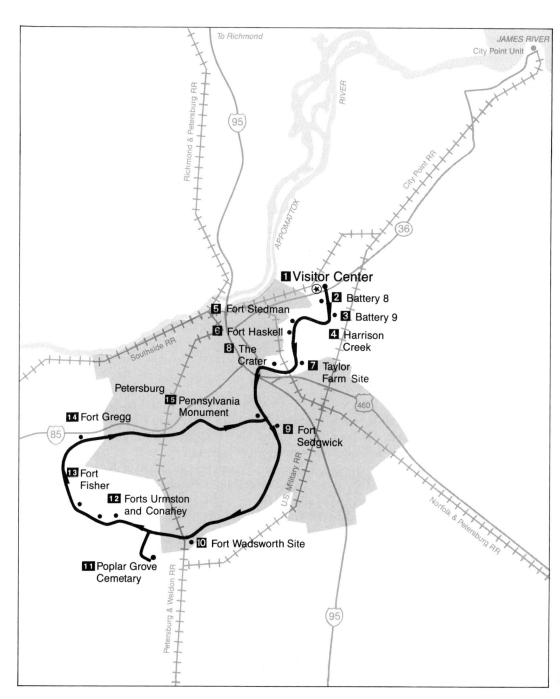

Petersburg National Battlefield

along the trail, give you some idea of what camp life was like for soldiers on the Petersburg siege lines.

Battlefield Tour Stop 4. Harrison Creek. When they abandoned the eastern portion of the Dimmock Line on June 15, 1864, the Confederates fell back and dug in along this creek. Two days later they withdrew again to a new defensive line closer to Petersburg, which they defended until April 1865.

Battlefield Tour Stop 5. Fort Stedman. At dawn on March 25, 1865, the Confederates attacked Fort Stedman in an attempt to pierce the Union line and break the siege of Petersburg. They seized the fort, but could advance no farther, and were eventually forced to retreat.

A loop trail leads from Fort Stedman to Colquitt's Salient, where the Confederate attack started.

Battlefield Tour Stop 6. Fort Haskell. After the Confederates captured Fort Stedman, just north of here, on the morning of March 25, 1865, Union artillery and infantry in this fort opened fire. The torrent of bullets and shells from Haskell devastated the attackers crowded into Stedman, and prevented them from scoring a breakthrough and lifting the siege of Petersburg.

Battlefield Tour Stop 7. Taylor Farm Site. Along this ridge, which was part of the Taylor Farm, nearly 200 pieces of Union artillery were lined up to provide fire support during the Battle of the Crater.

Battlefield Tour Stop 8. The Crater. Here, on July 30, 1864, a mine was exploded under a Confederate fort, gouging out an immense crater. Union infantry rushed forward, but instead of bypassing the crater and pouring through the gap opened in the enemy defensive line, they went down into the hole, where they were trapped and slaughtered by heavy Confederate artillery and musket fire.

A foot trail leads to the crater; its contours can still easily be seen.

To take the Siege Line Tour, turn left onto Crater Road (U.S. 301) when you exit the main unit.

Siege Line Tour Stop 9. Fort Sedgwick Site. Union troops built Fort Sedgwick on this site in July and August 1864 to control the Jerusalem Plank Road (now U.S. 301), one of the main roadways leading into Petersburg from the south. Nicknamed "Fort Hell" by its garrison, the post was subjected to almost continuous mortar and sniper fire from Confederate Fort Mahone (Stop 15) to the east. A major Union assault from Fort Sedgwick on April 2, 1865, succeeded in breaking through the Confederate line; a nearby monument honors Colonel George Gowan, commander of the Forty-eighth Pennsylvania Volunteers, who was killed in this attack. Another nearby marker identifies the site of Rives's Salient, an important part of the Confederate defensive line.

Siege Line Tour Stop 10. Fort Wadsworth. During three days of fierce fighting, beginning on August 18, 1864, Union soldiers extended the siege line south and west to cut the Petersburg & Weldon Railroad, which ran into Petersburg along the route now followed by the Halifax Road. Fort Wadsworth was built to strengthen the Federal hold on the strategically important rail line.

Siege Line Tour Stop 11. Poplar Grove Cemetery. This burial ground was established in 1868 to hold the remains of Union soldiers who died during the Petersburg siege. Of the 6,178 men interred here, 4,110 are unknown. Most of the Confederate dead were buried in Blandford Cemetery in Petersburg.

Siege Line Tour Stop 12. Forts Urmston and Conahey. In late September and early October 1864, Federal forces again extended the siege line westward, stretching the Confederate defenses even thinner. These two forts were built to hold the ground won during the Battle of Peeble's Farm, fought September 30–October 2, 1864.

Siege Line Tour Stop 13. Fort Fisher. Completed in March 1865, this was the largest earthen fort on the Petersburg siege line. Because the nearest Confederate work was more than a mile to the north, Fort Fisher saw little fighting.

Siege Line Tour Stop 14. Fort Gregg. On April 2, 1865, 600 Mississippians and North Carolinians defending Fort Gregg and Fort Whitworth (located just to the north) halted the advance of the 5,000-man Union Twenty-fourth Corps for two hours. Their gallant stand gave Lee time to rally the rest of his army and withdraw from Petersburg during the night.

Siege Line Tour Stop 15. Pennsylvania Monument. This monument stands on the site of Confederate Fort Mahone, known to its garrison as "Fort Damnation." The fort was captured on April 2, 1865, by Pennsylvanians of the Union Ninth Corps, attacking from Fort Sedgwick (stop 9), 600 yards to the east.

This ends the Siege Line Tour. You may wish to visit the City Point Unit, located approximately ten miles to the northeast. Follow Crater Road north to its intersection with East Washington Street (Virginia Highway 36). Turn right and follow Virginia Highway 36 northeast to its terminus at City Point.

City Point Unit. Between June 1864 and April 1865, this sleepy landing at the confluence of the Appomattox and James rivers was transformed into a huge supply depot for arming and provisioning the 120,000 soldiers of the Army of the Potomac who manned the siege lines in front of Petersburg. More than 280 buildings, a half mile of new wharves, and more than fifteen miles of railroad were built to carry out this massive logistical operation.

From his headquarters cabin, General Grant used an extensive telegraph system to issue orders to his field commanders along the siege line and to communicate with Washington, D.C., coordinating the war effort in other theaters.

President Lincoln visited City Point twice; he spent two of the last three weeks of his life here.

CHAPTER 12

RICHMOND NATIONAL BATTLEFIELD PARK

(Civil War)

3215 East Broad Street
Richmond, Virginia 23223
Telephone: (804) 226-1981

Between 1861 and 1865, Union generals launched no fewer than seven major campaigns against Richmond, capital of the Confederacy. Two of these—the Peninsular Campaign of 1862 and the Virginia Campaign of 1864—resulted in fierce battles being fought almost within eyesight of the city. Richmond National Battlefield Park preserves the sites of these battles as well as several historic buildings and forts associated with the struggle for Richmond.

Getting to the Park: Richmond National Battlefield Park consists of 9 separate units located south and east of the city of Richmond, Virginia. The Chimborazo Visitor Center, starting point for a tour of the park, is located at 3215 East Broad Street in Richmond. Take Exit 10 off I-95 and drive along 17th Street until it intersects Broad Street. Turn left on Broad and drive 16 blocks southeast. The Visitor Center is on the right.

Gas, food, lodging: In Richmond and vicinity.

Visitor Centers: Museum exhibits and gift shops; audiovisual programs.

Activities: Interpretive talks by park personnel. Living-history demonstrations during the summer months. Inquire at Visitor Centers for schedule and locations.

Handicapped Access: The Fort Harrison Visitor Center, Watt House and Garthright House grounds, and interpretive exhibits at Cold Harbor and Malvern Hill are accessible. The Chimborazo Visitor Center is not fully accessible. The foot trail at Fort Harrison can be traversed by wheelchair. Inquire at Visitor Centers for further information about specific tour stops.

O
n May 21, 1861, five weeks after the first shots of the Civil War were fired at Fort Sumter (see Chapter 21), Richmond replaced Montgomery, Alabama, as the capital

of the Confederacy. Conquest of the Virginia city immediately became the chief objective of Union armies in the east.

Located on the James River, a scant 110 miles from Washington, Richmond was a tempting target both strategically and psychologically. Its capture by Federal forces would deal a shattering blow to Confederate morale; destruction of its factories, warehouses, and arsenals would cripple the southern war effort.

Between 1861 and 1864, Union generals launched no fewer than seven major campaigns against the Confederate capital. Two of these—the Peninsular Campaign of 1862 and the Virginia Campaign of 1864—resulted in fierce battles being fought almost within eyesight of the city.

The Peninsular Campaign of 1862

Following the stunning Federal defeat at the First Battle of Manassas in July 1861 (see Chapter 10), President Lincoln appointed General George B. McClellan commander of Union forces in the east. For the next nine months McClellan worked tirelessly to assemble and train a flood of new recruits and to devise a plan for capturing Richmond. Rather than attacking straight overland he decided to make an end run, landing his troops on the peninsula between the York and James rivers and approaching Richmond from the southeast.

The Union Army of the Potomac, 120,000-men strong, began disembarking at Fort Monroe on the tip of the York-James peninsula in late March 1862. Had McClellan moved swiftly, he might have seized his objective before the surprised Confederates could mount an effective defense. Instead he advanced slowly and methodically, taking an entire month to cover the twenty miles between Fort Monroe and Yorktown. After occupying Yorktown, he took another month to march his army up the peninsula to a point seven miles from Richmond.

Union sluggishness gave the Confederates time to pull their troops out of fortifications near Manassas and bring them south to defend the capital. On May 31, General Joseph E. Johnston, commander of the Rebel army, ordered an attack against the Federals at Fair Oaks, east of the city. This thrust was repulsed and Johnston was critically wounded; with the fate of the Confederacy hanging in the balance, President Jefferson Davis called on General Robert E. Lee to assume command of Johnston's dispirited men and save Richmond.

The Seven Days' Battles

The Confederate capital was ripe for the taking after the Battle of Fair Oaks, but again McClellan failed to seize the initiative. He grossly overestimated his opponents' strength, and instead of driving ahead to victory, he ordered his troops to dig in, in a position straddling the Chickahominy River.

Given a breathing space, Lee hastily reorganized the Confederate forces, which he had designated the Army of Northern Virginia, and began preparing for a bold counteroffensive aimed at hurling the Union forces back from the gates of Richmond. The first step was to attack General Fitz-John Porter's corps, which was on the north bank of the Chickahominy, isolated from the rest of the Army of the Potomac on the

General Joseph E. Johnston, commander of the Confederate army, was severely wounded in the Battle of Fair Oaks; Robert E. Lee took his place. National Archives.

south bank. The Confederate divisions led by Generals A. P. Hill, D. H. Hill, and James Longstreet would make a frontal assault while Stonewall Jackson's corps fell on Porter's flank. If all went according to plan, the Union formation would be trapped and destroyed.

The attack on Porter, launched on June 26, 1862, began a week of fighting known as the Seven Days' Battles. A. P. Hill's division moved through the hamlet of Mechanicsville and advanced toward a broad, shallow swale cut by Beaver Dam Creek. The Federals were entrenched behind the creek, and they slaughtered the Confederates charging across the open ground. The bloody debacle was made worse by Jackson's failure to get his corps onto the battlefield in time to execute the scheduled flank attack.

During the night, Porter's soldiers retreated five miles to the east and formed a new defensive line on high ground near Gaines' Mill. The Confederates followed, and early in the afternoon on June 27 Lee ordered another assault. The sound of gunfire rose to a thunderous crescendo as 55,000 gray troops pushed through thick underbrush and charged toward the flickering cloud of powder smoke that marked the Yankee trenches.

Although outnumbered better than two to one, Porter's command stood its ground against the valiant but uncoordinated Rebel attacks. The bloodshed was even more terrible than the day before: wave after wave of Confederate attackers rolled up the hill only to disintegrate in the maelstrom of Union lead. At dusk, a final, desperate charge succeeded in breaking the blue line, but most of the Federals were able to

A Federal battery prepares to go into action at Fair Oaks, east of Richmond, May 31, 1862. Library of Congress.

escape across the Chickahominy under cover of darkness and rejoin the Army of the Potomac.

McClellan, alarmed by the Confederates' aggressive maneuvering, decided to retreat to Harrison's Landing, where artillery fire from Federal gunboats patrolling the James River would shield his army from further attacks. Lee ordered a rapid pursuit, hoping to cut the Union troops off before they reached the James, but fierce rearguard actions fought on June 29 at Savage Station, and on June 30 at White Oak Swamp and Glendale, slowed the Confederate advance and allowed McClellan to get his supply wagons and artillery train to Harrison's Landing unmolested.

On July 1, Lee made one last attempt to destroy his foe. The road to Harrison's Landing passed over a slope called Malvern Hill. On the open ground between this hill and a nearby swamp, Porter's corps was arrayed in parade-ground formation with 100 cannon lined up hub to hub to provide support. The position was much too strong to be taken by frontal assault, but Lee ordered one anyway. Fourteen Confederate brigades charged toward the Union line and were decimated by the rapid, deadly accurate fire of the massed Federal artillery. "It was not war," General D.H. Hill said of this hopeless attack. "It was murder."

The next day, the Army of the Potomac completed its retreat to Harrison's Landing. The Army of Northern Virginia, weakened by the Malvern Hill bloodbath and exhausted by seven days of nonstop marching and fighting, limped back to Richmond. Wrote a young Georgia soldier of the experience: "I have seen, heard, and felt many things in the last week that I never want to see, hear, nor feel again."

Chimborazo: Hospital on the Hill

Following the First Battle of Manassas on July 21, 1861, hundreds of Confederate casualties were sent to Richmond, swamping the city's modest medical facilities. Realizing that the capital was destined to be a collecting point for men wounded on the Virginia battlefields, the Confederate government authorized the construction of five general hospitals. The most famous of these was Chimborazo, known as the "hospital on the hill," located where the Richmond National Battlefield Park Visitor Center now stands.

Eighty whitewashed pine-board huts, each one big enough to house forty men, were erected on Chimborazo Hill (named after a South American volcano). Laundry, bathhouse, and kitchen facilities, as well as a dairy and a bakery, were also built, making the hospital a self-contained community.

Chimborazo opened for business in October 1861 with an all-male staff to care for the wounded. Within a few months, however, the heavy influx of patients and the army's insatiable demand for able-bodied men forced Confederate authorities to recruit Richmond ladies to serve as matrons and ward attendants. This was one of the first large-scale entrances of women into nursing, a profession they would soon come to dominate.

Conditions at Chimborazo left much to be desired: wards were "littered with piles of dirty rags, blood, and water," the stench of festering wounds filled the air, and flies hovered in great swarms. Nevertheless, the hospital was considered one of the finest in the South, and injured soldiers counted themselves lucky to be there rather than at an even more primitive facility.

Between 1861 and 1865, more than 76,000 Confederate casualties were treated at Chimborazo; of these, approximately 15,000 died, a mortality rate close to 20 percent. Such a record would be considered scandalous today, but by the standards of the nineteenth century—before the development of antibiotics and antiseptic surgical techniques—it was quite good. In fact, given the lack of medical supplies, the chronic shortage of basic foodstuffs, and the often overwhelming patient load, the performance of the hospital staff was extraordinary.

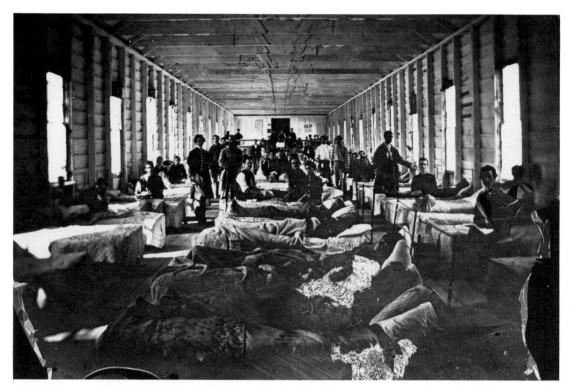

A Civil War hospital ward. National Archives.

Richmond Saved, the War Prolonged

Although it ended in stalemate, the Peninsular Campaign had a profound effect on the course and conduct of the Civil War. Richmond was saved for the Confederacy, Federal hopes for a quick victory were dashed, and leaders on both sides had to face the grim prospect of a bitter, bloody, open-ended struggle.

From a military standpoint, the vicious sustained combat of the Seven Days' Battles, which resulted in a total of 36,000 casualties, transformed the raw Union and Confederate armies into seasoned, professional fighting forces. In the months ahead, the lessons learned at Beaver Dam Creek, Gaines' Mill, and Malvern Hill would be applied with growing skill and ever more deadly effect.

The Virginia Campaign of 1864

On March 9, 1864, Ulysses S. Grant was given a commission as lieutenant general, a rank previously held only by George Washington, and made supreme commander of all Union armies. Two months later he took to the field with the Army of the Potomac, intent on crushing Lee's Confederates and capturing Richmond.

Where McClellan had tried an end run, moving his troops by water to the York-James peninsula, Grant set out on a straight-ahead overland campaign, taking advantage of his two-to-one edge in troop strength to smash forward and grind up Lee's army. At the Wilderness and Spotsylvania Court House (see Chapter 8), the Union forces suffered staggering casualties but maintained relentless pressure on the beleaguered Confederates. Grant concluded each battle by sidestepping around his opponent and pushing south, forcing Lee to fall back toward Richmond.

June 1, 1864, found the Rebels entrenched in a line extending from Totopotomoy Creek to the Chickahominy River on the same ground that had been fought over during the Peninsular Campaign two years before. The Federals were concentrating in the vicinity of Cold Harbor, preparing to deliver yet another sledgehammer blow aimed at pulverizing the Army of Northern Virginia and opening the way to Richmond.

Cold Harbor

The position at Cold Harbor was one of the strongest the Confederates held during the entire war. Taking maximum advantage of the terrain, they fortified to create

General Ulysses S. Grant (seated under the two trees) and his officers gather for a council of war prior to the Battle of Cold Harbor. Library of Congress.

clear, overlapping fields of fire that extended for some seven miles. Advancing into this broad killing zone was madness, yet that was precisely what Grant orderd. Three Union corps were to charge the gray line at dawn on June 3; there would be no attempt at deception and only minimal coordination between the attacking formations.

On the evening of June 2, Colonel Horace Porter, one of Grant's aides, rode through the Union camps near the front line. "I noticed that many of the soldiers had taken off their coats and seemed to be engaged in sewing up rents in them," he wrote. On closer inspection he "found that the men were calmly writing their names and addresses on slips of paper and pinning them on the backs of their coats so that their bodies might be recognized and their fate made known to their families at home."

At the appointed hour, 60,000 Federals surged forward and were hit by an awe-some fusillade that had, said one observer, "the fury of the Wilderness musketry, with the thunders of the Gettysburg artillery superadded." Wrote another: "It seemed more like a volcanic blast than a battle, and was just about as destructive."

In less than thirty minutes 7,000 Union soldiers were gunned down; the survivors dropped in their tracks and hugged the earth, trying to escape the snapping bullets until the order to withdraw came. Even Grant, whose hardened attitude toward ca-sualties was well known, was horrified by the Cold Harbor carnage. "I regret this

A Union soldier lounges amidst the ruins of Richmond. Library of Congress.

assault more than any one I ever ordered," he told his staff in an extraordinary admission of guilt and revulsion.

The Fall of Richmond

After the failed attack at Cold Harbor, the opposing armies squatted in their trenches and dugouts, enduring humid 100-degree weather and the suffocating stench of thousands of unburied bodies. "Grant intends to *stink* Lee out of his position, if nothing else will suffice," sneered an offended Richmond resident.

Finally, on June 13, the Federals pulled out of their fortifications and marched southeast toward the James River. Grant had decided to swing around Richmond, cross the James, and attack the important rail center of Petersburg, located twenty-three miles south of the Confederate capital (see Chapter 11).

On April 2, 1865, after a harrowing ten-month siege, Lee and the Army of Northern Virginia were forced to abandon Petersburg and retreat westward. With Richmond now defenseless in the face of advancing Union forces, officials of the Confederate government authorized the torching of its warehouses and arsenals.

Fires raged through the night, and dawn on April 3 revealed a scene of incredible devastation. It was, said one witness, like "all the horrors of the final conflagration. . . . The roaring, crackling and hissing of the flames, the bursting of shells at the Confederate Arsenal, the sounds of the instruments of martial music, the neighing of the horses, the shouting of the multitudes . . . 'The Yankees! The Yankees are coming!'"

Six days later, Lee surrendered to Grant at Appomattox Courthouse. The inferno that consumed Richmond had, fittingly, been the Confederacy's funeral pyre.

Touring the Park

Begin your tour at the Chimborazo Visitor Center, where exhibits and an audiovisual program will explain Richmond's role in the Civil War. From the Visitor Center a complete tour of the park involves a drive of approximately 100 miles. For the sake of convenience and clarity, the units are grouped according to the campaign in which they played a part. On the map, park units associated with the Seven Days' Battles of 1862 are marked in black and units associated with Grant's Virginia Campaign of 1864 are marked in blue.

1862 Units

Stop 1. Chickahominy Bluff. This high ground was part of the outer Confederate defensive line guarding the approaches to Richmond during the Peninsular Campaign of 1862. Not far from this position, General Robert E. Lee watched his soldiers advance against Union troops at Beaver Dam Creek, starting the Seven Days' Battles.

Stop 2. Beaver Dam Creek. The Confederates assaulted entrenched Union troops on June 26, 1862, here in the valley of Beaver Dam Creek. Heavy artillery and musket fire slaughtered the attackers before they could get across the stream and storm the earthworks. During the night, the outnumbered Union force withdrew five miles to the east and dug in near Gaines' Mill.

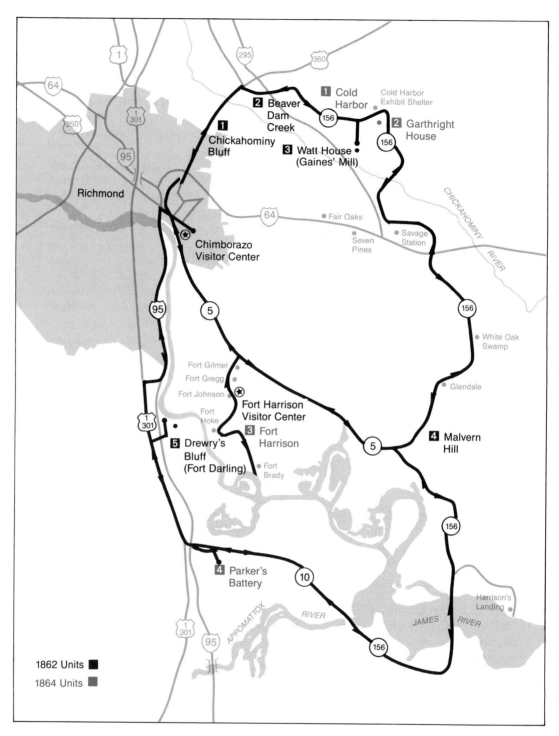

Richmond National Battlefield Park

Stop 3. Watt House (Gaines' Mill). The Watt House, built about 1835, served as Union general Fitz-John Porter's headquarters during the Battle of Gaines' Mill, fought on June 27, 1862. The exterior has been restored to its original appearance; the interior is closed to the public. From the house, take the short foot trail to Breakthrough Point, where the remains of shallow trenches manned by Union soldiers can be seen. It was at this point, late on the afternoon of the 27th, that Confederate troops finally pierced the blue line and forced Porter's corps to retreat south across the Chickahominy River.

Stop 4. Malvern Hill. The last of the Seven Days' Battles was fought here on July 1, 1862. Instead of digging in, the Union troops stood in massed, parade-ground formation, supported by 100 cannon. On their left was the steep slope of Malvern Hill and on their right a low, swampy area. Lee's Confederates, forced to advance across the open ground between the hill and the swamp, were struck by heavy, continuous fire from the Union artillery and repulsed in bloody disarray. After the failed attack, the Confederates limped back to Richmond while the Union forces completed their withdrawal to Harrison's Landing on the James River.

Stop 5. Drewry's Bluff (Fort Darling). This Confederate fort on the James River guarded the water approach to Richmond. On May 15, 1862, five Union gunboats, including the famous ironclad *Monitor*, tried to pound the fort into submission. They failed, and Richmond was spared a devastating naval bombardment.

Two years later, in May 1864, the fort was instrumental in blocking the Union land attacks by General Benjamin Butler's Army of the James. It also served as the Confederate Naval Academy and Marine Corps Camp of Instruction throughout the war.

1864 Units

Stop 1. Cold Harbor. On this ground, on June 3, 1864, Union forces launched a massive frontal assault against the well-entrenched Confederate Army of Northern Virginia. The assault failed, and over 7,000 Union soldiers were killed or wounded in less than thirty minutes. Stop at the Cold Harbor Visitor Center and then drive along the 1.25-mile tour road. Along the way you will see the remains of Confederate and Union earthworks and the field across which the ill-fated assault was made.

Stop 2. Garthright House. This restored house was used as a field hospital by the Union army during the Battle of Cold Harbor. The first floor and upstairs area were occupied by wounded soldiers, while the Garthright family used the basement as living quarters. The exterior has been restored to its Civil War appearance; the interior is closed to the public.

Stop 3. Fort Harrison. After the defeat at Cold Harbor, the bulk of the Union army crossed the James River and besieged Petersburg. To prevent Lee from shifting all of his troops away from the Richmond defenses, Grant ordered a surprise attack on Fort Harrison, an important link in the chain of earthworks guarding the Confederate capital. Federal forces, including several regiments of black soldiers, gallantly stormed and captured the fort on the morning of September 29, 1864. Nearby Forts Gilmer, Gregg, Johnson, and Hoke remained in Confederate hands, however, blocking further Federal advance toward Richmond. On the north bank of the James, Union soldiers built Fort Brady to neutralize Confederate Fort Darling (Stop 5), located across the river on Drewry's Bluff. Stop at the Fort Harrison Visitor Center, then follow the self-guided walking trail through the remains of the fort. Exhibits and interpretive signs along the way provide information about the battle and siege that followed.

Stop 4. Parker's Battery. This Confederate artillery emplacement helped to block the Union Army of the James from approaching Richmond in May 1864.

CHAPTER 13

YORKTOWN BATTLEFIELD, COLONIAL NATIONAL HISTORICAL PARK
(Revolutionary War)

P.O. Box 210
Yorktown, Virginia 23690
Telephone: (804) 898-3400

In September and October 1781, French and American land and naval forces trapped a 7,500-man British army in the village of Yorktown, on the York River near the mouth of Chesapeake Bay. After a three-week siege, Charles Lord Cornwallis was forced to surrender to General George Washington, effectively ending Britain's six-year-old effort to crush the American Revolution. Yorktown Battlefield preserves the scene of the siege as well as several historic buildings associated with the Yorktown campaign.

Getting to the Park: Yorktown Battlefield is a unit of Colonial National Historical Park, which is located approximately 60 miles southeast of Richmond, Virginia. From Richmond, take I-64 to Virginia 199 (Exit 57). Take Virginia 199 2 miles north to Colonial Parkway, turn right and drive east to the Yorktown Visitor Center.

Gas, food, lodging: In Yorktown.

Visitor Center: Museum, gift shop; twelve-minute film on the Yorktown siege; observation deck on roof of Visitor Center building.

Activities: Living-history demonstrations are presented by volunteers in period dress at the Moore House and the Nelson House in Yorktown. Each year on October 19, the anniversary of the British surrender is celebrated with a reenactment by volunteers in period uniforms and with patriotic festivities. Inquire at Visitor Center for more information.

Handicapped Access: The Visitor Center is fully accessible. Historic houses have one or two steps at their entrances.

Following the Battle of Guilford Courthouse on March 15, 1781 (see Chapter 22), British general Charles Lord Cornwallis withdrew his victorious but exhausted army to Wilmington on the North Carolina coast. The casualties suffered by the British force at Guilford had been so severe that Cornwallis felt compelled to abandon offensive operations in the Carolinas and march north to Virginia, where reinforcements awaited him.

In late May 1781, Cornwallis's troops linked up with another contingent of British soldiers at Petersburg, Virginia, and began campaigning against a small patriot army led by the Marquis de Lafayette. For the next two months the redcoats pursued Lafayette's men north and west into the Virginia backcountry, keeping them on the run but failing to bring them to battle.

Exasperated by the rebels' elusiveness, Cornwallis finally halted the chase. Recalling what had happened at Saratoga to another British expedition that had been lured deep into the American interior (see Chapter 4), he decided to return to the relative safety of the coast and establish a supply base there. His troops arrived at Yorktown, a small village on the York River near the mouth of Chesapeake Bay, during the first week of August.

Washington Moves South

On August 14 George Washington received electrifying news at his headquarters in the Continental Army's camp north of New York City. The French admiral Count de Grasse, with twenty-four ships of the line, would arrive within days in the waters of the Chesapeake, affording the Americans local naval superiority for the first time in the war. The advantage would be short-lived, however: the French fleet had orders to return to the Caribbean on October 15. "I shall be greatly obliged to you if you will employ me promptly and effectually within that time," de Grasse wrote in his dispatch to the patriot general.

Washington immediately consulted with the Count de Rochambeau, commander of the French army that had landed at Newport, Rhode Island, the preceding year. The two generals decided to move south and, with the help of de Grasse's fleet, trap Cornwallis at Yorktown. On August 21 the combined French and American force, totaling some 16,000 men, packed up and began a rapid march south toward Virginia.

As promised, de Grasse's warships sailed into Chesapeake Bay on August 30, breaking Cornwallis's seaborne supply line. The British navy counterattacked five days later, initiating a ferocious two-hour gun duel with the French ships off the Virginia Capes. There were no sinkings, but the British men-of-war were so badly damaged that they had to sail back to New York, leaving de Grasse in control of the Chesapeake.

With the retreat of the British fleet, Cornwallis was cut off from reinforcement or evacuation by sea; on September 28, when Washington and Rochambeau arrived with their armies from the north, he was also cut off by land.

The Siege of Yorktown

Cornwallis had chosen Yorktown as his base of operations because of its harbor facilities, not because it was well situated to withstand a siege. In fact, the low, swampy terrain surrounding the village was ill-suited for defense, especially by a force num-

Following the Battle of the Capes, British warships were forced to withdraw to New York, leaving Cornwallis's army cut off at Yorktown. U.S. Naval History Center.

bering only 7,500 men. Seeking to make the best of a bad situation, the British general put his soldiers to work constructing a chain of fortifications. An inner line of earthworks and gun emplacements encircled Yorktown; an outer line of detached redoubts was built to block the routes attackers would follow as they tried to approach the inner line.

On September 28, the newly arrived American and French troops formed a six-mile arc around the British outerworks and began siege operations. The Americans held the right wing extending from Wormley Creek to the marshes of Beaverdam Creek, while the French held the left which ran from Beaverdam Creek to the banks of the York River, northwest of town.

The night after the allies took up position, Cornwallis ordered the evacuation of all the outer works except the star-shaped Fusiliers' Redoubt northwest of Yorktown and Redoubts 9 and 10 to the southeast. These forts were the key to the British defensive scheme. As long as they held, the French and American soldiers would be unable to dig saps—zigzag approach trenches—toward the inner line of earthworks ringing Yorktown.

The Americans were not accustomed to siege warfare, but to the veteran French engineers and artillerymen it was old hat. Under their expert direction the first siege line—a trench running parallel to the enemy's works—was dug 1,200 yards from Redoubts 9 and 10. By the evening of October 9, batteries of cannon and mortars had been manhandled into the trench and were ready to blast the British redoubts. The French opened fire, and the Americans joined in several hours later, with General Washington personally applying the match that touched off the first shot.

For the next week the allied gunners kept up an incessant bombardment, raining cannonballs and explosive mortar shells on Cornwallis's forts and on Yorktown itself. The British guns were soon silenced, and the British soldiers were forced to seek cover wherever they could find it. "I now want words to express the dreadful situation of the garrison," wrote Lieutenant Bartholomew James of the Royal Navy. "Upwards of a thousand shells were thrown into the works this night, and every spot became alike dangerous. The noise and thundering of the cannon, the distressing cries of the wounded, and the lamentable sufferings of the inhabitants, whose dwellings were chiefly in flames, added to the restless fatigue of the duty."

Taking advantage of their superior firepower, the French and Americans began digging a second parallel siege line, this one just 300 yards from Redoubts 9 and 10. At 8 P.M. on the night of October 14, elite units from both armies gathered in this trench to storm the British fortifications. The American contingent, 400 New England and New York Continentals commanded by Colonel Alexander Hamilton, charged Redoubt 10 with fixed bayonets. The defenders were caught by surprise and quickly overwhelmed. Four hundred picked French troops assaulted Redoubt 9 at the same time, but they encountered much stiffer resistance and lost fifteen killed and seventy-seven wounded in a fierce fire fight before managing to secure their objective.

The British outer line had now been breached, and Cornwallis knew that his position in Yorktown would soon be untenable. He still had a few desperate gambits left to play, however. The first was a surprise raid on the allies' second siege line. It took place just before dawn on October 16. A party of 350 British soldiers slipped into the trench, bayoneted a handful of artillerymen and spiked several cannon, but then were driven off before they could do more damage.

Later that evening, Cornwallis tried to engineer an escape across the York River to Gloucester Point. He had only sixteen small boats available to transfer his entire army, however, and when the little flotilla embarked on its first run, disaster struck. "A most violent storm of wind and rain . . . drove all of the boats, some of which had troops on board, down the river," the British general wrote in his report of the campaign. All hope of escape was gone; surrender was the only option left.

The World Turned Upside Down

A British drummer boy, resplendent in a brilliant scarlet jacket, white leggings, and gleaming black gaiters, clambered to the parapet of an earthwork on the morning of October 17 and began beating the *chamade*, the signal for a parley. The allied guns ceased firing, and presently a British officer emerged and made his way across no-man's land into the American lines to request an armistice. Representatives from both sides met at the Moore House the next day and drafted the terms of surrender.

At 2 P.M. on October 19, 1781, the soldiers of Cornwallis's army marched out of their shot-scarred fortifications toward the surrender field a mile distant. Although they were smartly dressed in new uniforms, and stepped along with the smooth precision of professionals, they had a melancholy air about them. Regimental bands were playing the sad English drinking song, "The World Turn'd Upside Down," and as the redcoats passed through the allied siege line the watching Americans felt, in the words of one, "an awful sense of the vicissitudes of human life, mingled with commiseration for the unhappy."

All told, 7,247 British and German officers and men and 840 British sailors were surrendered along with 244 cannon, 24 sets of colors, thousands of muskets, and a huge store of gear and ammunition. It was one of the worst military defeats ever suffered by Great Britain, and it significantly changed the course of world history. The six-year-old British effort to crush the American Revolution had failed. Another two years would pass before a peace treaty was signed, but for all intents and purposes America had won its independence at Yorktown.

Touring the Park

Begin your tour at the Yorktown Visitor Center, where exhibits and an audiovisual program will help you understand the siege.

From the Visitor Center, the seven-mile Battlefield Tour and the nine-mile Allied Encampment Tour lead to various points of interest on the battlefield.

Battlefield Tour: Stop A. British Inner Defense Line and Hornwork. As you drive out of the Visitor Center parking lot, look to your left. The earthworks you see mark the location of the British inner defense line (these breastworks were enlarged by Confederate soldiers during the Civil War). When Washington's army arrived on September 28, 1781, Cornwallis ordered his soldiers to withdraw from most of the outer defense works to better guard this inner line, which extended about one and a half miles around Yorktown. The hornwork, which you will see on the left as you approach the first intersection, extended out from the main line to block the Hampton Road (now Virginia 238).

Battlefield Tour: Stop B. Grand French Battery. Beginning on October 6, the allied troops dug the first siege line, a trench running from this point eastward to the York River (all of the earthworks you see from here on in the tour have been reconstructed). Cannon and mortars were positioned in the siege line, and on October 9 they opened fire on the British fortifications. The largest gun emplacement was the Grand French Battery. The reconstructed battery you see here contains both original and reproduction artillery pieces.

Battlefield Tour: Stop C. Second Allied Siege Line. Heavy fire from the allies' first siege line battered Cornwallis's defenses and destroyed most of his artillery. By October 11, the French and American troops were able to advance and dig this second siege line, tightening the noose around Yorktown.

Battlefield Tour: Stop D. Redoubts 9 and 10. These two earthen forts were crucial to the British defense of Yorktown. On the night of October 14, American and French troops stormed them. After a fierce hand-to-hand fight, the allies captured the redoubts, allowing the completion of the second siege line. The Americans placed the largest of their artillery batteries between the two forts, in position to hammer the British inner defense line and Yorktown itself. The fall of Redoubts 9 and 10 and the point-blank fire of the allied artillery made Cornwallis's position untenable, and on October 17 he asked for an armistice.

The mortars and cannon you see here are reproductions.

Battlefield Tour: Stop E. Moore House. On the afternoon of October 18, British,

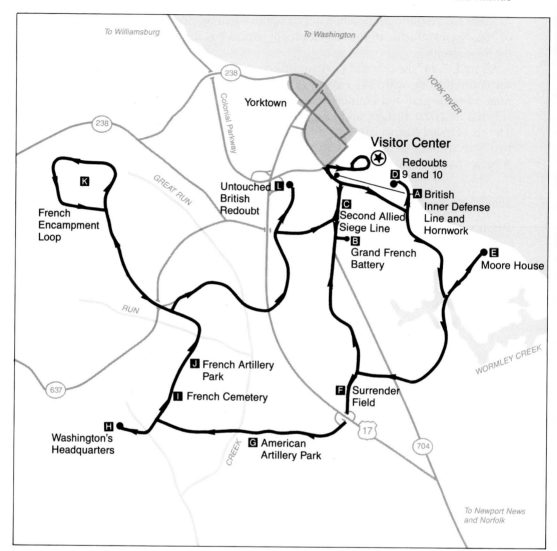

Yorktown Battlefield, Colonial National Historical Park

American, and French officers met in this house to draft the terms of surrender. The Articles of Capitulation called for the British to march out of Yorktown "with shouldered arms, colors cased, and drums beating a British or German march."

Battlefield Tour: Stop F. Surrender Field. On the afternoon of October 19, 1781, Cornwallis's soldiers marched onto this field and stacked their arms. Cornwallis himself declined to attend the ceremony, sending his second in command, General Charles O'Hara, instead. After the surrender, the British and German troops were sent to prisoner of war camps, while Cornwallis, who had been granted parole, departed for England by way of New York City.

The 7,247 British and German soldiers and 840 British sailors who surrendered here represented nearly one-third of all royal forces in America. Loss of this army crippled the British war effort and eventually led to the negotiation of a peace treaty recognizing American independence.

This ends the Battlefield Tour. If you wish to return to Yorktown, turn right as you leave the parking lot at Stop F and follow the red arrows. If you wish to take the Allied Encampment Tour, turn left and follow the yellow arrows.

Allied Encampment Tour: Stop G. American Artillery Park. When Washington's army broke camp in New York and set out for Yorktown in August 1781, its artillery was loaded aboard ships and transported down the coast to Trebell's Landing on the James River. From Trebell's Landing, the mortars and cannon were hauled to the siege area and placed in an artillery park from which they could be moved into the front line. The American Artillery Park was located in this area.

Allied Encampment Tour: Stop H. Washington's Headquarters. General Washington's headquarters tent was pitched on this site.

Allied Encampment Tour: Stop I. French Cemetery. French casualties of the Yorktown siege are buried in this cemetery.

Allied Encampment Tour: Stop J. French Artillery Park. The French concentrated their artillery pieces here before deploying them in the siege lines.

Allied Encampment Tour: Stop K. French Encampment Loop. The tour road loops through the area where the French army had its camp.

Allied Encampment Tour: Stop L. Untouched British Redoubt. This earthwork was part of Cornwallis's outer line of redoubts, built to block the approaches to Yorktown. It was abandoned on the night of September 29, 1781.

The George Rogers Clark Memorial stands on the site of Fort Sackville. National Park Service, photograph by Richard Frear.

CHAPTER 14

GEORGE ROGERS CLARK NATIONAL HISTORICAL PARK
(Revolutionary War)

401 South Second Street
Vincennes, Indiana 47591
Telephone: (812) 882-1776

During 1778–1779, George Rogers Clark and a small band of frontiersmen invaded the old Northwest Territory—present-day Ohio, Indiana, Michigan, Illinois, and Wisconsin—to attack British outposts. They captured the villages of Kaskaskia, Cahokia, and Vincennes, and ended royal domination over the region. George Rogers Clark National Historical Park, on the site of old Fort Sackville in Vincennes, Indiana, commemorates the seizure of the fort from the British on February 25, 1779, and the Clark expedition's role in conquering the old Northwest for the United States.

Getting to the Park: George Rogers Clark National Historical Park is located in Vincennes, Indiana. The park entrance is on Second Street, 4 blocks south of U.S. 50.

Gas, food, lodging: In Vincennes.

Visitor Center: Museum; film on George Rogers Clark.

Activities: Interpretive talks are given by park personnel during the summer months. Occasional living-history weapons-firing demonstrations are given. Inquire at Visitor Center for schedule.

Handicapped Access: Visitor Center is fully accessible. Most of the park grounds are accessible, with the exception of the George Rogers Clark Memorial, which can be entered only by a difficult 33-step climb.

The old Northwest Territory—present-day Ohio, Indiana, Michigan, Illinois, and Wisconsin—was dominated by Great Britain at the beginning of the American Revolution. From their military outpost at Detroit, the British dispatched Indian raiding parties to ravage American settlements on the Kentucky frontier. Their goal was to drive the Americans out of Kentucky and seize control of all the land west of the Appalachian Mountains.

In the winter of 1777–1778, a twenty-six-year-old frontiersman named George Rogers Clark went to the Virginia Legislature and offered to raise a small band of soldiers and invade the Northwest Territory. By carrying the fight to the British, the pressure on Kentucky (then a part of Virginia) would be relieved, and Virginia's postwar claim to sovereignty over the lands of the Northwest would be strengthened.

The legislature commissioned Clark a lieutenant colonel in the state's militia and authorized him to raise and equip a force of up to 350 men. When his troops were ready he was to mount an expedition against the British-held villages of Kaskaskia, Cahokia, and Vincennes in what is now southwestern Illinois and Indiana.

Clark's Western Campaign

In the spring of 1778, Clark and 170 followers boated down the Ohio River to Corn Island, near modern-day Louisville. They drilled and gathered supplies on the island until late June, then set off again, traveling to Fort Massac near Paducah. The boats were abandoned at the fort, and the little army marched overland to Kaskaskia, arriving at their destination on July 4.

The British garrison at Kaskaskia had not detected Clark's approaching column and were caught completely off guard by the frontiersmen's sudden appearance. They surrendered the fort and the village without firing a shot. Enlisting the aid of Kaskaskia's French inhabitants, the Americans next captured Cahokia, and then Vincennes on the banks of the Wabash. British control of the trans-Appalachian frontier had been dealt a severe blow; Clark's western campaign was a great success.

British Counterattack

At Detroit, the British lieutenant governor of the Northwest Territory, Colonel Henry Hamilton, prepared to counterattack. His first target was Fort Sackville at Vincennes, one of the posts recently captured by the Americans. On December 17, 1778, Hamilton's expeditionary force—a small contingent of British regulars augmented by hundreds of Indians—retook the fort from its tiny, five-man garrison.

From Vincennes, Hamilton intended to move into Illinois and drive Clark and his band from their stronghold in the Kaskaskia-Cahokia area. The onset of winter weather changed his mind, however. Convinced that the Americans would not fight until spring, he allowed most of his Indian allies to depart, while he remained at Fort Sackville with forty British regulars and forty French and Indian volunteers.

When Clark and his men learned that Hamilton was at Fort Sackville they decided to march at once. The frontiersmen loathed the British lieutenant governor, who was reputed to pay his Indian raiders for American scalps, and if there was a chance to capture or kill him they were not about to let bad weather stand in their way. The sympathetic citizens of Kaskaskia supplied them with ammunition and food, and on February 5, 1779, the little army set off for Vincennes, 180 miles to the east.

Snow and rain had swollen the creeks and rivers of southern Illinois, and much of the prairie the Americans traveled over was flooded. Slogging through freezing mud, wading through icy, chest-deep water, they moved steadily across the "drowned coun-try," spurred on by Clark and by the thought of catching Hamilton, the hated "hair buyer." On the night of February 23, after 18 days of suffering and privation, they reached Vincennes and surrounded the fort.

The Siege of Fort Sackville

One the morning of February 24, the Americans opened fire with their long rifles on Fort Sackville's flabbergasted British defenders. Outnumbered and pinned down, the British soon hoisted a flag of truce. Hamilton and Clark met in a nearby church, where Clark demanded unconditional surrender, but Hamilton angrily rejected these terms and the fighting resumed.

Chance soon gave Clark an opportunity to frighten the British into capitulation. A party of Hamilton's Indian allies returned to the fort during a lull in the firing and, unaware that a siege was in progress, approached the gates yelling and waving tro-phies from their latest raid. The Americans attacked them, killing and wounding sev-eral and taking most of the others prisoner.

Frontier vengeance was swift and cruel. Four of the bound Indian captives were dragged in front of the fort and savagely tomahawked to death in full view of the British garrison. This grisly scene had the desired effect. Hamilton asked for another truce, and this time he accepted Clark's terms of surrender. On the morning of Feb-ruary 25, the Union Jack was cut from the flag staff, and Hamilton and his troops marched from the fort and laid down their arms.

The Fruits of Victory

With the fall of Fort Sackville, the British effort to vanquish George Rogers Clark and keep the Americans out of the Northwest Territory was doomed. Detroit re-mained in British hands, but its value as a base for Indian raids was sharply reduced.

The full import of Clark's victory did not become evident until the war's final days, however. The presence of his soldiers in Illinois and Indiana enabled American ne-gotiators to insist that their British counterparts surrender all the lands west of the Appalachians. When the war-ending Treaty of Paris was signed in 1783, the old Northwest Territory was ceded to America. This rich prize instantly doubled the size of the new nation.

Touring the Park

Begin your tour at the Visitor Center, where exhibits and an audiovisual program provide information about the siege of Fort Sackville, the Revolutionary War in the old Northwest, and the territory's incorporation into the United States.

George Rogers Clark Memorial. From the Visitor Center you can walk to the memorial, which stands on the site of Fort Sackville. At the time of the siege, the rectangular fort was approximately 200 feet long and had 11-foot-high palisaded walls. Inside the walls were a powder magazine, a well, a guardhouse, two barracks, two blockhouses, and a headquarters building.

St. Francis Xavier Church and Old French Cemetery. West of the memorial are an old cemetery and a white-spired church, recalling the important role French Catholics played in settling southern Indiana and Illinois. Without the aid of French citizens, Clark and his soldiers would not have been able to defeat the British at Fort Sackville.

CHAPTER 15

BRICES CROSS ROADS NATIONAL BATTLEFIELD SITE

(Civil War)

C/O Natchez Trace Parkway
R.R.1, NT-143
Tupelo, Mississippi 38801
Telephone: (601) 842-1572

On June 10, 1864, General Nathan Bedford Forrest and 3,500 Confederate cavalrymen attacked and routed a Union force of 8,300. Students of military tactics consider Forrest's performance at this battle one of the greatest exhibitions of generalship in the annals of warfare. Brices Cross Roads National Battlefield Site consists of a one-acre piece of land from which much of the scene of action can be viewed.

Getting to the Park: Brices Cross Roads National Battlefield Site is located 6 miles west of Baldwyn, Mississippi, on Mississippi Highway 370.

Gas, food, lodging: In Tupelo, Mississippi, 25 miles south off U.S. 45.

Visitor Center: There are no visitor facilities or park personnel at the battlefield site. However, visitors may obtain information at the Natchez Trace Parkway Visitor Center, five miles north of Tupelo at the intersection of the Natchez Trace Parkway and U.S. 45. The Natchez Trace Parkway Visitor Center is open daily, 8 A.M.–5 P.M., except Christmas.

Activities: None.

Handicapped Access: The entire area is accessible.

The tide of war had turned in favor of the Union in the latter half of 1863. Capture of Vicksburg on the Mississippi River (see Chapter 32) gave Union gunboats undisputed control of that vital waterway, and victories at Gettysburg (see Chapter 9) and Chattanooga (see Chapter 17) bolstered Union morale and put Confederate forces on the defensive. As the winter of 1864 melted into spring, General Ulysses S. Grant planned a coordinated attack from east and west that would strike at the heart of the Confederacy, destroying its ability to wage war.

In the west, the plan called for armies commanded by General William T. Sherman to invade Georgia from bases at Nashville and Chattanooga, Tennessee. Sherman's troops were to defeat the Confederate soldiers led by General Joseph E. Johnston, capture the city of Atlanta, and then drive east to Savannah and the coast, devastating the countryside along the way.

The Confederate defenders of north Georgia were badly outnumbered, and when Sherman launched his invasion in early May, they fell back, fighting delaying actions as they grudgingly gave ground. Slowly but inexorably, the Union armies advanced southeast, pushing closer and closer to Atlanta, threatening the rich Georgia heartland.

To ease the pressure on their soldiers in front of Atlanta, the Confederate high command decided to strike at Sherman's exposed supply line, a single-track railroad running from Nashville to Chattanooga. General Nathan Bedford Forrest and his force of 3,500 cavalrymen camped near Tupelo, Mississippi, were ordered to ride northward into Tennessee and cut the track, disrupting the flow of food and ammunition to the Union army in Georgia.

The Wizard of the Saddle

Nathan Bedford Forrest was one the great commanders of the Civil War, a cavalryman whose military genius earned him the nickname the "Wizard of the Saddle."

Born in Chapel Hill, Tennessee, in July 1821, Forrest grew up in Tippah County, Mississippi. He became a successful slave trader, and amassed a fortune of over a million dollars before joining the Confederate army in June 1861.

Despite his lack of formal education, Forrest proved to be an adept organizer and a brilliant strategist and tactician. Uncompromisingly aggressive, he was committed to attacking his enemies, pursuing them relentlessly, and demanding their unconditional surrender under threat of total annihilation.

"Fierce and terrible" in battle, he was wounded four times during the course of the war, had twenty-nine horses shot from beneath him, and personally killed or wounded thirty Union troopers in hand-to-hand combat.

What his soldiers admired most about Forrest was his boundless energy and will to win, which inspired them again and again to perform seemingly impossible feats of marching and fighting. "His commission as General was signed not only by Mr. Jefferson Davis (president of the Confederacy), but by the Almighty himself," wrote one of his men.

The Union high command hated and feared the hard-hitting Mississippian, and specifically targeted him for destruction. "There will be no peace . . . . until Forrest is dead," General Sherman bluntly proclaimed, and sent expedition after expedition to hunt him down. Forrest managed to defeat or elude all his pursuers, however.

"I took a through ticket," he said of his participation in the war, "and I fought and lost as much as anyone else; certainly as much as I could."

Confederate general Nathan Bedford Forrest, the "Wizard of the
Saddle," won his greatest victory
at Brices Cross Roads. Library of
Congress.

Sherman knew that his supply line was vulnerable, and that the most feared of the
Confederate raiders—the man he called "that devil Forrest"—was lurking in northeastern Mississippi. To prevent him and his horsemen from raising havoc in Tennessee, he decided to mount a preemptive attack.

June 1864: Sturgis Moves against Forrest

The unenviable task of containing Forrest fell to Union general Samuel D. Sturgis.
With 8,300 troops, 22 cannon, and 250 supply wagons, he left Memphis on June 1
and moved into northern Mississippi, heading for the Confederate cavalry's stronghold near Tupelo.

The same day that Sturgis marched from Memphis, Forrest and his raiders broke
camp and rode east. They were at Russellville, Alabama, on June 3, preparing to cross
into Tennessee and smash Sherman's supply line, when word came that the blue column was threatening Tupelo. Hurrying back to Mississippi, the Confederates took
up positions near the towns of Rienzi, Booneville, and Baldwyn, north of Tupelo,
and waited for Sturgis to come on.

Although his cavalry was outnumbered and outgunned, Forrest was determined to
strike at the advancing Union troops. He devised a plan of attack and selected the
ground on which he would fight—Brices Cross Roads—a densely wooded area
where the Ripley-Guntown Road Sturgis was following was intersected by a road
running southwest from Baldwyn to New Albany.

On the evening of June 9, scouts arrived at the Confederate camps with news that

Sturgis's force would reach Brices Cross Roads around noon the next day. Forrest promptly set his plan in motion: the gray cavalry would ride for Brices at dawn.

June 10, 1864: Forrest Strikes

Heavy rains had been soaking northern Mississippi since June 2, turning roads into quagmires and sending normally sluggish creeks foaming over their banks. The downpour ended on the night of June 9, however, and the next day dawned bright and hot.

As he trotted down the Baldwyn Road toward Brices Cross Roads, Forrest explained his strategy to Colonel Edmund Rucker, commander of one of his cavalry brigades. "I know they greatly outnumber the troops I have at hand," he told Rucker, "but . . . when we strike them they will not know how few men we have. Their cavalry will move out ahead of their infantry and should reach the crossroads three hours in advance. We can whip their cavalry in that time. As soon as the fight opens they will send back to have the infantry hurried up. It is going to be hot as hell, and coming on the run for five or six miles, their infantry will be so tired out we will ride right over them."

This assessment was to prove uncannily accurate. At about 10 A.M., a mile east of Brices, Forrest and the lead elements of his force met and attacked the Union cavalry, which had ridden out ahead of the main body of infantry. For three hours the dismounted cavalrymen, blue and gray, fought savagely in the tangled thickets of scrub oak, blazing away at close range as the day grew hotter and hotter.

General Sturgis galloped up to look over the situation, and seeing his blue troopers hard pressed, ordered the infantry, straggling along several miles back, to advance on the double. "Make all haste," his message to them read. "Lose no time in coming up."

The foot soldiers obeyed, jogging forward in the sweltering heat, pulling their cannon and supply wagons through sticky mudholes, slogging ankle-deep across the flooded bottomland of Tishomingo Creek just west of the crossroads. Many men collapsed from sunstroke along the way; the rest arrived on the battlefield at 1 P.M., sweat soaked and out of breath.

This was the moment Forrest had been waiting for. His earlier attack had worn down the Union cavalry; now he was ready to launch the main effort against the exhausted infantry. Down the Confederate line he rode, shirt sleeves rolled up, saber in hand, "looking the very God of War," according to one of his soldiers.

"Get up men," he called. "When . . . the bugle sounds, every man must charge, and we will give them hell."

Moments later the attack began, a headlong rush at the center of the Union position. The fighting was hand to hand. "Guns once fired were used as clubs, and pistols were brought into play, while the two lines struggled with the ferocity of wild beasts," wrote one of the combatants.

Winded though they were, the Union infantrymen stubbornly resisted the Confederate assault. Finally, around 4 P.M., they began to give way. Forrest quickly ordered a flanking attack—"hit 'em on the e-e-end!" he yelled—and the blue line crumbled as whooping graybacks swept around the left and right.

"Order gave way to confusion and confusion to panic," recalled Sturgis. "Everywhere the army now drifted toward the rear and was soon altogether beyond control."

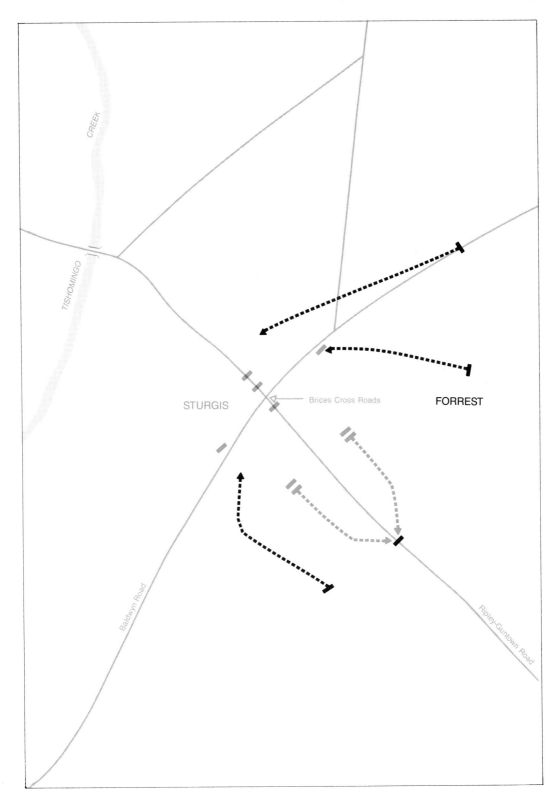

CREEK

TISHOMINGO

STURGIS

Brices Cross Roads

FORREST

Baldwyn Road

Ripley-Guntown Road

Brices Cross Roads, June 10, 1864

A wagon had overturned on the bridge spanning swollen Tishomingo Creek, obstructing the Union retreat. Caught in this bottleneck, hundreds of men threw down their weapons and plunged into the muddy torrent, floundering desperately for the other side. Others sought hiding places in the brush along the creek banks.

Hard on their heels came the jubilant Confederates. They heaved the tangle of debris off the bridge and raced on in hot pursuit of the panic-stricken bluecoats, stopping only to take prisoners and to loot abandoned supply wagons.

Forrest's orders to his men were simple: "Keep the skeer on 'em"—and this they did, hounding the fleeing Union troops the rest of the day and into the night. In the flooded morass of the Hatchie River bottom, eight miles from Brices, what was left of Sturgis's supply and artillery train bogged down and was abandoned.

"General, for God's sake don't let us give up so," pleaded a Union soldier as the rout continued, but Sturgis was too badly shaken to pull his command together.

"What can we do?" he said. "What can we do?"

The blue army, defeated and utterly humiliated, did not stop running until it reached Memphis on June 12. It had lost 200 wagons, all its artillery, and 2,240 men—223 killed, 394 wounded, and 1,623 captured or missing. The Confederates had suffered 492 casualties—96 killed and 396 wounded.

A Hollow Victory

Forrest's triumph at Brices Cross Roads was one of the most brilliant in the annals of warfare. On terrain of his choosing, he executed a daring battle plan to perfection and smashed a numerically superior force. The Confederate victory was so complete and so devastating that Union general Sturgis insisted, despite all evidence to the contrary, that he had been bested by a force of 15,000–20,000, not the 3,500 gray troops he actually faced.

Students of military tactics still study Forrest's performance at Brices Cross Roads, and consider it a masterpiece of generalship. But his achievement was a hollow one that brought no relief to the beleaguered Confederates in north Georgia. Supplies continued to flow through Tennessee to Sherman's armies around Atlanta, and in this, the critical theater of the western conflict, the Union kept rolling toward ultimate victory.

Touring the Park

The park consists of a one-acre piece of land situated at the crossroads. Monuments and markers provide interpretation. Much of the battlefield is visible from this point. A short drive northwest on the Ripley-Guntown Road brings you to Tishomingo Creek and the site of the bridge where the Union retreat became a rout.

CHAPTER 16

CHALMETTE UNIT, JEAN LAFITTE NATIONAL HISTORICAL PARK AND PRESERVE

(War of 1812)

8606 West St. Bernard Highway
Chalmette, Louisiana 70043
Telephone: (504) 589-4430

The Battle of New Orleans was fought on January 8, 1815 at Chalmette Plantation, six miles east of the city. General Andrew Jackson's ragtag force of American volunteers crushed an army of British regulars and saved the Mississippi Valley for the United States. Chalmette National Historical Park preserves the site of the battle as well as the historic Beauregard House, built in 1833.

Getting to the Park: Chalmette National Historical Park is located 6 miles east of downtown New Orleans, Louisiana. From downtown, take the St. Bernard Highway (Louisiana Highway 46) east 6 miles to the park entrance. From I-10, take the Chalmette exit, go south on Louisiana Highway 47 to the St. Bernard Highway, then turn right to the park entrance.

Gas, food, lodging: In New Orleans.

Visitor Center: Museum and gift shop; audiovisual displays.

Activities: Interpretive talks by park personnel. Inquire at Visitor Center for schedule.

Handicapped Access: The first floor of the Visitor Center is accessible. The museum exhibits on the second floor are accessible only by steep and winding stairs.

The Battle of New Orleans—the climactic struggle of the War of 1812—was fought on January 8, 1815, at Chalmette Plantation, a muddy strip of Mississippi bottomland six miles east of New Orleans. On this flat, swampy ground, a rabble of Louisiana, Kentucky, and Tennessee volunteers vanquished an army of British regulars and saved the Mississippi River Valley for the United States.

Ironically, British and American negotiators meeting half a world away in the Netherlands had signed a peace treaty fifteen days *before* the victory. Had rapid, transoceanic communication been possible, the battle would not have been fought.

The Gulf Coast Offensive

After forcing the French emperor Napoleon to abdicate in the spring of 1814, Great Britain turned its attention to the War of 1812, which had been dragging on for two and a half years. Battle-hardened British soldiers were dispatched from Europe to North America, and an ambitious three-pronged invasion of the United States was planned.

The first prong of the invasion—from Canada south toward New York City—was blunted by American naval forces at Lake Champlain in September 1814. The second prong—from Chesapeake Bay west into Virginia and Maryland—was blocked the same month at Fort McHenry in Baltimore Harbor (see Chapter 6). The third prong—from the Gulf Coast north up the Mississippi River Valley—was launched in late December when 10,000 British army regulars landed at Lake Borgne, Louisiana.

The commander of the Gulf Coast invasion force, General Sir Edward Pakenham, contemplated a quick campaign to seize New Orleans. Capture of the bustling port would give the British a stranglehold on the lower Mississippi Valley, allowing them to choke off commerce and cripple the economy of the western United States.

Standing in the way of this seasoned, well-equipped army was a ragtag force of 5,000 volunteers led by General Andrew Jackson, hero of the Creek War (see Chapter 23). Although most of his troops were without battle experience, Jackson was determined to fight: on December 23, 1814, he launched a surprise attack that rocked the British back on their heels. The outnumbered Americans could not sustain their attack, however, and Jackson ordered a withdrawal to Chalmette Plantation.

Prelude to Battle

General Pakenham reached Chalmette on Christmas Day, and carefully inspected the American defensive position. Jackson's battle line stretched across a neck of land barely half a mile wide, its southern flank anchored on the Mississippi River and its northern flank resting on the edge of an impenetrable cypress swamp. There was no room for an attacker to maneuver, and the only avenue of approach was across open sugarcane fields that could be swept by artillery and small-arms fire. The Americans were dug in behind a shoulder-high mud rampart, which was fronted by the Rodriguez Canal, an irrigation ditch linking the river and the swamp.

In hopes of panicking Jackson's green volunteers, Pakenham ordered his infantry to make a probing attack on December 28; they were beaten back by American cannon fire. On New Year's Day he tried to dislodge the Americans with an artillery barrage of his own; this effort also failed. The only options left were an all-out frontal assault or ignominious retreat. Without hesitation, Pakenham chose the former, counting on the discipline and fighting spirit of his combat-tested veterans to carry the day.

January 8, 1815: The Battle of New Orleans

At dawn on January 8, the British soldiers formed into two tightly massed columns and moved out across the sugarcane stubble toward the American line. The flash of their scarlet uniform jackets, the flicker of their steel bayonets, the measured rise and fall of their polished black boots, transformed the dreary plantation field into a parade ground.

The defenders, who had been breakfasting on whiskey and cornbread, admired this stately advance for a few moments. Then they unleashed their first volley, a smoky, thunderous explosion of musket and cannon fire that abruptly ended the pageantry. Wide gaps were torn in the British ranks, but still the regulars moved ahead, one column veering toward the American left flank, the other toward the right.

The left end of the line, near the cypress swamp, was held by the "Dirty Shirts," Tennessee and Kentucky riflemen under the command of General John Coffee, a blooded veteran of the Creek War. Coffee steadied his soldiers with a few words, and they responded by peppering the oncoming British formation with rapid, deadly-accurate fire. Hundreds of the red-coated soldiers, including General Samuel Gibbs, leader of the assault, were slain, and hundreds of others were wounded.

The second British column, moving against the south or river flank of the defensive line, was similarly punished. Units commanded by Colonel Robert Rennie managed to get across the Rodriguez Canal and clamber up onto the mud rampart, but they were hurled back in furious hand-to-hand fighting. Rennie was shot through the eye and killed, and the attack soon sputtered out.

The Ninety-third Highlanders were ordered to march diagonally across the length of the battlefield and attack the American left. They were exposed every step of the way to scathing flanking fire and suffered appalling casualties. Dixon Ticonderoga Company.

The Ninety-third Highlanders, a regiment being held in reserve near the river, was now ordered by General John Keane to go to the aid of Gibbs's faltering column. This was a disastrous tactical decision that condemned the Highlanders to march diagonally across the length of the battlefield, exposed every step of the way to scathing flanking fire from the entire American line. Keane soon paid for this folly with his life. The regiment continued on but suffered appalling casualties. Seven hundred forty soldiers were shot, and the 160 survivors never reached the far side of the field.

Seeing the assault stall, Pakenham rode forward to rally his troops for another charge. The Americans knew that mounted men were officers, and they opened up on the lone rider as he came galloping toward them. Down went Pakenham with a bullet through his left forearm; foolishly, he remounted and tried to ride on. Another shot hit him in the neck, and as he collapsed to the ground, a third bullet smashed into his thigh, severing the artery. He bled to death in a matter of seconds.

Now leaderless, the surviving British soldiers turned and fled from the killing field. More than 2,000 of their fellows had been cut down in barely half an hour's time. By contrast the Americans had lost only 13 men.

The Gulf Coast Offensive Thwarted

After the terrible butchery at Chalmette, the shattered British army limped back to Lake Borgne, where ships waited to evacuate them. The Gulf Coast offensive was over; New Orleans and the Mississippi River Valley had been saved.

News of the stunning victory had a tonic effect on the people of the United States. American confidence and pride—beaten down by the unpopular and heretofore unsuccessful war—were restored, and Andrew Jackson became a great national hero. Thirteen years after his triumph at Chalmette, he was elected the country's seventh president.

Touring the Park

Begin your tour at the Visitor Center located in the Beauregard House, a superb example of French-Louisiana architecture built in 1833. An audiovisual program and museum exhibits provide background on the War of 1812 and explain the Battle of New Orleans.

A 1.5-mile tour road runs through the park. Six numbered stops mark the key historic points on the battlefield.

Stop 1. American Left Flank. This section of Jackson's line, near the cypress swamp, was defended by the "Dirty Shirts," Tennessee and Kentucky volunteers commanded by General John Coffee. The deadly fire from their rifles and the cannon in Batteries 7 and 8 broke the back of the British attack, which came across the field directly in front of you.

Stop 2. Batteries 5 and 6. Cannon like the two reproduction 6-pounders you see here fired on the British column as it advanced toward Stop 1. The solid shot took a heavy toll on the tightly packed British formation.

Stop 3. March of the Ninety-third Highlanders. General John Keane ordered the Ninety-third Highlanders to go to the aid of Gibbs's attacking column. As they marched past this point, north across the open field toward Stop 1, the Highlanders

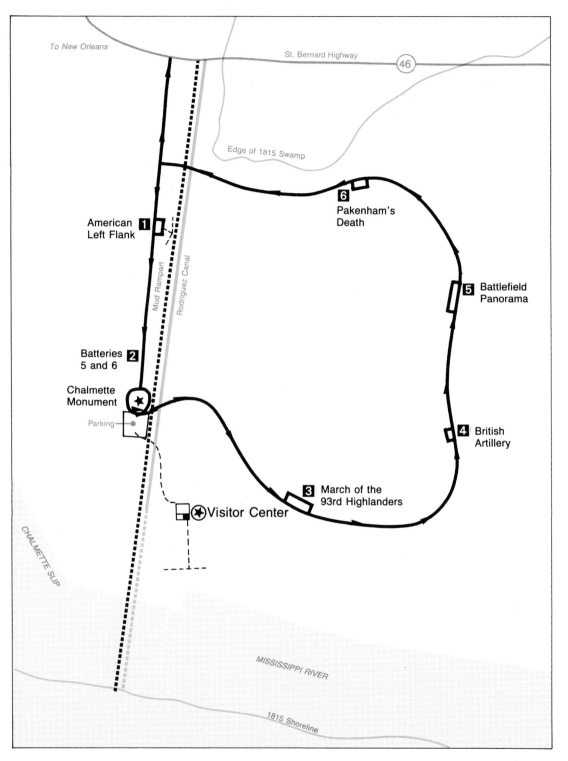

To New Orleans

St. Bernard Highway

46

Edge of 1815 Swamp

American
Left Flank **1**

6

Pakenham's
Death

Mud Rampart

Rodriguez Canal

5 Battlefield
Panorama

Batteries **2**
5 and 6

Chalmette
Monument

Parking

4 British
Artillery

3 March of the
93rd Highlanders

Visitor Center

CHALMETTE SLIP

MISSISSIPPI RIVER

1815 Shoreline

Chalmette Unit, Jean Lafitte National Historical Park and Preserve were hit by enfilading fire from the entire American line. They suffered terrible casualties and never reached their objective.

Stop 4. British Artillery. Because of poor positioning and a shortage of ammunition, British cannon played almost no part in the battle. The six-pounder has been placed here as an interpretive aid; during the battle the British batteries were located farther east, a greater distance from the American line.

Stop 5. Battlefield Panorama. From this point you can see the battlefield from the British perspective. In front of you and to the right, Gibbs's column advanced toward the mud rampart, only to be thrown back by heavy fire. To the far left, troops led by Colonel Robert Rennie briefly penetrated the American line but were beaten off in hand-to-hand fighting. In the center, the ill-fated Ninety-third Highlanders were slaughtered as they tried to link up with Gibbs's column.

Stop 6. Pakenham's Death. In a desperate effort to rally his army, General Pakenham rode onto the battlefield. Near this spot he was hit and mortally wounded by a hail of American bullets.

CHAPTER 17

CHICKAMAUGA AND CHATTANOOGA NATIONAL MILITARY PARK

(Civil War)

P.O. Box 2126
Fort Oglethorpe, Georgia 30742
Telephone: (404) 866-9241

In one of the hardest-fought battles of the Civil War, General Braxton Bragg's Confederate army vanquished Federal forces along Chickamauga Creek on September 19–20, 1863. The defeated Union army retreated to Chattanooga, where it was besieged by Bragg's command. On November 23–25, 1863, the Federals broke the siege and forced the Confederates to withdraw into Georgia, opening the way for a campaign against the city of Atlanta. Chickamauga and Chattanooga National Military Park preserves the sites of these critical Civil War battles.

Getting to the Park: Chickamauga and Chattanooga National Military Park is composed of several separate units. The Chickamauga Battlefield Unit is located near Fort Oglethorpe, Georgia, 7 miles south of Chattanooga, Tennessee, on U.S. 27. The Point Park and Lookout Mountain Units are located just west of downtown Chattanooga off U.S. 64/72. The Orchard Knob Unit is located in downtown Chattanooga off Orchard Knob Avenue. The Missionary Ridge Units are located just east of downtown Chattanooga on Crest Road.

Gas, food, lodging: In Chattanooga and Fort Oglethorpe.

Visitor Centers: Museum and gift shop; audiovisual programs.

Activities: Guided tours and living-history demonstrations are presented during the summer months. Inquire at Visitor Centers for schedule and location.

Handicapped Access: The first floor of the Chickamauga Visitor Center is accessible, but the second floor, where audiovisual programs are presented, is accessible only by a flight of steps. The park units can be seen by automobile. There are several tiers of steps along the Lookout Mountain foot trail.

The summer of 1863 marked a turning point in the two-year-old Civil War. At Gettysburg, in July, a Confederate invasion of the North was turned back (see Chapter 9). Half a continent away, Vicksburg, key to the Mississippi River, fell to a Union army (see Chapter 32). In Tennessee, another Union force, the Army of the Cumberland, occupied the town of Tullahoma and prepared to advance on the city of Chattanooga.

Chattanooga: Gateway to the Deep South

Situated near the Tennessee-Georgia border at the point where the Tennessee River flows west through gaps in the Cumberland Mountains, Chattanooga was a rail center of great strategic importance. Its loss would deal a crippling blow to the Confederate war effort and open the way for a Union thrust into the deep South.

On August 16, 1863, the 60,000-man Army of the Cumberland, commanded by General William S. Rosecrans, moved out of Tullahoma and marched southeast toward Chattanooga. Dug in near the Tennessee River crossings, both upstream and downstream of the city, were 43,000 Confederate soldiers led by General Braxton Bragg. Six months earlier, at the Battle of Stones River (see Chapter 30), Rosecrans had forced Bragg to give way after a bloody three-day struggle. Now, during the first week of September, he again compelled Bragg to retreat by crossing the Tennessee south of Chattanooga and threatening to cut his supply line.

The Confederates fell back toward Lafayette, Georgia, with Rosecrans in pursuit. Unbeknownst to the Federal commander, Bragg was being heavily reinforced—two divisions of General James Longstreet's corps had arrived from Virginia—and was preparing to counterattack and reoccupy Chattanooga. By mid-September, the ranks of the Confederate army had grown to more than 66,000, and a major battle was in the offing.

On September 18 Bragg ordered his rejuvenated command to take up position on the west bank of Chickamauga Creek several miles north of Lee and Gordon's Mill. He planned to strike the Union left, slash around it, and plant his army between the Federal soldiers and their supply base at Chattanooga. Rosecrans was alerted to the danger, however, and quickly extended his line northward so that Bragg could not outflank him.

When the sun rose on the 19th, 126,000 armed men were facing each other along a zigzag, four-mile-long front.

September 19, 1863: Chickamauga—Day One

The ground along Chickamauga Creek was so choked with brush and brambles that the opposing soldiers could not see each other, even though they were just a few hundred yards apart in places. When the fighting began shortly after dawn, units quickly became separated and officers lost tactical control of the battle. "There was no generalship in it," said one of the combatants of the death struggle on the banks of the Chickamauga. "It was a soldiers' fight, purely. . . . The two armies came together like two wild beasts, and each fought as long as it could stand up in a knock-down and drag-out encounter."

By mid-morning blinding clouds of powder smoke were billowing through the thickets as the troops blazed away at close quarters. The Federals tried to turn the Confederate right, then the Confederates tried to turn the Federal left, but neither

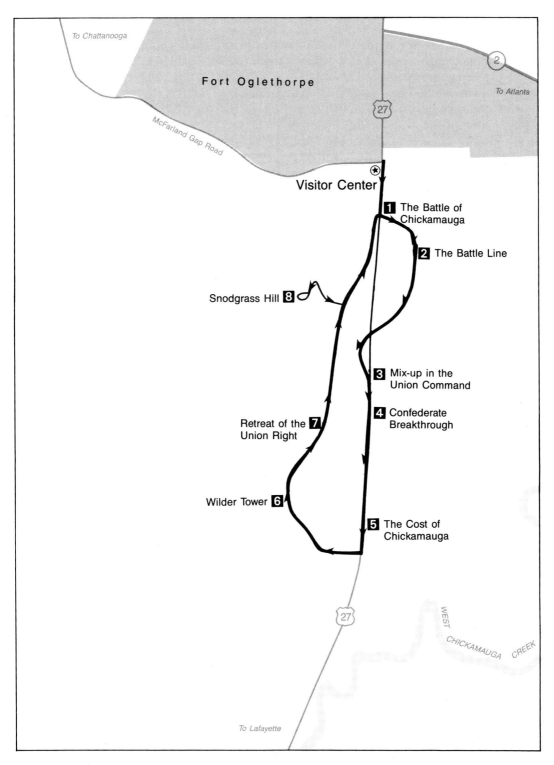

Chickamauga, September 20, 1863

side could make any headway. The bloody stalemate continued through the afternoon. At twilight, Confederate general Patrick Cleburne's division launched a final, savage assault on the Federal left flank.

The roar of musketry was terrifying in its intensity, "as if all the fires of earth and hell had been turned loose in one mighty effort to destroy each other." The impact of Cleburne's attack bent the Union line back nearly a mile, but failed to break it. Night brought an end to the bloodletting. While the Union soldiers felled trees and constructed breastworks, the Confederates regrouped and positioned themselves to resume the attack in the morning.

September 20, 1863: Chickamauga—Day Two

General Bragg's objective on the 20th was the same as it had been the day before: to turn the Federal left and get his army between the bluecoats and Chattanooga. The battle resumed at 9:30 A.M., but the furious Confederate attacks shattered against the breastworks Rosecrans's soldiers had erected during the night.

At 11 A.M. Bragg struck the center of the Union line with Longstreet's corps. As the orders went out and the three Confederate divisions gathered themselves for the charge, Rosecrans committed a terrible blunder. He received a message from a staff officer that one of the Union divisions was out of position, opening a gap in the center of his line. The staff officer was mistaken—there was no gap—but Rosecrans accepted his report as fact. He quickly ordered another division to fill the phantom gap, creating a real one in the process. With nearly perfect timing, Longstreet's corps rushed forward and punched through this hole, accomplishing a mile-deep penetration of the Union line in less than an hour.

The right half of the Federal army disintegrated as howling Confederates swarmed into the rear; soldiers threw down their weapons and fled in panic to the north and west. Rosecrans, his aides, and two of his three corps commanders were caught up in the flight and swept from the field, leaving General George Thomas in command of the units still intact and in position on the Federal left. Thomas faced a desperate situation: Longstreet's jubilant veterans were wheeling about and preparing to fall on his exposed flank. Thomas joined his troops at Snodgrass Hill, where he formed a new, hook-shaped battle line just before the storm of the Confederate attack broke around him.

The onslaught lasted all afternoon. Charge after charge was repulsed, the last one with bayonets and bare fists as ammunition ran out. At sundown Thomas finally pulled his exhausted soldiers out of the line and put them on the road to Rossville, where the rest of the Federal army was trying to reorganize. Henceforth he would be known as the "Rock of Chickamauga" in honor of his determined stand on Snodgrass Hill.

When Thomas's weary soldiers reached Rossville at about 11 P.M., they found a scene of chaos. "The army is simply a mob," observed a disgusted officer. "There appears to be neither organization nor discipline. The various commands are mixed up in what seems to be inextricable confusion." Wounded men lay everywhere, unaided and ignored in the general panic. "They had crawled or hobbled slowly away from the fury of the battle, become exhausted, and lain down by the roadside to die."

All told, the Army of the Cumberland had suffered 16,170 casualties, 28 percent of its strength. Morale had been shattered by the sudden rout, and a swift, determined push by the Confederates could easily have completed the destruction of the Union force. But the Confederates would not, perhaps could not, make that push. They had suffered appalling casualties, too—18,454 in total—and were just as spent as their opponents. Longstreet and General Nathan Bedford Forrest urged Bragg to seize the moment and resume the attack, but he refused to do it. "How can I?" he said. "Here is two-fifths of my army left [dead or wounded] on the field, and my artillery is without horses."

The Union army was allowed to retreat unchallenged into Chattanooga, where it regrouped and dug in. One of the greatest Confederate victories of the war, won at frightful cost, was squandered by indecision and excessive caution.

The Siege of Chattanooga

After the Battle of Chickamauga, General Rosecrans and his soldiers were besieged in Chattanooga. Bragg's Confederates entrenched on the heights of Lookout Mountain and Missionary Ridge and trained their guns on the city below, hoping to starve the Union army out.

Reinforcements were ordered to march to Rosecrans's aid; in early October, General Joseph Hooker arrived in Chattanooga with 20,000 troops from Virginia, and in mid-November General William T. Sherman and 16,000 additional men arrived from Mississippi. Rosecrans was relieved of his duties and George Thomas, "The Rock of Chickamauga," took his place. On October 23, General Ulysses S. Grant reached Chattanooga and assumed overall command of the campaign.

The first step in lifting the siege—opening a supply line—was achieved on October 28. The "Cracker Line," as this route was called, allowed Grant to build up his army's ammunition and food stocks in preparation for mounting an attack that would throw the Confederates from their positions on the high ground.

The Battle of Chattanooga

On the afternoon of November 23, two Union divisions launched a probing attack east from Chattanooga toward Missionary Ridge. They succeeded in capturing Orchard Knob, a little hill a mile from the base of the ridge, and setting up an artillery battery on its crest.

The next day, Hooker's troops assaulted Lookout Mountain. Climbing up the steep, rocky slopes, they were concealed from the defenders by a swirling fog. Halfway up, on a narrow bench of land, stood the Cravens Farm. Here the Federals and Confederates came to grips and fought what later came to be known as the "Battle above the Clouds." The fog continued to thicken, and at mid-afternoon both sides had to break off the combat because it was impossible to see. The Confederates had held their own, but they were outnumbered, and during the night they evacuated their entrenchments and slipped away to join their comrades on Missionary Ridge.

The climax of the battle, the Union assault on heavily defended Missionary Ridge, came on November 25. Grant's plan was to have Sherman's corps hit the enemy right while Hooker's force simultaneously hit the left. In the center, the troops led by General Thomas were to stay put until the flank attacks had run their course.

Sherman's veterans advanced on the Confederate fieldworks in their front just after sunrise, but were repulsed. Again they charged, only to be cut down by a sheet of musket fire that sliced through their ranks like a fiery scythe. More brave but foolhardy attacks were made, but by 3 P.M. it was clear to Grant that Sherman would not be able to win his objective. Meanwhile, Hooker's force had been delayed by a destroyed bridge and other road obstructions left by the retreating Confederates.

Desperate to relieve the pressure on Sherman, Grant ordered Thomas to advance from his outpost on Orchard Knob against the Confederate center. Four divisions numbering 25,000 men set off toward the rifle pits at the base of Missionary Ridge nearly a mile distant. These were the same soldiers who had been humiliated at Chickamauga, and they were eager to redeem themselves. Confederate artillery on the high ground opened up with "a crash like a thousand thunderclaps," raining hot iron on the blue ranks, but the attackers did not waver. Instead, they broke into a run, quickly covering the open ground between Orchard Knob and the foot of the ridge, sweeping through the line of rifle pits, routing the occupants.

What occurred next was one of the most extraordinary episodes of the war. Small groups of Union soldiers, exhilarated by the successful storming of the rifle pits, continued the charge up the precipitous slope of Missionary Ridge, without orders. Other soldiers followed, ignoring their officers' calls to stop, and shortly the entire force was surging forward, clambering over rocks and fallen trees, racing toward the crest.

The Confederates were stunned by this sudden, reckless advance. They tried to bring their guns to bear on the attackers, but the slope was so steep that much of their fire flew high. The momentum of the Union charge was irresistible; as the Federals neared the ridgetop, the gray line suddenly broke. Moments later, thousands of panting Union soldiers reached the crest and beheld a sight they would never forget: "Gray clad men rushed wildly down the hill and into the woods, tossing away knapsacks, muskets, and blankets as they ran. . . . Officers, frantic with rage, rushed from one panic-stricken group to another, shouting and cursing as they strove to check the headlong flight. . . . In ten minutes all that remained of the defiant Rebel army that had so long besieged Chattanooga was captured guns, disarmed prisoners, moaning wounded, ghastly dead, and scattered, demoralized fugitives. Mission[ary] Ridge was ours."

A Confederate Disaster

The storming of Missionary Ridge completed a remarkable, and for the Confederates a disastrous, turnaround in military fortunes. Despite winning a great victory at Chickamauga, they had been unable to break the Union grip on Tennessee. Now the battleground would shift to Georgia. In the spring of 1864, Sherman would move out of Chattanooga and begin his devastating march to Atlanta and the sea.

Visiting the Park

Chickamauga and Chattanooga National Military Park consists of several separate units. The main units are the Chickamauga Battlefield and Point Park (Lookout Mountain) in Chattanooga.

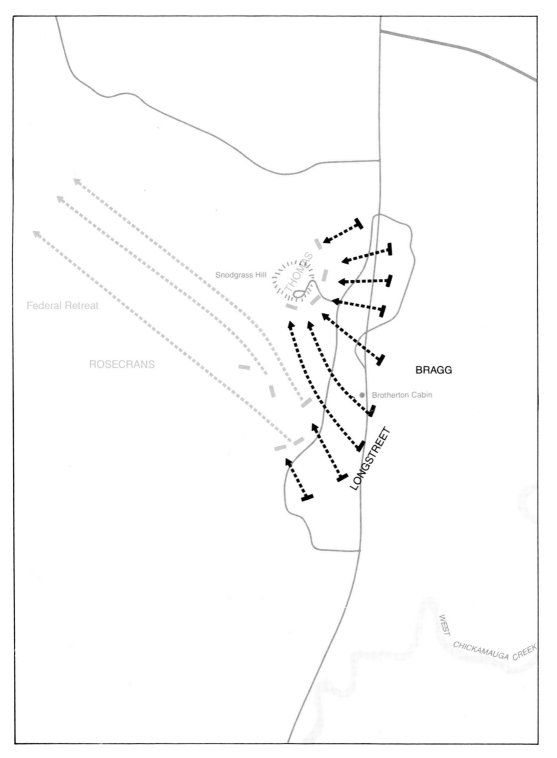

Federal Retreat

ROSECRANS

Snodgrass Hill

THOMAS

BRAGG

Brotherton Cabin

LONGSTREET

WEST CHICKAMAUGA CREEK

Chickamauga Battlefield, Chickamauga and Chattanooga National Military Park

Chickamauga Battlefield Tour. Begin your tour at the Visitor Center, where museum exhibits and audiovisual programs explain the battle and its significance in the Civil War. A seven-mile auto tour leads through the battlefield. There are eight numbered stops along the way, marking major points of interest.

Chickamauga Battlefield Tour Stop 1. The Battle of Chickamauga. Unlike most Civil War battles, which were fought in open farm fields, the Battle of Chickamauga was fought in woods and thick underbrush. Troops became separated and officers lost tactical control of the fight. As you drive along the tour road you will see metal tablets—blue for Union, red for Confederate—marking the location of various units.

Chickamauga Battlefield Tour Stop 2. The Battle Line. The second day of fighting began near this spot at 9:30 A.M. on September 20, 1863. The Confederates attacked from the northeast against breastworks the Union soldiers had erected during the night. Although the assault failed, the pressure it created forced Rosecrans to shift reinforcements up from the south, weakening his right flank and causing confusion among his commanders, leading to Longstreet's breakthrough.

Chickamauga Battlefield Tour Stop 3. Mix-up in the Union Command. At 11 A.M. on September 20, Rosecrans received a message from a staff officer that General John M. Brannan's division, which was deployed near here, was out of position, opening a gap in the center of the Union line. The message was wrong; there was no gap. Rosecrans accepted the report as fact, however, and shifted General Thomas J. Wood's division to fill the phantom gap, creating a real one in the process.

Chickamauga Battlefield Tour Stop 4. Confederate Breakthrough. When Wood's division pulled out of the Union line and moved north, it left an undefended gap. Longstreet's Confederate corps rushed forward from the woods behind you, past the Brotherton Cabin, and across the field to the trees, where the gap was. It accomplished a mile-deep penetration of the Union line in less than an hour.

Chickamauga Battlefield Tour Stop 5. The Cost of Chickamauga. Chickamauga was one of the bloodiest battles of the Civil War. The Union army lost 16,170 men, the Confederates 18,454. The rosters of some regiments were reduced more than 50 percent by the ferocious, seesaw combat.

The monuments across the road mark troop positions held on September 19, the first day of the battle.

Chickamauga Battlefield Tour Stop 6. Wilder Tower. This tall monument honors Colonel John Wilder and the 2,000 men of his mounted infantry brigade. When Longstreet's Confederates broke through the Union line on September 20, Wilder's brigade slowed their advance with rapid fire from seven-shot Spencer repeating carbines.

The monument stands on the ground where Rosecrans had his headquarters on September 19 and 20. The platform at the top offers an excellent panoramic view of the battlefield.

Chickamauga Battlefield Tour Stop 7. Retreat of the Union Right. Looking east from this point, you can see the Brotherton Cabin, site of the Confederate breakthrough on September 20. Longstreet's troops charged toward the spot where you are standing, catching Federal units by surprise. Many of the Union soldiers threw down their weapons and fled to the north and west. Others, including Rosecrans and two of his corps commanders, tried to halt the Confederate advance, but were driven from the field. To your left, on the knoll beyond the field, is a monument marking the site of Rosecrans's headquarters at the time of the breakthrough.

Chickamauga Battlefield Tour Stop 8. Snodgrass Hill. Longstreet's breakthrough shattered the right half of the Union line and left the other half exposed to a crushing flank attack. Union general George H. Thomas realized what had happened and ordered Union units still on the field to withdraw to this hill and form a new battle line. Longstreet's Confederates stormed the position again and again, but could not dislodge the Federals. In honor of his determined stand here, Thomas was nicknamed the "Rock of Chickamauga."

The log cabin you see marks the site of the 1863 home of the Snodgrass family.

Point Park (Lookout Mountain) Tour. The assault on Lookout Mountain was one of the major engagements in the Battle of Chattanooga. The Point Park Unit preserves a portion of the field on which the struggle for Lookout Mountain took place.

Begin your tour at the Visitor Center, where an eight-minute audiovisual program explains the Battle of Chattanooga and its significance in the Civil War. Across the street from the Visitor Center, a short foot trail leads to the point of Lookout Mountain. There are six numbered stops along the way.

Point Park Tour Stop 1. Entrance Gate. This impressive stone gate was constructed in 1905 by the U.S. Corps of Engineers.

Point Park Tour Stop 2. Siege Batteries. The three artillery batteries in this part of the park mark a small segment of the Confederate siege line that encircled Chattanooga from September to November 1863.

The first battery consists of two Parrott rifles, named after their inventor, Robert Parrott of New York. Weighing nearly one-half ton each, these guns had rifled barrels to improve accuracy. Their maximum range was two miles, firing at a five-degree elevation. The thick metal collar around the breech provided reinforcement against cracking from extreme heat.

The second battery, called Garrity's Battery, overlooks the Chattanooga River Valley. These guns are 12-pound Napoleons, so-called because their design was sponsored by Emperor Napoleon III of France. The 12-pound Napoleon was the standard cannon in both the Union and Confederate armies. It could fire a 12-pound iron ball 1,700 yards, but was most effective as a short-range weapon, firing shotgun-like blasts of canister against charging infantry.

The third battery, called Corput's Battery, is near the western overlook from which Sunset Rock may be seen. This rock was used as an observation point by Confederate general James Longstreet.

Point Park Tour Stop 3. New York Peace Memorial. This large monument, constructed of Tennessee marble and pink Massachusetts granite, features Union and Confederate soldiers shaking hands under one flag, signifying peace and national unity.

Point Park Tour Stop 4. Ochs Museum and Overlook. The exhibits in this museum tell the story of the Battle of Chattanooga.

Point Park Tour Stop 5. Cravens House. In the vicinity of this house, on November 24, 1863, Union and Confederate troops fought what later came to be known as the "Battle above the Clouds." Combat began in the morning and ended in midafternoon when the fog became too thick for the soldiers to see each other. That night

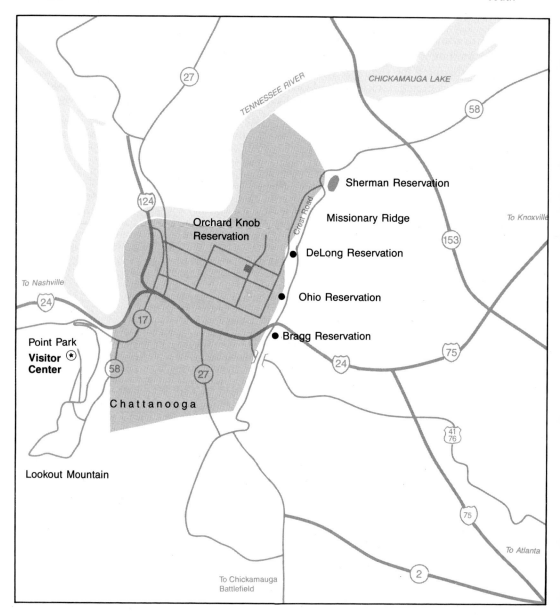

Chattanooga, Chickamauga and Chattanooga National Military Park

the Confederates withdrew from the mountain and joined their comrades on Missionary Ridge.

Point Park Tour Stop 6. Bluff Trail. The main hiking trail in the park begins here. Well-marked side trails branch off from the main trail. It was at this spot that Union soldiers climbed up to the point of the mountain and planted the Union Stars and Stripes.

Related Units. The National Park Service maintains several other areas that played important parts in the Battle of Chattanooga. **Orchard Knob Reservation** marks the site of Grant's field headquarters on November 25, 1863. It was from this high ground that he directed the attack on Missionary Ridge. **Bragg Reservation** on Missionary Ridge marks the site of the Confederate commander's headquarters during the siege of Chattanooga. The monument honors Illinois troops who participated in the Missionary Ridge assault. The **Ohio Reservation** honors Ohio troops who took part in the Battle of Chattanooga. **DeLong Reservation** is the site of a large monument to the Second Minnesota Regiment, which fought at both Chickamauga and Missionary Ridge. The **Sherman Reservation** marks the area where Sherman's troops made a series of unsuccessful assaults against the Confederate line.

CHAPTER 18

COWPENS NATIONAL BATTLEFIELD
(Revolutionary War)

P.O. Box 308
Chesnee, South Carolina 29323
Telephone: (803) 461-2828

On this field on January 17, 1781, a small American army commanded by Brigadier General Daniel Morgan defeated a larger force of British regulars led by Colonel Banastre Tarleton. This stunning patriot victory was a turning point in the struggle to keep the American Revolution alive in the South. Cowpens National Battlefield preserves the scene of the fighting.

Getting to the Park: Cowpens National Battlefield is located 2 miles southeast of Chesnee, South Carolina. Leave I-85 at Gaffney, South Carolina, and drive 11 miles northwest on South Carolina Highway 11 toward Chesnee. The park entrance is on the left, approximately ½ mile east of the intersection of South Carolina 11 and 110.

Gas, food, lodging: In Gaffney, 11 miles southeast on South Carolina 11.

Visitor Center: Museum and audiovisual program.

Activities: Ranger-conducted walking tours.

Handicapped Access: Visitor Center is fully accessible. Inquire at Visitor Center about accessibility of the Walking Tour trail.

On December 2, 1780, when General Nathanael Greene arrived in Charlotte, North Carolina, to take command of the patriot southern army, he inherited a strategic situation so desperate that it would have caused a less determined officer to contemplate surrender. His new command was "but the shadow of an army," leading "only an imaginary existence." Its 2,000 soldiers were hungry, sick, clad in rags, and utterly despondent after the crushing defeat they had suffered three months earlier at the Battle of Camden. With this pitifully weak force Greene somehow had to fend off Charles Lord Cornwallis and his British troops, who were poised to seize North Carolina and Virginia and stamp out the Revolution in the South.

Cornwallis's legions were arrayed across upland South Carolina in a broad arc, with the western flank at the settlement of Ninety Six, the center at Winnsboro, and the eastern flank at Camden. It was a powerful command—much too strong for the ragtag patriot army to confront in a set battle—so Greene was compelled to adopt an unorthodox and highly risky strategy. He would divide his force into two detachments and launch a raid deep behind British lines. One column, which he would lead personally, would circle around the British right at Camden, while the other, commanded by General Daniel Morgan, would sweep around the British left at Ninety Six.

The goal of this movement was to confound and ultimately paralyze Cornwallis's army with a series of quick marches and lightning, hit-and-run strikes. The danger was that the British might trap one of the small detachments and destroy it piecemeal: if this happened, the patriot cause in the South would be doomed.

Morgan vs. Tarleton

At the Battle of Saratoga (see Chapter 4), Daniel Morgan had emerged as one of the Continental Army's best field officers. A tough, hard-drinking Virginia woodsman, he was greatly admired by his soldiers, who affectionately called him the "Old Wagoner" and fought hard under his spirited leadership.

Morgan was an adept raider, so the assignment General Greene gave him on December 16, 1780, was much to his liking. He was to take 600 men across the Catawba River into South Carolina and move rapidly southwest toward Ninety Six, "spirit[ing] up the people" and "annoy[ing] the enemy in that quarter."

On December 30, the cavalry wing of Morgan's corps—120 riders led by Colonel William Washington—ambushed a force of Georgia loyalists at Hammond's Store and killed or wounded 150 of them. News of this bloody attack did more than just annoy the British: it infuriated them. At his headquarters in Winnsboro, Cornwallis sent for his most aggressive commander, Colonel Banastre Tarleton, and ordered him to go after Morgan. "Wipe him out," the British general said. "Catch him and smash him!"

Like Daniel Morgan, twenty-six-year-old Banastre Tarleton was a hard fighter, a man of "sanguinary and resentful temper," who showed no mercy to his enemies. As commander of the British Legion, a mixed force of cavalry and light infantry, he had become the scourge of South Carolina, earning the nicknames "Bloody Tarleton," and "Barbarous Benny," for his ruthless forays through the backcountry. Now he set off in hot pursuit of Morgan, eager to execute Cornwallis's harsh orders to the letter.

Rendezvous at the Cowpens

The 1,100 men of Tarleton's British legion moved fast, marching northwest through heavy rain, fording the Enoree, Tyger, and Pacolet rivers, heading for the patriot camp that was reported to be somewhere along the banks of Thicketty Creek.

Morgan did not learn of Tarleton's approach until the afternoon of January 15, when the British column was barely a day's march from his bivouac. He knew immediately that he was in deep trouble. His force was outnumbered two to one, and to make matters worse a third of his troops were inexperienced militiamen who were likely to run from a cavalry or bayonet charge.

The next morning scouts dashed into the Thicketty Creek camp with news that the British were now only a few hours away. Morgan's men left their breakfast fires burning and took flight, heading northeast toward the Cowpens, a frontier pasturing ground near the Broad River ford. Tarleton kept his legion hard on the heels of the retreating Americans, determined to catch them and bring them to battle.

Morgan halted his force when it reached the Cowpens on the afternoon of January 16. He could not hope to outrun Tarleton's fast-moving legionnaires, and this was the place he had chosen for making a stand. The terrain of the Cowpens favored the kind of defensive battle he wanted to fight: the wide, grassy meadow sloped up from the south—the direction the British would come from—and ended in two low ridges separated by a shallow swale.

That evening Morgan deployed his men and explained what part he expected them to play in the coming battle. One hundred twenty sharpshooters were placed in a skirmish line at the base of the slope. They would slow the British charge with accurate rifle fire, then fall back behind the second line, which was drawn up 100 yards to their rear. This formation was composed of South Carolina and Georgia militia commanded by Colonel Andrew Pickens. Knowing the militiamen's propensity to run from a charging foe, Morgan asked them to fire just two volleys and then retire.

The heart of Morgan's defense-in-depth was the third line, manned by the army's best troops, the Maryland and Delaware Continentals commanded by Colonel John Eager Howard, and by the well-seasoned Virginia militia. Morgan ordered this 500-man detachment to hold its ground. If pressed hard the Continentals and Virginians had permission to move back across the swale to the second ridgetop, but under no circumstances were they to break and run. In the rear, the cavalry was told to wait in reserve, ready to ride into the battle when the moment was right.

January 17, 1781: The Battle of Cowpens

Shortly after 7 A.M. on January 17, the advancing British Legion made contact with Morgan's skirmish line at the south end of the Cowpens. Fifty cavalrymen resplendent in green jackets and brass helmets galloped forward to reconnoiter the American position. Fifteen were shot from their saddles by the concealed riflemen, who then retreated, according to plan, behind the militia's line.

Tarleton was unperturbed by this rude reception. After two weeks of pursuit he had caught his foe, and now he was eager to press the attack. On his orders, 1,000 red-coated infantrymen, escorted on each flank by 50 dragoons, lowered their bayonets and advanced toward the patriot battle line 400 yards distant.

Following Morgan's instructions, the South Carolina and Georgia militia waited until the British were within musket range; they raked the red ranks with two killing volleys, then filed off the field, reforming in the swale behind the ridge held by Colonel Howard's Continentals.

Thinking that the patriot army was on the verge of collapse, Tarleton threw his reserve—a battalion of Highlanders—into the assault against the third American line. The Scottish soldiers struck the Continentals' right flank hard and threatened to turn it. Colonel Howard ordered the men on that end of the line to wheel about to face

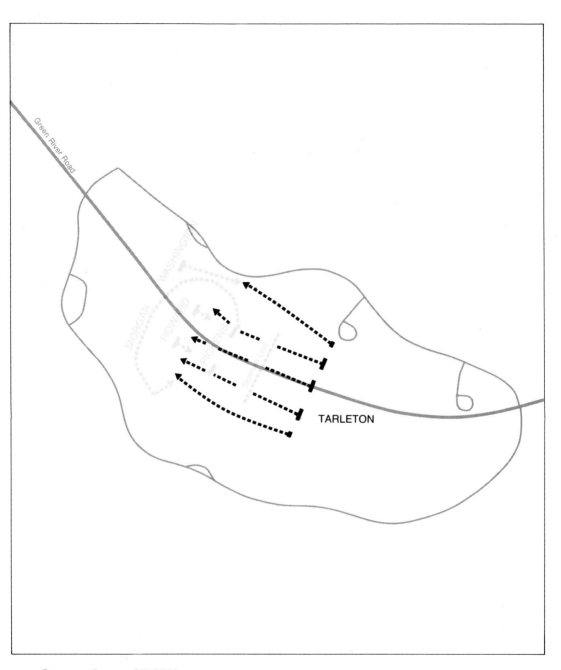

Cowpens, January 17, 1781

the threat, but his command was misunderstood and the entire patriot formation began to withdraw.

For an instant the outcome of the battle—and the fate of the Revolution in the South—hung in the balance. The Americans were retreating in confusion, and the redcoats were charging forward to seize victory. Just when it seemed a rout was inevitable, Daniel Morgan galloped onto the field and rallied the Continentals. They stopped, turned, and fired into the tightly packed British formation, which was barely thirty yards away. At the same moment the patriot cavalry struck the British right and Colonel Pickens's reorganized militia moved up and blasted the Highlanders on the British left.

This powerful triple punch staggered Tarleton's men, and in his words "an unaccountable panic extended itself along the whole line." In a twinkling, roles were reversed. The patriots surged forward triumphantly while the British fled helter-skelter back the way they had come.

Morgan had turned impending defeat into stunning, glorious victory: 110 redcoats were dead, 200 were wounded, and 500 had been taken prisoner. The patriots had lost only 12 killed and 60 wounded.

An Important Morale Builder

By taking advantage of terrain, tailoring tactics to fit his troops' strengths and weaknesses, and providing courageous leadership at the critical juncture, Daniel Morgan scored a triumph that was as important psychologically as it was strategically. The spirits of South Carolinians were lifted by Tarleton's humiliation, and the patriot soldiers gained new confidence in their fighting ability. Coming barely three months after the American victory at Kings Mountain (see Chapter 25), the Battle of Cowpens was a turning point in the struggle to keep the Revolution alive in the South.

Touring the Park

Begin your tour at the Visitor Center, where maps and exhibits describe the Battle of Cowpens and explain its significance.

A three-mile tour road runs through the park. There are four numbered stops.

Auto Tour: Stop 1. Prelude to Cowpens. The meadow in front of you was a frontier pasturing ground in the eighteenth century. Farmers herding their cattle into this area to graze called it the Cowpens. Daniel Morgan was familiar with the open, sloping terrain of the Cowpens and knew it would be a good place to fight a defensive battle.

Auto Tour: Stop 2. Robert Scruggs House. This log cabin was built beside the old Green River Road several years after the battle. It is an outstanding example of backcountry architecture and demonstrates the building techniques used on the eighteenth-century frontier.

Auto Tour: Stop 3. Battlefield Overlook. Directly in front of you is the place where Tarleton formed his line of battle on the morning of January 17, 1781. The British advanced from your left to your right, where Morgan had his skirmishers positioned.

Auto Tour: Stop 4. Battlefield Overlook. From this vantage point, looking

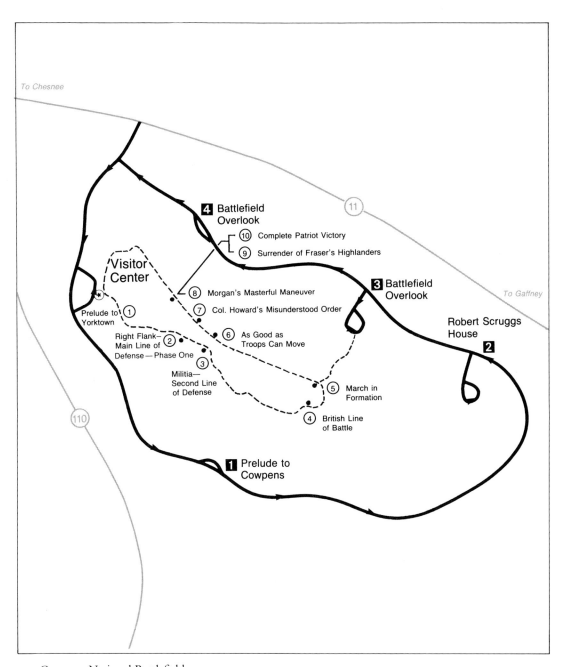

To Chesnee

4 Battlefield Overlook

⑩ Complete Patriot Victory

⑨ Surrender of Fraser's Highlanders

11

3 Battlefield Overlook

To Gaffney

Visitor Center

⑧ Morgan's Masterful Maneuver

⑦ Col. Howard's Misunderstood Order

Prelude to Yorktown ①

Right Flank— Main Line of Defense—Phase One ②

⑥ As Good as Troops Can Move

Robert Scruggs House

2

Militia— Second Line of Defense ③

⑤ March in Formation

④ British Line of Battle

110

1 Prelude to Cowpens

Cowpens National Battlefield

south, you can see the low ridges where Pickens's militia and Howard's Continentals were drawn up to meet the British attack.

A walking trail begins at the Visitor Center and leads through the heart of the battlefield. Exhibits along the way explain the troop movements in detail and describe the events that culminated in the patriot victory.

Walking Tour: Stop 1. Prelude to Yorktown. The Battle of Cowpens was an important link in a chain of British military disasters in the South. These setbacks frustrated Cornwallis and caused him to revamp his strategy, a change that ultimately led him and his army to Yorktown and final defeat.

Walking Tour: Stop 2. Right Flank—Main Line of Defense—Phase One. Colonel Howard's Maryland and Delaware Continentals, the best soldiers in the American army, were formed in a line that extended some 700 feet from this point northeast along the ridge. Morgan was counting on the Continentals to hold their ground at all costs.

Walking Tour: Stop 3. Militia—Second Line of Defense. The South Carolina and Georgia militia, commanded by Colonel Andrew Pickens, were arrayed in battle formation here. Militia units were notoriously unsteady under fire, so Morgan did not expect the Georgians and South Carolinians to make a stand. He asked only that they deliver two volleys at killing distance (100 yards or less) before retiring from the field.

Walking Tour: Stop 4. British Line of Battle. On this ground, in the gray half light of dawn, Tarleton deployed his troops for the attack. The infantry and artillery straddled the Green River Road; 50 mounted dragoons guarded each flank. Behind this line, a battalion of Highlanders and 200 cavalrymen waited in reserve.

Walking Tour: Stop 5. March in Formation. After forming his battle line, Tarleton ordered the infantry to march in formation toward the American position 400 yards up the Green River Road. From this point on, the walking trail follows the old road, the route along which the British advanced.

Walking Tour: Stop 6. As Good as Troops Can Move. When the approaching British infantry came within musket range, the Georgia and South Carolina militia opened fire, concentrating on the officers, who stood out because of their epaulettes. After delivering two volleys, they filed off to the left, "moving as good as troops can move" around the ridge held by the Continentals to the safety of the swale behind.

Walking Tour: Stop 7. Colonel Howard's Misunderstood Order. When the American militia retreated in apparent disorder, the British infantry sensed that victory was in their grasp. They lowered their bayonets and charged up the hill toward the Continentals. When a crashing volley halted this assault in its tracks, Tarleton threw in his reserve. The British cavalry struck the American left flank while the battalion of Highlanders attacked the right.

To fend off the Highlanders, Colonel Howard ordered the soldiers on the right flank to turn and reform at a right angle to the original battle line. His command was misunderstood, and the entire formation began to retreat toward the second ridge line.

Walking Tour: Stop 8. Morgan's Masterful Maneuver. When Morgan saw the Continentals withdrawing, he rode forward to rally them. At his command, the seasoned soldiers from Maryland and Delaware abruptly about-faced, fired a murderous point-blank volley into the ranks of pursuing redcoats, then charged with their bayonets leveled. At almost the same moment, Colonel Washington and the patriot cavalry struck the British right, scattering Tarleton's cavalry and panicking his infantry.

Walking Tour: Stop 9. Surrender of Fraser's Highlanders. After being reorganized by Colonel Pickens, the Georgia and South Carolina militia units advanced back into the fray, circling all the way around the battle ridge and coming up on the exposed British left flank. They poured heavy fire into the ranks of the Highlanders, and in the words of Tarleton, "threw them into confusion." Moments later, the entire British force broke and ran, and "neither promises nor threats" could stop them. The Highlanders were cut off, and most of them threw down their weapons and surrendered.

Walking Tour: Stop 10. Complete Patriot Victory. With skill and luck, Daniel Morgan achieved a perfect concentration of forces at the battle's critical moment. Hit simultaneously by the patriot cavalry, the Continentals, and the militia, the British army collapsed.

In all, Tarleton lost 810 men killed, wounded, or taken prisoner, an astonishing 74 percent of his command, while Morgan lost just 12 men killed and 60 wounded. It was a remarkable victory, as complete as any in the Revolutionary War.

CHAPTER 19

FORT DONELSON
NATIONAL BATTLEFIELD
(Civil War)

P.O. Box F
Dover, Tennessee 37058
Telephone: (615) 232-5706

In a two-day battle fought on February 14–15, 1862, a Union army captured Confederate-held Fort Donelson on the Cumberland River, opening the way for an invasion of the South. Triumph at Fort Donelson gave the Union its first major victory of the Civil War and its first real war hero, General Ulysses S. Grant. Fort Donelson National Battlefield preserves the scene of the battle as well as the historic Dover Hotel, where the Confederate commander had his headquarters and where he surrendered to General Grant.

Getting to the Park: Fort Donelson National Battlefield is located 1 mile west of Dover, Tennessee, on U.S. 79.

Gas, food, lodging: In Dover.

Visitor Center: Museum and gift shop; audiovisual program on the battle.

Activities: Living-history demonstrations are presented during the summer months. Inquire at Visitor Center for schedule and locations. A short film on the surrender of Fort Donelson is presented at the Dover Hotel.

Handicapped Access: Visitor Center is accessible, but rest rooms are down two flights of stairs. All significant battlefield features can be seen from a car.

A pall of gloom and frustration hung over the North as the new year of 1862 began. After nine months of war Union forces had yet to win a major victory, and confident Confederate armies, arrayed in a defensive line stretching from Missouri to Virginia, stood ready to thwart any attempt to bring the rebelling southern states to heel.

In the West, Union general Henry W. Halleck—nicknamed "Old Brains" because of his encyclopedic knowledge of military science—and his subordinate, General Ulysses S. Grant, looked for a way to pierce the Confederate line. Their attention was drawn to the Cumberland and Tennessee rivers. From the Union base at Paducah, Kentucky, the Cumberland led south and east to the important Confederate manufacturing center of Nashville. The Tennessee, an excellent natural highway for transporting troops and supplies, led due south to Mississippi and Alabama.

Near the town of Dover, Tennessee, just south of the Kentucky state line, the two streams ran parallel to each other, separated by a neck of land only twelve miles wide. Here, the Confederates had built a pair of earthen forts—Fort Henry on the Tennessee and Fort Donelson on the Cumberland. If Halleck and Grant wanted to use the rivers as avenues of invasion, they would first have to break through this well-guarded choke point.

Fort Henry Falls

On January 30, 1862, Halleck ordered Grant to move against Fort Henry. The campaign was to be a joint army-navy operation involving 15,000 troops, led by Grant, and four ironclad gunboats commanded by Flag Officer Andrew H. Foote. The attack plan called for the gunboats to steam up the Tennessee River and bombard the fort, pinning down its garrison until the infantry arrived to deliver the coup de grace.

Foote's armor-plated steamboats, each one mounted with thirteen cannon, opened fire on Fort Henry at noon on February 6. The Confederate defenders promptly answered with their nine heavy guns, and a noisy artillery battle ensued. The ironclads closed to almost point-blank range, and one by one the Confederate guns were knocked out. At 2 P.M. the fort struck its colors, but less than 100 of the garrison remained to be taken prisoner. The remaining 2,500 men had escaped to Fort Donelson, twelve miles to the east.

Grant Surrounds Fort Donelson

If Grant was perturbed that the gunboats had captured Fort Henry without any assistance from his infantry, he did not admit it. He quickly shifted his attention from the Tennessee to the Cumberland, and announced his intention to surround and seize Fort Donelson.

Donelson was a more daunting objective than Fort Henry. Situated on the brow of a high bluff, it commanded the river with a dozen large cannon. On the landward side, it was protected by a three-mile arc of rifle pits and log-and-earth breastworks, extending from flooded Hickman Creek on the north to the town of Dover on the south. Some 15,000 Confederates, commanded by Generals John Floyd, Gideon Pillow, Simon Buckner, and Bushrod Johnson, occupied this imposing defensive position.

On the morning of February 11, Grant's troops set out for Fort Donelson. The day was sunny and unseasonably warm, and many of the soldiers threw away their heavy blankets and overcoats as they marched along. The next day, the Union army encircled Fort Donelson's outerworks and launched several exploratory attacks, which were thrown back with heavy casualties.

During the night the weather turned wintry. The temperature plummeted to 12 degrees fahrenheit, the wind howled out of the north, and snow began to fall, punishing the men who had foolishly discarded their warm clothing. In the morning, the chilled soldiers beheld a ghostly landscape shrouded in ice and snow; there would be no fighting that day.

General Simon B. Buckner was one of four generals commanding the Confederate forces at Fort Donelson. It fell to him to surrender the Confederate garrison. Cook Collection, Valentine Museum, Richmond, Virginia.

February 14–15, 1862: The Battle of Fort Donelson

Flag Officer Foote's gunboats had moved from the Tennessee River to the Cumberland, and on February 14 Grant decided to give them a chance to duplicate their Fort Henry exploit. The gun battle began shortly after noon, but this time the results were different. Fort Donelson's cannon battered the ironclads with heavy fire and forced them to withdraw downriver.

The Confederate generals were elated by this success, but they knew they had to break Grant's siege soon or face starvation. When darkness fell, they massed their troops against the Union right, just south of Dover, in preparation for an attack the next morning.

At daybreak on February 15, the gray troops surged forward. Fierce fighting raged across the snowy fields, and slowly, grudgingly, the blue line fell back. It appeared that the Confederates were going to make a successful breakout and escape to Nashville, but Grant arrived at the scene of the battle and rallied his faltering soldiers. He then ordered the Union division on the far left to storm the Confederate breastworks, which had been stripped of troops to reinforce the morning attack.

The blue ranks swarmed over the lightly defended Rebel entrenchments and threatened to seize Fort Donelson itself. Faced with this sudden, dire threat, the Confederate generals called off their assault and returned their men to the outerworks to meet Grant's counterattack. The Union charge was stopped short of the fort, but the Confederates found themselves bottled up again.

During the night, 2,000 men led by Generals Floyd and Pillow crossed the Cumberland in boats, escaping Grant's trap. Another 1,000 troops followed cavalryman Nathan Bedford Forrest through the Union line below Dover, evading capture. Command of the fort and the remaining 12,000 troops was left to General Simon Buckner.

Early on the morning of February 16, Buckner sent a message to Grant asking for terms. "No terms except an unconditional and immediate surrender can be accepted," Grant brusquely replied. "I propose to move immediately on your works."

Recognizing the hopelessness of his situation, and wishing to avoid further bloodshed, Buckner capitulated.

"Unconditional Surrender" Grant

Church bells rang in celebration across the North when the fall of Fort Donelson was announced. At long last, the Union had its first major victory. It also had its first real war hero, U. S. Grant, whose initials, the newspapers said, stood for "unconditional surrender."

For the Confederacy, the defeat at Donelson was a major setback. The vaunted gray defensive line had been breached, most of northern Tennessee was in Union hands, and an invasion of the Deep South along the Cumberland and Tennessee rivers was now inevitable.

Touring the Park

Begin your tour at the Visitor Center, where museum displays and an audiovisual program describe the battle and its significance in the Civil War.

A self-guided auto tour leads through the park. There are eleven numbered stops along the way.

Stop 1. Fort Donelson. The grass-covered earthen parapets you see are the remains of Fort Donelson, built by Confederate soldiers and slaves over a seven-month period in 1861. The fort's ten-foot-high walls encompassed fifteen acres and protected the Cumberland River batteries from landward attack.

Stop 2. Log Huts. During the winter months, soldiers of Fort Donelson's Confederate garrison lived in log huts like this one. Sometime after the surrender, the Federals burned the 100 log huts in an attempt to halt an outbreak of measles. This structure is a reproduction.

Stop 3. River Batteries. The Confederates placed guns here to prevent the Union navy from using the Cumberland River as an invasion route. On February 14, 1862, the inexperienced Rebel gunners fought an artillery duel with Union flag officer Andrew Foote's fleet of gunboats. After a thunderous exchange that could be heard thirty-five miles away, the Federal fleet was forced to withdraw.

Stop 4. Buckner's Final Defense. After blunting the Confederate breakout at-

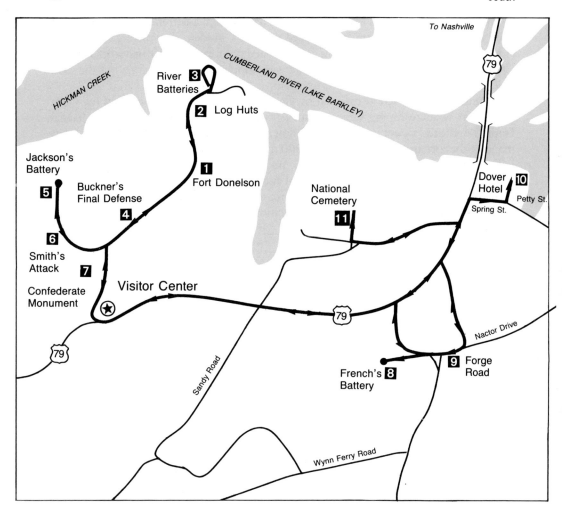

Fort Donelson National Battlefield

tempt on February 15, Grant ordered the Union division of General C. F. Smith to attack the far right flank of the Rebel line. The Federal troops drove the Confederates back to this ridge, where they made a desperate stand until reinforcements arrived.

Stop 5. Jackson's Battery. This four-gun battery supported the right flank of the Confederate defensive line. It was withdrawn early on the morning of February 15, and was not in position to meet the Union attack in this sector.

Stop 6. Smith's Attack. The Federals of General C. F. Smith's division charged up these snow-covered slopes on February 15 in an all-out assault against the right flank of the Confederate outerworks.

Stop 7. Confederate Monument. This monument to the Confederate soldiers who fought and died at Fort Donelson was erected in 1933 by the Tennessee Division of the United Daughters of the Confederacy.

Stop 8. French's Battery. This four-gun battery, in conjunction with Maney's Battery to the west, was positioned to prevent a Union attack down Erin Hollow toward Fort Donelson.

Stop 9. Forge Road. Early on the morning of February 15, the Confederates launched an attack in this area and succeeded in opening a hole in the Union siege line. The chance for a clean breakout was lost, however, when Grant rallied his troops and launched a swift counterattack.

Stop 10. Dover Hotel. This structure, built between 1851 and 1853, served as Confederate general Simon B. Buckner's headquarters during the Battle of Fort Donelson. It was here, on February 16, 1862, that Buckner surrendered to Union general Ulysses S. Grant.

At the river landing just north of the hotel, 13,000 Confederate prisoners were loaded on transports for the journey north to Federal prison camps. Following the battle, the hotel was converted into a Union hospital.

Stop 11. National Cemetery. In 1867, 655 Union soldiers killed in the Battle of Fort Donelson were reburied in this cemetery. Five hundred four of them are unknown.

CHAPTER 20

FORT PULASKI NATIONAL MONUMENT

(Civil War)

P.O. Box 98
Tybee Island, Georgia 31328
Telephone: (912) 786-5787

On April 10, 1862, Union artillery batteries located on the northwest shore of Tybee Island opened fire on Confederate-held Fort Pulaski. Pulaski's defenders believed that the fort's seven-and-a-half-foot-thick brick walls were impregnable, but shells from the Union force's rifled cannon proved them wrong. The Confederate garrison was forced to surrender on April 11, and the era of masonry forts came to an abrupt end. Fort Pulaski National Monument preserves the fort.

Getting to the Park: Fort Pulaski National Monument is located 14 miles east of Savannah, Georgia, on U.S. 80.

Gas, food, lodging: In Savannah.

Visitor Center: Exhibits and gift shop; audiovisual program.

Activities: Interpretive talks by park personnel and occasional living-history demonstrations. Inquire at Visitor Center for schedule.

Handicapped Access: Visitor Center is fully accessible. The fort's parade ground and first-tier casemates are accessible, but assistance may be required over the ramp through the sally port. Inside the fort, some rooms are separated by minor barriers, such as high thresholds or small steps. The doors of some rooms are too narrow to admit wheelchairs.

Throughout history, military strategists have proclaimed the development of the "ultimate" weapon or the "impregnable" defense, only to see their faith in its invincibility shattered by the sudden, shocking appearance of new technology. Such an event occurred on April 10–11, 1862, when Union gunners, firing rifled cannon, blasted gaping holes in the walls of Confederate-held Fort Pulaski and rendered an entire generation of masonry fortifications obsolete.

The Third System Forts

Following the War of 1812, U.S. military engineers began constructing an elaborate network of coastal fortifications known as the Third System. Anchoring this chain of defensive works were more than thirty large masonry forts sited at strategic locations along the Gulf and Atlantic coasts.

One of the new forts, begun in 1829 and finished in 1847, was Fort Pulaski, erected on Cockspur Island to guard the river approaches to Savannah, Georgia. Designed by General Simon Bernard, a famous French engineer, and requiring 25 million bricks to build, the pentagonal fort was considered a masterpiece of military engineering, one of the "most spectacular harbor defense structures" in the United States. Many believed that its seven-and-a-half-foot-thick walls, reinforced by massive masonry piers, were impervious to cannon fire: "You might as well bombard the Rocky Mountains," proclaimed Joseph G. Totten, U.S. Chief of Engineers.

On January 3, 1861, two weeks after South Carolina seceded from the Union, Georgia governor Joseph E. Brown ordered the state militia to seize Fort Pulaski to prevent Federal troops from reinforcing it, as they had done at Fort Sumter in Charleston Harbor the week before (see Chapter 21). The militia followed Brown's instructions, and when Georgia seceded on January 19, 1861, Fort Pulaski was turned over to the Confederate States of America.

Union Blockade

Following the outbreak of hostilities between North and South in the spring of 1861, President Abraham Lincoln ordered the U.S. Navy to blockade the southern coast in an effort to strangle the Confederate economy. Savannah, one of the largest and busiest of the southern harbor cities, was targeted for special attention.

On November 7, 1861, a Union task force sailed into Port Royal Sound, South Carolina, and dropped anchor off Hilton Head Island, just fifteen miles north of Fort Pulaski. Navy warships bombarded Forts Walker and Beauregard, driving the Confederate defenders away, and Union infantry landed and established a beachhead from which they could mount campaigns against targets up and down the South Carolina and Georgia coasts.

Alarmed by the growing Union presence on Hilton Head, the Confederates decided to evacuate Tybee Island at the mouth of the Savannah River. This withdrawal gave the Federals the site they needed to lay siege to Fort Pulaski. Early in December, Navy ships isolated the fort from the mainland, and in February, Union soldiers commanded by Engineer Captain Quincy A. Gillmore moved onto Tybee Island to begin siege operations.

The Fall of Fort Pulaski

During February and March 1862, the northwest shore of Tybee Island was a scene of feverish activity as Captain Gillmore's soldiers hacked gun emplacements out of the swamp and then manhandled thirty-six mortars and cannon into place. Across the sluggish, blue-green expanse of Tybee Roads, the 384 officers and men of Fort Pulaski's garrison watched these preparations with considerable interest but little con-

Captain Quincy A. Gillmore led the Union expeditionary force that captured Fort Pulaski. Library of Congress.

cern. A mile of water and seven and a half feet of solid brick separated them from the muzzles of the Union guns; all previous military experience indicated that smooth-bore artillery firing from a range of over 1,000 yards had no chance of breaching the fort's heavy masonry walls.

Confident that the Federal batteries posed no threat, Colonel Charles Olmstead, commander of the Confederate garrison, rejected Captain Gillmore's formal demand that Fort Pulaski surrender. What Olmstead did not know was that among the thirty-six guns positioned on Tybee Island were ten new rifled cannon. Unlike conventional smoothbore artillery, these pieces had spiraled, or rifled, grooves inside their barrels. The bullet-shaped projectiles they fired engaged this rifling and left the muzzle with a rapid spin, greatly increasing their range, accuracy, and penetrating power.

Thus, when the Union siege batteries began the bombardment of Fort Pulaski on the morning of April 10, 1862, the Confederate defenders were flabbergasted. Instead of enjoying the spectacle of cannonballs falling short in Tybee Roads, they had to dive for cover as screaming projectiles smashed into the parade ground. The Federal gunners soon adjusted their fire and began to concentrate on hitting the angle formed by the south and southeastern walls. Projectile after projectile slammed into the fort at this point, pulverizing the brick and mortar with sledgehammer force. By noon on April 11, the southeastern casemates had been breached in several spots, and the rifled cannon were firing explosive shells through the holes, trying to hit the fort's main powder magazine.

Olmstead and his men were utterly demoralized by the events of the past thirty hours; their faith in Fort Pulaski's invincibility had been shattered along with the brick bastions, and to make matters worse, they had no way of fighting back. When Union projectiles began to explode against the walls and roof of the magazine, which held more than twenty tons of gunpowder, they knew the jig was up. "That the fort could and would be absolutely destroyed by the force of the enemy was a demonstrated fact," Olmstead later wrote. "I did not feel warranted in exposing the garrison to the hazard of the blowing up of our main magazine—a danger which had just been proved well within the limits of probability."

He ordered the Confederate colors to be struck and the white flag of surrender hoisted in its place.

End of an an Era

The fall of Fort Pulaski created a sensation: Gillmore was breveted a brigadier general for his bold use of a new weapon, while Olmstead and his command were ignominiously loaded aboard a ship to be transported north to a prison in New York.

Exhibiting the same industriousness that had enabled them to carve gun emplacements out of the muck of Tybee Island, the Union soldiers quickly repaired the damage their bombardment had caused. With Fort Pulaski in hand, they had no need to march against Savannah. Sealed off from the ocean by the guns of the fort and the ships of the U.S. Navy, the port was no longer of any strategic value.

To military men, both Union and Confederate, the significance of Fort Pulaski's

Rifled cannon like this one blasted gaping holes in Confederate-held Fort Pulaski and rendered an entire generation of masonry fortifications obsolete. Copyright 1983 Eastern National Parks and Monuments Association, photograph by Ed Elvidge.

destruction went far beyond the blockading of Savannah and crippling of the southern economy, however. The strategic dogma of half a century, and a vast outpouring of money and labor, had gone up in smoke: rifled cannon had made an entire generation of masonry forts obsolete. "The result of this bombardment," summed up a perceptive Union officer, "must cause a change in the construction of fortifications as radical as that foreshadowed in naval architecture by the conflict between the *Monitor* and the *Merrimac*. No works of stone or brick can resist the impact of rifled artillery of heavy calibre."

The siege of Fort Pulaski marked the end of one era and the beginning of another.

Touring the Park

Begin your tour at the Visitor Center, where exhibits and an audiovisual program provide background on the siege of Fort Pulaski, the history of masonry forts, and the impact of rifled cannon on nineteenth-century military strategy.

From the Visitor Center a paved foot trail leads to the fort. There are twelve numbered stops along the way.

Stop 1. The Moat. The fort is surrounded by a water-filled ditch, seven feet deep and from thirty-two to forty-eight feet wide. The water enters through a canal from the Savannah River.

Stop 2. The Demilune. This large triangular earthwork—called a demilune—was built after the Civil War to guard the rear, or gorge, wall of the fort. The earthen mounds covered four powder magazines and the passageways to several gun emplacements.

During the 1862 siege, the area was flat and surrounded by a parapet, which shielded a number of storage buildings.

Stop 3. The Drawbridge. The drawbridge and sally port were designed to make forced entry into the fort impossible. When the drawbridge was raised, a sturdy wooden grille, called a portcullis, dropped into place through the granite lintel above. Bolt-studded wooden doors closed behind that.

If attackers somehow managed to get through the portcullis, they still had to pass two rows of rifle slits in the sally port walls, then break through another set of doors.

Stop 4. Gorge Wall. The gorge, or rear, wall housed the officers' quarters. Several of the rooms have been furnished to illustrate what life was like for the occupants during the Civil War.

Stop 5. The Northwest Magazine. The magazine, with its twelve- to fifteen-foot-thick walls, was the storage place for ammunition and gunpowder. When projectiles from the Federal rifled cannon struck the magazine walls on April 11, threatening to blow up the 40,000 pounds of powder inside, the Confederate commander decided to surrender.

Stop 6. Confederate Defense System. Fort Pulaski's Confederate defenders made a number of modifications to protect themselves from the effects of a bombardment. Earthen traverses were built between the guns and over the magazine, ditches were dug in the parade ground to catch rolling cannonballs, and a heavy timber blindage was erected to shield the interior perimeter from flying shell fragments.

Stop 7. The Prison. During the winter of 1864, the northeast, southeast, and

A Fort Pulaski casemate. National Park Service, photograph by Cecil W. Stoughton.

part of the south casemate were used to house Confederate prisoners of war. The living conditions were terrible. After the war, several political prisoners were incarcerated here.

Stop 8. The Breach. Union gunners on Tybee Island concentrated their fire on this section of the fort. Over a thirty-hour period, the rifled artillery projectiles smashed several holes through the seven-and-a-half-foot-thick wall. The gaps were repaired within six weeks of the fort's surrender.

Stop 9. Southwest Bastion. After a fire in 1895, this bastion was left unrepaired. It reveals details of the fort's construction. The brick arches under the rampart carry weight to the counterarches in the floor, which are supported by a timber framework and pilings driven seventy feet into the mud of Cockspur Island.

Stop 10. Cistern Room. The cistern you see here is one of ten that were used to store fresh water. Rain ran down through lead pipes in the brick piers into the tanks, which could hold more than 200,000 gallons.

Stop 11. Exhibits and Rest Room. This section of the gorge wall contains exhibits on the fort, its garrison, and the artillery that was its downfall.

Stop 12. Damaged Wall. From this vantage point you can see the craters made by Union artillery hits on the south and southeast walls. Some of the projectiles are still embedded in the brick. A total of 5,275 rounds were fired at Fort Pulaski in thirty-odd hours—more than two rounds per minute.

CHAPTER 21

FORT SUMTER NATIONAL MONUMENT
(Civil War)

1214 Middle Street
Sullivan's Island, South Carolina 29482
Telephone: (803) 883-3123

On April 12, 1861, the first shots of the Civil War were fired when Confederate batteries ringing Charleston Harbor opened up on Union-held Fort Sumter. The bombardment lasted for thirty-four hours and ended with the garrison's surrender. For the next four years the fort remained in Confederate hands despite determined Union attempts to retake it, both by bombardment and by storm. Fort Sumter National Monument preserves the remains of the historic fort.

Getting to the Park: Fort Sumter is located on an island in Charleston Harbor and can be reached only by boat. Tour boats operated by a National Park Service concessionaire leave from the City Marina on Lockwood Drive, just south of U.S. 17 in Charleston. For boat schedules call (803) 722-1691 or write Fort Sumter Tours, Inc., P.O. Box 59, Charleston, S.C. 29402. The Visitor Center is located at 1214 Middle Street on Sullivan's Island. From Charleston, take U.S. 17 to its intersection with South Carolina Highway 703 in Mount Pleasant. Take South Carolina 703 south, across the Intercoastal Waterway, until it intersects Middle Street on Sullivan's Island. Turn right on Middle Street. The Visitor Center is approximately 2 miles ahead.

Gas, food, lodging: In Charleston.

Visitor Center: Museum and gift shop; audiovisual programs. There is a separate museum at Fort Sumter.

Activities: Upon your arrival at the fort a park ranger presents a brief history and orientation lecture.

Handicapped Access: Visitor Center is fully accessible. Fort Sumter's parade ground level and the rest rooms are fully accessible. Boarding and disembarking from the tour boat may present some difficulties to visitors in wheelchairs because of steep gangways, but assistance is available.

At 4:30 A.M. on April 12, 1861, a single mortar shell rose above the city of Charleston, South Carolina. It zoomed upward in a fiery red arc, hung momentarily, then burst directly over the walls of Fort Sumter in Charleston Harbor. Moments later forty-two other guns joined in the bombardment, and streaks of light flashed in great parabolic curves across the dark sky. The thunder of heavy explosions rumbled over the water, and clouds of powder smoke drifted like sulfurous fogbanks in the cool morning air. The Civil War—America's bloodiest and most divisive armed conflict—had begun.

"The Gage Is Thrown Down"

Four decades of sectional strife between North and South came to a head with the election of President Abraham Lincoln in November 1860. Certain that the triumph of Lincoln and the Republican Party meant an end to slavery, South Carolina seceded from the Union on December 20, 1860. Within six weeks six other southern states— Mississippi, Alabama, Florida, Georgia, Louisiana, and Texas—followed suit, and in early February 1861, they joined with South Carolina in forming the Confederate States of America. All Federal military installations in the seceded states were surrendered to the new government, with two important exceptions: Fort Pickens at Pensacola, Florida, and Fort Sumter at Charleston.

Fort Sumter was part of the Third System of American coastal defenses, a chain of forts authorized by Congress after the War of 1812. Started in 1828, and still under construction when it was occupied by Federal troops in December 1860, Sumter squatted on a swampy shoal at the entrance to Charleston Harbor. Built of bricks on a granite foundation, the five-foot-thick walls loomed nearly fifty feet above the water level at low tide, enclosing a pentagonal parade ground of one acre. The three-story-high barracks could house 650 men, and the casemates and terreplein had space for 135 pieces of coastal artillery.

Despite its formidable appearance, Fort Sumter was in poor condition for defense when Major Robert Anderson and two companies of the U.S. First Artillery—about eighty-five officers and men—moved into it on December 26, 1860. Only fifteen cannon had been mounted, workmen were camping in the unfinished barracks, and the parade ground was littered with "building materials, guns, carriages, shot, shell, derricks, timbers, blocks and tackle, and coils of rope in great confusion."

Nevertheless, Anderson had been given instructions to "hold possession of the fort . . . and if attacked . . . to defend yourself to the last extremity." He put his command and the eighty laborers who had been occupying the fort to work, bricking up open embrasures, removing debris from the parade ground, mounting additional guns, and distributing ammunition in anticipation of a Confederate attack.

These warlike preparations infuriated the citizens of Charleston: "loud and violent were the expressions of feeling against Major Anderson and his action," wrote one Charlestonian. Militia units occupied Fort Moultrie, Fort Johnson, and Castle Pinckney, three older harbor fortifications, and began building batteries on Morris Island and Sullivan's Island, directly across the water from Fort Sumter. South Carolina governor Francis Pickens demanded that the Federal government evacuate Charleston Harbor, but lame duck president James Buchanan refused. "If I withdraw Anderson

Major Robert Anderson commanded the Fort Sumter garrison during the 1861 siege. Library of Congress.

from Sumter," he said, "I can travel home . . . by the light of my own burning effigies." Instead he dispatched the ship *Star of the West*, carrying 200 men, small arms and ammunition, and several months' provisions, to the relief of the fort.

The *Star of the West* sailed into Charleston Harbor on January 9, 1861, but cannon mounted on Morris Island opened fire and drove the ship away. Two days later, Governor Pickens called on Major Anderson to surrender. Anderson declined and stepped up his preparations for meeting an attack. More guns were mounted in the first tier of casemates and along the fort's parapet, bombproofs and covered traverses were constructed on the parade ground, and several cannon were set up to serve as mortars.

The South Carolinians also made preparations. An "ironclad" battery made of logs armored with plate iron was erected at Cummings Point on Morris Island, and work began on new batteries on Sullivan's Island, James Island, and near the village of Mount Pleasant.

On March 1, the Confederate States government, in the person of General Pierre G. T. Beauregard, took control of military operations at Charleston. West Point graduate, Mexican War hero, and late captain in the U.S. Army, Beauregard had once studied artillery tactics under Major Anderson. Now student and teacher readied themselves for a high-stakes confrontation.

On April 4, 1861, a month after his inaugural, President Lincoln decided to resupply Fort Sumter. When informed of this, Confederate president Jefferson Davis ordered Beauregard to demand Sumter's surrender, "and if this is refused proceed . . . to reduce it." The fort's supply of fresh meat and vegetables was cut off on April 7, and its mail was seized. On the afternoon of April 11, three of Beauregard's staff officers rowed out to Sumter under a flag of truce and presented Major Anderson with an ultimatum: evacuate or face dire consequences. Anderson refused. "The gage is thrown down," blared the Charleston *Mercury*, "and we accept the challenge. . . . God and Battle must decide the issue between the hirelings of Abolition hate and

Northern tyranny, and the people of South Carolina defending their freedom and homes."

The Bombardment of Fort Sumter

The Confederate guns went into action at 4:30 A.M. on April 12, and for two and a half hours ordnance rained down on the fort without drawing a response. Then, shortly after 7 A.M., Captain Abner Doubleday, Anderson's second in command, ordered a shot fired at the ironclad battery on Cummings Point. The ball "bounded off from the sloping roof . . . without producing any apparent effect." Nine other cannon in the casemates joined in, but their fire was also largely ineffective.

In Charleston, the battery, the wharves, and the rooftops were jammed with spectators, one of whom wrote: "There were prayers from the women and imprecations from the men; and then a shell would light up the scene." Another eyewitness described the heavy bombardment as follows: "Showers of balls . . . poured into the fort in one incessant stream, causing great flakes of masonry to fall in all directions. When the immense mortar shells, after sailing high in the air, came down in a vertical direction, and buried themselves in the parade ground, their explosion shook the fort like an earthquake."

Damage to Sumter during the first day was not as severe as might have been expected given the intensity of the Confederate cannonade. The barracks were set on fire three times, but the flames were quickly extinguished. The wall around one embrasure was penetrated to a depth of twenty inches by projectiles from a rifled cannon, one gun on the parapet was destroyed and another damaged, but otherwise the fort was still intact as the sun set on April 12.

All through the night, members of the garrison worked to make cartridge bags—cloth containers full of gunpowder—for the artillery duel that would resume in the morning. When the gray light of dawn lit Charleston Harbor, the Federal guns opened "early and spitefully," maintaining a steady rate of fire for several hours. The Confederates also kept up a brisk fire, and at midmorning their "hotshot"—iron cannonballs heated red hot—ignited the officers' quarters. This time the flames could not be doused, and they spread into the enlisted men's barracks and forced the closure of the powder magazine. By noon the smoke on the parade ground was so thick that those men not actively engaged in loading and firing the guns were forced to lie on the ground near open embrasures with wet handkerchiefs over their mouths.

At 1:30 P.M. Sumter's flag was shot away. Colonel Louis T. Wigfall, an aide to General Beauregard, rowed out to the fort to see if the sudden disappearance of the colors meant the garrison wished to surrender. While he was on his way across the harbor a new flag was raised, but he bravely rowed on and entered the fort through an embrasure on the left flank. Realizing that his situation was hopeless, Major Anderson agreed to Wigfall's surrender proposal, provided that his command be allowed to salute the U.S. flag as it was lowered and then depart in safety for a northern port with all their property. At about 7:30 that evening, Beauregard agreed to these terms and the bombardment came to an end. Although more than 3,000 shells had been fired at Fort Sumter, the garrison had suffered no casualties.

On Sunday, April 14, Major Anderson and his men stood at attention while the

The Fort Sumter parade ground following the Confederate bombardment in April 1861. National Archives.

U.S. flag was lowered to the accompaniment of a fifty-gun salute. They then marched out of the fort with drums beating to board a steamer that would take them north to a hero's welcome. As the steamer stood down the channel toward the sea, the Confederate soldiers manning the battery at Cummings Point doffed their caps in tribute to the brave defenders. Fort Sumter had fallen, and the Civil War had begun.

Battle for Charleston Harbor

On April 19, 1861, five days after the fall of Fort Sumter, President Lincoln proclaimed a blockade of the southern coast. Charleston Harbor, less than 700 miles from Nassau in the Bahamas, became one of the main ports of entry for Confederate blockade runners, and a prime target for the Union military.

On November 7, 1861, a Federal fleet captured Hilton Head at Port Royal Sound and established a base for land and sea operations against Charleston. Seven months later, in mid-June 1862, Union infantry commanded by General Henry Benham moved against the city by way of James Island, but were bloodily repulsed at the Battle of Secessionville. This setback only served to whet the Navy Department's "morbid appetite" to seize Charleston, where "rebellion first lighted the flame of civil war."

On the afternoon of April 7, 1863, nine Union ironclads steamed up the main ship channel between Morris Island and Sullivan's Island. The Confederate guns at Cummings Point, Fort Moultrie, and Fort Sumter opened fire, the ironclads answered, and a two-and-a-half-hour-long artillery duel ensued. When it was over, the badly battered ironclads withdrew (one, U.S.S. *Keokuk*, sank the following morning); Sumter had been hit by thirty-four shells, but was only superficially damaged.

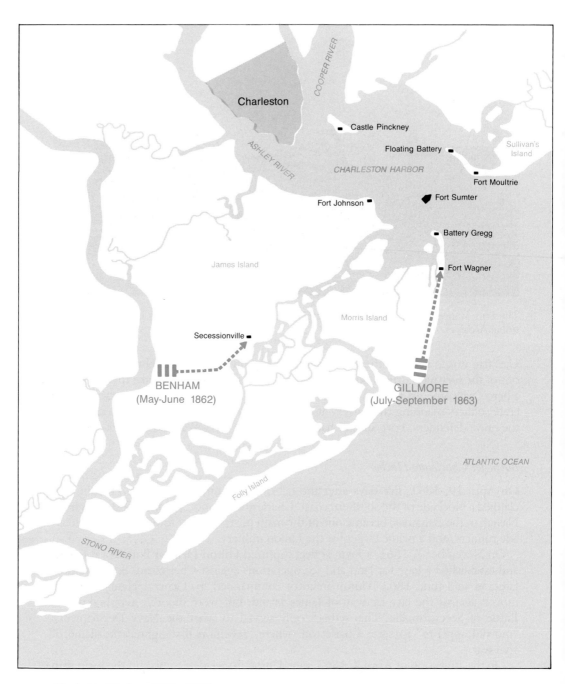

Charleston Harbor, 1861–1865

Union batteries on Morris Island turned Fort Sumter into a "heap of rubbish" with their continuous fire. Library of Congress.

Undeterred by this failure, Federal officers next planned a joint army-navy campaign to capture Morris Island and use its batteries to bombard Fort Sumter and gain control of Charleston Harbor. General Quincy Gillmore, conqueror of Fort Pulaski (see Chapter 20), led 3,000 Union infantrymen onto the island on July 10, 1863. Supported by artillery fire from navy gunboats offshore, the invasion party advanced toward Cummings Point, where its progress was blocked by Fort Wagner, a Confederate earthwork mounting about fifteen cannon. Gillmore called for reinforcements, and on July 18, following an intense preliminary barrage, the fort was stormed. The all-black Fifty-fourth Massachusetts Infantry spearheaded the attack, which was repelled after a brief, ferocious fight on the fort's parapet.

Having lost 1,500 men in the failed assault, Gillmore decided to abandon his efforts to seize Fort Wagner and begin siege operations against Fort Sumter, using the ground he already held. Union engineers set up eight batteries of long-range rifled cannon in a swamp west of Morris Island, and on August 17 they opened fire on Fort Sumter. Nearly 1,000 shells were fired on the first day of the bombardment, and 5,000 more slammed into the fort during the week that followed.

Sumter's masonry walls could not stand up to the explosive impact of rifled-cannon projectiles, and on August 24 Gillmore reported the "practical demolition" of the fort to his superiors. Another 1,300 shells were lobbed into the smoking rubble for good measure, reducing the once-proud citadel into a "shapeless and harmless mass of ruins." The Union gunners then turned their attention to Fort Wagner and Battery Gregg on Morris Island, blasting them relentlessly until the defenders were forced to evacuate on the night of September 6.

The fall of Charleston appeared imminent, but the 320 Confederate soldiers manning Fort Sumter refused to surrender. In the course of leveling the fort's walls, Gillmore's rifled cannon had created a virtually impregnable earthwork, a "heap of rubbish" in which the members of the garrison could burrow like moles, safe from the effects of artillery fire. On the night of September 8, 400 Union sailors and marines attempted a landing, but were beaten back with heavy casualties.

Stalemate had been achieved; the Confederates could not be pried out of the wreck of Sumter, but neither could they mount any offensive operations against the Federals on Morris Island. For the next seventeen months the fort was bombarded sporadically, but the stream of projectiles served only to make the mountain of debris higher and more difficult for infantry to assault.

It was not until February 1865 that the defenders of Fort Sumter were forced to evacuate. The approach of General William T. Sherman's army, advancing north from Georgia into the South Carolina interior, finally accomplished what a year and a half of nearly continuous shelling had failed to do.

On April 14, 1865, exactly four years after he was forced to surrender his post, Robert Anderson, now retired from the army, returned to raise the Stars and Stripes over Charleston Harbor. "I thank God I have lived to see this day," he said as he hoisted the flag to the top of the staff. Fort Sumter belonged to the United States once again.

Touring the Park

Fort Sumter National Monument is located in Charleston Harbor and can be reached only by boat. Tour boats leave from the Charleston City Marina. For boat schedules and ticket information, call (803) 722-1691 or write Fort Sumter Tours, Inc., P.O. Box 59, Charleston, S.C. 29402.

When the tour boat arrives at the fort, a park ranger will give a brief orientation talk. A foot trail leads around the fort grounds. There are ten numbered stops along the way.

Stop 1. Sally Port. This entrance, called a sally port, was built after the Civil War. It replaced a gun embrasure. The wall here is about half its original height.

Stop 2. Left Flank Casemates. The first tier of gun rooms, called casemates, was topped by a second tier identical in appearance. On April 12, 1861, when the Confederate bombardment began, these casemates housed several 32-pounders. Each gun could be moved on a track to adjust the angle of fire through the embrasure.

The gun you see mounted to the left of the sally port is a rifled 42-pounder; the one on the right is a smoothbore 42-pounder. During the 1863–1865 siege of the fort, the Confederates used these casemates as headquarters and hospital.

Stop 3. Enlisted Men's Barracks. These are the ruins of the three-story-high enlisted men's barracks. The building had a mess hall on the first floor and sleeping quarters on the upper two floors. Another enlisted men's barracks, identical to this one, was located on the right flank, directly opposite this wall.

Stop 4. Officers' Quarters. These ruins were the officers' quarters, a three-story building that extended the entire length of the gorge (back) wall. In it were rooms for the officers, administrative offices, storerooms, the guardhouse, and powder magazines. The wooden portion of the building burned during the 1861 bombardment.

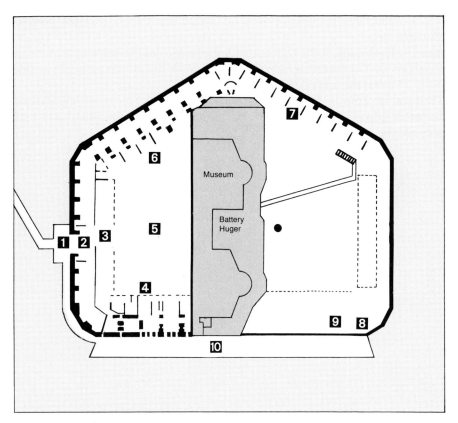

Fort Sumter National Monument

On December 11, 1863, the small-arms magazine here exploded, killing eleven Confederates and wounding forty-one more. The effects of that explosion are still visible today.

Stop 5. Parade Ground. The Fort Sumter parade ground originally encompassed an acre. When Battery Huger, a coastal defense installation, was built in 1899, the parade ground was filled with sand. This portion was excavated by the National Park Service in 1959.

Stop 6. Left Face. During the 1863–1865 siege, fire from Federal rifled cannon on Morris Island destroyed the left face casemates. Several projectiles still protrude from the walls of the ruins. Outside the ruins are two 15-inch Rodman guns, an 8-inch columbiad, and a 10-inch mortar.

Stop 7. Right Face. The eleven 100-pounder Parrott guns you see here were used by Union batteries on Morris Island to bombard Fort Sumter from 1863 to 1865. After the war they were moved here.

Stop 8. Right Gorge Angle. From a gun in the first-tier casemates here, Captain Abner Doubleday fired the first Union shot from Fort Sumter on April 12, 1861.

Stop 9. Mountain Howitzer. Light fieldpieces, like this 12-pounder, were used by the Confederates to repel a surprise assault by Union marines during the 1863–1865 siege.

Stop 10. Esplanade. A 25-1/2-foot-wide esplanade ran the full length of the gorge wall exterior. A 171-foot-long wharf extended from the sally port in the middle of the wall. This was the fort's original entrance.

When you have finished the walking tour, be sure to visit the museum in the center of the parade ground. It contains many interesting artifacts of the 1861 battle for Fort Sumter and the 1863–1865 siege.

CHAPTER 22

GUILFORD COURTHOUSE NATIONAL MILITARY PARK

(Revolutionary War)

P.O. Box 9806
Greensboro, North Carolina 27408
Telephone: (919) 288-1776

On March 15, 1781, a British army commanded by Charles Lord Cornwallis attacked a patriot force led by General Nathanael Greene at Guilford Courthouse, North Carolina. After a ferocious, day-long battle the Americans were forced to retire from the field, but Cornwallis's army was so battered that it had to abandon its Carolina campaign, allowing the Americans to go on the offensive in the South. Guilford Courthouse National Military Park preserves the scene of this decisive battle.

Getting to the Park: Guilford Courthouse National Military Park is located 6 miles north of Greensboro, North Carolina, off U.S. 220 on New Garden Road.

Gas, food, lodging: In Greensboro.

Visitor Center: Museum; interpretive film.

Activities: Interpretive talks are given by park personnel. Living-history demonstrations are presented during the summer. Inquire at Visitor Center for schedule and locations.

Handicapped Access: Visitor Center is fully accessible. Tour stops may be seen by automobile. Some foot trails are paved but others are surfaced with coarse gravel. Visitors in wheelchairs may need assistance; inquire at Visitor Center.

By 1778, British plans for crushing the American Revolution had been thoroughly frustrated. The dramatic American victory at Saratoga (see Chapter 4), and France's decision to enter the war on the American side, had ended all hopes for a decisive British victory in the northern colonies. The high command decided to turn its attention to the South, mounting a campaign to recapture South Carolina and Georgia.

General Nathanael Greene, commander of the patriot army at Guilford Courthouse, was a shrewd tactician and tenacious fighter. Painting by C. W. Peale, Independence National Historic Park Collection.

Cornwallis's Southern Campaign

The southern strategy was successful at first. British authority was reestablished in coastal South Carolina and Georgia, and by the fall of 1780, Charles Lord Cornwallis was positioning his army for a thrust northward into Virginia. The conquest of Virginia, Cornwallis believed, would deal the patriot cause a mortal blow. Before he could start the campaign, however, his forces suffered two stunning setbacks. At Kings Mountain in October, a large loyalist detachment was wiped out by a band of patriot irregulars (see Chapter 25); three months later, another British detachment was soundly beaten by the Americans at the Battle of Cowpens (see Chapter 18).

Despite these reversals, Cornwallis was determined to forge ahead with the Virginia invasion, and in late January 1781 he set out at the head of approximately 2,000 troops. Opposing his advance was a small patriot army commanded by General Nathanael Greene, a shrewd tactician and tenacious fighter. Greene knew that his force was too weak to stop Cornwallis so he retreated toward the North Carolina–Virginia border, drawing the British army away from its base of supplies while positioning himself to receive reinforcements.

Cornwallis took the bait, and for three long weeks he and his soldiers slogged through mud and snow in pursuit of the elusive Americans. On February 14, Greene got his men across the swollen Dan River where Cornwallis, who had no boats, could not follow. There he was joined by fresh troops—600 Virginia riflemen—and with a force now totaling some 2,100 soldiers, he recrossed the Dan to harry the British.

Cornwallis was anxious to come to blows with the patriot army, but Greene, who was expecting even more reinforcements, refused to stand and fight. He continued to maneuver until the second week of March, when the size of his command was doubled by the arrival of militia units from Virginia and North Carolina. Strong enough at last to give battle, he halted his army near Guilford Courthouse, only twelve miles from the British camp at Deep River, and waited for Cornwallis to attack.

Greene Deploys his Troops

The ground Greene had selected straddled the New Garden Road, part of the main east-west artery through North Carolina. The British, approaching along the road from the west, would have to cross Little Horsepen Creek and then advance across an open farm field to get at the Americans.

Greene placed his first battle line, composed of 1,000 North Carolina militiamen, behind a rail fence at the east end of the field. Two 6-pounder cannon were placed on the road, in the line's center. Three hundred yards farther to the east, along a low, wooded knoll, he formed a second line, manned by Virginia riflemen. Behind this line, on an open hillside near the courthouse, he positioned his best troops, the Maryland and Virginia Continentals. The cavalry was placed on the wings, where it could ride to the infantry's support.

The tactics Greene meant to use were almost identical to those employed so successfully by Daniel Morgan at the Battle of Cowpens. Knowing that the inexperienced North Carolina militia in the first line would run from a bayonet charge, he asked only that they slow the British advance. "Two rounds, my boys, and then you may fall back," he told them. The second line also was expected to give ground after bleeding the British. The hard fighting would be left to the disciplined, battle-tested Continentals in the third line.

The Battle of Guilford Courthouse

The morning of March 15, 1781, was clear and cold. In their lines, the 4,400 American soldiers checked their muskets and nervously waited for the arrival of Cornwallis's army, which, cavalry scouts reported, was approaching along the New Garden Road.

Around noon, the British column emerged from the woods and forded Little Horsepen Creek. The Americans opened fire with their two small cannon, and the British brought three guns forward and replied. This noisy exchange lasted a half hour and did no damage to either side, but it gave Cornwallis's infantry time to form into ranks. To the beat of drums and squeal of fifes, the redcoats moved out across the open field toward the rail fence and Greene's first line.

At a range of 150 yards, the patriots fired a volley; gaps opened in the British ranks, but still the redcoats came forward, moving at a steady, measured pace. When they were less than 100 yards from the fence, they halted, fired their muskets, gave a loud cheer, and charged with bayonets lowered. This was too much for the North Carolina militiamen. They threw down their arms and rushed helter-skelter toward the rear.

Excited by the sight of the fleeing patriots, the British dressed their ranks and plunged ahead into the woods toward Greene's second line. Hidden by trees and thick underbrush, the Virginia riflemen "kept up for a considerable time a galling fire, which did great execution." The weight of British numbers soon told, however, and the main portion of the patriot formation gave way.

Tired but triumphant, the redcoats again reformed and moved into the courthouse clearing to make a bayonet charge against the third American line. This time their opponents were not raw militiamen: the Maryland and Virginia Continentals, the

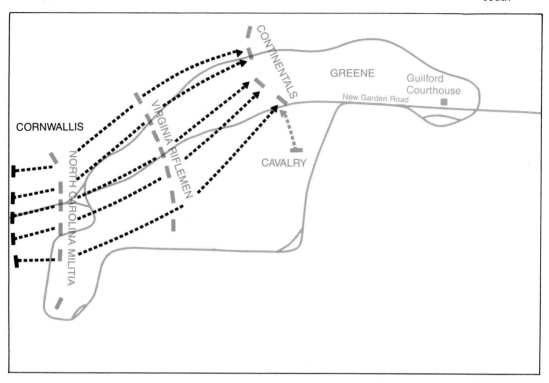

Guilford Courthouse, March 15, 1781

cream of the American army, waited until the British soldiers were only 100 feet away, blasted them with a crashing volley, then followed up with a bayonet charge of their own. The redcoats bravely rallied, and there was hand-to-hand fighting as the battle lines swayed back and forth.

Patriot cavalrymen, led by Colonel William Washington, now charged into the fray, slashing left and right with their long, curving sabers. Still the redcoats held their ground. "Never, perhaps, has the prowess of the British soldier been seen to greater advantage than in this obstinate and bloody combat," a British military historian said of the fight.

Cornwallis surveyed the vicious melee near the courthouse and realized that his army was in trouble. A little more pressure by the Americans and the red ranks would break. Quickly he ordered his artillery to move up and fire grapeshot into the seething mass of men, cutting down British and American soldiers alike. It was a cruel, desperate measure, but it broke up the fight and prevented the total collapse of his command.

Greene could not risk the loss of his army—the only patriot force in the South— and at 3:30 P.M. he ordered a withdrawal from the battlefield. The sky clouded over as the American troops filed east along the New Garden Road toward a camp fifteen miles distant. Soon a cold, soaking rain was falling, and Cornwallis, if he had had any thoughts about pursuing his foe, was forced to give them up.

The Maryland and Virginia continentals, the cream of the patriot army, fought hand to hand with Cornwallis's redcoats. Dixon Ticonderoga Company.

A Costly Victory

The Americans had been vanquished at Guilford Courthouse, but the price paid by the victors was extremely high. More than a quarter of the British army, 532 men, had been killed or wounded. These crippling losses, combined with lack of supplies, compelled Cornwallis to embark on a painful, depressing retreat to Wilmington, on the North Carolina coast.

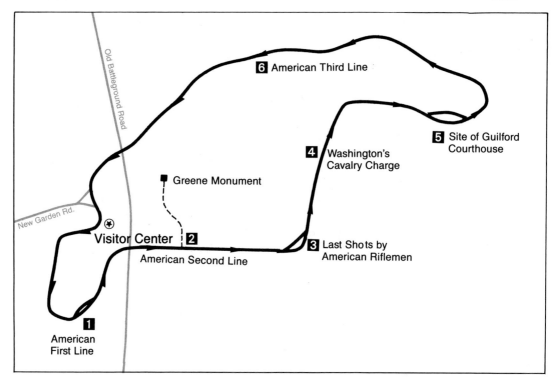

Guilford Courthouse National Military Park

Greene, whose casualties numbered only 261, took advantage of this British retreat to lunge south and begin liberating South Carolina. He had lost the fight at Guilford Courthouse, but he won the campaign. Britain's hold on the South would soon be permanently broken.

Touring the Park

Begin your tour at the Visitor Center, where exhibits and an audiovisual program explain the battle and its significance in the American Revolution.

A 2.25-mile tour road runs through the park. There are six numbered stops; foot trails lead from several of the stops to points of historic interest.

Stop 1. American First Line. From this point, the patriots' first battle line extended a quarter mile to the north. One thousand North Carolina militiamen stood behind rail fences and fired at Cornwallis's soldiers advancing from the west. When the redcoats charged ahead with their bayonets fixed, the North Carolinians turned and ran.

Stop 2. American Second Line. Virginia riflemen, shielded by trees and brush, took a heavy toll on the British troops as they advanced past this point. The foot trail follows the line held by the Virginians.

Stop 3. Last Shots by American Riflemen. Most of the Virginia riflemen retreated in the face of the British advance, but on the left side of the line several groups held their ground and kept on firing, pinning down a substantial number of redcoats.

Stop 4. Washington's Cavalry Charge. From this hill, Colonel William Washington's patriot cavalry charged into the battle raging in the open field below. The foot trail leads to the hill from which Cornwallis ordered his artillery to fire grapeshot into the melee, slaughtering British and American soldiers alike, and ending the battle.

Stop 5. Site of Guilford Courthouse. The courthouse for which the battle was named was built on this site in 1775. About 100 people lived in a small village nearby. The courthouse was closed and the town abandoned in 1808; today, nothing remains of either.

Stop 6. American Third Line. The Maryland and Virginia Continentals, among the best soldiers in the American army, fought a pitched battle with the British Guards in this clearing. The fierce fighting continued until Cornwallis's cannon opened fire on British and American soldiers alike, forcing the antagonists to break off the combat.

The cannon on the field are reproductions of the 6-pounders used by the patriots. The foot trail follows the historic New Garden Road to the Delaware and Maryland monuments and returns along the left flank of the British line.

Greene Monument. From the parking area, the foot trail leads to the Greene Monument, a large equestrian statue of the patriot general.

CHAPTER 23

HORSESHOE BEND NATIONAL MILITARY PARK
(Indian Wars)

Route 1, Box 103
Daviston, Alabama 36256
Telephone: (205) 234-7111

In a bloody battle at the Horseshoe Bend of the Tallapoosa River on March 27, 1814, General Andrew Jackson's Tennessee Volunteers broke the power of the Creek Indian Confederacy and opened Alabama to white settlement. Horseshoe Bend National Military Park preserves the scene of the battle.

Getting to the Park: Horseshoe Bend National Military Park is located approximately 94 miles southeast of Birmingham, Alabama. Take U.S. 280 from Birmingham to Dadeville, then drive 12 miles north on Alabama Highway 49 to the park.

Gas, food, lodging: In Dadeville.

Visitor Center: Museum and gift shop; audiovisual displays.

Activities: Interpretive talks by park personnel. Occasional flintlock-rifle demonstrations. Inquire at Visitor Center for schedule.

Handicapped Access: Visitor Center is fully accessible. Paved paths lead to the roadside exhibits.

The Tallapoosa River flows across the flatlands of eastern Alabama, winding snake-like through dense forests of loblolly pine and scrub oak. Twisting and turning back on itself as it rolls south and west toward the Gulf of Mexico, the stream incises a series of tortuous loops and bends in the sandy, red soil.

On a narrow peninsula formed by one of the river's horseshoe-shaped bends, the Creek Indians established a stronghold in the late 1700s. It was called Toho-peka—"the fort"—and its defenders believed it to be impregnable. On March 27, 1814, an army of Tennessee frontiersmen led by General Andrew Jackson attacked this bastion; the ensuing battle was one of the fiercest and most decisive in the history of the American Indian Wars.

The Creek War

The Creek Nation was a loose confederacy of fifty villages spread across Alabama and western Georgia. The 40,000 tribesmen who populated this network of towns maintained good relations with the Spanish, French, and British traders who came into their territory beginning in the mid-1500s, and with the Americans who came later.

In 1790, the Creeks signed a treaty of friendship with the fledgling government of the United States. Not long after, an Indian agent named Benjamin Hawkins moved to Creek country and began encouraging the Indians to forsake their old tribal ways and adopt white American culture.

The Lower Creeks of Georgia, who lived closer to white settlements, were receptive to Hawkins's blandishments, but the Upper Creeks, who inhabited the more remote sections of Alabama, resisted them. Tension between the two factions gradually mounted, and in the summer of 1813 it erupted into open warfare. The Red Sticks, as the rebellious Upper Creeks were called, repudiated agent Hawkins and his Lower Creek followers and vowed to resist further white encroachment on their territory.

Late in August 1813, a Red Stick war party attacked Fort Mims on the lower Alabama River, twenty-odd miles north of Mobile. Five hundred fifty-three white settlers who had sought refuge in the fort were brutally killed; only thirty-six escaped to carry word of the massacre to American authorities in Georgia and Tennessee.

The Tennessee Volunteers March

News of the carnage at Fort Mims shocked and enraged the people of Tennessee. The state legislature quickly authorized the raising of a 3,500-man army and asked Andrew Jackson, forty-six-year-old major general in the Tennessee militia, to lead it against the Upper Creeks. "I indulge the grateful hope of sharing with you the dangers and glory of prostrating those hell hounds," Jackson told his eager volunteers as they set out for Alabama in October 1813. They reached the heart of Red Stick country, between the Coosa and Tallapoosa rivers, in early November, and promptly attacked the Red Sticks at the villages of Tallushatchee and Talladega.

"We shot them like dogs," wrote frontiersman Davey Crockett of the Tallushatchee fight in which 200 Creeks were killed. The Tennessee volunteers were also victorious at Talladega, and the remaining Red Stick warriors, numbering about 1,000, fled south to the citadel of Tohopeka, inside the horseshoe bend of the Tallapoosa.

Jackson wanted to follow at once, but lack of supplies and the desertion of 1,500 of his troops prevented him. Finally, after three hard months during which the army nearly disbanded for want of food, Jackson was resupplied. He ordered the advance on Tohopeka to begin, and on March 26, 1814, the Tennessee militiamen—thin, ragged, but spoiling for a fight—arrived at Horseshoe Bend.

March 27, 1814: Jackson Storms the Horseshoe

The Horseshoe was a natural fortress, a 100-acre peninsula encircled almost completely by the muddy Tallapoosa River. Across the narrow neck of the peninsula the Red Sticks had erected a stout seven-foot-high log barricade. The barricade was

Forty-six-year-old General Andrew Jackson
led 3,500 Tennessee volunteers into Alabama's Creek Indian country in the fall of 1813.
Painting by Ralph E. W. Earl. Copyright The
Hermitage, 1988.

pierced with loopholes and laid out in a zigzag fashion so that approaching attackers
would be exposed to a deadly cross fire.

On the morning of March 27, Jackson sent General John Coffee with 700 cavalrymen and 600 Cherokee Indian allies across the Tallapoosa to surround the bend,
cutting off any possible Red Stick retreat. Meanwhile he and 2,000 infantrymen
marched onto the peninsula and prepared to assault the log barricade.

In his wagon train Jackson had two small cannon, which he planned to use to punch
a hole in the Indians' wall. When the little battery opened fire, however, the cannonballs either stuck in the soft logs or bounced off harmlessly. For two hours the 1,000
Red Stick defenders, led by Chief Menawa, exchanged rifle and musket fire with the
Tennesseans, but no one was hurt.

At 12:30 P.M. Jackson decided that he had had enough of the bloodless stalemate and ordered his men to storm the barricade. A drum roll sounded, and with
fierce shouts the militia rushed forward and clambered over the stockade. "Never was
more bravery displayed," the general said of this headlong charge into the teeth of
heavy fire.

As fate would have it, Coffee's force had recrossed the Tallapoosa and launched an
assault on the rear of the Red Sticks' redoubt at almost the same time Jackson's men
were attacking the barricade. The Indians were caught between the hammer of Jackson's infantry and the anvil of Coffee's cavalry. Hand-to-hand fighting raged for several hours, with no quarter asked or given: "Arrows and spears and balls were flying;
swords and tomahawks were gleaming in the sun and the whole peninsula rang with
the yell of savages and the groans of the dying," recalled one of the combatants.

The issue was never in doubt, however. By dusk 800 Red Stick warriors had been killed, and 350 Creek women and children had been taken prisoner. Forty-nine Tennesseans lay dead; 154 were wounded, many of them mortally.

Downfall of the Creek Nation

When the sun dipped below the horizon on March 27, 1814, it set not only on the smoldering ruins of Tohopeka but on the Creek Nation as well. In the span of five hours the fighting strength of the Red Sticks had been decimated, and there was nothing left for the survivors to do but capitulate. In August 1814 they signed the Treaty of Fort Jackson, ceding 23 million acres of Creek land to the government of the United States. Most of this verdant territory was incorporated into the State of Alabama when it was admitted to the Union five years later.

The destruction of the Creek Nation was the making of Andrew Jackson. His victory over the Red Sticks at Horseshoe Bend, and his triumph at the Battle of New Orleans nine months later (see Chapter 16), brought him national fame and started him on the road to the White House. When he became president in 1829, he finished the job he had begun at Horseshoe Bend: the Indian Removal Bill, passed at his instigation in 1830, forced all the Indian tribes east of the Mississippi to relocate to the Indian Territory, in present-day Oklahoma and Kansas, opening the entire Southeast to white settlement.

Touring the Park

Begin your tour at the Visitor Center, where exhibits and audiovisual programs on Creek Indian culture, frontier life, and the Creek War of 1813–1814 will help you gain a better understanding of the Battle of Horseshoe Bend.

A three-mile tour road loops through the battlefield. There are six numbered stops; a 2.8-mile nature trail starts and ends at Stop 1.

Stop 1. Cotton Patch Hill. Andrew Jackson deployed his army in this area at about 10 A.M. on March 27, 1814, and prepared to attack the village of Tohopeka in the Horseshoe Bend. Straight ahead, approximately half a mile to the south, was a log barricade defended by 1,000 Creek warriors. General John Coffee's cavalry and Cherokee scouts had already forded the Tallapoosa three miles downstream and were in position to prevent any villagers from escaping by swimming the river.

Stop 2. The Island. From this vantage point you can see a heavily wooded fifteen-acre island in the Tallapoosa River. General Coffee detached Lieutenant Jesse Bean and forty Tennessee riflemen to hold this island and stop any Creeks from taking refuge there. It was an astute move. As Coffee later wrote: "many of the enemy did attempt their escape to the island but not one ever landed—they were sunk by Lt. Bean's command ere they reached the bank."

Stop 3. Gun Hill. Jackson's army had an artillery battery consisting of two small cannon—a 3-pounder and a 6-pounder. They were placed on this hill and aimed at the Creeks' log barricade. The bombardment produced a great deal of noise and smoke, but caused very little damage. Most of the cannonballs either stuck in the logs or bounced off. At 12:30 P.M. Jackson lost patience with his artillerymen and ordered the infantry to storm the barricade.

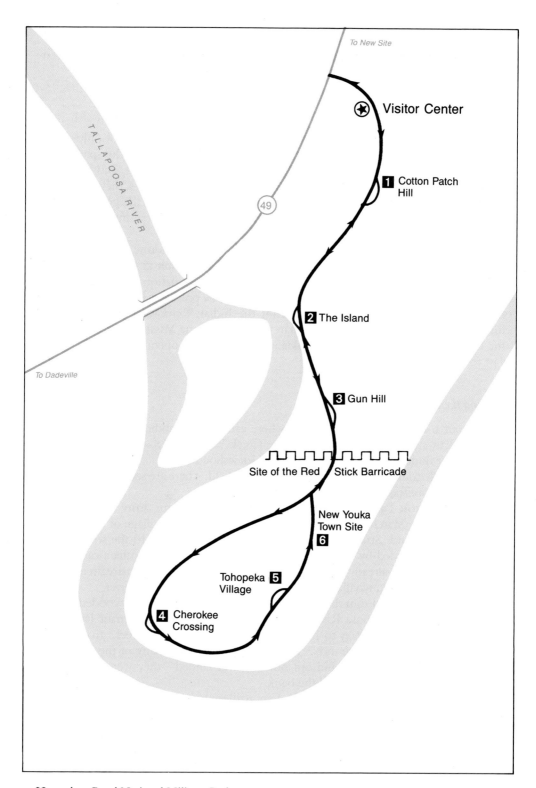

Visitor Center

1 Cotton Patch Hill

TALLAPOOSA RIVER

49

To Dadeville

2 The Island

3 Gun Hill

Site of the Red   Stick Barricade

New Youka Town Site **6**

Tohopeka Village **5**

4 Cherokee Crossing

Horseshoe Bend National Military Park

Stop 4. Cherokee Crossing. The Cherokees of General Coffee's force heard the crescendo of firing as Jackson's troops charged the barricade and became worried that they would miss out on the looting of the captured Creek village. As Coffee described it, they "plunged into the water and swam over for canoes that lay at the other shore in considerable number and brought them over, in which craft a number of them embarked." The Cherokees landed on the bank in front of you, swept past this point, and attacked Tohopeka from the rear. Trapped between two forces, the Creek army was doomed.

Stop 5. Tohopeka Village. This was the site of the Creek village, in the middle of the Horseshoe Bend. When Coffee's Cherokees attacked from across the river, they plundered the settlement, set the log huts on fire, and took 350 Creek women and children prisoner.

Stop 6. New Youka Town Site. As you look east from this point, across the Tallapoosa, you see the site of the Creek village of New Youka, named after the 1790 Treaty of New York. Ironically, this treaty guaranteed Creek sovereignty over the lands of southeastern Alabama and pledged friendship with the United States. New Youka was burned before the battle, and its residents fled to Tohopeka.

CHAPTER 24

KENNESAW MOUNTAIN NATIONAL BATTLEFIELD PARK
(Civil War)

P.O. Box 1610
Marietta, Georgia 30061
Telephone: (404) 427-4686

During the spring and summer of 1864, Union general William T. Sherman and an army of 100,000 men moved against the strategically vital city of Atlanta. At Kennesaw Mountain, a Confederate army led by General Joseph E. Johnston tried to block the Federal advance. After bloody battles on June 22 and June 27, Johnston was forced to retreat, and Atlanta fell to Sherman. Kennesaw Mountain National Battlefield Park preserves the scene of the fiercest fighting of the Atlanta Campaign.

Getting to the Park: Kennesaw Mountain National Battlefield Park is located three miles northwest of Marietta, Georgia. Take Exit 116 off I-75 and drive approximately 1 mile northwest on U.S. 41 to its intersection with Old U.S. 41. Drive approximately 2 miles northwest on Old U.S. 41 to its intersection with the Stilesboro Road. Turn left on the Stilesboro Road and drive 1/4 mile west to the park entrance.

Gas, food, lodging: In Marietta.

Visitor Center: Museum and gift shop; audiovisual programs.

Activities: Interpretive talks by park personnel, living-history demonstrations during the summer months. Inquire at Visitor Center for schedule.

Handicapped Access: Visitor Center is fully accessible. Braille park folders are available on a loan basis. Foot trails at tour stops range from easy to difficult; some are level, while others are steep and rough. Inquire at Visitor Center whether assistance will be needed.

In the spring of 1864 the Union brought the full weight of its military might to bear on crushing the Confederacy. From Chattanooga, Tennessee, 100,000 Federal troops led by General William T. Sherman marched southeast into Georgia. Their mission was simple: "Get into the interior of the enemy's country as far as you can, inflicting all the damage you can against their war resources." It was obvious to Sherman and his battle-hardened veterans where they could do the most damage. "Atlanta was too important a place in the hands of the enemy to be left undisturbed, with its magazines, stores, arsenals, workshops, foundries, and more especially its railroads," wrote the general. His army would move against that city, lying beyond the mountainous barrier of Rocky Face Ridge, 100 miles from Chattanooga.

The Atlanta Campaign

A Confederate army 60,000 men strong was dug in along Rocky Face Ridge, near the town of Dalton, waiting to contest Sherman's advance. Its commander, General Joseph E. Johnston, had brushed aside suggestions that he preempt the Federal invasion by marching north into Tennessee. Instead, he had chosen to employ a defensive strategy, entrenching and waiting for the Union force to come to him.

On May 8, Sherman reached the foot of Rocky Face with two-thirds of his army. The other third marched south toward Snake Creek Gap, trying to circle around the Confederate left flank. Faced with the prospect of being cut off from his supply base in Atlanta, Johnston ordered his men to retreat to Resaca on May 12. Three days later, this chain of events was repeated. Sherman pinned the Confederates in place with the bulk of his force while sending a column around their flank to cut the supply line. Again Johnston was forced to retreat, and a pattern was established: the Confederates would entrench, the Federals would manuever around their flank, the Confederates would withdraw and entrench again.

By mid-June, Johnston's troops had fallen back to a position only twenty miles from Atlanta. Here they dug in, in a defensive line anchored by Kennesaw Mountain, a rocky, forested knob that rose abruptly from the surrounding countryside. The mountain's twin peaks were "crowned with batteries," Sherman wrote, and "the spurs were alive with men busy felling trees, digging pits, and preparing for the grand struggle impending." Despite the forbidding nature of this obstacle, the Union general was determined to drive on and seize Atlanta.

June 22, 1864: Clash at Kolb's Farm

Sherman's first attempt to neutralize the Kennesaw Mountain defenses followed the familiar pattern established the preceding month. He sent two corps south to try to get around the Confederate left flank, but this time Johnston anticipated the move and sent a corps of his own—20,000 men under General John Bell Hood—to meet the threat.

Shortly after noon on June 22, Hood's skirmishers encountered the advance elements of the Union column. Believing that he had outflanked Sherman's flankers, the combative Hood attacked at once and rapidly pushed the blue soldiers back until he encountered the main body of Federals, entrenched on the farm of Peter Valentine Kolb. The sporadic banging of musket fire merged into a solid roar as the Confederates charged forward, trying to break through the Union line. They were bloodily repulsed. Just before sundown Hood ordered a second assault, which was hurled back like the first.

Sherman's flanking attempt had been thwarted, but the Confederates had lost 1,000 irreplaceable troops in the attack against the Kolb Farm earthworks.

June 27, 1864: The Battle of Kennesaw Mountain

After the fight at Kolb's Farm, Sherman had to revamp his tactics. The blocking movement of Hood's corps and the rain-soaked condition of the roads ruled out further attempts at getting around the Rebel line. The choice was stalemate or frontal attack, and Sherman promptly chose the latter. He suspected that the Confederates were stretched thin and resolved "to feign on both flanks and assault the center," the center being the area around Kennesaw Mountain.

At precisely 8 A.M. on Monday, June 27, over 200 Union cannon thundered into action, hammering the Confederate line with shot and shell. "Hell has broke loose in Georgia, sure enough!" exclaimed one Rebel as he and his comrades scrambled for shelter. The furious bombardment lasted exactly one hour; then two groups of blue-shirted infantry moved forward, one column attacking down the Burnt Hickory Road that ran past the southern flank of Kennesaw Mountain, the other attacking down the Dallas Road half a mile farther south.

The artillery fire had shattered trees and plowed up earth, but it had failed to weaken the Confederate defenses. Secure in their rifle pits and log redoubts, the Rebel troops loaded their muskets and waited for the Federals to draw near. When the blue assault force came within range it was savaged by massed fire that produced "a roar as constant as Niagara and as sharp as the crash of thunder with lightning in the eye."

Along Burnt Hickory Road over 550 Union soldiers were cut down in almost an hour, and the rest were obliged to dive for cover. "It was almost sure death to take your face out of the dust," remembered one of the pinned-down attackers.

South of the Dallas Road the fighting was even bloodier. Five thousand Federals made for a salient in the Confederate line held by General Benjamin Cheatham's division. "Dead Angle," as the soldiers named this zigzag in the fortifications, became a slaughter pen for the troops in blue, who "seemed to walk up and take death as coolly as if they were automatic or wooden men."

In less than a half hour the Union attack column suffered nearly 1,500 casualties without coming close to making a breakthrough. The only thing accomplished, their commander bitterly remarked, was to prove "now, as never before, the futility of direct assault upon entrenched lines already well prepared and well manned."

The Federals retreated at 11 A.M., and the battle was over. "When the Yankees fell back and the firing ceased, I never saw so many broken down and exhausted men in my life," wrote a Confederate. "I was sick as a horse, and as wet with blood and sweat as I could be, and many of our men were vomiting with excessive fatigue, overexhaustion, and sunstroke; our tongues were parched and cracked for water, and our faces blackened with powder and smoke, and our dead and wounded were piled indiscriminately in the trenches."

Among the Union generals the results of the bloody, failed assault were accepted with grim stoicism. Sherman defended his decision to attack: "I had to do it," he wired Washington. To his wife he wrote these chilling lines: "I begin to regard the death and mangling of a couple of thousand men as a small affair. . . . It may be well that we become hardened. . . . The worst of the war has not yet begun."

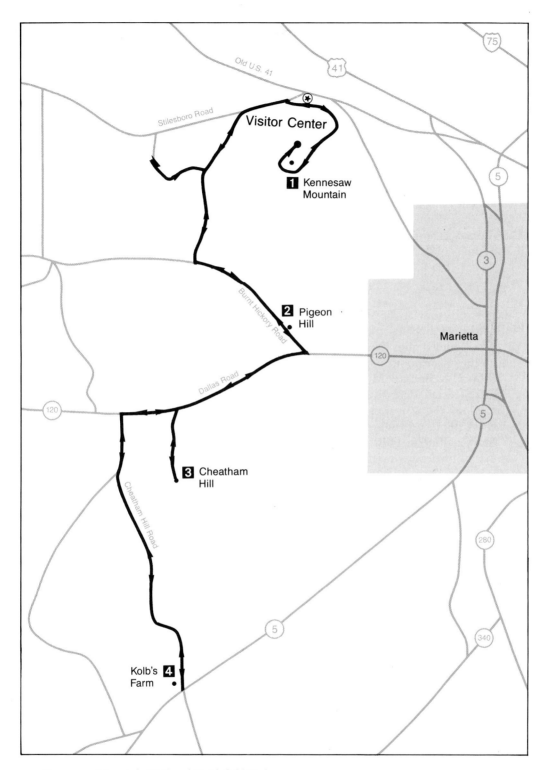

Kennesaw Mountain National Battlefield Park

Atlanta Falls

The Confederates had stopped the Federal assault in its tracks, but they could not stop the sun from drying the roads. Just as soon as the mud hardened, Sherman resumed his flanking tactics and Johnston resumed his retreat, this time to Atlanta itself.

On July 17, the Confederate high command replaced Johnston with the more aggressive Hood, but efforts to push the Union army back failed. Atlanta was besieged, and on September 2 it fell to the Federals.

The loss of the city with its rail links and vital war industries was a staggering blow to the Confederacy. Conversely, it was a great morale booster in the North, helping President Lincoln win reelection, and convincing the public that the war's end was in sight. Sherman was determined to do his part to bring about that end: on November 15 he put Atlanta to the torch and set off with his army on the devastating "March to the Sea."

Touring the Park

Begin your tour at the Visitor Center, which provides background information on the Atlanta Campaign and the Battle of Kennesaw Mountain.

A self-guided auto tour will take you around the battlefield. Five numbered stops mark the major points of interest.

Stop 1. Kennesaw Mountain. The twin peaks of Kennesaw Mountain anchored the Confederate defensive line. A short trail leads from the parking area to the summit. Along the way are gun emplacements dug by the Confederate artillerymen, as well as exhibits explaining the significance of this position during the battle.

Stop 2. Pigeon Hill. From trenches and dugouts on this mountain spur, Johnston's Confederates ravaged the Union attackers advancing along Burnt Hickory Road. A foot trail leads from the parking area to the site of the entrenchments.

Stop 3. Cheatham Hill. The battle's bloodiest fighting took place here, at a salient in the Confederate defensive line known as "Dead Angle." On this ground, 1,500 Union soldiers were killed or wounded in less than two hours of combat. A short trail leads to the Illinois Monument, the site of the Confederate earthworks, and to markers showing where the Union attackers fell. Near the base of the monument is the mouth of a tunnel dug by Union engineers planning to blow up the Confederate position with a mine. The remains of Union trenches can be seen nearby.

Stop 4. Kolb's Farm. Sherman's flanking maneuver was thwarted here on the afternoon of June 22, 1864. Confederate general John Bell Hood tried to turn the tables, but his attack was repulsed with heavy casualties. The log house you see was built in 1836 by Peter Valentine Kolb; during the battle it served as headquarters for Union general Joseph Hooker.

CHAPTER 25

KINGS MOUNTAIN NATIONAL MILITARY PARK
(Revolutionary War)

P.O. Box 31
Kings Mountain, South Carolina 28086
Telephone: (803) 936-7921

On October 7, 1780, a force of American frontiersmen attacked and defeated a loyalist army that had been attempting to subjugate upcountry South Carolina. This victory strengthened the resolve of southern patriots to fight against British rule. Kings Mountain National Military Park preserves the scene of the battle.

Getting to the Park: Kings Mountain National Military Park is located 15 miles southwest of Gastonia, North Carolina. From Gastonia, take I-85 to the Kings Mountain Exit and then drive 10 miles southeast on South Carolina Highway 216 to the park.

Gas, food, lodging: In Gastonia.

Visitor Center: Museum and audiovisual programs.

Activities: Interpretive programs and living-history demonstrations are presented periodically by park personnel. Inquire at Visitor Center for schedule.

Handicapped Access: The Visitor Center is fully accessible. The 1.5-mile foot trail is paved, but quite steep in spots. Visitors in wheelchairs will need assistance. A handrail is provided on the steepest part of the trail.

It is a little-known fact that the Revolutionary War's bitterest combat did not involve the British army; rather, it pitted American against American in ferocious local struggles that were fought by the code of an eye for an eye, a tooth for a tooth. On the southern frontier in particular, American loyalists and patriots met in vicious clashes in which quarter was given only grudgingly and atrocities were commonplace. One such engagement was the Battle of Kings Mountain, fought in the wild hill country along the border of North and South Carolina on October 7, 1780.

The over-mountain men were fiercely independent hunters and farmers who
came from the Watauga, Holston, and Nolichucky river valleys on the western
slope of the Appalachians. Dixon Ticonderoga Company.

Bull Dog Ferguson and the Over-Mountain Men

In May 1780, after a lengthy siege, a British army captured the city of Charleston, South Carolina. Not content with overrunning the coastal area, the army's commander, Charles Lord Cornwallis, decided to extend his control to the upcountry by purging it of all rebels who dared defy royal authority.

The man who would carry out this mission was Major Patrick "Bull Dog" Ferguson, commander of a battalion of American loyalists. Strong and athletic, a crack shot, skilled swordsman, and daring equestrian, the aggressive, energetic Ferguson seemed a perfect choice for subjugating South Carolina's recalcitrant rebels. In June 1780 he and his battalion set out from Charleston, riding toward the country between the Catawba and Saluda rivers, burning and plundering as they went.

Opposing Ferguson and his loyalists were small bands of "over-mountain" men, fiercely independent hunters and farmers who came from the Watauga, Holston, and Nolichucky river valleys on the western slope of the Appalachians in what is now Tennessee. These hardy Scotch-Irish frontiersmen reviled the British Crown and were determined to protect their settlements from tory depredations. They crossed the mountains in July and intercepted Ferguson's detachments along the headwaters of the Saluda. Neither side could gain the upper hand in the contest that followed, but the bloody skirmishing, the looting and arson, the torture and execution of prisoners, served to kindle a burning hatred in the hearts of patriot and loyalist alike.

Ferguson Throws Down the Gauntlet

In late August, as the harvest time approached, the over-mountain men broke off the fighting and returned to their homes beyond the Appalachians. Meanwhile, Cornwallis was planning an invasion of North Carolina. A large British army would move north from Camden to Charlotte in September; Major Ferguson and his loyalist battalion were ordered to shield the invasion column's left flank from guerilla attacks.

Ferguson knew exactly where such hit-and-run raids would come from, and he decided to issue a peremptory warning. A messenger was dispatched westward bearing an ultimatum: if the people of the Watauga, Holston, and Nolichucky valleys did not desist from their opposition to British arms, Ferguson and his loyalists would cross the mountains, hang their leaders, and "lay their country waste with fire and sword."

This harsh threat infuriated the over-mountain men, and during the last week of September they began to assemble at Sycamore Shoals on the Watauga, bringing their horses, hunting knives, and long-barreled rifles. On September 26, 1780, they set out— a mounted column of 800 men—riding southeast over the wind-whipped Appalachian passes, grimly determined to track down Bull Dog Ferguson and kill him.

The army of frontiersmen arrived at Quaker Meadows, near present-day Morganton, North Carolina, on September 30. There they were joined by 350 more volunteers, bringing their strength to over 1,000. Led by Isaac Shelby, John Sevier, and William Campbell, they then turned southwest and rode around Pilot Mountain toward the hamlet of Gilbert Town, where Ferguson had his headquarters.

When scouts informed the British major that his bitter enemies were only a day's ride away, he panicked. His intemperate threat had backfired and now he and his

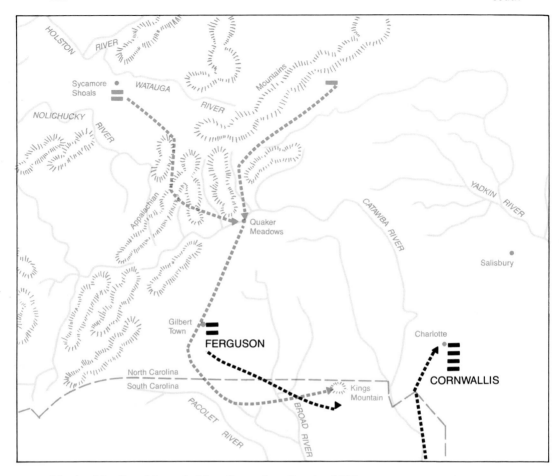

March of the Over-Mountain Men, September–October 1780

battalion were in mortal danger. Calling on Cornwallis for reinforcements, he beat a hasty retreat south and east, warning British sympathizers who lived along the way to "run to camp" to escape the wrath of the "backwater men . . . a set of mongrels." Arriving at Kings Mountain just south of the North Carolina line on October 6, he called a halt and deployed his 1,100 loyalists.

Kings Mountain was a natural fortress, a rocky scarp that jutted from the surrounding forest like an island rearing out of a broad green sea. Its steep, sixty-foot-high flanks were covered with brush and boulders, and its long, flat summit offered clear fields of fire. When Ferguson had finished positioning his men in this wilderness stronghold, his confidence returned and he brazenly "defied God Almighty and all the rebels out of Hell to overcome him."

The over-mountain men intended to accept his challenge. Riding day and night through cold, soaking rainstorms, stopping just long enough to partake of parched corn and squirrel stew, they pursued their quarry relentlessly. Shortly after noon on October 7, they caught up with him. Tying their horses in the woods, they formed a horseshoe-shaped battle line around the foot of the mountain, and waited in a light drizzle for the signal to attack.

The Battle of Kings Mountain

Except for the steady plop of raindrops falling on the sodden forest floor, all was quiet on Kings Mountain as dusk approached on October 7. Then a keening war whoop shattered the stillness, and the over-mountain men began to clamber up the steep slopes, their horseshoe-shaped line closing like a hangman's noose around Ferguson's perimeter.

The Long Rifle

The Long Rifle—also known as the Pennsylvania or Kentucky Rifle—is perhaps the most fabled firearm in American history. A muzzle-loading, flintlock piece with an octagonal iron barrel three to four feet long, it evolved from the German Jaeger, a short, heavy, large-caliber hunting rifle brought to America by European immigrants around 1710.

Gunsmiths in Pennsylvania changed the design of the Jaeger to better suit the conditions found on the American frontier. They lengthened the barrel to improve accuracy and range, reduced the caliber to lessen weight and conserve gunpowder, and reshaped the stock to improve handling. The result was a long, slender, beautifully proportioned rifle that was light enough at eight to ten pounds to be carried through the forest all day, but powerful enough to shoot a .50-caliber lead ball over 200 yards with incredible accuracy.

Superb as it was for hunting, the Long Rifle had several serious shortcomings as a military weapon. It took a full minute to load properly, as compared to twenty seconds for a smoothbore musket, thus greatly reducing the rate of fire. Furthermore, a rifle could not be fitted with a bayonet, and bayonet charges were often decisive in eighteenth-century battles. Finally, because each rifle was handmade and had a slightly different caliber, supplying ammunition to a large body of riflemen was extremely difficult.

In spite of these drawbacks, the Long Rifle could be a spectacular combat weapon when employed under the right conditions. At Saratoga, Cowpens, and Guilford Courthouse, the lethal long-range fire of the American rifle companies devastated exposed British formations, taking a particularly heavy toll of royal officers, who made tempting targets because of the gaudy epaulettes on their uniforms.

Nowhere was the Long Rifle used to more deadly effect, however, than at Kings Mountain. On its steep, forested slopes, frontier marksmen, aiming at targets silhouetted against the skyline, shot down 388 loyalists in less than an hour, and delivered a crushing blow to British plans for conquering the South.

A stone monument stands on the flat summit of Kings Mountain, not far from the spot where the over-mountain men gunned down their hated enemy, Patrick "Bull Dog" Ferguson. National Park Service, photograph by Richard Frear.

The startled loyalists discharged a volley at their assailants, but the cliffs were so steep and the brush so thick that most of the musket balls flew high and wide. The distinctive, sharp crack of rifle fire was now heard as the over-mountain men fought their way uphill Indian-style, moving from tree to tree and rock to rock, sharpshooting as they went.

Major Ferguson, dressed in a checked hunting shirt and blowing on a large silver whistle, rallied his troops and led them on a bayonet charge that pushed the attackers away from the lip of the summit. The deadly accurate rifle fire of the concealed frontiersmen was taking a heavy toll, however, and several loyalists tried to raise a white flag. Ferguson galloped over and cut the flag down, swearing angrily that he would "never surrender to such bandits." Shrilling his whistle and waving his sword, he led another bayonet charge, but a hail of bullets ripped into his body and he pitched dead from the saddle, one foot still caught in a stirrup.

The over-mountain men howled in triumph as the bleeding corpse of their hated enemy was dragged across the battlefield by his panic-stricken horse. They swept to the crest of the mountain, herded the terrified loyalists into a hollow, and opened fire at point-blank range. White flags went up and cries for mercy were heard, but the furious riflemen continued to blaze away, shooting down their helpless foes.

Darkness finally ended the slaughter; 225 loyalists had been killed and 163 wounded. The over-mountain men had lost just 28 killed and 62 wounded.

Patriots' Revenge

The rage of the over-mountain men did not subside with the conclusion of the battle. All through the night they refused to give aid to the wounded loyalists, whose anguished groans and pleas for water were ignored or cruelly mocked. The next morning the frontiersmen piled the bodies of Ferguson's slain in great heaps where scavenging animals could get at them and, leaving the wounded behind to die, began herding the remainder of the loyalist battalion—some 700 cold, hungry, bedraggled men—northward toward the Continental Army's encampment at Hillsboro, North Carolina.

During the trek north many of the captives were beaten and some were mutilated and killed. When the column reached Gilbert Town, the citizens of that village demanded retribution for the execution earlier that summer of several local patriots. An outdoor trial was held in a driving rainstorm, thirty-six prisoners were convicted of various offenses, and nine were summarily hanged.

The surviving loyalists were finally delivered to the Continental Army, and the overmountain men dispersed, returning to their farms beyond the Appalachians. The aftershocks of the Battle of Kings Mountain, and of the terrible death march that followed it, reverberated through the Carolinas long after they had disbanded, however. Loyalists, fearing for their lives, became reluctant to enlist in the British army or to offer it aid; patriots were heartened, and they turned out in ever greater numbers to fight against Cornwallis and his lieutenants. At Kings Mountain, the tide of war in the South had begun to turn against the British.

Touring the Park

Begin your tour at the Visitor Center, where exhibits help explain the battle. A one-and-a-half-mile foot trail loops through the battlefield; unnumbered displays along the way describe the troop movements and the tactics employed. The spot where Major Patrick Ferguson was killed, and his grave site, are prominently marked.

CHAPTER 26

MOORES CREEK
NATIONAL BATTLEFIELD
(Revolutionary War)

P.O. Box 69
Currie, North Carolina 28435
Telephone: (919) 283-5591

On February 27, 1776, patriots and loyalists clashed in a brief, violent battle on the banks of Moores Creek in southeastern North Carolina. The patriot victory forestalled a British invasion of the South and encouraged North Carolinians to instruct their delegation to the Continental Congress to support total independence—the first colony to so act.

Getting to the Park: Moores Creek National Battlefield is located 20 miles northwest of Wilmington, North Carolina. From Wilmington, take U.S. 421 to North Carolina 210. Turn left on 210 and drive 5 miles west to the park.

Gas, food, lodging: In Wilmington, 20 miles to the southeast on U.S. 421.

Visitor Center: Museum, audiovisual program.

Activities: Interpretive programs and living-history demonstrations. Inquire at Visitor Center for schedule and locations.

Handicapped Access: The Visitor Center is fully accessible. The History Trail is hard-surfaced, but the spur trail to the Bridge Monument and the Tarheel Trail are sand covered. Return route of the History Trail over Slocumb Hill may be difficult because of a fairly steep grade. There are benches along the trail for resting.

North Carolina was a colony divided in the spring of 1775. Many North Carolinians wanted to repudiate British rule and seek independence, but many others remained staunchly loyal to the Crown and were determined to preserve the political status quo. As America drifted toward open rebellion against Great Britain, a struggle for supremacy between these two groups became inevitable.

Gathering of the Highlanders

News of the Battle of Lexington and Concord (see Chapter 3) galvanized the North Carolina patriots into action. They drove Josiah Martin, royal governor of the colony, from the capital at New Bern, established a provincial council to rule in his place, and began raising two regiments for the newly formed Continental Army as well as several battalions of militia.

The colony's loyalists were not about to let this "most daring, horrid, and unnatural Rebellion" go unchallenged, and they began organizing a militia force of their own. General Donald MacDonald was dispatched to south-central North Carolina, an area populated by fiercely loyal Scottish Highlanders, to recruit a battalion and lead it to the coast where a British army was expected to land.

Offering 200 acres of free land and a twenty-one-year tax exemption as an inducement, MacDonald enlisted some 1,600 Highlanders in his battalion. On February 20, 1776, they set out from Cross Creek, near present-day Fayetteville, and marched southeast toward Cape Fear, where they were to link up with the British invasion force.

Widow Moore's Creek

When the patriots learned of the Highlanders' march to the sea, they took steps to block it. Approximately 1,000 militiamen, led by Colonel Richard Caswell and Colonel Alexander Lillington, moved to "take possession of the bridge over Widow Moore's creek," a span the loyalists would have to cross on their way to the coast. Earthworks were dug on both the east and west banks of the meandering, thirty-five-foot-wide stream, and the patriots took cover behind them and waited for the Highlanders to arrive.

On the night of February 26, MacDonald halted his battalion near the Moores Creek Bridge and convened a council of war. Should the Highlanders swing wide around the patriots and avoid an engagement or should they attack? After a spirited debate the decision was made to attack at dawn on the 27th.

The Battle of Moores Creek Bridge

The patriots defending the earthworks on the west side of Moores Creek got wind of the impending attack and withdrew across the stream on the night of February 26. They tore up the bridge's planks and greased the girders to make it difficult for the Highlanders to follow them. Then they moved into the east bank earthworks, cleaned their muskets, and readied themselves for battle.

Around 1 A.M. on the 27th the Highlanders began their advance, moving slowly through the chill darkness toward the bridge. Leading the way was a company of seventy-five broadswordsmen commanded by Captain John Campbell; this picked group of fighters would spearhead the assault on the patriot position.

The attackers reached the banks of the creek an hour before dawn. The plan called for them to wait there until daylight, but a sudden sputter of musket fire and the shout "King George and broad swords!" sent them plunging forward toward the bridge. Bagpipes skirled in the rear as the Highlanders crawled over the slippery girders or waded through the dark water and gathered on the east bank. Waving their basket-hilted claymores overhead and bellowing fiercely, they charged toward the shadowy outline of the earthworks.

The 1,000 patriots massed in the fortifications kept their heads down until the Scotsmen were only thirty yards away. Then they rose as one, leveled their muskets, and opened fire.

Bright as lightning, a sheet of flame rippled along the line, and a deep-throated boom like a clap of thunder enveloped the onrushing Highlanders. Musket and cannonballs smashed flesh and bone, and the attack was shattered. A second volley, heavy as the first, crashed into the Highlander ranks, and the rout was on.

The British Cancel Their Invasion

When the sun finally rose on February 27, it revealed the terrible toll taken by the patriot guns: thirty loyalists were dead and forty wounded. The remainder of MacDonald's battalion was fleeing westward; most of its members would be captured and disarmed within a few days.

Although brief, the skirmish at Moores Creek was decisive. Denied loyalist support, the British decided to cancel their invasion of North Carolina. Without the threat of British intervention, the patriots were free to consolidate their control over the colony, and on April 12, 1776, they took the momentous step of instructing their delegation to the Continental Congress in Philadelphia to vote for independence from Britain.

Touring the Park

Begin your tour at the Visitor Center, where exhibits, an audiovisual program, and a large diorama explain the Battle of Moores Creek and provide background on the Revolutionary War in North Carolina.

History Trail. A .7-mile foot trail connects the key historic points on the battlefield. Starting at the Visitor Center, the trail follows the trace of the old Negro Head Point Road, the route the Highlanders were following on their march to the sea. When you reach the east bank of Moores Creek you will see the remains of earthworks that were reconstructed in the 1930s. This was the position held by the patriots on the morning of February 27, 1776. A short side trail leads to the site of the Moores Creek Bridge, focal point of the fighting.

Return to the History Trail and follow it back to the Visitor Center. You will pass a number of monuments, including the Grady Monument honoring Private John Grady, the only patriot to die in the battle, and the Loyalist Monument dedicated to those North Carolinians who supported the British and "did their duty as they saw it."

Tarheel Trail. This .3-mile foot trail begins near the end of the History Trail. Interpretive exhibits along the trail describe the production of naval stores (timber and pitch), which was an important industry in this region during the Revolutionary War.

CHAPTER 27

NINETY SIX NATIONAL HISTORIC SITE
(Revolutionary War)

P.O. Box 496
Ninety Six, South Carolina 29666
Telephone: (803) 543-4068

In May and June 1781, General Nathanael Greene's patriot army besieged the British outpost at Ninety Six. Although the American attempt to storm the fortifications was repulsed, the British were ultimately forced to abandon Ninety Six and retreat to the South Carolina coast. Ninety Six National Historic Site preserves the site of the crossroads hamlet of Ninety Six and the earthworks and other historic features dating to the 1781 siege.

Getting to the Park: Ninety Six National Historic Site is located 2 miles south of the town of Ninety Six. From Greenwood, South Carolina, drive 10 miles east on South Carolina highway 34 to Ninety Six, then south 2 miles on South Carolina Highway 248 to the park.

Gas, food, lodging: In Greenwood.

Visitor Center: Museum and audiovisual program.

Activities: Interpretive talks by park personnel. Historical Heritage Festival held in May to commemorate the siege of Ninety Six features living-history demonstrations. Autumn Candlelight Tour held in October features nighttime guided candlelight tours of the park grounds. Costumed volunteers portray Revolutionary War era residents and soldiers. Holiday Open House held in December is a Christmas celebration. Park personnel in period dress tell of the holiday legends and traditions of eighteenth-century backcountry South Carolina. Inquire at Visitor Center for dates and additional information.

Handicapped Access: Visitor Center is accessible. Inquire about accessibility of the one-mile loop trail.

Patriot general Nathanael Greene and his southern army emerged from the Battle of Guilford Courthouse on March 15, 1781 (see Chapter 22), tactical losers but strategic victors. The British force that drove them from the battlefield suffered such heavy losses that it was forced to withdraw to Wilmington, on the North Carolina coast. This left the way open for the Americans to drive south and begin retaking the South Carolina backcountry. The first target in this campaign of liberation was the British outpost at Ninety Six.

Frontier Crossroads

In the early 1700s, traders traveling back and forth along the Cherokee Path, a frontier road that linked the coastal city of Charleston with Indian villages in the South Carolina backcountry, regularly stopped over at a place where several side trails intersected the main path. They called the spot Ninety Six because they believed it was ninety-six miles from Keowee, a large Cherokee town in the foothills of the Blue Ridge Mountains.

A businessman named Robert Gouedy opened a trading post at Ninety Six in 1751, and a wave of settlers moved into the fertile lands nearby. By 1775, at least 100 people lived in the vicinity of Ninety Six, and the village proper boasted a dozen homes, a blacksmith shop, a courthouse, and a two-story brick jail.

The outbreak of hostilities between American patriots and the British army in the northern colonies divided the citizens of Ninety Six along political and economic lines. Some were wholeheartedly in favor of seeking independence, while others were adamantly opposed to breaking ties with the British Crown. Still others—perhaps a majority—remained neutral, waiting to see which way events would break and hoping to stay out of trouble.

Whatever their feelings about independence, the people of Ninety Six soon found themselves embroiled in the Revolutionary War. The village's strategic location and its importance as a regional trading center guaranteed that the British and the Americans would vie for its control. The first clash took place on November 18, 1775, when 1,800 loyalists attacked 600 patriots who had gathered at Ninety Six. After several days of skirmishing the two armies agreed to a truce, but there would be no lasting peace. For the next five years, bitter, fratricidal fighting wracked the South Carolina backcountry, with neither side able to gain the upper hand.

In June 1780, a mixed force of British soldiers and American loyalists occupied Ninety Six and turned it into a base for controlling upland South Carolina. The British commander, Charles Lord Cornwallis, planned to garrison the town with 550 loyalists while he and his redcoats moved on to the north to duel with the patriot regular army. A New York tory, Lieutenant Colonel John Harris Cruger, was put in charge and instructed to be "vigorous" in suppressing all rebel guerilla activity.

During the next year, Cruger and his loyalists diligently carried out their assignment. They also worked hard to strengthen Ninety Six's defenses, building a log stockade west of town and a star-shaped earthen fort to the northeast. When news of the battle at Guilford Courthouse reached them, they occupied these fortifications and prepared to defend them against Greene's advancing patriot column.

The Siege of Ninety Six

The American army, numbering about a thousand men, arrived at Ninety Six on May 22, 1781, and surrounded the stockade and star fort. Greene had no heavy artillery

Capture of this star-shaped earthen fort at Ninety Six was the chief goal of the thirty-day siege mounted by the patriot army in the spring of 1781. National Parks and Monuments Association, photograph copyright William A. Bake.

with which to batter the enemy into submission, so he turned to his engineering officer, Polish general Thaddeus Kosciuszko, who was an expert in siegecraft.

Kosciuszko set the patriot soldiers to digging a network of zigzag approach trenches that connected with parallels, ditches long and deep enough to shelter large numbers of infantrymen from hostile fire. On June 10, the third parallel, located less than 100 feet from the north parapet of the star fort, was completed. The Americans then erected a log tower from which their riflemen could shoot down at the loyalists inside the fort.

Hunger, thirst, and sniping from the rifle tower eventually would have forced Colonel Cruger to surrender his garrison, but Greene did not have the luxury of time. During the second week of June he received word that a large British relief column, led by Lord Rawdon, was marching rapidly toward Ninety Six. He had to take the fortifications quickly or face the prospect of being trapped between the forces of Rawdon and Cruger. Reluctantly, he decided to launch frontal attacks against the stockade and star fort.

At noon on June 18, American troops led by Major Henry "Light-horse Harry" Lee stormed the stockade and captured it. The star fort would be a more difficult objective, however: a fraise of sharpened stakes bristled from its high, steeply angled ramparts, and a barrier of sandbags ringed its parapets. Greene's plan called for squads of sappers to advance from the third parallel to the north wall of the fort. While sharpshooters in the rifle tower pinned down the defenders, the sappers would chop through the sharpened stakes and pull down the sandbags with long hooks, clearing the way for a general infantry assault.

Under cover of fire from the rifle tower, the axemen and hookmen ran forward and began the job of dismantling the star fort's defenses. Colonel Cruger refused to let them work unmolested, however. He ordered his soldiers to counterattack, and a brief, furious, hand-to-hand struggle ensued in the ditch beneath the north rampart. After suffering heavy casualties, the patriot sappers retreated; with the fraise and sand-bag barrier still intact, Greene knew that it would be useless to go ahead with the main assault. Instead, he commanded his troops to pack up their gear and prepare to move out.

The weary, dispirited patriot army broke camp before dawn on June 20, and marched north toward the Saluda River. Hours later, Lord Rawdon's column of red-coats arrived at Ninety Six. The thirty-day siege was over.

Ninety Six Abandoned

Cruger and his band of loyalists had made one of the great defensive stands of the Revolutionary War, but in the end their courage and determination came to naught. Lord Rawdon assessed the strategic situation and decided to abandon Ninety Six. With Greene's army lurking nearby, and the patriot guerilla bands of Francis Marion, Andrew Pickens, and Thomas Sumter growing ever bolder, it was useless to try to hang on to the isolated post.

On July 3, after wrecking the star fort and burning the few buildings still standing in the village, the British and their loyalist allies departed for the coast. With their retreat all of the South Carolina backcountry was under patriot control again, this time for good. Greene had failed to take Ninety Six by force of arms, but had achieved his ultimate goal nonetheless.

Touring the Park

Begin your tour at the Visitor Center, where interpretive displays describe the history of Ninety Six and explain the important role it played in the Revolutionary War.

A one-mile loop trail begins and ends at the Visitor Center. There are seven numbered stops along the way.

Stop 1. Historic Island Ford Road. This road was the main street of old Ninety Six. Seven miles to the north, it crossed the Saluda River at Island Ford and then intersected with roads leading to Charlotte and Camden. Erosion and heavy wagon traffic cut the Island Ford Road below the level of the surrounding ground.

Stop 2. Siege Lines. From this vantage point you can see the outline of the approach trenches and parallels dug by the patriots, under the direction of Thaddeus Kosciuszko, in May and June 1781. Just behind the third parallel is the spot where the wooden rifle tower was erected.

Stop 3. Star Fort. Capture of this large earthwork was the chief goal of the thirty-day siege mounted by the patriot army in the spring of 1781. The loyalist garrison suffered great privation during the siege, but managed to hold out, successfully repelling the only assault, made on June 18.

Stop 4. Site of Ninety Six. The village of Ninety Six stood on this site from 1751 to 1781. A dozen buildings flanked the Island Ford Road, which was an important trade route linking Charleston on the coast with various communities in the South Carolina interior.

The Revolutionary War brought an abrupt end to Ninety Six's prosperity, and when the British abandoned the town after the 1781 siege, they set fire to the few buildings that were still standing.

Stop 5. Jail Site. The South Carolina colonial legislature made Ninety Six the seat of a backcountry judicial district in 1769. A courthouse was built and, in 1772, a two-story brick jail was erected on this site. The jailer and his family lived on the first floor while the prisoners were housed on the second floor.

During the siege the jail was used as a loyalist strongpoint. It was guarded on the north side by a V-shaped earthwork.

Stop 6. Stockade Redoubt. Cruger and his loyalists built this stockade to guard Spring Branch, the only reliable source of water for the village. Patriot troops led by "Light-horse Harry" Lee captured it on June 18.

Stop 7. Site of Cambridge. At the conclusion of the Revolutionary War, people began to drift back to Ninety Six. Instead of rebuilding on the old site, they decided to start a new town, which they called Cambridge.

For a time Cambridge flourished, but in 1815 a deadly epidemic ravaged the population. The little village never recovered, and by the 1840s it had disappeared completely.

CHAPTER 28

PEA RIDGE NATIONAL MILITARY PARK
(Civil War)

Highway 62 East
Pea Ridge, Arkansas 72751
Telephone: (501) 451-8122

In a bitter two-day battle fought on March 7–8, 1862, in the hill country of northern Arkansas, Federal forces commanded by General Samuel Curtis defeated a Confederate army led by General Earl Van Dorn. This decisive victory ended the Confederate threat to Missouri and permanently secured the state to the Union. Pea Ridge National Military Park preserves the scene of the fighting as well as Elkhorn Tavern, a historic building associated with the battle.

Getting to the Park: Pea Ridge National Military Park is located 28 miles north of Fayetteville, Arkansas. Take U.S. 62 from Fayetteville to Rogers. The park is 10 miles north of Rogers off U.S. 62.

Gas, food, lodging: In Rogers.

Visitor Center: Museum and gift shop; audiovisual program.

Activities: Interpretive talks by park personnel.

Handicapped Access: Visitor Center is fully accessible with the exception of the observation deck, which is reached by three steps up from the foyer. Elkhorn Tavern is entered by two narrow steps to the porch. Foot trail at Stop 12 (Little Sugar Creek Trenches) has a very steep incline, and may not be suitable for wheelchairs. Inquire at Visitor Center.

After their defeat at Wilson's Creek in August 1861 (see Chapter 33), Union forces in Missouri regrouped and made preparations for a second campaign into the Confederate stronghold in the state's southwestern corner. Commanding the 10,500-man Federal army was General Samuel R. Curtis, West Point graduate, Mexican War veteran, and ex-Republican congressman from Iowa.

Curtis began his offensive on Christmas Day 1861, pushing General Sterling Price's pro-Confederate Missouri State Guard before him as he moved southwest toward the town of Springfield. By mid-February 1862, the 7,000 guardsmen had been driven

242

out of their home state and into neighboring Arkansas. Curtis also crossed into north-western Arkansas, but instead of staying on the enemy's heels he halted and ordered his army into camp.

March 1862: The Confederates Counterattack

As it turned out, Curtis's caution was justified. Fifty miles from his bivouac, in the Boston Mountains south of Fayetteville, three separate Confederate units were co-alescing into a formidable new army. Price's Missourians had been joined by 8,000 Confederate regulars from Texas, Louisiana, and Arkansas, commanded by General Ben McCulloch, and by 1,000 Cherokees from the Indian Territory, led by politician Albert Pike.

On March 3, forty-one-year-old Earl Van Dorn—recently promoted to general in recognition of his military success in Texas—arrived to take charge of this polyglot force. Thirsting for action, he announced that he would move immediately against the Union army, crush it, and then conquer Missouri. "I must have St. Louis—then huzza!" was the way he summed up his strategy in a letter to his wife.

When Curtis was informed by scouts that the 16,000 Rebels had broken camp and were marching north through a heavy snowstorm, he ordered his troops to fall back and entrench on the bluffs overlooking Little Sugar Creek, approximately five miles south of the Missouri state line. This was a naturally strong defensive position, guarded in the front by a stream and in the rear by a rugged escarpment called Pea Ridge. The Federals turned to with shovels and axes, and they were snug behind earth-and-log breastworks, ready to beat off any attacks, when the Confederates arrived on March 6.

Van Dorn reconnoitered this bristling position at dusk on the 6th and decided against launching a frontal assault. Instead, he would lead half his troops—Price's Missourians—on a night march around Pea Ridge into the Union rear. At dawn on March 7 they would advance south, down the Telegraph Road past Elkhorn Tavern, and take the Yankees by surprise.

Meanwhile, McCulloch and Pike would lead the other half of the Confederate army on a shorter march to the west end of Pea Ridge. When Van Dorn began his attack at daylight, they would move southeast through the hamlet of Leetown and hit the right rear of the Union line. Caught between two attacking forces, Curtis's army would be rolled up and destroyed.

March 7, 1862: Pea Ridge—Day One

Van Dorn's troops were hungry and tired after their grueling three-day trek up from the Boston Mountains, and the night march around Pea Ridge proved extremely difficult for them to execute. They were hours late arriving at the jump-off point for their attack, and this gave Curtis time to pull his army out of the Little Sugar Creek trenches and turn it around to meet the threat from the north.

At 10:30 A.M., more than three hours after the appointed time, Price's Missourians began their advance down the Telegraph Road, only to be confronted by Union troops arrayed in battle formation. The Confederates attacked, charging against the blue ranks in a determined thrust; the Federals slowly gave ground, fighting every inch of the way. Three times in the span of six hours the Missourians surged forward,

General Samuel R. Curtis led a 10,500-man Federal army into the Confederate stronghold of southwestern Missouri during the winter of 1861–1862. Library of Congress.

Dashing General Earl Van Dorn intended to crush Curtis's army, and then conquer Missouri for the Confederacy. "I must have St. Louis—then huzza!" he wrote to his wife. Cook Collection, Valentine Museum, Richmond, Virginia.

and three times their opponents retreated, only to stop and form another, more deadly defensive line. The final assault of the afternoon carried the Confederates a half mile past Elkhorn Tavern, but that was the limit of their endurance, and the banging of musketry slowly sputtered to a halt.

The other prong of Van Dorn's attack, from the west end of Pea Ridge, was met by two of Curtis's divisions in a meadow north of Leetown. Albert Pike's Cherokees began the combat by capturing a Union artillery battery; they were then hit by a terrific barrage from other cannon, which frightened them so badly that they fled and refused to fight any more.

Ben McCulloch's Texans and Arkansans tried their hand next, but the Federals, massed behind a split-rail fence, cut them down as they advanced across the open field. McCulloch was shot and killed as he urged his men forward. Minutes later his successor, General James McIntosh, was also mortally wounded. A third officer took charge but was quickly taken prisoner, and the leaderless Confederate soldiers broke off the attack and retreated in disorder. Some took the opportunity to desert; others waited for sundown, then set out to join Van Dorn's force at Elkhorn Tavern.

March 8, 1862: Pea Ridge—Day Two

The gray army had shot its bolt in the attack of March 7. The troops had been marching or fighting for four days, and the only food they had eaten in the last forty-eight hours was what they could scavenge from the knapsacks of the enemy dead. Ammunition was running low and the supply wagons, left behind during the nighttime march around Pea Ridge, were now lost somewhere in the Union rear. Too tired to retreat, too weak to advance, they spread out in a defensive line and waited to see what the Federal forces would do.

In the wan light of early morning, Curtis examined the Confederate position, which stretched from the base of Pea Ridge on his left to the Telegraph Road and Elkhorn Tavern on his right. Sensing its vulnerability, he decided to attack at once. A brisk preparatory bombardment wreaked havoc on the Confederate artillery emplacements, and then long ranks of cheering Union infantrymen advanced toward the enemy formations positioned at the base of Pea Ridge. Bayonets glittering, the bluecoats bore down on the gray line, which bent backward and then broke under the irresistible pressure.

As the Confederate right gave way, Curtis signaled for the remainder of his army to strike the left at Elkhorn Tavern. With excited shouts, the Federals charged up the Telegraph Road toward the shot-scarred, white frame building, eager to deliver the coup de grace to the reeling Rebel army.

Curtis—normally quiet and reserved—was beside himself with excitement as his

Fierce fighting raged around Elkhorn Tavern on March 7–8, 1862. Arkansas Department of Parks and Tourism.

assault swept the enemy from the field. "Victory!" he bellowed in exaltation. "Victory!"

The Federal formations converged, and the Confederate line disintegrated, its fragments fleeing north, east, and west in a desperate effort to avoid capture. The Union army was triumphant; Earl Van Dorn's bold prediction: "St. Louis—then huzza!" had been hurled back in his face.

Missouri Saved for the Union

"The vulture and the wolf have now communion, and the dead, friends and foes, sleep in the same lonely grave," Curtis wrote the day after the battle. Casualties totaled 2,684, split almost evenly between the two sides.

For his part, Van Dorn tried to explain, both to himself and his superiors, just what had happened at Pea Ridge. "I was not defeated," he concluded, "but only foiled in my intentions." The Confederate high command failed to appreciate the difference, and ordered him to abandon his designs on St. Louis and march with the remnants of his army south and east into Mississippi.

Thus, the Federal victory at Pea Ridge was decisive: it ended the Confederate threat to Missouri and secured the state to the Union.

Touring the Park

Begin your tour at the Visitor Center, where exhibits will help you understand the struggle for Missouri and the role the Battle of Pea Ridge played in it. A loop road runs through the park. Twelve numbered stops mark the major historic points on the battlefield.

Stop 1. General Curtis Headquarters Site. The Union commander had his headquarters near this spot. Two miles south of here, the Union army entrenched along Little Sugar Creek, anticipating a Confederate attack from the south against their fortified line.

Stop 2. Winton Spring. Union soldiers drew water from this spring, located on the Ruddick Farm. The house you see, which stands on the site of the old Ruddick cottage, dates from the early 1900s.

Stop 3. Leetown. The tiny village of Leetown was located a short distance from here. Except for a few gravestones, nothing remains of the settlement.

Stop 4. Leetown Battlefield. Union soldiers crouched behind a split rail fence on the southern edge of this field and repelled the attack of General Ben McCulloch's Texans and Arkansans. McCulloch and his successor, General James McIntosh, were killed near the tree line at the north end of the field. After their charge was halted, the Confederates retreated north and east into the woods, eventually making their way around Pea Ridge to Elkhorn Tavern.

Stop 5. The Indians at Pea Ridge. One thousand Cherokees from the Indian Territory fought with the Confederate army at Pea Ridge. Late on the morning of March 7, the Indians captured a Union artillery battery in the field to your left. When they were hit by cannon fire from other Union batteries, they fled in terror into the woods and refused to rejoin the fighting.

Stop 6. Pea Ridge—West Overlook. On the night of March 6, half of the Con-

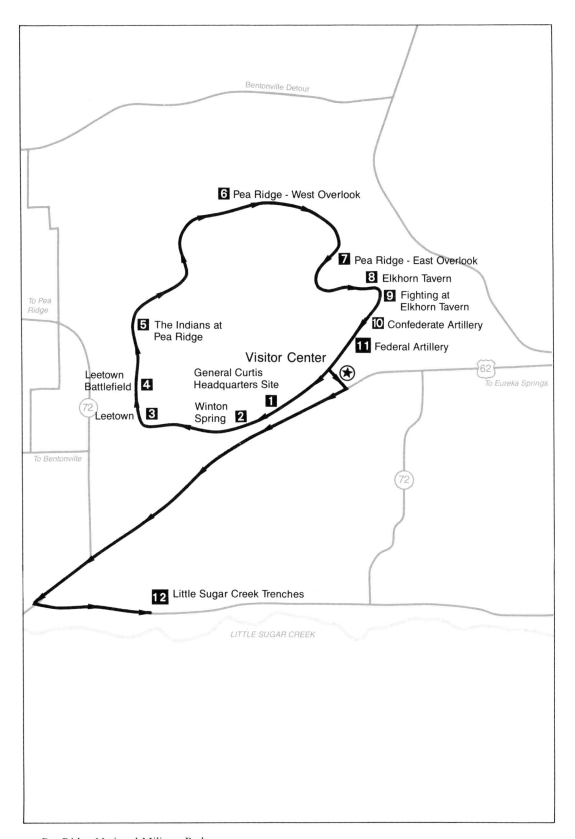

Pea Ridge National Military Park

federate army marched around this high ground to get into the rear of the Union position.

Stop 7. Pea Ridge—East Overlook. Walk down the gravel path to the shelter. From this point you can see most of the battlefield. A tape recording explains the troop movements.

Stop 8. Elkhorn Tavern. Fierce fighting raged around this building. On March 7 the Confederates made a series of attacks south down the Telegraph Road toward the tavern, pushing the Union forces back about half a mile from where you are standing. On March 8, the Federals charged north up the Telegraph Road toward the tavern and routed the Confederate defenders who were stationed near this spot. Walk 100 yards east to Stop 9.

Stop 9. Fighting at Elkhorn Tavern. Displays explain the fighting that took place in this area.

Stop 10. Confederate Artillery. Tull's Missouri battery was located here, anchoring the left end of the Confederate defensive line, on the morning of March 8.

Stop 11. Federal Artillery. On the morning of March 8, a line of Union cannon extending from the hill on your right to a point almost directly behind the Visitor Center pounded the Confederate position to the north. The bombardment ended about 10 A.M., and the Union infantry charged and routed the Confederate defenders.

From here, return to the park entrance, turn right on U.S. 62, and drive 2.8 miles west to where a sign directs you to Stop 12.

Stop 12. Little Sugar Creek Trenches. Walk along the trail to the crest of the bluff above Little Sugar Creek. If you look carefully you will see the eroded remnants of the Union earthworks.

CHAPTER 29

SHILOH NATIONAL MILITARY PARK

(Civil War)

Shiloh, Tennessee 38376
Telephone: (901) 689-5275

On April 6–7, 1862, Union and Confederate armies fought a savage battle near Shiloh Church in southern Tennessee. More men were killed or wounded in the two days of combat than in all three of America's previous wars combined. The Confederate failure to drive the Federal army out of Tennessee led, ultimately, to Union control of the Mississippi River and the splitting of the Confederacy. Shiloh National Military Park preserves the site of this crucial Civil War battle.

Getting to the Park: Shiloh National Military Park is located 10 miles south of Savannah, Tennessee, and 22 miles north of Corinth, Mississippi. From Savannah, take U.S. 64 4 miles west to its intersection with Tennessee Highway 22. Drive south on Tennessee 22 approximately 6 miles to the park. From Corinth, take U.S. 45 5 miles north to its intersection with Tennessee Highway 22. Drive north and east on Tennessee 22 approximately 18 miles to the park.

Gas, food, lodging: In Corinth, Mississippi, and Savannah, Tennessee.

Visitor Center: Museum; twenty-five-minute film on the battle. The gift shop is located in a separate building.

Activities: Interpretive talks by park personnel. Living-history demonstrations. Inquire at Visitor Center for schedule and locations.

Handicapped Access: Visitor Center is fully accessible. All major points of interest may be seen by car.

Capture of Forts Henry and Donelson in February 1862 (see Chapter 19) opened the Tennessee and Cumberland rivers to navigation by Union gunboats and compelled Confederate forces to abandon middle and western Tennessee.

Withdrawing to the town of Corinth in northeastern Mississippi, the Rebel troops

General Albert Sidney Johnston, commander in chief of Confederate forces in the West, was determined to attack the Union army at Pittsburg Landing. "I would fight them if they were a million," he declared. Cook Collection, Valentine Museum, Richmond, Virginia.

deployed along a defensive line covering the Memphis & Charleston Railroad. This vital rail link, connecting Memphis on the Mississippi River with Charleston and Richmond on the Eastern Seaboard, had been called "the vertebrae of the Confederacy." General Albert Sidney Johnston, commander in chief of Confederate armies in the West, was determined to shield it.

Johnston's Union counterpart, General Henry W. Halleck, also recognized the importance of the Memphis & Charleston. In the spring of 1862, he launched an offensive aimed at cutting the strategic railroad, dividing the Confederacy, and ending the war.

The campaign began during the third week of March when a fleet of transports left Fort Henry and steamed up the Tennessee River, carrying Federal troops to establish a base of operations near the Mississippi-Tennessee border. The site chosen for the base was Pittsburg Landing, twenty-two miles northeast of the main Confederate encampment at Corinth. Major General Ulysses S. Grant, commander of the expedition, bivouacked his 40,000 soldiers in the woods and fields around Shiloh Church, a few miles from the Landing. His instructions from Halleck were to wait there, postponing any attack, until he was joined by General Don Carlos Buell's 30,000-man army, which was marching overland from Nashville to link up with him.

Meanwhile, in Corinth, Confederate general Johnston was drilling his army in preparation for taking the offensive. Although worried about the greenness of his 40,000 troops—"this mob we have miscalled soldiers," chief of staff Braxton Bragg sourly called them—he believed he had no choice but to attack Grant before he was reinforced by Buell. On April 3 he put the Rebel army on the road to Pittsburg Landing; it was poised on the perimeter of the Union camp, ready to launch an assault, two days later.

As the sun went down on April 5, several of Johnston's senior officers pleaded with the general to cancel the attack and withdraw to Corinth. They were convinced that the element of surprise had been lost and that the alerted enemy would be found "entrenched to the eyes."

Johnston was firm, however. The attack would go ahead at daylight, as planned. "I would fight them if they were a million," he bluntly proclaimed.

April 6, 1862: Shiloh—Day One

Sunrise on April 6 revealed a grand and ominous panorama: 40,000 Confederates were massed in battle formation in the underbrush southwest of Shiloh Church. Less than a mile away, Federal troops were sitting around their tents eating breakfast, unaware that they were about to be plunged into the deadly maelstrom of combat.

Grant and his commanders had decided against fortifying the Shiloh camp because they wanted the soldiers to spend their time drilling rather than digging. The possibility of a Confederate attack had been dismissed, and all reports of Confederate troops in the vicinity had been scoffed at as the nervous imaginings of inexperienced pickets.

The first warning of the impending attack came at 5:15 A.M. when a Union patrol encountered Confederate skirmishers in Fraley Field, just southwest of the main Federal encampment. An officer rushed back to the bivouac, shouting that "the Rebels are out there thicker than fleas on a dog's back!" Moments later, as the startled soldiers fumbled for their weapons, the Confederates burst into view, yelling and shooting.

Johnston's plan called for the assault to be concentrated on the Union left. He hoped to seize Pittsburg Landing, separating Grant's army from the river and its base of supplies. His soldiers charged along the entire length of the Federal position, however, advancing in a blaze of gun flashes and a rolling cloud of powder smoke.

The Union troops were stunned by the sudden onslaught; a few fought desperately, but most fled for their lives. "Everybody was running . . . so I ran too," recalled one private. The Rebel forces surged ahead through the camp, sweeping the panicking Federals before them. Not until 9 A.M. did Union soldiers manage to form a line of resistance, stretching from Shiloh Church on the right, along a sunken wagon road, to a peach orchard on the left.

Trying to break through the blue line in a brush-choked area in front of the sunken road, the Confederates were hit by scathing volleys of musket fire. The bullets swarmed through the undergrowth, humming and cracking like angry insects; again and again Johnston's men rushed into this "Hornets' Nest," only to be cut down by a hail of metal. The crash of the guns was terrific, "one never-ending, terrible roar, with no prospect of stopping," wrote an Illinois soldier.

To the right of the Hornets' Nest, Union forces began to retreat under pressure. Grant galloped over the battlefield trying to steady his troops, but he needed time to organize another defensive line. He ordered General Benjamin Prentiss, commander of the 5,000 men in the Hornets' Nest, to hold the position "at all hazards" while the rest of the army regrouped behind him. Prentiss and his soldiers obeyed, repulsing eleven headlong charges over the next four hours.

At 2 P.M., General Johnston personally led a furious bayonet assault on the Union stronghold near the Peach Orchard, on the left flank of the Hornets' Nest. The attack was a success, but as Johnston tried to rally his troops for another push, a minié ball ripped through the back of his right knee, severing the artery.

No one present knew how to apply a tourniquet, and within minutes the Confederate commander bled to death.

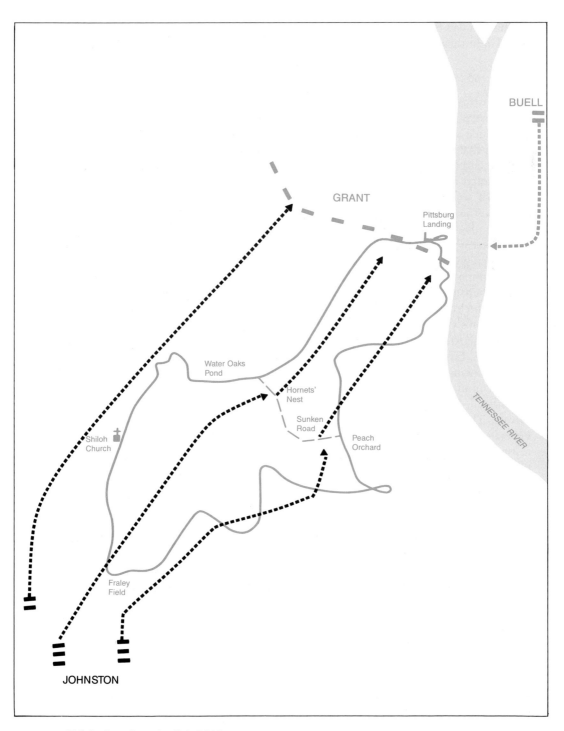

Shiloh, Day One, April 6, 1862

During the Battle of Shiloh, wounded soldiers crawled to this pond to drink and wash their wounds. Men and horses died in the pond, staining its waters a muddy red. Photograph by Joseph E. Stevens.

The Rebels had suffered terrible casualties in their attempts to seize the Hornets' Nest. Now they adopted a new tactic: General Daniel Ruggles massed sixty-two cannon, the largest artillery concentration yet seen on a North American battlefield, and opened fire. The big guns bucked and thundered, and rocks, dirt clods, splintered trees, and body parts exploded into the air as a hurricane of cannonballs, shells, and canister tore through the Union position.

The blue troops who survived this terrible barrage tried to retreat toward Pittsburg Landing, but were quickly cut off and captured by onrushing Confederates. In the smoking ruins of the Hornets' Nest, 2,800 of their comrades—nearly 60 percent of Prentiss's command—lay dead or wounded. Their determined stand had not been in vain, however: they had bought with blood the time Grant needed to form a new defensive perimeter on the bluff above the Landing. They had also worn out the Confederates, who were unable to press their advantage any further that afternoon.

A Night of Suffering

General Pierre G. T. Beauregard, who had assumed command of the Confederate army when Johnston was killed, went to sleep on the evening of April 6 convinced that victory was at hand. His troops had driven the Yankees to the brink of disaster, and he was sure that when the battle resumed in the morning, they would finish the job.

At Pittsburg Landing, General Grant was assessing his situation. The Union army had been caught by surprise and forced back two miles, suffering heavy casualties. Of the men left unscathed, thousands were cowering along the riverbank, "frantic with fright and utterly demoralized," refusing to obey their officers and move into the defensive line.

Still, Grant had an ace in the hole. Buell's army had arrived from Nashville and was being ferried across the Tennessee. By morning there would be 20,000 fresh troops on hand, more than making up for today's losses. Then it would be the Union's turn to launch a surprise attack.

The soldiers on both sides knew nothing of their commanders' strategic thinking. They squatted around smoky fires, trying to ignore the cries of the wounded and the whiz and crash of shells fired into the Confederate camp every fifteen minutes by Union gunboats on the Tennessee. Misery was made nearly complete by a cold rain that began falling at midnight and did not let up until after 3 A.M.

April 7, 1862: Shiloh—Day Two

At dawn, Grant issued orders to his reinforced army: "Advance and recapture our original camps." The gunboats stopped their shelling, and at 7 A.M. Federal troops moved forward, retracing the path of yesterday's rout.

The Rebels were caught off guard, and Union formations rolled ahead, taking back much of the territory lost in the April 6th fighting. By noon the left flank had advanced beyond the Peach Orchard and Hornets' Nest and the right flank was approaching Shiloh Church.

The patchwork Confederate battle line reeled on the verge of collapse. Ammunition was running perilously low and hundreds of exhausted, discouraged men had given up the fight and were straggling toward the rear. Beauregard refused to panic, however. He ordered a series of counterthrusts that halted the Union surge and gave his army a brief breathing spell.

The tempo of the battle picked up again after 1 P.M., with the fiercest combat taking place in the vicinity of Water Oaks Pond, 700 yards northeast of Shiloh Church. In a final, desperate bid to regain the initiative, a Confederate brigade charged through this marsh and hit the Federal right. "The fires from the contending ranks were two continuous sheets of flame," wrote a Union officer who was in the thick of the fighting.

The blue troops were pushed back, but the Rebel assault soon ran out of steam. Beauregard realized that the jig was up, and at 2 P.M. he ordered his battered army to retire. Weary but unbowed, the Rebels slowly withdrew toward Corinth, leaving the Federals in possession of the battlefield.

As the sound of gunfire died away and gray twilight settled over the smoldering, shot-scarred landscape, burial parties went on their grisly rounds. Smoke from burning tents eddied among the splintered tree stumps and hung like a shroud over hundreds of bodies; the cries of the wounded swelled into a ghastly chorus of pain and anguish.

The bone-tired survivors—Union and Confederate—huddled in their bivouacs and tried to sleep. After two days of carnage, they were back where they had started. The battle was over, and there was no clear-cut victor.

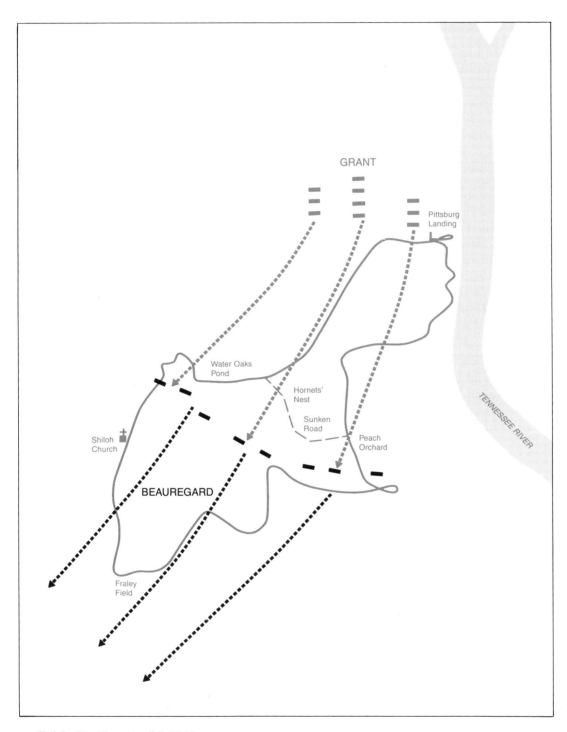

GRANT

Pittsburg
Landing

Water Oaks
Pond

Hornets'
Nest

Sunken
Road

Peach
Orchard

Shiloh
Church

TENNESSEE RIVER

BEAUREGARD

Fraley
Field

Shiloh, Day Two, April 7, 1862

The Butcher's Bill

Roll call on April 8 revealed the terrible dimensions of the Shiloh slaughter: 3,482 men had been killed; 16,420 were wounded; 3,844 were missing. In two days of combat, more blood had been spilled than in all three of America's previous wars combined; approximately one out of every four men who had gone into battle had become a casualty.

Reaction to these shocking losses was particularly strong in the North, where Grant, erstwhile hero of Fort Donelson, was now denounced as a bungler and a butcher. "Those who continue General Grant in active command will . . . carry on their skirts the blood of thousands of their slaughtered countrymen," declared an Iowa congressman. President Lincoln stood by his beleaguered commander, however, rebuffing the calls for Grant's removal with the stark observation: "I can't spare this man. He fights."

Meanwhile, General Halleck hastened to Pittsburgh Landing to reorganize the battered Federal army. In late April he began a cautious, creeping advance toward the Rebel stronghold at Corinth. He captured it without a fight a month later, and cut the Memphis & Charleston Railroad. This achievement, coupled with the Union navy's seizure of Memphis on the Mississippi River, set the stage for Grant's epic campaign against Vicksburg (see Chapter 32) and the cutting in half of the Confederacy.

Touring the Park

Begin your tour at the Visitor Center, where museum exhibits and a twenty-five-minute film provide background information on the Battle of Shiloh and its significance in the Civil War.

A tour road loops through the battlefield. There are fifteen numbered stops along the way, marking major points of interest.

Stop 1. Grant's Last Line. The Confederate attack on April 6, 1862, caught the Union army by surprise. Federal troops fled in panic toward Pittsburg Landing, in what appeared to be a disastrous rout. A determined stand by Union divisions in the Hornets' Nest (Stop 2) gave Grant time to rally his men and form a defensive line along this low ridge.

The line of cannon marks the final position of the Union army at sundown on April 6. The Federals began their counterattack from this line early the next morning.

Stop 2. Hornets' Nest. Caught completely off guard by the Confederate attack on the morning of April 6, Union soldiers abandoned their camps and retreated to this area. They formed a defensive line along the sunken road you see here, extending into the woods to the east. Between 9 A.M. and 3 P.M., the Confederates made eleven frontal assaults against this position, advancing across the open fields in front of you, suffering heavy losses. To the soldiers the whining, snapping sound of flying bullets sounded like a swarm of angry insects, and so they called the area the "Hornets' Nest."

Stop 3. Ruggles' Battery. After their repeated attacks into the Hornets' Nest failed to dislodge the stubborn defenders, the Confederates adopted a new tactic. General Daniel Ruggles massed sixty-two pieces of artillery in a line, like the one you see here, and opened fire on the Union position, which was only a few hundred yards to the east. The hurricane of cannonballs, shells, and canister shattered the blue ranks and allowed the Confederates to overrun the Hornets' Nest.

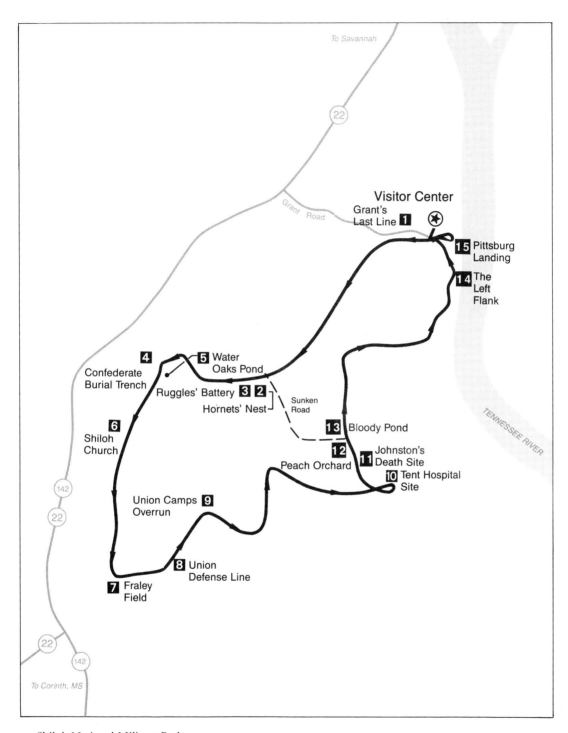

Shiloh National Military Park

Stop 4. Confederate Burial Trench. Immediately after the battle the bodies of the Confederate dead were gathered and buried in five mass graves. This is the largest of those graves; it holds the bodies of more than 700 soldiers, stacked seven deep.

Stop 5. Water Oaks Pond. At dawn on April 7, the Union army counterattacked and regained much of the ground it had lost the day before. In a desperate attempt to blunt the momentum of the blue assault, a Confederate brigade struck the Federals in the vicinity of this wet-weather pond. The Union attack was halted, but the Confederates lost heavily in the process and were forced to break off the fighting and withdraw to the southwest.

Stop 6. Shiloh Church. This is the site of Shiloh Church, for which the battle was named. It was a one-room log structure built by Southern Methodists around 1854. Ironically, Shiloh is a Hebrew word meaning "peace." The present church was built in 1949.

Stop 7. Fraley Field. A short walk down the foot trail takes you to Fraley Field, where, at 5:15 A.M. on April 6, a Federal patrol encountered the advancing Confederates and fired the first shots of the battle.

Stop 8. Union Defense Line. On the low ridge in front of you, on the morning of April 6, surprised Union soldiers tried to form a battle line to halt the Confederates who were advancing rapidly from the southwest. Outnumbered and outgunned, the Federals were swept aside in a matter of minutes.

Stop 9. Union Camps Overrun. Union soldiers were sitting around their tents in this area, eating breakfast, when they were struck by the Confederate onslaught on April 6. Most of the men panicked and ran; a few tried to make a stand and were either killed or captured. The upright cannon marks the spot where Union colonel Everett Peabody was shot while trying to rally his command.

Stop 10. Tent Hospital Site. Union surgeons established one of the first tent hospitals of the Civil War on this site. By bringing the wounded to a central location, where all medical services could be concentrated, the death rate was lowered.

Stop 11. Johnston's Death Site. The tree stump you see marks the spot where General Albert Sidney Johnston, commander of the Confederate army, was mortally wounded by a minié ball. He was taken to a ravine about 100 yards south of this monument, where he bled to death. "When he fell," wrote Confederate president Jefferson Davis, "I realized that our strongest pillar had been broken."

Stop 12. Peach Orchard. This orchard marked the left flank of the defensive line formed by Union soldiers around 9 A.M. on April 6. It was the scene of desperate, seesaw fighting, as the Confederates tried to break through to Pittsburg Landing to the north. The peach trees were in bloom, and the shower of white petals, cut from the branches by the flying bullets, reminded observers of a sweet-smelling snowstorm.

Stop 13. Bloody Pond. During the battle, wounded soldiers of both sides crawled to this pond to drink and wash their wounds. Men and horses died in the pond, staining its waters a muddy red.

Stop 14. The Left Flank. After breaking the Union line in the vicinity of the Hornets' Nest (Stop 2) and Peach Orchard (Stop 12) at approximately 4 P.M. on April 6, a portion of the Confederate army drove on to the north trying to reach Pittsburg Landing. It struck the left flank of Grant's final defensive line in this area and was repulsed.

Stop 15. Pittsburg Landing. This steamboat landing, which served as the Union army's supply depot, was the primary objective of the Confederate assault. During the night of April 6, 20,000 fresh Federal troops were ferried across the river from the east bank and put into the battle line. These reinforcements permitted Grant to counterattack the next morning.

The steep bluffs lining the river in this area also provided shelter to thousands of panic-stricken Union stragglers who, "frantic with fright and utterly demoralized," refused their officers' commands to rejoin the fighting.

CHAPTER 30

STONES RIVER NATIONAL BATTLEFIELD

(Civil War)

RT #10, Box 495
Old Nashville Highway
Murfreesboro, Tennessee 37130
Telephone: (615) 893-9501

On December 31, 1862 and January 2, 1863, Union and Confederate armies clashed in a fierce midwinter battle on the banks of Stones River, near the town of Murfreesboro, Tennessee. The Confederates' inability to drive their enemy from the field opened the way for a Federal campaign against Chattanooga in the summer of 1863. Stones River National Battlefield preserves the scene of the fighting.

Getting to the Park: Stones River National Battlefield is located northwest of Murfreesboro, Tennessee. Leave I-24 at Exit 78 and drive east on U.S. 231 to its intersection with U.S. 70s/41. Drive northwest on U.S. 70s/41 and follow signs to the park.

Gas, food, lodging: In Murfreesboro.

Visitor Center: Museum and gift shop; audiovisual program.

Activities: Interpretive talks by park personnel; living-history demonstrations. Inquire at Visitor Center for schedule and locations.

Handicapped Access: Visitor Center is fully accessible. Some foot trails are surfaced with wood chips. Most of the historic features can be viewed from a car.

The South suffered a disastrous series of setbacks in the western theater during the first four months of 1862. Surrender of Fort Henry and Fort Donelson in February (see Chapter 19), defeat at Pea Ridge in March (see Chapter 28), and a bloody reversal at Shiloh in April (see Chapter 29) sapped the strength and fighting spirit of Confederate forces. Arkansas and western Tennessee were lost, and it seemed only a matter of time before the entire Mississippi River Valley would fall into Union hands.

As spring turned to summer, a Union army 120,000-men strong stood poised in Corinth, Mississippi, ready to thrust south and finish the job of cutting the Confederacy in two. But at this decisive moment General Henry W. Halleck surrendered the initiative and divided his command. One detachment was given the task of occupying western Tennessee, while the other, led by General Don Carlos Buell, was sent east to seize the important railroad junction at Chattanooga.

Braxton Bragg, commander of the 45,000 Confederate troops in Mississippi, was relieved by the sudden dismemberment of the powerful force that had been threatening him. Against the whole he had been hopelessly outnumbered, but against one of the parts he had a fighting chance. In late July, he transferred two-thirds of his army east, by rail, from Tupelo, Mississippi, to Chattanooga, blocking the Union advance on that strategic city. Rather than offering a fight, Buell withdrew northwest to Nashville.

Buoyed by the bloodless defense of Chattanooga and encouraged by the timidity of his opponent, Bragg decided to take the offensive. During the last week of August, his army headed north toward Kentucky, bidding to conquer (or liberate according to the southern point of view) that border state and then invade southern Ohio, capturing Cincinnati.

The Confederate troops got as far as Lexington, in the center of the Bluegrass State, before Buell's Union army caught up with them. On October 8 a battle was fought near Perryville; the result was inconclusive, but Bragg was sufficiently discouraged to call off the invasion and order a retreat back to middle Tennessee. At the end of November the Confederates went into winter quarters on the banks of Stones River, near the town of Murfreesboro.

December 1862: Rosecrans Advances on the Rebel Bivouac

After the Battle of Perryville, the Union high command relieved the overly cautious Buell and replaced him with General William S. Rosecrans. "Old Rosy," as the Union

General William S. Rosecrans—called "Old Rosy" by his soldiers—commanded the Union army at the Battle of Stones River. Library of Congress.

troops called their new leader, was reputed to be a fighting general, and his superiors hoped he would exhibit this aggressiveness in a prompt attack on Bragg.

Rosecrans moved his army to Nashville in November and began stockpiling supplies for an offensive. He planned to hit the Confederates in their Stones River camp, sweep them aside, and march on to Chattanooga, gaining control of the railroads and farms of middle Tennessee.

The day after Christmas he set his troops in motion toward Murfreesboro; they arrived on December 30 and took up a position about half a mile from the hastily formed Confederate battle line.

That night, the soldiers could see the enemy's campfires and hear the tunes played by their military bands. The Confederate musicians played "Dixie," and their Union counterparts responded with "Yankee Doodle." The Confederates' "Bonnie Blue Flag" was followed by the Union's "Hail Columbia." Finally, the bands played "Home Sweet Home," and the men of the two armies sang along, recalling home and loved ones and forgetting, at least for a moment, the dangers they would face on the morrow.

December 31, 1862: Stones River—Day One

At dawn the Confederates charged the Union right flank. "We swooped down on those Yankees like a whirl-a-gust of woodpeckers in a hailstorm," wrote one private. The blue soldiers were caught off guard and hurled backward by this sledgehammer attack, suffering heavy casualties as they retreated through dense thickets of scrub cedar. By 10 A.M., their once straight battle line had been bent into a J-shape and was in danger of breaking.

The entire Union army was tottering on the brink of disaster, but a division commanded by General Philip H. Sheridan made a desperate stand, beating back three separate assaults and blunting the momentum of the Confederate attack. Given a respite by Sheridan's brave fighters, Rosecrans rallied the rest of his troops and organized a new defensive line.

The heart of this position was a rocky, tree-topped knoll known locally as the "Round Forest." Here the blue infantry, supported by fifty cannon, braced to meet the next Rebel onslaught.

It came just before noon, a brigade of Mississippians—about 800 men—rushing across a field of unpicked cotton toward the bristling outcrop. A withering, point-blank blast of cannon and musket fire left a third of their number dead or wounded. The survivors retreated, stopping just long enough to stuff wads of the cotton into their ears to dampen the terrible thunder of the Union guns.

A half hour later, a Tennessee brigade tried a second assault on "Hell's Half Acre," as the Mississippians had dubbed the Round Forest. They too were beaten back, losing more than half their strength to the crashing Federal volleys. A third wave moved across the cotton field at 2 P.M., only to be repulsed like the first two.

Once more, at 4 P.M., the Confederates tried to dislodge the Federals from the Round Forest. Two brigades marched forward toward the muzzles of the waiting Union guns, moving "steadily and, as it seemed, to certain victory," wrote one officer. But valor was no match for massed firepower, and as the winter sun set on the blood-soaked turf of Hell's Half Acre, this last attack was shattered by a barrage of bullets.

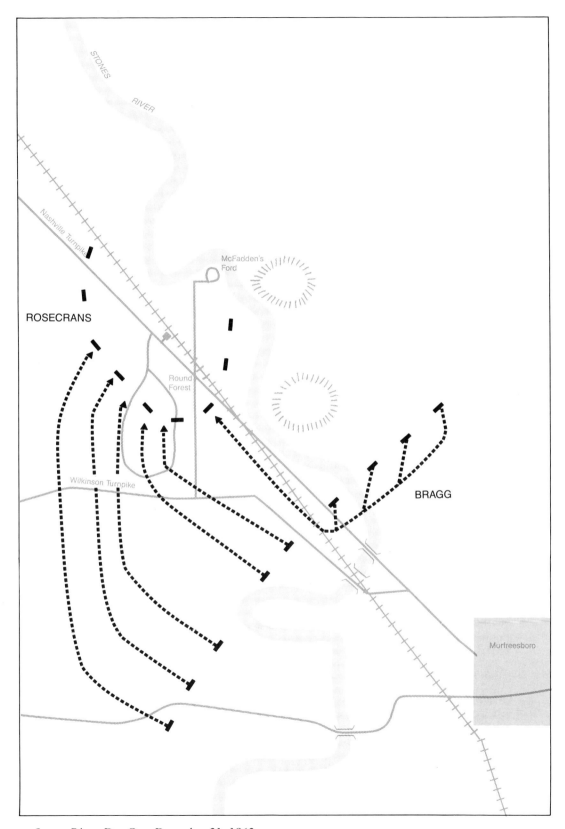

Stones River, Day One, December 31, 1862

In this densely wooded area, soldiers of General Philip Sheridan's division made a desperate stand against the onrushing Confederates. Photograph by Joseph E. Stevens.

Bragg Claims Victory

In eleven hours of fighting, Bragg had lost 10,000 men—nearly a quarter of the Confederate army—but had inflicted 12,000 casualties on his opponent. With the exception of the Round Forest, his troops had overrun every Yankee position they had attacked, and he was sure that Rosecrans would order his battered force to retreat to Nashville. In a telegram to Richmond, he proudly claimed victory: "The enemy has yielded his strong position and is falling back. . . . God has granted us a Happy New Year."

But Rosecrans was not going anywhere: sunup on New Year's Day revealed his army still in battle formation, much to Bragg's chagrin. The Confederate commander remained hopeful that the Federals would admit defeat and withdraw, but after the fierce and costly fighting of the 31st he was not about to push them. Rosecrans also wished to avoid an engagement, so the weary soldiers spent the day resting and foraging for food.

January 2, 1863: Stones River—Day Two

The armies remained in their respective positions on the morning of January 2, eyeing each other warily but making no move to attack. Neither Rosecrans nor Bragg seemed to have any idea what to do next. Bragg was still perplexed by the Union force's failure to retreat; Rosecrans was determined to hold his ground.

Late in the afternoon the Confederate commander concluded that he would have to resume the offensive if he was to validate his premature claim of victory. He or-

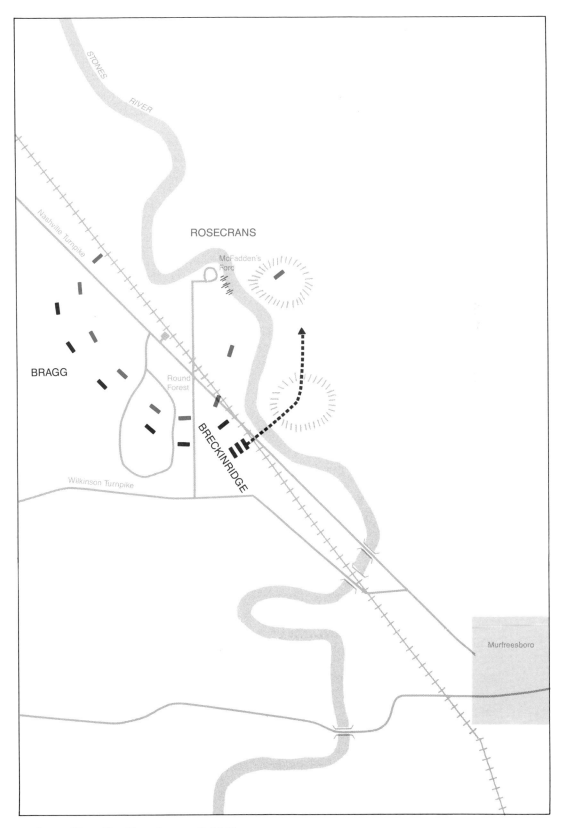

Stones River, Day Two, January 2, 1863

dered General John C. Breckinridge—former vice president of the United States—to assault an area of high ground anchoring the Union left. This hill was defended by a reinforced Federal division, supported by fifty-eight heavy guns.

Breckinridge protested that the position was impregnable, but the grim-faced Bragg cut him short. "I have given the order to attack the enemy in your front and expect it to be obeyed," he snapped.

At 4 P.M. Breckinridge's 4,500 troops set out across the broad swale that separated their line from the hill that was their objective. The Federals opened fire, but the Confederates continued to move forward, maintaining their ranks. As bullets hissed over the field, terrified rabbits scampered in all directions.

"Go it cottontail!" hollered one of the Rebels. "I'd run too if I hadn't a reputation."

Taking heavy losses, Breckinridge's soldiers crossed the valley and started up the hill. Halfway to the crest they discharged a volley, then leveled their bayonets and charged. Thoroughly intimidated by this display of raw courage, the Union defenders turned and fled.

Whooping in triumph, the Confederates pursued them, sweeping over the hilltop, down the rearward slope, and into the field of fire of the fifty-eight cannon. There was a terrific roar as the big guns belched flame, hurling clouds of canister into the onrushing gray ranks. The effect was instantaneous and terrible: "Thinned, reeling, broken under that terrible hail," the Rebels milled about in confusion, then stumbled back the way they had come. The attack was finished; in little over an hour 1,700 Confederates had been killed, wounded, or captured.

Bragg Retreats

On the morning of January 3, Bragg received word that Rosecrans's army had been reinforced. Discouraged, he wrote: "Common prudence and the safety of my army . . . [leave] no doubt on my mind as to the necessity of my withdrawal from so unequal a contest."

That night his troops began a retreat that would eventually take them to a new winter encampment at Tullahoma, thirty-five miles southeast of Stones River. Rosecrans did not follow. He set his soldiers to fortifying Murfreesboro, transforming the town into a huge supply depot from which further attacks could be mounted in the spring.

The Battle of Stones River was judged a victory for the North, cementing as it did Union control of middle Tennessee. The cost was fearful, however. In little more than a day's fighting, the Federals had lost 13,249 men killed, wounded, or captured. The Confederates had lost 11,739, bringing the total for both sides to nearly 25,000.

This horrific casualty figure underscored the lesson learned eight months earlier at Shiloh, and put into words by Confederate cavalryman Nathan Bedford Forrest: "War means fighting, and fighting means killing."

Touring the Park

Begin your tour at the Visitor Center, where museum exhibits and an audiovisual program explain the battle and its significance in the Civil War.

A tour road loops through the battlefield. There are nine numbered stops along the way.

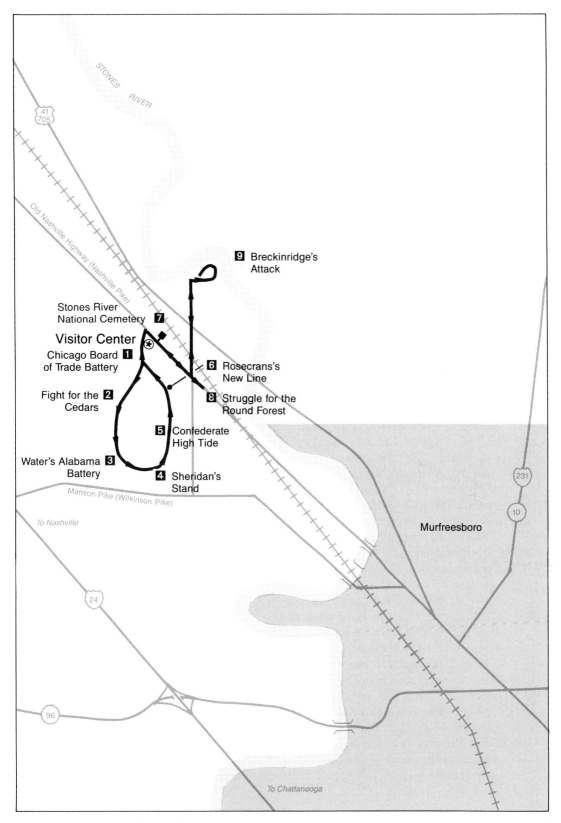

Stones River National Battlefield

Stop 1. Chicago Board of Trade Battery. At 8 A.M. on December 31, 1862, thousands of panicky Union troops came running out of the line of cedars located across the field behind the Visitor Center, pursued by yelling Confederates. This six-gun artillery battery, called the Chicago Board of Trade Battery because it had been paid for by the Board of Trade, went into action. Firing canister into the onrushing gray line, it broke up the attack and gave the retreating Federals a chance to regroup.

Stop 2. The Fight for the Cedars. Rosecrans had planned to attack the Confederate right on the morning of December 31, but the Rebels beat him to the punch. Their assault penetrated as far as this grove of cedars. Artillery fire from Federal batteries near the Visitor Center (Stop 1), and the arrival of Union reserves, finally checked the Confederate drive.

Stop 3. Water's Alabama Battery. Around noon on December 31, the Confederate infantry resumed its attacks against Union positions along the Nashville Pike. This Confederate artillery battery tried to move up to the battle line, but could not get through the thick cedar forest and jumbled limestone outcroppings. Without artillery support to suppress the fire of the Union batteries, the Confederate infantry assaults were doomed to failure.

Stop 4. Sheridan's Stand. In this area, the soldiers of General Philip H. Sheridan's division made a desperate stand, trying to halt the Confederate attack. In an effort to break through, the Confederates brought their cannon up to within 200 yards of the Union position, but the point-blank artillery fire and three separate assaults failed to dislodge Sheridan's determined fighters. Eventually, Sheridan was forced to withdraw, but his stand had given the rest of the Union army time to form a new defensive line along the Nashville Pike.

Stop 5. Confederate High Tide. This segment of the Union defensive line was held by troops of General Thomas Crittenden's corps. They repelled one Rebel assault, but another attack forced them to retreat around 4 P.M.

Stop 6. Rosecrans's New Line. After seeing his army thrown back on the morning of December 31, Rosecrans established a new defensive line along the Nashville Pike. This line was anchored by a rocky, tree-topped knoll called the "Round Forest." Confederate efforts to pierce this line failed.

Stop 7. Stones River National Cemetery. Union cannon were arrayed across this hill, supporting the defensive line which stretched from the vicinity of the Visitor Center, along the Nashville Pike in front of you, to the Round Forest on your left.

Following the war, a National Cemetery was established on these grounds. The Union dead were disinterred from their graves on the battlefield, and reburied here. Of the more than 6,100 soldiers buried here, 2,562 are unidentified. The Confederate dead were not buried in this cemetery, but were taken to their hometowns or the nearest southern community, or were buried in mass graves on the battlefield.

Stop 8. Struggle for the Round Forest. This tree-crowned knoll was the anchor of the Union defensive line. Confederate infantry brigades assaulted it repeatedly on December 31, but were repulsed every time with extremely heavy casualties.

Stop 9. Breckinridge's Attack. At 4 P.M. on January 2, 1863, Bragg ordered General John C. Breckinridge's 4,500 troops to attack this position. They routed one Union division, but then were hit by the massed fire of fifty-eight Union cannon arrayed on the hillside above McFadden's Ford. The blasts of canister, shot, and shell ravaged the gray ranks, killing or wounding hundreds of men and checking the attack.

CHAPTER 31

TUPELO NATIONAL BATTLEFIELD

(Civil War)

C/O Natchez Trace Parkway
R.R.1, NT-143
Tupelo, Mississippi 38801
Telephone: (601) 842-1572

On July 13–14, 1864, General Nathan Bedford Forrest's Confederate cavalry battled a Union force sent to keep Forrest from cutting the railroad supplying General William T. Sherman's army in Georgia. The battle was a draw, but the Federals succeeded in frustrating the Confederate attempt to interfere with the Union supply line. Tupelo National Battlefield consists of a small park within the city limits of Tupelo.

Getting to the Park: Tupelo National Battlefield is located on Mississippi Highway 6, approximately one mile west of the intersection with U.S. 45.

Gas, food, lodging: In Tupelo.

Visitor Center: There are no visitor facilities or park personnel at the battlefield site. However, visitors may obtain information at the Natchez Trace Parkway Visitor Center, 5 miles north of Tupelo at the intersection of the Natchez Trace Parkway and U.S. 45.

Activities: None.

Handicapped Access: The entire area is accessible.

"Forrest is the very devil, and I think he has got some of our troops under cower," wrote Union general William T. Sherman on June 14, 1864. Four days earlier, at the Battle of Brices Cross Roads in northeastern Mississippi, Nathan Bedford Forrest and 3,500 Confederate cavalrymen had smashed a large Federal column sent by Sherman to track them down and destroy them (see Chapter 15).

As crushing as the defeat at Brices had been, the Union commander was determined to keep dogging Forrest. It was the only way to stop the bold Confederate raider from riding into Tennessee and savaging the Nashville-to-Chattanooga supply line that was supporting Federal armies campaigning in northwest Georgia.

"I have two officers at Memphis that will fight all the time," Sherman concluded.

"I will order them to make up a force and go out and follow Forrest to the death, if it costs 10,000 lives and breaks the Treasury. There will never be peace in Tennessee until Forrest is dead."

July 1864: Smith Punishes Northern Mississippi

On July 5, 1864, 14,000 Union troops commanded by General A. J. Smith left La Grange, Tennessee, fifty miles east of Memphis, and marched south into Mississippi. Their instructions from Sherman were blunt: "pursue Forrest on foot, devastating the land over which he passed or may pass. . . . If we do not punish Forrest and the people [of Mississippi] now, the whole effect of our past conquests will be lost."

Smith's veteran soldiers cheerfully obeyed the order to scourge Mississippi. They razed the hamlet of Ripley on July 8, then moved south through New Albany, leaving a ten-mile-wide trail of desolation in their wake. At Pontotoc, on the 13th of July, the blue column veered east, intending to lay waste the railroad town of Tupelo.

Forrest, his superior General Stephen Lee, and 8,000 Confederate troopers were camped at Okolona, twenty miles south of Tupelo. Learning of Smith's plan, they set out to intercept him. The gray troops moved swiftly, and at nightfall on the 13th they caught up with the Union invaders on the western outskirts of Tupelo.

Although the Confederates were outnumbered, General Lee would not hold back:

"Go out and follow Forrest to the death, if it costs 10,000 lives and breaks the Treasury," General William T. Sherman told a subordinate. "There will never be peace in Tennessee until Forrest is dead." Library of Congress.

Smith's army, he said, had to be "dealt with vigorously and at once." This was music to the ears of the bellicose Forrest, and the two officers agreed to mount an all-out assault the next morning.

July 14, 1864: "Useless Sacrifice"

Sunup, July 14, revealed the 14,000 Union soldiers dug into a strong position along the crest of a low ridge. The Confederates attacked anyway, dashing toward the Federal breastworks, "yelling and howling like Comanches." They were struck and flung back by a flickering sheet of musket fire. Again they attacked and again they were repulsed, suffering terrible casualties.

"It was all gallantry and useless sacrifice," wrote one of the participants. Two more charges were made with the same bloody result, and the day ended with 1,326 Confederate soldiers killed, wounded, or missing.

The Union troops had beaten Lee's army and suffered relatively few casualties in the process, but their food and ammunition were running low. On the morning of July 15, Smith ordered them to leave the wounded behind and retreat to a campsite on Town Creek, four miles to the north.

Forrest followed, and despite the severe losses his cavalry had suffered at Tupelo, struck the Federals hard on the morning of July 15. In the fierce fighting that followed, the gray troopers were again held at bay; Forrest was wounded in the foot and forced to retire from the field.

With their leader unable to ride, the Confederates broke off the chase, and Smith and the blue column returned to La Grange on July 21, sixteen days after setting out.

Forrest Frustrated

Both sides were able to claim a partial victory at the Battle of Tupelo. Smith and his men had "punished" northern Mississippi, looting and burning over a wide area, and had inflicted heavy casualties on the Confederates. However, far from "following Forrest to the death" as Sherman wished, they had retreated at the conclusion of the fighting, even though they outnumbered their bloodied opponents two-to-one.

For his part, Forrest could take satisfaction in having driven another invader out of northeastern Mississippi, but he had been frustrated from performing his primary task, striking the Union supply line in Tennessee. Bullets and hardtack were still flowing to the blue armies in Georgia, and the noose around Atlanta was tightening.

Touring the Park

The park consists of a small plot of ground located near the place where the Confederate line was formed to attack the Union position. Signs and markers provide interpretation.

CHAPTER 32

VICKSBURG NATIONAL MILITARY PARK
(Civil War)

3201 Clay Street
Vicksburg, Mississippi 39180
Telephone: 601-636-0583

In the spring of 1862, the Union army and navy began a series of joint operations aimed at capturing Vicksburg, key to controlling the Mississippi River. For fourteen months Vicksburg's Confederate defenders frustrated every Federal thrust; then, on July 4, 1863, after a grueling forty-seven-day siege, the city fell to an army led by Ulysses S. Grant. Vicksburg National Military Park preserves the site of the siege.

Getting to the Park: Vicksburg National Military Park is located just outside Vicksburg, Mississippi, on U.S. 80 (Clay Street). See map.

Gas, food, lodging: On Clay Street, just outside the park entrance.

Visitor Center: Located at the park entrance. Museum and gift shop; film on the Vicksburg campaign and siege.

Museum: U.S.S. *Cairo* Museum, adjacent to Stop 8 on the battlefield tour.

Activities: Civil War weapons demonstrations. Inquire at Visitor Center for schedule and locations.

Handicapped Access: Visitor Center, U.S.S. *Cairo* Museum, and rest rooms are accessible. Tour stops can all be viewed from inside an automobile.

From the outset of hostilities in the spring of 1861, Union strategy for winning the Civil War centered around two key objectives. The first was capture of Richmond, Virginia, capital of the Confederacy; the second was control of the Mississippi River from Illinois to the Gulf of Mexico.

To the northern press and public, Richmond, located only 110 miles from Washington, was a tantalizing target, but to professional soldiers, domination of the Mississippi was the real prize. The great river formed a natural highway for transporting troops and supplies into the deep South while at the same time serving as a formidable barrier to east-west movement. If the Union controlled the river, Texas, Arkansas, and most of Louisiana would be cut off from the rest of the South, depriving the Confederacy of critically needed food and manpower. Little wonder then that Union general in chief Henry W. Halleck wrote: "In my opinion, the opening of the Mississippi River will be of more use to us than the capture of forty Richmonds."

Vicksburg: Key to the Mississippi

By the summer of 1862, Union forces had made good progress in their drive to open the Mississippi. From the stream's mouth north to Port Hudson, Louisiana, and from its headwaters south to Vicksburg, Mississippi, Federal gunboats steamed with impunity. Between Vicksburg and Port Hudson, however, the Confederates still held sway, and as long as they commanded this 250-mile stretch, normal river traffic would be impossible.

For the Confederates, the key to obstructing the Mississippi was Vicksburg, known to its residents as the "Queen City of the Bluffs." Perched high on the river's eastern bank, it had been transformed by southern engineers into a citadel. Batteries of heavy artillery glowered down on the town's water approaches and a chain of sturdy earthen forts guarded its landward side. The "Gibraltar of America" the Confederates proudly called this bastion, and to Union officers charged with devising plans for its capture, it appeared virtually impregnable.

The first attempt to reduce Vicksburg was made by the Union navy in June 1862. A fleet commanded by Admiral David Farragut sailed upriver from New Orleans to bombard the city into submission. A torrent of shot and shell rained down on the Confederate defensive works as Farragut's ships floated by on June 28, but the damage inflicted was minimal and the admiral concluded that Vicksburg could only be taken by a powerful land force.

The Union high command agreed, and on October 25, 1862, General Ulysses S. Grant was ordered to seize the strategic river city with his Army of the Tennessee. Eleven days earlier, General John C. Pemberton had been placed in command of Confederate troops in western Mississippi and given the assignment of holding Vicksburg at all costs. Thus the stage was set for one of the Civil War's most decisive campaigns.

The Vicksburg Campaign

Barely a week after receiving his orders, Grant had hatched a plan for a two-pronged attack on Vicksburg. From his supply base at Holly Springs in northern Mississippi, he would lead 40,000 troops south to Jackson, then swing west against the main objective. At the same time his subordinate, General William T. Sherman, would take 32,000 troops downriver on transports from Memphis to a point a few miles north of Vicksburg. While Grant's column diverted the attention of the Confederate defenders, Sherman would attack and capture the city.

The plan appeared sound on paper, but it quickly went awry in the field. Confederate cavalry led by General Earl Van Dorn rode around Grant's advancing army and destroyed the supply depot at Holly Springs. Without sufficient food and ammunition to continue the offensive, Grant was forced to retreat to Memphis. Sherman went ahead with his attack on December 29, hitting the Confederates at Chickasaw Bayou five miles northeast of Vicksburg, but his command was beaten back with heavy losses.

As the new year of 1863 began, Grant reassembled his forces at Milliken's Bend on the Louisiana side of the Mississippi and prepared to try again. This time he planned to use the skein of lakes and bayous north and west of Vicksburg as a water route to get his troops safely past the city's artillery batteries and into position for an attack from the south and east. Opening a waterway through the tangled, flooded swamps proved impossible, however, and spring found the Federals still in camp at Milliken's Bend.

Grant now resolved to gamble. On the nights of April 16 and April 22, Union transports convoyed by gunboats dashed downriver past the deadly Vicksburg batteries. Meanwhile the infantry was marching overland from Milliken's Bend to a point across the river from Grand Gulf, thirty miles below Vicksburg. There they rendezvoused with the transports, and on April 30 they crossed to the Mississippi's east bank, landing at the hamlet of Bruinsburg.

The bulk of Pemberton's Confederate army was at Vicksburg, but smaller Rebel forces were scattered thoughout central Mississippi. Grant decided to move swiftly against these units, attacking them piecemeal before they could concentrate against him or be reinforced by Pemberton. On May 1, 1863, his army moved inland from Bruinsburg, whipping 8,000 Confederates in a day-long clash known as the Battle of Port Gibson.

From Port Gibson, the blue columns marched northeast toward Jackson. On May 12, a Confederate brigade tried to halt their advance at the town of Raymond. The fighting was fierce, but the small Rebel force was no match for Grant's 45,000 men and was soon forced to retreat. Two days later the Union army reached Jackson, handily defeated its 6,000 defenders, and occupied the city, destroying its warehouses, factories, and railroad facilities.

The fragmented Confederate forces in central Mississippi had been routed, and the blue formations could now wheel about and head west toward their primary objective. Pemberton, belatedly recognizing the danger posed by Grant's maneuvering, pulled 23,000 of his troops out of the Vicksburg defenses and moved to block the Federals' westward advance at Champion Hill on May 16.

The ensuing battle was, according to a veteran officer, "one of the most obstinate and murderous conflicts of the war." Grant's soldiers applied relentless pressure, charging again and again in an attempt to dislodge the stubborn Rebel force, which held a position on a crescent-shaped ridge.

"The rattle of musketry was incessant for hours," wrote correspondent Sylvanus Cadwallader in his account of the Champion Hill fight. "Cannons thundered 'til the heavens seemed bursting. Dead men, and wounded, lay strewed everywhere." Eventually the weight of numbers told, and Pemberton's Confederates fell back, withdrawing to new positions along the Big Black River, twelve miles east of Vicksburg. They left behind 4,000 of their comrades, dead, wounded, or captured; Union losses totaled 2,500.

Grant resumed his march on Vicksburg the next day, getting his army on the road before dawn. At midmorning, advance units discovered the Confederate defensive line along the Big Black River and promptly attacked it. A brigade led by General Michael

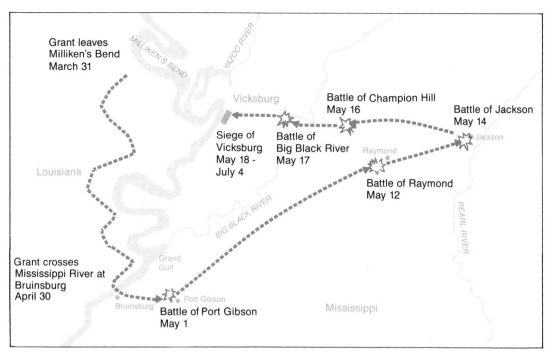

Vicksburg Campaign, March–July 1863

Lawler broke through, and the entire Rebel position crumbled, leaving Pemberton no choice but to retreat all the way back to the Vicksburg forts.

The triumphant Union troops followed hard on his heels, arriving in the city's outskirts on the afternoon of May 18. Pemberton and his officers held a hasty council of war: should they evacuate Vicksburg and save their army or should they stay and fight? Just as they reached a unanimous decision—to stay and fight—the first Union cannonball whistled into the breastworks. Vicksburg was under attack.

May 18–22, 1863: Assault on Fortress Vicksburg

The fortifications protecting Vicksburg's landward side had been constructed in the fall of 1862. Carefully sited on the spine of a high ridge overlooking deep ravines and gullies, they stretched in a curving, nine-mile line from Fort Hill, on the Mississippi one and a half miles north of Vicksburg, inland along the high ground and then back to the river at South Fort, three miles below town.

Three types of earthworks had been built: redoubts, which were square or rectangular in shape; redans, which were triangular; and lunettes, which were crescent shaped. The parapets of these works were twenty feet thick, and most of them had deep ditches dug in front so that would-be attackers would have to scale a long, nearly vertical slope to gain entrance. One hundred fifteen cannon were interspersed among the forts, and the whole line was tied together by a network of mutually supporting trenches and rifle pits manned by upwards of 30,000 Confederate infantrymen.

The terrain in front of the Rebel entrenchments strongly favored the defense. "The approaches to this position were frightful—enough to appall the stoutest heart," said one Union staff officer. Grant decided to launch an immediate assault nevertheless, reasoning that the defenders were demoralized by their defeats at Champion Hill and Big Black River and might collapse if subjected to vigorous offensive pressure.

At 2 P.M. on May 19, Union troops of General Sherman's corps moved down into the ravine fronting Stockade Redan, a strong point on the left side of the Confederate line. A tangle of felled timber slowed the advance, and when the soldiers finally hacked their way through and began climbing up the slope toward the fort, they were hit by a withering blast of musket fire. A few got as far as the ditch under the fort's parapet, but there they were pinned down and had to wait for cover of darkness before retreating back to their starting point.

One thousand men had been lost in this failed attack, but Grant was determined to try again. He believed that a successful assault, even if very bloody, would be less costly in the long run than a protracted siege. Furthermore, he was itching to seize the prize that had eluded him for over seven months, and so he ordered a second, more powerful thrust at the Confederate perimeter.

Union artillery began to bombard a three-and-one-half-mile sector of the Rebel line early on the morning of May 22. For four hours shells arced into the Confederate defenses. Then, at exactly 10 A.M., the barrage lifted and the infantry advanced all along the front, simultaneously attacking Stockade Redan, Third Louisiana Redan, Great Redoubt, Second Texas Lunette, Railroad Redoubt, and Square Fort in an effort to prevent the Confederate commanders from shifting forces from one threatened point to another.

The morale of the Union assault troops was high, but their task was made extraordinarily difficult by the deep, brush-choked gullies they had to cross and the steep parapets they had to scale, all while being subjected to galling fire.

At Stockade Redan, 150 volunteers calling themselves the "Forlorn Hope" rushed along Graveyard Road toward the Confederate revetment, carrying planks to bridge the ditch at its base. The gray defenders waited until the attackers drew to within 500 feet, then loosed a tremendous volley that littered the road with bodies. Two Ohio regiments followed the "Forlorn Hope" down the road, but they too were cut to pieces by the deadly fire from inside the redan. The few Federals who managed to reach the ditch were slaughtered when the Confederates rolled grenades and fused artillery shells down into their midst.

The assaults on the other Rebel forts encountered equally ferocious resistance. Only at the Railroad Redoubt was the defensive line breached, and a determined counterattack by Waul's Texas Legion quickly closed the gap. By 5:30 P.M., Grant's attack had ground to a halt. Union casualties were 3,200, the Confederate perimeter was intact, and it was obvious that further attempts to pierce it would also fail.

Reluctantly, Grant decided to forsake further frontal attacks against the hilltop citadel. "The nature of the ground about Vicksburg is such that it can only be taken by siege," he wrote, and resolved to starve the defenders into submission.

May 23–July 4, 1863: Vicksburg under Siege

After storming Vicksburg twice and being bloodily repulsed both times, Grant's troops willingly laid down their muskets and took up shovels to begin siege operations. During the last week of May and the first week of June they spaded their way through the sandy yellow soil of the Mississippi bluffs, laying out a network of entrenchments roughly parallel to those of the Confederates.

Reinforcements arrived from Memphis in mid-June, bringing the strength of the Union army to 71,000 men, more than double that of the encircled Rebels. "The enemy are now undoubtedly in our grasp," claimed Grant in a dispatch to Washington. "The fall of Vicksburg and the capture of most of the garrison can only be a question of time."

Inside the beleaguered city, General Pemberton insisted that he had made the right decision when he ordered his army to stand and fight. "I have decided to hold Vicksburg as long as possible," he wrote. "I still conceive it to be the most important point in the Confederacy." He knew that the odds were stacked against him, however, and that unless relief came soon, the supply situation would become desperate. "Am I to expect reinforcements?" he anxiously inquired of his superiors. "From what direction, and how soon?"

General Joseph E. Johnston, who was raising a new Confederate army in the vicinity of Jackson, sought to reassure Pemberton: "I am trying to gather a force which may attempt to relieve you. Hold out." His subsequent letters were less encouraging, however, and in a message to the Confederate secretary of war on June 15, he flatly stated: "I consider saving Vicksburg hopeless."

Meanwhile, the Union besiegers were working diligently to tighten their stranglehold on the river city. On May 27, the navy tried to neutralize the water batteries anchoring the left end of the Confederate line at Fort Hill. The gunboat *Cincinnati* steamed into range and opened fire, only to be struck repeatedly by Rebel cannonballs and sent to the bottom of the river.

On the landward side, Grant's army burrowed its way closer to the Confederate defenses, excavating zigzag approach trenches called "saps" and tunneling underneath several Rebel forts. While all this digging was going on, Federal artillerymen and sharpshooters blazed away, forcing the Confederate soldiers to take cover in dugouts and behind barricades. Even if the defenders had not been pinned down they would not have returned fire, as their ammunition supply was precariously low and could only be expended in the event of an all-out attack.

The Union batteries suffered no such shortage, and continued to bombard the forts, and Vicksburg itself, day and night. For the town's residents the fiery stream of incoming shells—"rising steadily and shiningly in great parabolic curves, descending with ever-increasing swiftness, and falling with deafening shrieks and explosions"—was terrifying. Many of them moved into caves quarried out of the hillsides, causing the Federal artillerists to jeeringly rename Vicksburg "Prairie Dog Village."

The gibes of their tormentors aside, the townspeople managed to endure the shelling. A far worse enemy was hunger. Rations grew shorter and shorter as the siege progressed, and by the end of June civilians and soldiers alike were subsisting on bits of mule meat and handfuls of dried corn and peas. Still, there was little complaining and no public outcry for Pemberton to surrender and end the harrowing ordeal. The citizens of Vicksburg bravely carried on, facing danger and deprivation with humor and determination.

The soldiers carried on, too, the Confederates fighting hunger, the Federals battling boredom. "The history of a single day was the history of all the others," wrote a

This wartime lithograph shows Union artillery and sharpshooters firing at the Confederate forts ringing Vicksburg. Anne S. K. Brown Military Collection, Brown University.

Union officer, and another lamented that "the excitement . . . has worn away, and we have settled down to our work as quietly and as regularly as if we were hoeing corn." Opposing pickets fraternized openly, arranging informal truces so they could visit and trade coffee and tobacco, and a sense of apathy spread through both armies as the siege dragged on and the summer heat intensified.

One group that did not fall prey to the prevailing lethargy was the Union engineers, who persisted in tunneling under the Confederate forts. On June 25, a huge mine consisting of over a ton of gunpowder was exploded beneath the Third Louisiana Redan, gouging out a crater forty feet wide and twelve feet deep. An Illinois regiment rushed forward to try to exploit the breach, but was raked by murderous fire from a trench dug at the rear of the redan. The bluecoats were forced to take cover in the smoking crater, and the assault fizzled out. Six days later a second mine was detonated, but it too accomplished little.

Starvation was a far more potent weapon than mines, artillery, or muskets, and its effect on the gray troops became evident to Union and Confederate officers alike. A Federal engineer remarking on the Rebels' lassitude said that "their indifference to our approach became at some points almost ludicrous." A Texas colonel wrote that his men had "swollen ankles and symptoms of incipient scurvy," and observed that even the lightest work left them exhausted.

On June 28, the thirty-fifth day of the siege, a letter was delivered to Pemberton from his troops. It read, in part, "If you can't feed us, you had better surrender us, horrible as the idea is, than suffer this noble army to disgrace themselves by deser-tion." The general had been clinging to the hope that another Confederate army would soon march to Vicksburg's relief, but now he had to face reality. The garrison's food was almost gone, and no help was on the way.

On July 1, he asked his division commanders whether their troops were fit enough to try a break-out. All but two replied that six weeks of reduced rations had left the men too weak to fight their way through the blue ring encircling them. Surrender was the only option.

White flags appeared up and down the Confederate line at midafternoon on July 3. The guns became quiet, and slowly, cautiously, soldiers on both sides clambered out of their trenches and moved about. Pemberton and several aides rode out past the Vicksburg ramparts to meet with Grant and his staff. The two generals sat in the shade of an oak tree and discussed the terms of capitulation. Their negotiations did not produce an agreement, but early the next morning, after an exchange of notes, the final details of surrender were worked out.

At 10 A.M. on July 4, 1863, the flag of the Confederacy, which had fluttered over the Vicksburg courthouse for forty-seven days of siege, came down and the Stars and Stripes rose in its place. The gaunt, ragged Confederate troops stacked their weapons and proudly marched out of their forts under the respectful gaze of massed Union formations.

"Men who have shown so much endurance and courage will always challenge the respect of an adversary," wrote Grant. "When they passed out of the works they had so long and gallantly defended . . . not a cheer went up, not a remark was made that would give pain."

Turning Point of the Civil War

If the surrender of Vicksburg was accepted quietly and matter-of-factly by the Union army in the field, it was greeted with jubilation in the North. Coming at the same time as the Confederate defeat at the Battle of Gettysburg (see Chapter 9), it seemed to mark a psychological turning point in the war. As one southern leader put it: "Yesterday we rode on the pinnacle of success—today absolute ruin seems to be our portion. The Confederacy totters to its destruction."

Vicksburg's fall marked an important strategic turning point as well. After two years of hard fighting, Union land and naval forces in the West had finally realized their great objective. The Confederacy had been cut in two, and the Mississippi River—father of waters, key to the continent—was once again entirely in Federal hands.

Touring the Park

Begin your tour at the Visitor Center, where museum exhibits and a film explain the campaign and siege of Vicksburg. A self-guided, sixteen-mile auto tour will take you around the battlefield. During the tour you will see metal markers painted either blue or red. The blue markers denote positions held by Union forces, the red, positions held by the Confederates. There are fifteen numbered stops marking points of particular interest.

Stop 1. Battery DeGolyer. From this position, the Eighth Michigan Artillery,

Ghost Gunboat: U.S.S. Cairo

On the morning of December 12, 1862, the Union ironclad *Cairo*, steaming up the Yazoo River eight miles north of Vicksburg, struck and detonated two Confederate mines. Powerful explosions ripped through the gunboat's hull, and within minutes she was resting on the river bottom, covered by six fathoms of water. Miraculously, none of her crewmen were killed, but all of their personal gear, as well as the boat's entire inventory of naval stores, guns, and machinery, were lost.

For ninety-four years the *Cairo*'s hulk lay undisturbed in the Yazoo River mud; then, on November 12, 1956, a party of Civil War historians rediscovered the wreck and launched a campaign to raise it. The salvage operation began in the autumn of 1963 and culminated the following year with the hoisting of the *Cairo* from its watery grave.

The shattered gunboat was loaded on a barge and towed to a shipyard in Pascagoula, Mississippi. There it sat moldering while politicians and historic preservationists tried to find money to pay for its restoration and display. Finally, in 1977, the *Cairo* was returned to Vicksburg, and the National Park Service began the long and difficult task of refurbishing it.

The remarkable results of that effort can be seen today at the U.S.S. *Cairo* Museum adjacent to Vicksburg National Cemetery (Stop 8 on the battlefield tour). High on a grassy bluff overlooking the Mississippi, the partially restored Civil War gunboat floats on a bayou of red bricks, an oak-and-iron ghost that has navigated down the river of time and dropped anchor at this final resting place.

Next to the hulking ironclad, in a striking triangular-shaped visitor center, *Cairo* artifacts, including weaponry, tools, hardware, medical supplies, and personal belongings of the crewmen, are on display. Photo exhibits, audio tapes, and a film tell the story of the *Cairo*'s resurrection, explain the significance of the relics, and provide insight into the role Union gunboats played on the Mississippi during the Civil War.

The exhibition area and the remains of the *Cairo* form one of the most fascinating naval museums in the United States. No visit to the Vicksburg battlefield would be complete without a stop at it.

commanded by Captain Samuel DeGolyer, bombarded the Confederate Great Redoubt 700 yards to the west. (The site of the Great Redoubt is marked by the tall, white-marble pillar of the Louisiana Monument.) Union infantry, supported by DeGolyer's battery, stormed the redoubt in the general attack of May 22 but were repulsed with heavy casualties.

During the siege that followed, as many as twenty-two cannon were massed here. They kept up a steady harassing fire until Vicksburg surrendered on July 4. Captain DeGolyer did not live to see the surrender; he was mortally wounded by Confederate gunners while directing his battery's fire.

Stop 2. Shirley House. This is the only surviving wartime structure in the park.

A wartime photograph of the U.S.S. *Cairo*. Library of Congress.

Called the "White House" by Union troops, it served as headquarters for the forty-fifth Illinois Infantry Regiment. The soldiers from Illinois dug hundreds of bomb-proof shelters around the house to protect themselves from Confederate artillery fire.

The exterior has been restored to its 1863 appearance; the interior is closed to the public.

Stop 3. Third Louisiana Redan. This large earthen fort, which guarded the Jackson Road leading into Vicksburg, was one of the most important in the entire Confederate line. After failing to capture it in the assault of May 22, Union troops began digging an approach trench from the Shirley House (Stop 2) toward the redan's east parapet, following the line of the present-day park road. The trench ended just outside the fort; from there, Union engineers tunneled forty feet under the Confederate position and placed a mine consisting of 2,200 pounds of black powder.

The mine was exploded at 3:30 P.M. on June 25, gouging out a huge crater. The Confederates had heard the sounds of tunneling, however, and had withdrawn to a position in the rear of the redan before the explosion. Thus, when Union troops rushed forward to try to exploit the breach, they were blasted by musket fire and forced to withdraw.

A second mine was exploded on July 1; the huge detonation virtually destroyed the redan, but this time there was no follow-up assault.

Stop 4. Ransom's Gun Path. Union infantry commanded by General Thomas Ransom needed additional artillery support in this portion of the siege line. To provide it, men of the Second Illinois Artillery dismantled two 12-pounder cannon and dragged the pieces across the ravine in front of you to an earthen parapet just 100 yards from the Confederate position. There the guns were reassembled and returned to action.

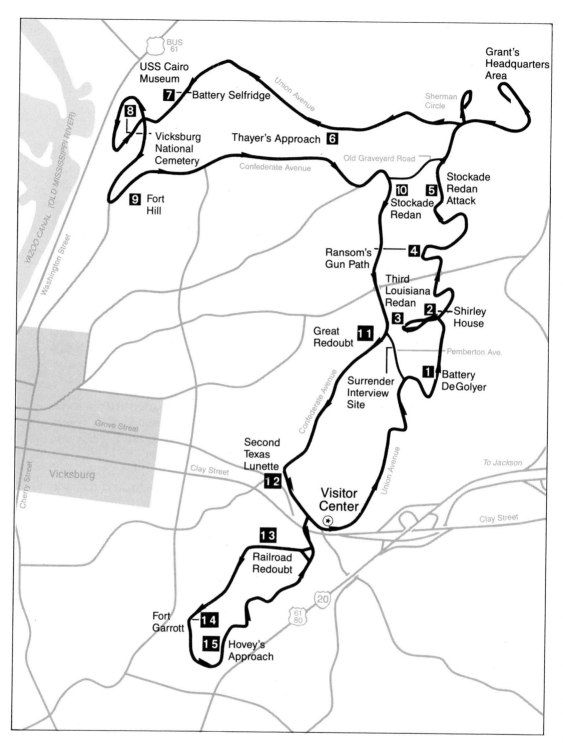

Vicksburg National Military Park

Most of the heavy tree cover seen here and in other parts of the park did not exist during the siege in 1863. It dates to a Civilian Conservation Corps erosion-prevention project in the 1930s.

Stop 5. Stockade Redan Attack. From this point, on the afternoon of May 19, troops of General Sherman's corps moved to attack Stockade Redan, visible directly ahead. Brush and felled trees in the ravine in front of you slowed the advance of the Federal formations, and when they finally approached the redan's parapet, they were devastated by Confederate musket fire. The attack failed, and 1,000 Union soldiers were killed, wounded, or captured.

On May 22, Stockade Redan was again attacked as part of the general Union assault all along the Confederate line. This time a group of 150 volunteers, mordantly dubbed the "Forlorn Hope," rushed along Old Graveyard Road (the narrow paved road you see in front and to the right of you) carrying planks to bridge the ditch in front of the redan and ladders to scale its walls. The Confederates waited until the attack force was within point-blank range, then opened fire, littering the road with the bodies of dead and wounded men. Two Federal color bearers managed to plant their flags on the parapet of the redan, but the Confederate position was never in serious danger of being captured.

Stop 6. Thayer's Approach. During the attack on Stockade Redan on May 22, Union troops commanded by General John Thayer crossed the ravine and charged up the hillside in front of you toward a line of Confederate earthworks. The steep terrain and the defenders' fire combined to defeat the assault.

Following this setback, Thayer and his men began to dig a six-foot-deep approach trench up the slope toward the Confederate position. They used round, tightly wrapped bundles of cane called *fascines* to cover the trench and protect themselves from harassing fire while they worked.

The tunnel beneath the tour road was built so that the Union soldiers would not be exposed to Confederate snipers as they crossed the ridge that now forms the roadbed.

Stop 7. Battery Selfridge. This Union siege battery consisted of naval cannon and was manned by sailors of the U.S. Navy. The position was named in honor of Thomas O. Selfridge, the battery commander and former captain of the U.S.S. *Cairo*, an ironclad sunk in the Yazoo River in December 1862.

Stop 8. Vicksburg National Cemetery. The remains of 17,000 Union soldiers, 13,000 of whom are unknown, are buried here. Many of the Confederates who died during the siege are buried in the Vicksburg City Cemetery.

Stop 9. Fort Hill. This position overlooking the Mississippi anchored the left end of the Confederate line. Confederate artillery here, in conjunction with the heavy guns of the Water Battery located at river level below Fort Hill, shelled and sank the Union gunboat *Cincinnati* on May 27, 1863.

Stop 10. Stockade Redan. Confederate infantry holding this earthwork repulsed Union attacks on May 19 and May 22 (see Stop 5). The bloody failure of these assaults convinced Grant to give up his notion of taking Vicksburg by storm and to resort to siege operations instead.

Stop 11. Great Redoubt. The defenders of this earthen fort beat off a determined Union attack on May 22. Thereafter they were subjected to almost continuous artillery bombardment from Battery DeGolyer, 700 yards to the east (Stop 1).

This view from the parapet of Fort Garrott shows one of the zigzag approach trenches dug by General Alvin Hovey's Union soldiers. Photograph by Joseph E. Stevens.

Stop 12. Second Texas Lunette. This crescent-shaped earthwork was manned by soldiers of the Second Texas Volunteer Infantry. They repelled a ferocious Federal assault on May 22, inflicting hundreds of casualties. Wrote the commander of the Texans: "for more than 200 yards the bodies lay so thick that one might have walked the whole distance without touching the ground."

Stop 13. Railroad Redoubt. Built to guard the route of the railroad leading into Vicksburg, this was the only Confederate fort that Union infantry succeeded in entering during the May 22 assault. Before the bluecoats could consolidate their position, however, they were counterattacked by Colonel Thomas Waul's Texas Legion. A savage hand-to-hand fight ensued, and the Federals were forced to retreat.

Stop 14. Fort Garrott. Colonel Isham W. Garrott's Twentieth Alabama Regiment defended this fort during the siege. The Alabamans were plagued by the fire of Union snipers, and Colonel Garrott himself was shot and killed on June 17. From the fort's parapet you can see two restored approach trenches that were dug by Federal troops.

Stop 15. Hovey's Approach. From this position Union troops commanded by General Alvin P. Hovey dug the two approach trenches you saw at the previous stop. The zigzag design of the trenches helped protect the diggers from Confederate fire.

CHAPTER 33

WILSON'S CREEK NATIONAL BATTLEFIELD

(Civil War)

Route 2, Box 75
Republic, Missouri 65738
Telephone: (417) 732-2662

Along the banks of Wilson's Creek on August 10, 1861, a Union army led by General Nathaniel Lyon met a Confederate force led by General Benjamin McCulloch in a battle for control of Missouri. The Confederates were victorious, but their failure to follow up allowed the Federals to regroup and hold the important border state for the Union. Wilson's Creek National Battlefield preserves the scene of the fighting.

Getting to the Park: Wilson's Creek National Battlefield is located 10 miles southwest of Springfield, Missouri. Take I-44 to Exit 77 and drive 5 miles south on Missouri Highway 13 (Kansas Expressway) to U.S. 60. Turn right on U.S. 60 and drive 7 miles west to Missouri Highway ZZ. The park is 3 miles south on Missouri ZZ.

Gas, food, lodging: In Springfield and Republic.

Visitor Center: Museum and gift shop; film on the battle and the struggle for Missouri; electric map.

Activities: Living-history demonstrations are presented on weekends in the summer. Other special interpretive programs are offered periodically. Inquire at Visitor Center for schedule and locations.

Handicapped Access: The Visitor Center is fully accessible.

As the Civil War got underway in the spring of 1861, the loyalties of three states—Maryland, Kentucky, and Missouri—remained divided. These so-called border states were still part of the Union, but southern sympathizers were active in each, and the Lincoln administration feared that in time they might try to secede and join the Confederacy.

The allegiance of Missouri, with its rich farmland and strategic position on the

Mississippi River, was of particular concern to Union war planners. The state's governor, Claiborne F. Jackson, had refused President Lincoln's request to raise four regiments to help put down the southern rebellion. Even worse, he was threatening to use the Missouri State Guard to seize the U.S. arsenal at St. Louis and turn the weapons over to the Confederacy.

General Nathaniel Lyon, commander of Federal forces in Missouri, moved promptly to prevent this calamity. On May 10, his 7,000-man army surrounded the Missouri State Guard's camp on the outskirts of St. Louis and forced the guardsmen to surrender. Several weeks later he marched on the state capital in Jefferson City, deposed Governor Jackson and the pro-Confederate legislature, and installed a new Unionist government.

Determined to finish the job of securing Missouri, Lyon next headed for the Confederate hotbed in the southwestern corner of the state. Here he would face organized and determined opposition. Five thousand secession-minded Missouri State Guardsmen led by General Sterling Price, and 7,000 Confederate regular army troops led by General Benjamin McCulloch, were drilling there in preparation for an advance on St. Louis.

The first week of August found the opposing armies bivouacked within a day's march of each other. The Federals were in the small town of Springfield, the Confederates ten miles to the southwest along the banks of Wilson's Creek.

August 10, 1861: Lyon Attacks

Forty-three-year-old Nathaniel Lyon was a West Pointer, a veteran of the Seminole and Mexican wars, and an aggressive, hard-driving commander. Although outnumbered two to one, he was determined to attack the Confederate encampment at Wilson's Creek, relying on the element of surprise to make up for his army's numerical inferiority.

The plan he concocted was audacious. Dividing his already small force on August 9, he ordered Colonel Franz Sigel to lead a column on a perilous night march around the Confederate position. At dawn on August 10, Sigel and his 1,200 men were to hit the enemy rear while Lyon and the main body struck the front, catching and crushing the Rebels in a vise.

Maneuvering a large body of inexperienced troops at night was an exceedingly difficult undertaking, but Sigel managed to get his column into position to launch the attack at the appointed time. The muzzle flashes of his guns, flickering like lightning in the gray half-light of dawn, were the cue for Lyon's 4,000 soldiers to begin their advance.

The crash of cannon and crackle of musketry roused the slumbering Confederates and sent them scampering, half-dressed and half-asleep, in all directions. Taking advantage of this momentary panic, both Lyon and Sigel surged forward. Lyon's force overran the northern end of the Rebel camp and occupied a strong position along a ridge that would soon be known as Bloody Hill. Sigel's men charged into the camp's southern end, sweeping across open fields for nearly a mile before halting and deploying in battle line across the Wire Road near the Sharp Farm.

The Union attack plan had worked to perfection: the enemy had been caught off guard, and the jaws of the vise were in place. However, the Federals simply

The Ray House, scene of skirmishing early in the Battle of Wilson's Creek. Missouri Division of Tourism.

did not have enough troops to squeeze them shut, and their assault quickly lost momentum. General McCulloch, a veteran Indian fighter and former Texas Ranger, rallied the frightened Confederate soldiers, formed them into units, and prepared to counterattack.

Colonel Sigel and his 1,200 men were the first to bear the brunt of the Rebel onslaught. A Confederate formation that Sigel mistook for a Federal regiment approached his position on the Wire Road and opened fire. Shocked, devastated by the sudden storm of bullets, Sigel's green troops broke and ran, abandoning their guns and colors in a desperate rush toward the rear. This rout turned the tide of the battle, for it meant that McCulloch and Price could now hit Lyon's 4,000 soldiers on Bloody Hill with the entire 12,000-man Confederate force.

A thick cloud of gun smoke blanketed Bloody Hill's south slope as the Rebel troops charged again and again, trying to throw the badly outnumbered Federals from the high ground. Minié balls whined through the air like angry bees, and the bodies of dead and wounded men littered the field. There was no place to seek cover from the vicious cyclone of lead, and General Lyon was hit twice.

Seeing their commander fall, the blue soldiers wavered, but Lyon somehow pulled himself back into the saddle and returned to the fray. Waving his hat over his head and bellowing exhortations, he led a fierce countercharge that threw the Confederates back on their heels. It seemed that Lyon's valor and inspirational leadership might, against all odds, carry the day, but at that instant a bullet ripped through his heart and killed him.

Major Samuel Sturgis assumed command and tried to hold the ground that had been regained, but the Union soldiers—outnumbered, running low on ammunition, and utterly demoralized by Lyon's horrible death—had had enough. They turned and

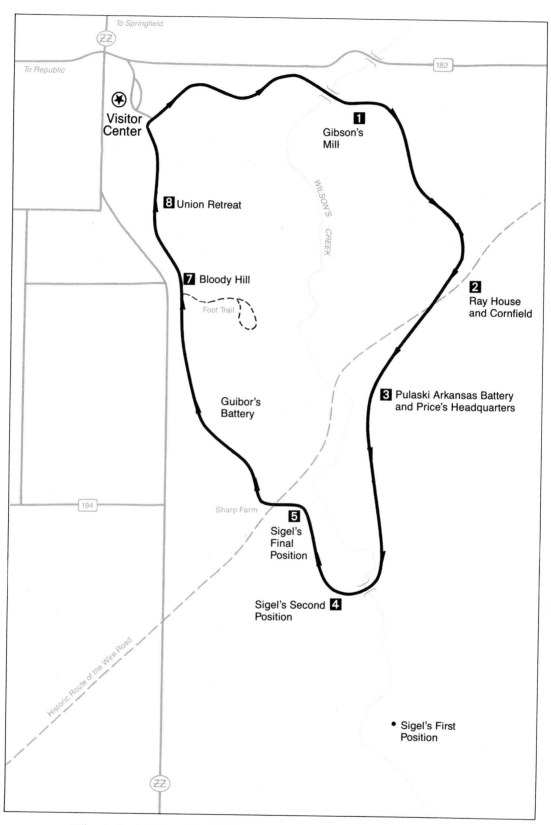

Wilson's Creek National Battlefield

fled, leaving their wounded comrades behind in their haste to get back to Springfield and safety.

As suddenly as it had begun, the Battle of Wilson's Creek was over. In four hours' time the Confederates had suffered 1,222 casualties, the Federals 1,317.

An Inconclusive Victory

The Confederates had routed the Union army at Wilson's Creek, and they justly claimed victory, boasting that once again, as at the Battle of Manassas two weeks earlier (see Chapter 10), the southern fighting man had shown himself to be superior to his northern counterpart.

The victory was inconclusive, however, because the Rebels failed to pursue the disorganized Federals and deliver the decisive blow that might have given them control of the state. Instead, the blue army was given time to recover and to organize a second, more powerful thrust against the Confederates.

Nathaniel Lyon had lost the battle and his life, but the goal of his campaign—keeping Missouri under Union control—had been achieved.

Touring the Park

Begin your tour at the Visitor Center, where museum exhibits, an electric map, and a short film provide background on the Civil War in Missouri and the Battle of Wilson's Creek.

A 4.9-mile, one-way loop road winds through the park. Eight numbered stops mark the major historic points on the battlefield.

Stop 1. Gibson's Mill. The north end of the Confederate encampment was located here, on the grounds of the Gibson Farm. Union general Nathaniel Lyon's dawn attack sent 2,500 Missouri State Guardsmen scurrying from their tents in this area, south down Wilson's Creek. A short walking trail leads to the sites of the Gibson House and Mill.

Stop 2. Ray House and Cornfield. The Ray House, built in 1852, is the only surviving wartime structure in the park. The Confederates used it as a field hospital; the corpse of General Nathaniel Lyon was brought here when the fighting ended. The cornfield to the northwest of the house was the scene of fighting between Union and Confederate soldiers early in the battle.

Stop 3. Pulaski Arkansas Battery and Price's Headquarters. The cannon of the Pulaski Arkansas Battery, arrayed along the wooded ridge to the northwest, opened fire on Lyon's charging troops, checking their advance just as they reached Bloody Hill. This gave the panicking Confederate infantry a chance to regroup and prepare to launch a counterattack. Just west of here, across Wilson's Creek, General Sterling Price, commander of the Missouri State Guard, had his headquarters in the front yard of the Edwards Cabin. The cabin marked the center of the Confederate camp.

Stop 4. Sigel's Second Position. Half a mile south of this point, across Wilson's Creek to the left, is the ridge from which Colonel Franz Sigel's 1,200-man column began its dawn attack on the Confederate camp. The Federals forded the creek and routed 2,300 Confederate cavalrymen who were sleeping in the field in front of you.

Sigel halted 100 yards south of the point where you are standing, reformed his battle line, then resumed the northward advance in the face of stiffening opposition.

Stop 5. Sigel's Final Position. Colonel Sigel's column stopped here, at the site of the Sharp Farm, and formed a battle line running west across the Wire Road. When a force of Confederate soldiers that Sigel mistook for a Federal regiment opened fire at close range, the Union soldiers broke and ran. After this rout the Confederates were able to throw the full weight of their numbers against Lyon on Bloody Hill.

Stop 6. Guibor's Battery. Cannon under the command of Captain Henry Guibor bombarded the Union position on Bloody Hill from this point. In the woods and fields in front of you, the Confederate infantry assembled to mount repeated assaults on the Federal line.

Stop 7. Bloody Hill. On this high ground, General Lyon's 4,000 troops fought desperately to repel three separate Confederate charges. Bullets and bursting shells took a fearsome toll on both sides; a granite monument marks the approximate spot where Lyon was shot and killed. As you follow the trail along the crest of Bloody Hill, put yourself in the soldiers' place—try to imagine the deafening noise, the choking smoke, the confusion and terror of the battle.

Stop 8. Union Retreat. Following the death of General Lyon, the surviving Union soldiers streamed down from Bloody Hill and retreated past this point, heading north toward Springfield. The Confederates failed to pursue vigorously, and this allowed the defeated Federal army to regroup and maintain control of Missouri.

CHAPTER 34

BIG HOLE NATIONAL BATTLEFIELD
(Indian Wars)

P.O. Box 237
Wisdom, Montana 59761
Telephone: (406) 689-3155

The Battle of the Big Hole, fought on August 9–10, 1877, was a turning point in the Nez Perce War, a tragic four-month-long struggle in which the U.S. Army tried to force one-third of the Nez Perce Indian tribe onto a reservation. Big Hole National Battlefield preserves the site of the battle.

Getting to the Park: Big Hole National Battlefield is located approximately 85 miles south and west of Butte, Montana. From Butte, take I-15 south to the Divide Exit. From Divide drive west and south 53 miles on Montana Highway 43 to Wisdom. The park is 10 miles west of Wisdom on Montana 43.

Gas, food, lodging: In Wisdom and Butte.

Visitor Center: Museum; audiovisual program.

Activities: Interpretive talks by park personnel. Inquire at Visitor Center for schedule.

Handicapped Access: Visitor Center is partially accessible. Foot trail to the siege area is steep and assistance may be required. Check at Visitor Center.

In July 1877, a band of 800 Nez Perce Indians began an epic, 1,700-mile trek from eastern Oregon, across the mountains of Idaho and Montana, toward the Canadian border. Hot on their trail were U.S. Army troops bent on capturing them and forcing them to live on a reservation in northern Idaho.

While the fleeing Nez Perce hoped to avoid bloodshed, they were prepared to fight for their freedom. Nine times they clashed with the pursuing soldiers. The most important of these battles was fought on the banks of Montana's Big Hole River on August 9–10, 1877.

The Nez Perce War of 1877

The Nez Perce were a peaceful, seminomadic people who inhabited the area where the Idaho, Washington, and Oregon borders meet. During the mid-1850s white settlers moved into this territory, and the Nez Perce agreed to confine themselves to a large reservation that included most of their ancestral homeland. Ranchers and miners soon wanted access to more of this territory, however, and in 1863 a second treaty was proposed, greatly reducing the size of the Nez Perce reservation. Two-thirds of the tribe accepted the new treaty, but the other third—about 800 people—refused to sign and continued to live outside the reservation boundaries.

Friction between whites and the nontreaty Nez Perce increased until 1877, when the Indian Bureau decreed that all the Indians were to move onto the reservation. In early May, General Oliver O. Howard, commander of the army troops in the area, issued an ultimatum: the nontreaty Nez Perce were to be on the reservation within thirty days or hostilities would commence.

The Indians decided to comply, but on June 14 three warriors attacked and killed four white settlers. Certain that Howard would seek retribution for these killings, the nontreaty Nez Perce sought shelter in White Bird Canyon. A detachment of army troops followed them and attacked their encampment on June 17. In the battle that ensued, the army troops were beaten off after suffering heavy losses. Alarmed, General Howard called for reinforcements and began preparing for war.

Escape to Montana

After the fight at White Bird Canyon and a skirmish on the Clearwater River in early July, the nontreaty Nez Perce made a fateful decision: they would abandon their homeland and head east toward Montana, where, they hoped, the U.S. Army would leave them alone. Led by Chief Joseph and Chief Looking Glass, they crossed the high mountains along the Idaho-Montana border and descended into the Bitterroot Valley. From there they crossed the Continental Divide and continued east until they came to the headwaters of the Big Hole River.

Thinking they had eluded Howard and were out of danger, the Indians set up their tipis on the east bank of the Big Hole's North Fork and rested after their long journey. No scouts were sent to look for enemy soldiers and no guards were posted around the encampment. This uncharacteristic lack of caution was to prove disastrous. Elements of the U.S. Seventh Infantry, commanded by Colonel John Gibbon, had left Fort Shaw near Great Falls, Montana, several days earlier and advanced up the Bitterroot Valley. They discovered the Big Hole camp on August 8, and deployed to launch a surprise attack in the early morning hours of August 9.

The Battle of the Big Hole

In the predawn darkness of August 9, Gibbon's 149 infantrymen, accompanied by 35 civilian volunteers, crept around the base of Battle Mountain, waded through a swamp, and formed a skirmish line on the west bank of the Big Hole River. They were so close to the Nez Perce camp that they could see the embers of the cooking fires and smell the pungent woodsmoke.

Chief Joseph, one of the chiefs who led the nontreaty Nez Perce on their epic march from eastern Oregon, across the mountains of Idaho and Montana, toward the Canadian border. Copyright Smithsonian Institution.

Just before sunup, a single Indian came out of a tipi, mounted a horse, and rode straight toward the concealed soldiers. A shot rang out, the Indian fell dead, and the assault began. The infantrymen splashed across the river and fired a series of volleys into the cluster of tipis. Within minutes scores of Nez Perce, including many women, children, and old people, had been killed or wounded, and the rest were fleeing in panic.

After twenty minutes of confusion, Chief Looking Glass managed to rally his warriors. They took up concealed positions and began shooting at the exposed army troops. Their fire was heavy and accurate and Colonel Gibbon was forced to order a retreat. The soldiers recrossed the river and headed for a wooded area at the foot of Battle Mountain, where they took cover behind fallen trees and in hastily dug trenches.

Lodge poles mark the site of the Nez Perce encampment along the banks of the North Fork of the Big Hole River. National Park Service, photograph by Ken West.

For the rest of the day and on into the night, the Nez Perce kept Gibbon's command pinned down with sniper fire. On the afternoon of August 10, the main body of the Indian band packed up and moved off to the south, leaving a handful of warriors to hold the infantry at bay. As the sun set, this rear guard fired its last rounds of ammunition and then slipped away to join the retreat.

Trail to Surrender

Despite being caught by surprise, the Nez Perce had vanquished Gibbon's soldiers in the Battle of the Big Hole. The price was high, however: ninety Indians were dead and many more were wounded. Equally damaging was the knowledge that the army intended to pursue them relentlessly. There would be no peace as long as they remained in U.S. territory, and in desperation they decided to go to Canada.

Gibbon and his soldiers were heartened by the results of the Big Hole fighting. Their attack had been repulsed, but they had inflicted severe casualties on the Nez Perce. A strategy of pursuit and pressure eventually would wear down the retreating Indians, the army commanders believed, and several separate units took up the chase.

The Nez Perce managed to evade the soldiers for a month and a half as they made their way east and north toward Canada. On September 30 they were in the Bear Paw Mountains, just a few miles south of the international border, when troops led by Colonel Nelson Miles caught up with them. After a five-day siege the exhausted Indians finally gave up. Their gallant bid for freedom was over.

Touring the Park

Begin your tour at the Visitor Center, where museum displays and an audiovisual program provide information about Nez Perce culture, the Nez Perce War, and the Battle of the Big Hole.

From the Visitor Center drive to the lower parking area. There are two short foot trails that lead from the parking area to points of interest on the battlefield.

Nez Perce Camp. The first foot trail leads along the east bank of the Big Hole River to the site of the Indian camp. The battle began here when Gibbon's soldiers crossed the river and fired into the Nez Perce tipis.

Siege Area. The second foot trail leads over the Big Hole to the wooded area where Gibbon's command sought shelter from the Indian sharpshooters. The soldiers were besieged for nearly two days.

Howitzer Capture Site. From the siege area a side trail leads uphill to the place where the Nez Perce captured and destroyed Gibbon's lone artillery piece. They also seized 2,000 rounds of rifle ammunition, which they used to keep the army troops pinned down.

CHAPTER 35

CUSTER BATTLEFIELD NATIONAL MONUMENT
(Indian Wars)

Post Office Box 39
Crow Agency, Montana 59022
Telephone: (406) 638-2622

On June 25, 1876, Lieutenant Colonel George Armstrong Custer and 215 troopers of the U.S. Seventh Cavalry were annihilated by several thousand Sioux and Cheyenne Indian warriors in the Battle of the Little Bighorn. Custer Battlefield National Monument preserves the site where Custer and his men made their last stand, as well as the separate Reno-Benteen defense perimeter, where the remainder of the Seventh Cavalry was besieged by the Indians.

Getting to the Park: Custer Battlefield National Monument is located 65 miles southeast of Billings, Montana. From Billings, take I-90 to the Custer Battlefield Exit, then drive 1 mile east on U.S. 212 to the park entrance.

Gas, food, lodging: In Hardin, Montana, 15 miles north on I-90.

Visitor Center: Located at the park entrance. Museum and bookstore; film on the battle.

Activities: Interpretive talks; hikes led by park personnel. Inquire at Visitor Center for schedule and locations.

Handicapped Access: Assistance may be needed to enter Visitor Center over three steps. Access to rest rooms is difficult because of narrow corridor. Entrenchment Trail is surfaced and accessible; Deep Ravine Trail is steep and unsurfaced and assistance will be required. Tour stops may be viewed from inside an automobile.

On the afternoon of June 25, 1876, on a bare, windswept ridge overlooking Montana's Little Bighorn River, five companies of the U.S. Seventh Cavalry commanded by Lieutenant Colonel George Armstrong Custer were attacked and overwhelmed by several thousand Sioux and Cheyenne Indian warriors. Officially called the Battle of the Little Bighorn, but more commonly known as Custer's Last Stand, this brief, desperate struggle has inspired more study and provoked more debate than any other armed clash in American history. At the heart of the battle's enduring fascination is an unanswerable question: what happened to Custer and his soldiers on that fateful afternoon? The mystery will never be solved, for of the 215 cavalrymen who rode into the fight, not one survived to tell the tale.

A Clash of Cultures

The Battle of the Little Bighorn was the culmination of a long, tragic struggle for possession of a vast territory encompassing much of present-day North Dakota, South Dakota, Wyoming, and Montana. For white Americans, control of this territory meant the opening of mines, establishment of ranches, and laying of railroads. For the Sioux and Cheyenne Indians, the stakes were even higher: they were fighting to safeguard their ancestral homeland and to preserve their free way of life.

The hostilities began after the Civil War when a flood of white prospectors, traders, and settlers swept across the northern plains, disrupting the nomadic existence of the Sioux and Cheyenne tribes. The Indians took up arms in 1866, and in a conflict called the Red Cloud War, brought white movement through their domain to a virtual standstill. The Red Cloud War ended in 1868 with the signing of the Fort Laramie Treaty in which the U.S. government agreed to set aside much of present-day South Dakota as a permanent reservation and to guarantee the Indians safety from "all depredations by people of the United States." For their part, the Sioux and Cheyenne promised to stop hostilities with whites and to confine themselves to the new reservation.

For six years a shaky peace was maintained. Then, in 1874, gold was discovered in the Black Hills of Dakota Territory, part of the Sioux reservation. Thousands of miners descended on the reservation in violation of the Fort Laramie Treaty, and in turn, thousands of Sioux and Cheyenne abandoned the reservation for the open grasslands of Wyoming and Montana. In December 1875, the Commissioner of Indian Affairs issued an ultimatum: all the Indians were to return to the reservation by January 31, 1876, or be considered hostile. The Sioux and Cheyenne ignored this order, and in the spring of 1876 the army began a campaign to round them up and bring them back to the reservation by force.

The Sioux Campaign of 1876

The army's plan called for three separate columns to converge on the Montana-Wyoming border, where the Indians were believed to be.

General Alfred Terry's column would march west from Fort Abraham Lincoln, located near present-day Bismarck, North Dakota; Colonel John Gibbon's column would move east from Fort Ellis in Montana; General George Crook's column would push north from Fort Fetterman in Wyoming.

Terry's Dakota Column, consisting of three infantry companies and the Seventh Cavalry Regiment, commanded by Lieutenant Colonel George Armstrong Custer, set out from Fort Lincoln on May 17, 1876. Although Terry was in charge of the expedition, he intended to let Custer and his fast-moving cavalrymen take the lead in finding and attacking the Sioux and Cheyenne.

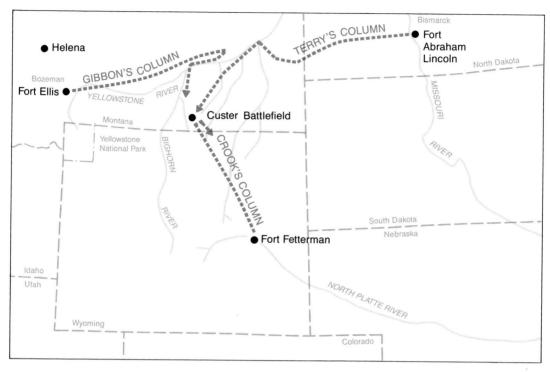

Sioux Campaign of 1876

In mid-June, Terry linked up with Gibbon's column on the banks of the Yellow-stone River in southeastern Montana. Scouts had discovered a fresh Indian trail lead-ing up Rosebud Creek. Terry promptly ordered Custer to take the Seventh Cavalry and follow the trail. He was to cross over into the Little Bighorn Valley, where the Indians were thought to be, and move downstream. Meanwhile, Terry and Colonel Gibbon would march with the infantry and remaining cavalry west along the Yellow-stone to the mouth of the Bighorn, then up to the Little Bighorn. Caught between these two forces, the Indians would be forced to fight or surrender.

Terry based his strategy on the assumption that there were no more than 800 war-riors, and that they were more likely to run than to stand and fight. This was a terrible miscalculation, for in reality there were between 2,000 and 4,000 Sioux and Chey-enne fighting men in the Little Bighorn Valley.

Custer Marches

On June 22, Custer and the Seventh Cavalry broke camp and headed up Rosebud Creek, following the trail of the Indians. The Crow and Arikara Indian scouts accom-panying the troopers grew increasingly restive as they saw how big this trail was, and they tried to tell Custer that the Sioux and Cheyenne badly outnumbered him. The confident lieutenant colonel brushed aside these warnings, however, and ordered his men to ride on to the summit of the divide separating the Rosebud from the Little Bighorn Valley. He intended to halt there and rest before moving down into the valley

The Boy General

Few men in American history have been so extravagantly admired or so bitterly reviled as George Armstrong Custer. To his partisans he was a dashing, heroic figure, the "Roland of the western plains," the "ablest Indian fighter we have ever had . . . . a man whose life was a perfect romance." To his detractors he was a brutal, reckless egomaniac, a man who "followed glory all his days" and "displayed in the violence and unscrupulousness of his search the aberration of a deprived addict."

Born in rural Ohio in 1839, Custer began his military career at West Point in 1857. A lackadaisical, insubordinate cadet with a penchant for adolescent pranks, he was in constant trouble with his instructors. He barely avoided expulsion and graduated last in his class in the spring of 1861.

After receiving his commission as a second lieutenant, Custer plunged headlong into the Civil War, distinguishing himself in combat and winning the attention and approbation of his superiors. In 1863, at the tender age of twenty-three, he was made a brigadier general, the youngest in the Union army, and barely a year later he was awarded his second star and given command of the Third Cavalry Division. By war's end the dashing, long-haired horseman had become a national hero, celebrated by press and public alike as the "Boy General."

The postwar years were difficult ones for Custer. His rank was reduced to lieutenant colonel in the army reorganization of 1866, and he was sent to join the Seventh Cavalry on the remote frontier, far from the adoring throngs of Washington and New York. He managed to keep himself in the public eye by writing magazine articles and a popular book about his western experiences, but military success proved more elusive. Despite his reputation as the army's best Indian fighter, he achieved only one victory in his ten years on the plains, the destruction of a Cheyenne village on Oklahoma's Washita River in 1868.

To make matters worse, the careless, insubordinate spirit that had characterized his West Point days resurfaced. He was court-martialed in 1867 for disobedience and desertion of his command, found guilty, and suspended from rank for a year. When he marched with General Terry's Dakota Column in the spring of 1876, he was again under a cloud, this time for accusing the administration of President Ulysses S. Grant of fraud.

Such contretemps were part and parcel of the Custer persona: in politics as in war he always charged ahead, heedless of the consequences. Spontaneous, fearless, utterly contemptuous of authority, he had much in common with the Sioux and Cheyenne warriors he battled in the Valley of the Little Bighorn. "In studying the Indian character . . . I find much to be admired," he wrote two years before his death. "If I were an Indian, I would greatly prefer to cast my lot among those of my people who adhered to the free open plains rather than submit to the confined limits of a reservation. . . . The fearless hunter, the matchless horseman and warrior of the plains. . . . nature intended him for the savage state. . . . He cannot be himself and be civilized: he fades away and dies."

A Civil War photograph of George Arm-
strong Custer, the "Boy General." National
Park Service, photograph by Matthew B.
Brady.

on June 26, the day Terry and Gibbon were scheduled to arrive at the mouth of the
Little Bighorn, cutting off the Indians' escape route.

This plan was discarded on the morning of the 25th when several Sioux warriors
were spotted near the cavalry's bivouac. Certain that his command had been discovered and that the Indians would get away unless he took quick action, Custer decided
to advance at once. He divided his command into three battalions: Captain Frederick
Benteen and 125 men were sent southwest with orders to "pitch into" any Indians
they might find. Major Marcus Reno with 140 men, and Custer with 215, would
march west along opposite banks of a small creek until they came to the Little Bighorn
River.

Reno Routed

Shortly after 2 P.M. on June 25, Custer and Reno approached the Little Bighorn.
In the distance they saw a cloud of white dust billowing up from a huge Sioux and
Cheyenne encampment. Custer immediately issued orders to Reno: "Charge the In-
dians, and you will be supported by the whole outfit."

Reno's soldiers forded the Little Bighorn and galloped down the valley toward the
distant line of tipis. As they drew closer they were startled to see a mass of Indian
warriors swarming out of the village to meet their attack. Believing it was suicidal to
continue the charge, Reno ordered his men to dismount and form a skirmish line.
Within minutes this line crumbled; frantically seeking cover, the cavalrymen retreated
into a stand of timber beside the river.

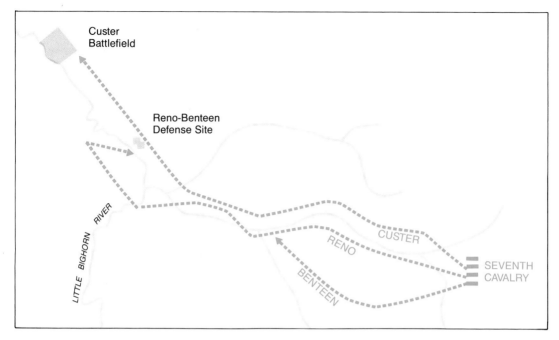

Custer Divides His Command, June 25, 1876

Without the promised support from Custer, Reno's tiny command was now in an extremely precarious position. In desperation, the major ordered his troopers to re-mount and make a dash for the high bluffs on the far side of the river, but the retreat degenerated into a rout as screaming warriors pursued the panicky soldiers, shooting down many of them as they floundered through the stream. The survivors, gasping with exhaustion and terror, regrouped atop the bluffs and prepared to face a fresh onslaught. The Indians suddenly broke off the fight, however, and galloped away to the north, where the sound of continuous, heavy firing could be heard.

"Gentlemen," panted one of Reno's officers, "in my opinion General Custer has made the biggest mistake of his life."

Custer's Last Stand

After separating from Reno's battalion, Custer and his 215 men rode north along the high ground above the Little Bighorn. Their exact movements and plan of action will never be fully known, but it seems likely that they were trying to descend to the river and attack the village in support of Reno's charge when they were met by a horde of warriors led by the Sioux chief Gall.

Badly outnumbered, the troopers fell back toward a long, high ridge until their line of retreat was cut off by another large force of warriors led by Chief Crazy Horse. More and more Indians poured onto the field, attacking from all directions, and the companies of Custer's battalion became separated and had to fight individual holding actions on foot against heavy odds. The Sioux and Cheyenne tide engulfed them, and they were annihilated in quick succession.

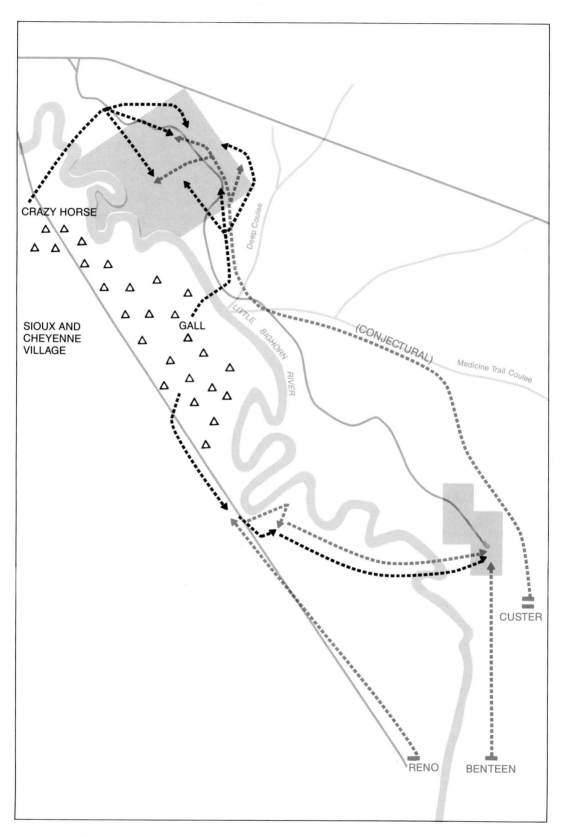

CRAZY HORSE

SIOUX AND
CHEYENNE
VILLAGE

GALL

Deep Coulee

LITTLE BIGHORN RIVER

(CONJECTURAL)

Medicine Trail Coulee

CUSTER

RENO

BENTEEN

Battle of the Little Bighorn, June 25, 1876

Sioux chief Gall. Copyright Smithsonian Institution.

Sioux chief Crow King. Copyright Smithsonian Institution.

At the north end of the high ridge, a cluster of fifty troopers gathered around Custer. They shot their mounts to make breastworks, and prepared to meet the final Indian charge. It came with frightening suddenness. The Sioux and Cheyenne swept over the horse-corpse barricade and made short work of the remaining soldiers, including Custer, who was shot through the temple and chest. The entire battle, from river to ridge, probably lasted less than an hour.

Reno and Benteen Besieged

Around 4:30 P.M., Benteen's battalion and the regimental pack train joined Reno's battered command on the bluffs above the Little Bighorn. The sharp report of firing rifles could still be heard in the distance, and the soldiers began riding north toward the sound, hoping to find Custer. They got as far as a high promontory, now called Weir Point, before hundreds of advancing Indians forced them to retreat back to the bluffs and form a defensive perimeter.

The Sioux and Cheyenne quickly surrounded this position and began blasting away as Reno and Benteen's men frantically dug rifle pits to protect themselves. The firing continued until sunset, when most of the Indians withdrew to the village to take part in a great victory dance. The soldiers spent the night speculating about what had become of Custer and deepening their trenches and rifle pits in anticipation of further combat in the morning.

The battle resumed at dawn on June 26. The Indians kept up a steady barrage of fire through the morning and into the afternoon; on several occasions they threatened

Archaeology at the Little Bighorn

During the summer of 1983 a prairie fire ignited by a tourist's cigarette swept across Custer Battlefield National Monument, incinerating 600 acres of grass and sagebrush. When the fire burned itself out archaeologist Rich Fox, a resident of nearby Hardin, Montana, walked across the freshly exposed ground in the vicinity of Last Stand Hill and the Deep Ravine. He was startled to see spent bullets, brass cartridge casings, bone fragments, and other artifacts from the Custer battle strewn across the scorched soil.

Fox's extraordinary discovery prompted the National Park Service to conduct a full-fledged archaeological survey of the battlefield in 1984 and 1985. Volunteers operating electronic detection devices made systematic sweeps across the terrain, locating metallic artifacts which were then excavated by a second group of volunteers. Other archaeological teams searched for human remains around the marble tablets that mark the locations where the bodies of Custer's men were found.

When the survey was over more than 4,000 artifacts had been unearthed, including bullets and cartridge casings, buttons and coins, pieces of firearms and horse gear, spurs, belt buckles, a watch, and a silver-plated wedding ring. Hundreds of human bones were also discovered, including the almost complete skeleton of an unidentified trooper.

By mapping artifact locations, particularly the patterns of spent ammunition, the achaeologists have been able to create a battle scenario. One interesting revelation that has emerged from the data is that the Indians were much better armed than previously thought. As many as 200 warriors may have been carrying Henry or Winchester repeating rifles, weapons superior to the single-shot Springfield carbines issued to the cavalry. The archaeologists have also learned that Custer's soldiers fought a relatively stationary battle, dismounted and in small defensive clusters, while their Indian opponents roamed freely across the field, attacking first one position, then another.

More valuable information will undoubtedly come to light as the archaeological analysis of the Custer battlefield continues. However, the tantalizing questions about Custer's intentions, the movements of his command, and its ultimate fate will never be completely answered.

to storm the perimeter, but were driven back by determined counterattacks. As the day wore on, thirst plagued the soldiers. Dr. Henry R. Porter, one of the regimental surgeons, told Reno that the wounded had to have water soon or they would die. Kettles and canteens were collected, and while four sharpshooters stood up to draw Indian fire, fifteen volunteers ran down a steep ravine to the river to fill the containers. This water sortie saved the lives of the wounded, and the men who made the desperate sprint to the Little Bighorn were later awarded Medals of Honor for heroism.

In the middle of the afternoon, the warriors began leaving the field, and the stream

A solitary headstone marks the spot where a Seventh Cavalry soldier died. National Park Service, photograph by William S. Keller.

of bullets that had kept the soldiers pinned down slackened and finally stopped. The Indians, alerted to the approach of Terry and Gibbon's infantry, were breaking camp; after setting fire to the prairie grass to create a smoke screen, they rode off to the southwest in a long, majestic procession. By dusk the entire village was gone; the battle was over.

A Short-lived Triumph

In a day and a half of fighting the Sioux and Cheyenne had achieved a stunning victory over the U.S. Army. At a cost estimated to be less than 100 men they had smashed the Seventh Cavalry, killing or wounding half the regiment.

Their triumph was short-lived, however. An enraged American public demanded vengeance for Custer's death, and the army redoubled its efforts to find and crush the hostiles. Within the year most of the Indians had grown so weary of running and fighting that they voluntarily returned to the reservation. Ironically for the Sioux and Cheyenne, the great victory at the Little Bighorn had hastened, rather than postponed, their final subjugation.

Touring the Park

Begin your tour at the Visitor Center, where museum exhibits and a film will help you understand the battle.

From the Visitor Center, a short walk takes you to Last Stand Hill. The white marble markers scattered across the battlefield show where the bodies of Custer's men were found. On the west side of the hill, just below the granite monument, a cluster of fifty-two markers shows where Custer and the remnants of his battalion made their "last stand."

After visiting Last Stand Hill, walk back to the Visitor Center. The Deep Ravine Trail, a three-quarter-mile footpath that leads across the lower portion of the battlefield, begins just south of the Visitor Center. There are nine numbered stops along the trail.

Deep Ravine Trail: Stop 1. Placement of Headstones. The mutilated, decomposing bodies of Custer and his 215 men were discovered two days after the battle by General Terry's infantry. Sickened by what they saw and fearful that the Indians would return, the soldiers threw a few spadefuls of dirt over the dead, marked the grave sites with wooden stakes, and hastily departed.

A burial detail returned to the battlefield in 1877 to exhume the officers' bodies and ship them east for reinterment by their families. Four years later, the remains of the enlisted men were collected and reburied in a mass grave at the base of the granite monument on Last Stand Hill. The wooden stakes that marked the original grave sites were replaced in 1890 with the marble headstones you see here.

There are no markers showing where Sioux and Cheyenne warriors fell. The Indians removed their battle dead (believed by some historians to number as few as thirty) and placed them on scaffolds or in caves in the nearby mountains.

Deep Ravine Trail: Stop 2. Sturgis Marker. The body of Lieutenant James G. Sturgis was never identified, although remnants of his bloodstained uniform were found in the Indian village. His mother was not told this gruesome fact, and when she came to visit the battlefield in 1881, soldiers decided to erect a marker on this spot rather than tell her that Sturgis's remains were missing.

Deep Ravine Trail: Stop 3. Companies C and E. An Indian charge led by Lame White Man split the two cavalry troops that were trying to hold this ridge. Company E was driven into the large ravine at the foot of the trail while Company C tried to retreat toward Last Stand Hill. As the marble markers indicate, most of the soldiers were killed here.

Deep Ravine Trail: Stop 4. Lame White Man's Charge. From near this spot, according to Indian testimony, Lame White Man led the charge that obliterated Companies C and E. "All around, the Indians began jumping up, running forward, dodging down, jumping up again, down again, all the time going toward the soldiers,"

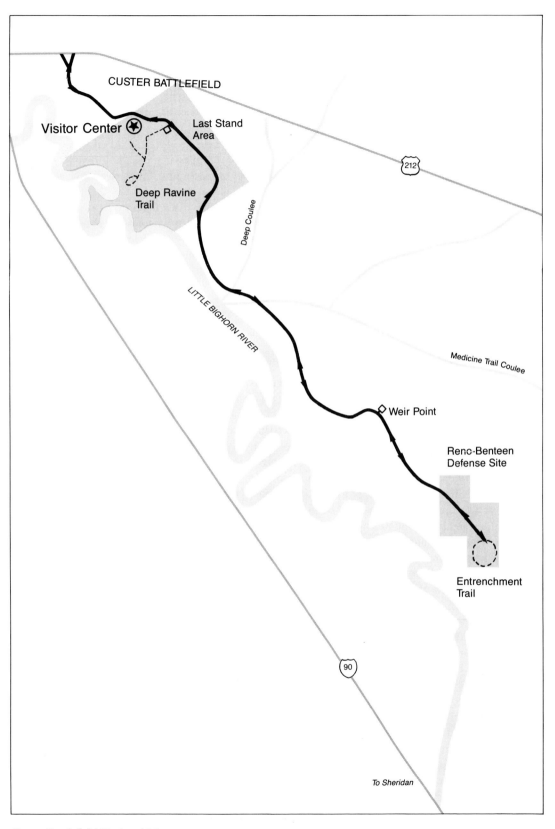

CUSTER BATTLEFIELD

Visitor Center

Last Stand
Area

Deep Ravine
Trail

Deep Coulee

LITTLE BIGHORN RIVER

Medicine Trail Coulee

◇ Weir Point

Reno-Benteen
Defense Site

Entrenchment
Trail

212

90

To Sheridan

Custer Battlefield National Monument

recalled Wooden Leg, a Cheyenne warrior who participated in the attack. Lame White Man was killed leading the charge.

Deep Ravine Trail: Stop 5. Indian Village. South and west of this point, on the bottomland along the far bank of the Little Bighorn, stood the Sioux and Cheyenne village. The encampment extended for three miles and was populated by 10,000–12,000 people.

Deep Ravine Trail: Stop 6. Surgeon George E. Lord. George E. Lord was one of three surgeons serving with the Seventh Cavalry. He was sick on the morning of the battle, and Custer offered to let him stay with the pack train. Lord declined, and paid for his decision with his life.

Deep Ravine Trail: Stop 7. Deep Ravine. A ferocious Indian charge (see Stops 3 and 4) drove the troopers of Company E into this steep gulch where all of them were killed. Oddly, no marble markers appear in the ravine, even though historical evidence suggests that as many as twenty-eight bodies are buried here. This mystery may be cleared up in the future by an archaeological investigation.

Return by the same trail to Stop 8.

Deep Ravine Trail: Stop 8. Custer's Last Stand. From this point, looking northeast, you see Last Stand Hill as the Indians saw it moments before they rushed forward and ended the battle.

Deep Ravine Trail: Stop 9. National Cemetery. The large, tree-shaded cemetery next to the Visitor Center contains the remains of over 5,000 veterans and their dependents. Soldiers from abandoned military posts in Montana, Wyoming, and North Dakota are buried here along with service members who fought in the Spanish-American War, World Wars I and II, and the Korean and Vietnam conflicts.

After walking the Deep Ravine Trail, return to your car and and drive south along the Battlefield Road. There are several pullouts, where interpretive signs identify the positions held by various companies of the Seventh Cavalry during the battle.

Continue along the Battlefield Road approximately 3.5 miles to the Reno-Benteen Defense Site. This is the area that Major Reno's battalion retreated to after its disastrous attempt to attack the Indian village in the Little Bighorn Valley below. From the parking area the Reno-Benteen Entrenchment Trail loops around the Defense Site. There are eighteen numbered stops along the trail.

Entrenchment Trail: Stop 1. Reno's Retreat. From this point looking west you see the stand of timber along the Little Bighorn River where Reno's command sought shelter after its failed charge against the Indian village. A powerful Sioux and Cheyenne counterattack forced the troopers to abandon the timber and flee across the river. They galloped up the ravines in front of you to this position on the bluffs, pursued by the Indian warriors.

Entrenchment Trail: Stop 2. M Company's Position. During the early morning hours of June 26, Indian riflemen took up concealed positions close to this side of the cavalry perimeter and pinned down the men of Captain Thomas H. French's M Company.

Entrenchment Trail: Stop 3. Field Hospital. Regimental surgeon Henry R. Porter gathered the wounded and set up a field hospital in the swale between this point and the memorial monument.

Entrenchment Trail: Stop 4. H Company Trench. This shallow trench was dug under fire on the morning of June 26 by the men of H Company. They used their knives and mess gear to mound up the dirt and then threw dead horses and mules on the parapet for added cover. The trench was restored to its original dimensions in 1958.

Entrenchment Trail: Stop 5. Indian Firing Positions. Armed with the carbines and ammunition they had taken from the Custer dead, the Indians sniped at the Reno-Benteen force from the ridges approximately 500 yards east and southeast of this point.

Entrenchment Trail: Stop 6. Medal of Honor Point. It was from this point on the morning of June 26 that fifteen volunteers ran down to the Little Bighorn, fully exposed to Indian fire, to fill kettles and canteens with water. Their action saved the lives of several of the wounded, and they were awarded the Medal of Honor for bravery.

Entrenchment Trail: Stop 7. Restored Trench. This L-shaped trench was restored to its original dimensions in 1958. During the restoration the skeletal remains of Privates Julian Jones and Thomas Meador, killed on the firing line thirty-five yards farther south along the trail, were discovered. They were buried in the trench after the fight ended on June 26.

Entrenchment Trail: Stop 8. Death of Jones and Meador. In the 1950s, Private Charles Windolph, Medal of Honor winner and the last survivor of the Reno-Benteen force, pointed out this spot as the location where Privates Jones and Meador were shot and killed on the morning of the 26th.

Entrenchment Trail: Stop 9. The Perimeter Threatened. A bold group of warriors crawled close enough to this point on the morning of June 26 to throw rocks at the soldiers. Captain Benteen saw that they were preparing to storm the perimeter and led a desperate countercharge that forced the warriors back (see Stop 11).

Entrenchment Trail: Stop 10. Route of the Seventh Cavalry, June 25. Looking east from this high point, you can see the tree-lined valley of Reno Creek and, in the distance, the Wolf Mountains. The Seventh Cavalry crossed the mountains and rode down Reno Creek on the morning of June 25 on their way to attack the Indian village.

Entrenchment Trail: Stop 11. Cavalry Counterattack. It was from this point that Captain Benteen launched the counterattack that saved the southern end of the perimeter (see Stop 9). The yelling troopers charged around the point of the hill to the right, caught the Indians by surprise, and sent them scurrying back to safety. Only one soldier was killed.

Entrenchment Trail: Stop 12. A Company Barricade. Seeking shelter from the heavy Indian fire coming from the east, the soldiers of A Company erected a barricade of pack saddles, boxes, sides of bacon, and dead mules and horses across this low area. The tablet behind you marks the spot where the skeletal remains of an unidentified soldier were found in 1958.

Entrenchment Trail: Stop 13. G Company Rifle Pit. This rifle pit was restored to its original dimensions in 1958.

Entrenchment Trail: Stop 14. K Company Rifle Pits. These rifle pits were restored to their original dimensions in 1958. Lack of shovels prevented the K Company soldiers from digging them any deeper.

Entrenchment Trail: Stop 15. Unrestored Rifle Pits. These shallow, almost imperceptible depressions are original rifle pits.

Entrenchment Trail: Stop 16. K Company Rifle Pit. This rifle pit was restored to its original dimensions in 1958.

Entrenchment Trail: Stop 17. Mass Grave. The granite marker to the left of the trail marks the site of a mass grave where casualties of the Reno-Benteen fight were buried. The remains were removed in 1881 to the mass grave on Last Stand Hill.

Entrenchment Trail: Stop 18. Sharpshooter Ridge. The high ground 500 yards north of this spot was occupied by Indian sharpshooters on June 25–26. Fortunately for the cavalrymen, most of the warriors were poor long-range marksmen.

CHAPTER 36

LAVA BEDS NATIONAL MONUMENT
(Indian Wars)

P.O. Box 867
Tulelake, California 96134
Telephone: (916) 667-2282

On November 29, 1872, a small group of Modoc Indians clashed with an army patrol on the shore of Tule Lake in northeastern California. Following this skirmish, the Modocs retreated into the rugged lava beds south of the lake, where, for six months, they held off an attacking force that at times outnumbered them twenty to one. Eventually the Modocs were forced to surrender; their leaders were hanged and the remaining members of the band were deported to Oklahoma. Lava Beds National Monument preserves several sites associated with the Modoc War, the only major Indian war fought in California.

Getting to the Park: Lava Beds National Monument is located 58 miles southeast of Klamath Falls, Oregon. From Klamath Falls, take Oregon Highway 39 to the California-Oregon border, where it becomes California Highway 139. Five miles south of Tulelake, California, signs point the way to the park's northeast entrance.

Gas, food, lodging: In Tulelake, California, and Klamath Falls, Oregon.

Visitor Center: Museum and gift shop.

Activities: Ranger-led hikes and cave trips during summer. Inquire at visitor Center for location and schedule.

Handicapped Access: Visitor Center is accessible. Some of the Modoc War sites can be seen from a car, but others involve short hikes. Inquire at Visitor Center about condition of foot trails.

In the long, checkered history of the American Indian Wars, perhaps no conflict was more unnecessary or more depressing than the six-month Modoc War, which began on November 29, 1872, and ended on June 1, 1873. Bad judgment and military incompetence dogged the U.S. Army throughout this sorry affair, but the army's bungling was more than matched by the Indians' mendacity; as one historian bluntly put it, "the Modoc War bathed none of its participants in glory, or even credit."

Captain Jack and the Modocs

The Modoc Indians were a tough, warlike people who inhabited the rugged, arid plateaus along the Oregon-California border. From small villages scattered along the banks of Lost River and the shores of Tule Lake they embarked on raids against neighboring Indian tribes and, beginning in the 1850s, against white settlers who had begun to encroach on their homeland.

In 1864, responding to the protests of the white immigrants, the U.S. Office of Indian Affairs imposed a treaty on the Modocs that compelled them to leave their ancestral domain and move to the Klamath Indian reservation in Oregon. The Modocs and the Klamaths were historic enemies, and conflict between the two tribes soon flared anew. Growing weary of Klamath harassment, a large band of Modocs, led by a young man the whites called Captain Jack, returned to the Tule Lake basin in 1865.

Four years later Indian Superintendent Alfred Meacham persuaded Captain Jack and his followers to go back to the Klamath reservation, but once again the Modocs were bullied by the more numerous Klamaths. In April 1869, Captain Jack and 371 Modocs fled the reservation for the second time; back in their villages, they asked Meacham to give them their own reservation on the Lost River.

Meacham's successor, Thomas B. Odeneal, denied this request, and in the fall of 1872 he decided to remove the Modocs to the Klamath reservation by force. Troop B of the First U.S. Cavalry—three officers and forty enlisted men—rode from Fort Klamath to Captain Jack's village on the west bank of the Lost River. At dawn on November 29, 1872, the cavalrymen confronted the Modocs and gunfire was exchanged; one trooper was killed and seven were wounded. Jack and his followers fled to Tule Lake, where they embarked in boats for the lava beds on the lake's south shore.

Meanwhile, white settlers attacked another Modoc village on the Lost River. This attack, like the cavalry's, was a bloody failure; two whites were killed and one was wounded. The Modoc band, led by Hooker Jim, escaped on horseback, riding east around Tule Lake, massacring white homesteaders as they went. By the time they united with Captain Jack's group in the lava beds on the south shore of the lake, fourteen settlers were dead and the entire region was in an uproar.

Captain Jack's Stronghold

The Modocs, numbering about 160, took shelter in a region of the lava beds known as Captain Jack's Stronghold. This area reminded army officers of a wind-tossed sea that had suddenly been frozen into black rock; it was a natural fortress of volcanic trenches, caves, and tunnels, complete with patches of grass to provide feed for the Modocs' livestock and sagebrush and greasewood to provide fuel for their campfires.

Cavalry, infantry, and militia units from posts all over northern California and southern Oregon converged on the lava beds during December 1872, and by the new year approximately 325 soldiers were camped a few miles east and west of the strong-

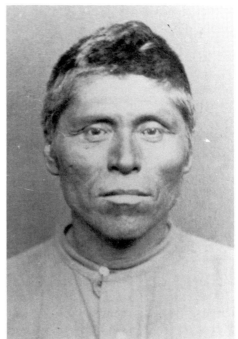

Above left: Captain Jack, leader of the Modocs. National Park Service, photograph by Louis Heller.

Above right: Modoc Indian medicine man, Curly Headed Doctor, hatched the plot to kill the peace commissioners. National Park Service, photograph by Louis Heller.

Left: General Edward Canby was one of the peace commissioners shot by the Modocs on April 11, 1873. National Park Service, photograph by Matthew B. Brady.

hold. Colonel Frank Wheaton, the commander of this polyglot force, devised a strategy for encircling the badly outnumbered Modocs and forcing them to surrender.

Two columns of troops advanced into the lava beds on the foggy morning of January 16, 1873, intending to execute a pincers movement that would trap the Indians. The rugged, confusing terrain and heavy, accurate rifle fire of the Modocs stalled the advance, however, and when the fog lifted it was the soldiers, not the Indians, who were pinned down. Nightfall finally enabled Wheaton's men to withdraw to safety, but they had lost nine killed and twenty-eight wounded. The Modocs not only suffered no casualties—they were never even seen by their befuddled and demoralized opponents.

Modoc Treachery

After the army's costly and humiliating defeat in the Battle of the Stronghold, President Ulysses S. Grant appointed a peace commission to negotiate an end to the fighting. The talks went nowhere, however, as Captain Jack continued to demand a reservation on the Lost River for his people, while the commissioners insisted that the Indians surrender unconditionally.

As the months passed without an end to the standoff, Captain Jack came under terrific pressure from militants in his band to end the negotiations. Hooker Jim and a Modoc medicine man called Curly Headed Doctor wanted to kill the peace commissioners and fight it out with the soldiers, and they eventually talked Captain Jack into going along with them.

On Good Friday, April 11, 1873, the peace commission—General Edward Canby, former Indian Superintendent Alfred Meacham, Reverend Eleaser Thomas, and L. S. Dyar—went to the council site to meet with Captain Jack and the Modoc negotiators. Once again Captain Jack asked for a Lost River reservation, and when Canby refused, Jack pulled a pistol from his coat and shot the general in the head. Meacham and Thomas were also shot and stabbed, while Dyar ran for his life.

This act of treachery stunned and infuriated the army and the Grant administration, and orders went out to crush the Modocs whatever the cost. On April 15, troops led by Colonel Alvin Gillem advanced into the lava beds, using mortars and mountain howitzers to drive the Modocs back. On the 17th the Indians abandoned the stronghold and retreated south to another lava fortress, leaving behind the bodies of three men and eight women.

On April 26, Gillem sent Captain Evan Thomas and a sixty-four-man patrol to scout the Modocs' new position. While resting in the shade of Hardin Butte near the western edge of the Schonchin Lava Flow, Thomas and his men were suddenly struck by a deadly fusillade of rifle bullets fired by Modoc warriors who had crept to within nearly point-blank range. When the deadly ambush was over, Thomas and twenty-four other soldiers were dead, and sixteen were wounded.

This startling success emboldened Captain Jack, and on May 10 he launched a surprise attack against the army camp at Dry Lake, hoping to drive the soldiers out of the Modoc homeland once and for all. The attack was repulsed, however, and the tired, discouraged Modocs began to quarrel among themselves. The argument ended with Hooker Jim and thirteen other warriors breaking off from the main group and heading west toward the present-day town of Dorris; Captain Jack, unable to defend the lava flow with only thirty-odd warriors, led his band east toward Clear Lake.

The army overran the abandoned Modoc fortress in Schonchin Lava Flow on May 14 and continued west, pursuing Hooker Jim's party. Jim surrendered on May 22, and offered to help track down Captain Jack in exchange for clemency; this offer was accepted, and the army turned east, following Captain Jack's trail toward Clear Lake.

The Modoc camp was discovered on May 28, and attacked the next morning. When the startled Indians scattered, the cavalry took up the pursuit, embarking on a four-day hunt that the army commander grouchily described as "more of a chase after wild beasts than a war." One by one, the Modocs were killed or taken prisoner. Captain Jack surrendered on June 3, explaining to his captor, Captain David Perry, that "his legs had given out."

Demise of the Modocs

Captain Jack and five other Modoc warriors were tried and found guilty of the assassination of the peace commissioners. Two of the men had their death sentences commuted by President Grant, but the other four, including Captain Jack, were hung at Fort Klamath on October 3, 1873. The rest of the Modocs—155 men, women, and children—were shipped off to the Quapaw Agency in Oklahoma, where they soon succumbed to disease.

The final act of the Modoc War was fittingly barbaric: Captain Jack's head was hacked from his body and boiled to remove the flesh. The skull—a grisly trophy of one of the most shameful and senseless armed conflicts in American history—was then shipped to Washington, D.C., and put on display at the Army Medical Hospital.

Touring the Park

Begin your tour at the Visitor Center, where museum displays and an audiovisual program provide information about the geology of the lava beds, Modoc culture, and the Modoc War.

From the Visitor Center drive north on the Park Road. Signs point the way to the Modoc War sites.

Thomas-Wright Battlefield. It was here, on April 26, 1873, that Captain Evan Thomas and his sixty-four-man patrol were ambushed by Modoc warriors. Thomas and twenty-four of his soldiers were killed in this brief clash.

Gillem's Camp. One of the two camps occupied by the army during the Modoc War was located here.

Canby's Cross. This memorial marks the council site where General Edward Canby was murdered by Captain Jack. Canby was the only general officer ever killed in the American Indian Wars.

Captain Jack's Stronghold. Captain Jack and his Modoc followers took shelter in this rugged area of the lava beds in December 1872. They held the numerically superior army forces at bay for five months, but were forced to withdraw after the murder of General Canby.

Hospital Rock. The army had its headquarters and hospital here.

CHAPTER 37

U.S.S. *ARIZONA* MEMORIAL
(World War II)

No. 1 Arizona Memorial Place
Honolulu, Hawaii 96818
Telephone: (808) 422-2771

On December 7, 1941, the Imperial Japanese Navy launched a surprise aerial attack against the U.S. naval base at Pearl Harbor, Hawaii. Eight ships, including the battleship U.S.S. *Arizona*, were sunk; 188 aircraft were destroyed; 2,403 American sailors, soldiers, and marines were killed. The U.S.S. *Arizona* Memorial spans the sunken battleship. It commemorates the heroism and sacrifice of the men who lost their lives aboard it.

Getting to the Park: U.S.S. *Arizona* Memorial and National Park Service Visitor Center are located within the boundaries of the Pearl Harbor Naval Base, Oahu, Hawaii. From Waikiki, take Ala Moana Boulevard, which becomes the Nimitz Highway, toward Honolulu International Airport. At Puuloa Road, get on H1, the elevated freeway above Kamehameha Highway. Leave the freeway at the Stadium exit, turn left at the fourth traffic light, and follow the signs. Although Pearl Harbor is a military installation, no pass or special document is needed to visit the *Arizona* Memorial.

Gas, food, lodging: In Honolulu.

Visitor Center: Museum and gift shop; film on the Pearl Harbor attack.

Activities: Interpretive talk by park personnel and boat trip to the memorial. (Please note: for safety reasons, visitors must be at least forty-five inches tall to ride the navy shuttle boats.)

Handicapped Access: The Visitor Center, shuttle boats, and memorial are all accessible. Assistance may be required boarding the shuttle boat; inquire at Visitor Center.

By the fall of 1941, relations between the United States and Japan had been strained to the breaking point. Economic sanctions aimed at forcing Japan to abandon its campaign of conquest in China had failed, and the island nation was now girding to invade Southeast Asia and seize strategic raw materials needed to fuel its war industries.

Japan's military leaders knew that their thrust into Southeast Asia would, in all likelihood, cause the United States to declare war. They decided to gain the upper hand by launching a surprise attack on the U.S. Pacific Fleet at Pearl Harbor. A decisive victory in Hawaii would paralyze the American navy and make possible the capture of the Philippines, Malaya, Hong Kong, and the Dutch East Indies. After consolidating its new empire, Japan could then negotiate a favorable peace with the demoralized United States.

The Japanese Fleet Sails

During the last week of November, a thirty-ship Japanese naval task force rendezvoused in the Kuril Islands, north of Hokkaido. On the 26th it set sail for Hawaii, following a route that took it far north of the usual trans-Pacific shipping lanes. Maintaining strict radio silence and utilizing storms and fog for cover, the task force steamed undetected to a point 240 miles north of Oahu.

Just before 6 A.M. on December 7, Vice Admiral Chuichi Nagumo ordered his six aircraft carriers to turn into the wind. The first wave of fighters, bombers, and torpedo planes took off in the predawn darkness and winged south toward their target. Five midget submarines had been launched earlier and already were lurking near the entrance to Pearl Harbor, waiting to strike.

On Oahu all was quiet. A message from Washington warning of hostile actions by the Japanese had been received several days earlier, but it had caused no great sense of alarm. The commanders of the island's army and navy installations believed that if an attack came it would be in the Philippines, not Hawaii.

Off Ford Island, in the middle of Pearl Harbor, the U.S. Pacific Fleet's big battleships were tied up in a row. The anchorage also was crowded with cruisers, destroyers, submarines, and auxiliary ships, but the fleet's aircraft carriers were not in port. At the Army Air Corps' Hickam, Wheeler, and Bellows fields, planes were parked wing tip to wing tip; sabotage, not attack from the sky, was the main concern of Oahu's defenders.

Tora, Tora, Tora

Shortly after 7 A.M., a radar operator at Opana Point observed a blip on his screen indicating that a large flight of airplanes was approaching from the north. His superiors, assuming that the planes either belonged to the carrier *Enterprise* or were a wing of B-17 bombers scheduled to arrive from the mainland, took no action. At almost exactly the same time, the destroyer *Ward*, patrolling near the entrance to Pearl Harbor, radioed that it had fired at a small, unidentified submarine. Nothing was done about this report, either.

Just before 8 A.M., the aircraft of the Japanese first wave arrived over Pearl Harbor. The flight leader, Commander Mitsuo Fuchida, saw that complete surprise had been achieved and transmitted the coded signal, "Tora, Tora, Tora," to inform the Japanese fleet. The bombers and torpedo planes then began their attacks, concentrating on the eight battleships moored near Ford Island.

The U.S.S. *Arizona*, on fire and sinking, following the Japanese attack on Pearl Harbor, December 7, 1941. National Archives.

Barely ten minutes after the raid began, a 1,760-pound armor-piercing bomb smashed into the U.S.S. *Arizona*. A tremendous explosion ripped through the ship and a pillar of black smoke boiled up into the sky. The *Arizona* sank almost instantly; 1,100 of her crew were killed.

Farther down battleship row, the *Oklahoma* was holed by several torpedos. It rolled completely over, trapping many sailors and marines who were still below decks. The *California* and *West Virginia* also were hit and sunk, while the *Maryland, Tennessee,* and *Pennsylvania* were severely damaged by the torrent of bombs. Only one of the battleships, the *Nevada*, got underway and tried to escape out to sea. As it moved down the channel, the Japanese airplanes swarmed over it like angry hornets, scoring several hits. Taking on water and in danger of foundering, the *Nevada* was run aground so that it would not block the harbor entrance.

Even as the battleships were being pummeled, other Japanese aircraft were bombing and strafing Hickam, Wheeler, and Bellows fields; the Kaneohe Naval Air Station; the Ewa Marine Corps Air Station; and Schofield Army Barracks. Hundreds of American planes were destroyed on the ground, runways, hangars, and maintenance facilities were damaged; and hundreds of men were killed or wounded.

American sailors, soldiers, marines, and airmen were stunned by the Japanese onslaught, but they did their best to fight back. Antiaircraft guns were manned, and when the second wave of attacking planes hit Pearl Harbor at 8:50 A.M. they were greeted by exploding shells and machine-gun fire. Several Army Air Corps pilots got their fighters off the ground and were able to shoot down a number of enemy planes before being knocked down themselves.

The fighting continued until about 10 A.M., when the last of the Japanese attackers turned and headed north, back to their carriers. Behind them, a pall of oily black smoke hung in the sky, marking the smoldering ruins of the U.S. Pacific Fleet's once proud battleships.

The Aftermath

At a cost of 29 airplanes and 5 midget submarines, the Japanese had inflicted a staggering defeat on the United States. Eight ships (including 5 battleships) had been sunk and 13 severely damaged; 188 aircraft had been destroyed and 159 damaged; 2,403 men were dead and 1,178 wounded.

The Japanese victory was not complete, however. The American aircraft carriers had escaped harm, and Pearl Harbor's submarine base, fuel depots, dry docks, and repair yards were virtually intact. With the ships and facilities that survived the attack, the Pacific Fleet would be able to regroup and carry on the fight. Even more ominously for the Japanese, the sneak attack had aroused the American people to action, inspiring in them a commitment to total victory. Japan had sowed the wind at Pearl Harbor; during the next four years she would reap the bloody whirlwind of American vengeance.

Touring the Memorial

Begin your tour at the Visitor Center information desk. Obtain a ticket for the interpretive program, and when your number is called, proceed to the theater entrance. (While waiting for your ticket number to be called, visit the museum and bookstore.)

The interpretive program consists of a short talk by a National Park Service Ranger and a documentary film. After the film, a navy shuttle boat will take you to the *Arizona* Memorial, a white, 184-foot-long concrete structure that spans the sunken battleship. The memorial has a large central assembly area for observation and a smaller shrine chamber where the names of 1,177 sailors and marines killed aboard the *Arizona* on December 7, 1941, are inscribed.

The next shuttle boat will take you back to the Visitor Center. (Please note: for safety reasons, visitors must be at least forty-five inches tall to ride the navy shuttle boats.)

CHAPTER 38

WAR IN THE PACIFIC NATIONAL HISTORICAL PARK
(World War II)

P.O. Box FA
Agana, Guam 96910
Telephone: Guam 477-8528

On December 10, 1941, a Japanese invasion force seized the U.S. Territory of Guam. Two and a half years later, American forces landed on the island and retook it in a bitter three-week struggle. War in the Pacific National Historical Park preserves several sites where heavy fighting took place in July and August 1944.

Getting to the Park: War in the Pacific National Historical Park is located on the island of Guam, a U.S. territory in the central Pacific. The park consists of seven physically separated units located near the villages of Asan, Piti, and Agat on the western side of the island. The Visitor Center is located in the Asan Beach Unit, approximately 3 miles west of the capital of Agana. From Agana, drive west on Guam Highway 1 (Marine Drive) to the park.

Gas, food, lodging: In Agana.

Visitor Center: Located in the Asan Beach Unit. Museum; short film on the Pacific War and the battle for Guam.

Activities: Snorkeling and diving at the Asan Beach Unit and Agat Unit.

Handicapped Access: War in the Pacific National Historical Park is a new and developing area, and is generally unimproved. Handicapped individuals should contact park personnel for up-to-date information about the accessibility of the various park units.

Japan's surprise attack at Pearl Harbor on December 7, 1941 (see Chapter 37), plunged the United States into World War II. In the Pacific theater, air power was the key to victory, and the Japanese moved swiftly to seize island bases from which their fighters and bombers could hold American naval forces at bay. One of the islands slated for conquest was Guam, in the southern Marianas.

Guam Falls to Japan

The U.S. Navy maintained an anchorage at Apra Harbor on Guam, but it was lightly defended: only 153 marines, armed with rifles and 30-caliber machine guns, were on hand to meet the 5,000-man Japanese invasion force when it landed on December 10, 1941. After offering token resistance, the Americans surrendered, and the Japanese troops occupied the island.

Guam was destined to remain in Japanese hands for two and a half years. For the people of the island the occupation was a harrowing ordeal, a time of restrictions and food rationing, of curfews and private property confiscation. Young and old alike were forced to study Japanese language and customs and to attend mass meetings where they were forcibly indoctrinated in *Nippon Seishen*, "spirit of Japan."

In 1944, as the threat of an American invasion loomed, the Japanese army compelled the Guamanians to perform slave labor, building gun emplacements and pillboxes and digging hundreds of caves. Those who complained about the harsh treatment or refused to work were beaten and in some instances executed. When the entrenchments were completed, the people were herded into concentration camps on the east side of the island. Conditions in these camps were terrible, but the incarceration did have one positive result: it removed the civilians from the areas hit hardest by the preinvasion bombardment, saving hundreds of lives.

Guam Recaptured

Beginning in August 1942, the U.S. Navy and Marine Corps went on the offensive in the Pacific. New tactics, equipment, and weapons were developed for storming Japanese-held islands, and by the summer of 1944 the techniques of amphibious assault had been refined to a high degree. The Guam invasion would demonstrate vividly the American forces' skill at planning and executing this most difficult form of warfare.

A thunderous naval barrage, one of the longest and heaviest of the war, pounded Japanese positions on Guam during the second week of July 1944. At 8:30 A.M. on July 21, landing craft carrying 55,000 men of the 3rd Marine Division, 1st Provisional Marine Brigade, and 305th Regimental Combat Team of the 77th Army Division ground onto the coral reefs ringing the Asan and Agat invasion beaches.

The Americans waded ashore under heavy machine-gun, mortar, and rifle fire, and took cover in shell holes and behind shattered palm trees. Presently they began moving inland across the narrow beach and up onto the cliffs and ridges that rose toward the island's interior. Using grenades, flamethrowers, and TNT charges, they burned and blasted the stubborn Japanese defenders out of their bunkers. By nightfall the beaches had been secured and more men, ammunition, and supplies were coming ashore.

Surrounded by the might of the American navy and cut off from reinforcements, the Japanese were in a hopeless position. Their cultural traditions and military training forbade surrender, however, and so they continued fighting, trying to inflict as many casualties as possible before giving up their own lives. During the next three weeks, the marines and army infantrymen would slowly advance up the ridges and across the 212-square-mile island, moving from cave to cave and pillbox to pillbox, exterminat-

Air power was the key to victory in the Pacific theater. Here, a U.S. Navy dive bomber flies over a Japanese-held island. U.S. Navy.

ing the Japanese to the last man. It was a hellish, deadly exercise; when it was finally over, on August 10, 1944, 7,000 Americans had been killed or wounded in the process of wiping out 17,500 Japanese soldiers.

Death Knell for Japan

The futile, suicidal resistance of Guam's Japanese defenders and the grim, relentless advance of the American attackers were entirely typical of the war in the Pacific. So, too, were the appalling casualties. The strategic value of Guam was clear, however. Within weeks of the island's capture, airfields were being constructed from which a devastating B-29 bomber offensive would be launched against the Japanese home islands. There would be more bloody invasions—Peleliu, the Philippines, Iwo Jima, and Okinawa—but with the fall of Guam and the rest of the Marianas, Japan's fate had been sealed.

United States Marines used grenades, flamethrowers, and TNT charges to burn and blast stubborn Japanese defenders out of their bunkers. U.S. Marine Corps.

Touring the Park

Begin your tour at the Visitor Center, which is located at the Asan Beach Unit. Exhibits and a short film provide background on the Pacific war and explain the battle for Guam. You will have to drive between units. At present there are few interpretative signs and hiking trails are generally unimproved. **WARNING:** Danger exists from unexploded ammunition. If you find ammunition, *do not touch it*. Inform a ranger about its location so that qualified personnel can remove it.

Asan Beach Unit. It was on this beach that the men of the Third Marine Division stormed ashore to begin the invasion. The remains of Japanese fortifications are still visible on Asan and Adelup points.

Asan Inland Unit. Directly opposite the Asan Beach Unit, across Marine Drive, this unit encompasses the cliffs and hillsides up which the Americans fought. Historic sites, including Japanese gun emplacements, caves, pillboxes, and a 75-millimeter mountain gun, are located at each end of the unit.

Piti Unit. On a ridge behind the village of Piti, three Japanese coastal defense guns can be seen.

Mt. Tenjo/Mt. Chachao Unit. From this ridge linking Mt. Tenjo and Mt. Chachao there is an excellent view of Asan Beach, Apra Harbor, and the Orote Peninsula, scene of heavy fighting during the invasion.

Agat Unit. This was the southern invasion beach where the First Provisional Marine Brigade and the 305th Regimental Combat Team of the Army's 77th Division came ashore. On Apaca, Bangi, and Gaan Points, caves, bunkers, and pillboxes can be seen.

Mt. Alifan Unit. Located behind the village of Agat, this commanding elevation was the scene of heavy fighting. Today the area is covered with historic sites and debris, but access is difficult, allowing only limited hiking.

Fonte Plateau Unit. This unit is still under development and is not yet open to the public.

INDEX